REALISM AND INTERNATIONAL POLITICS

Realism and International Politics brings together the collected essays of Kenneth N. Waltz, one of the most important and influential thinkers of international relations in the second half of the twentieth century. His books *Man, the State and War* and *Theory of International Politics* are classics of international relations theory and gave birth to the school of thought known as neo-realism or structural realism, out of which many of the current crop of realist scholars and thinkers has emerged. Waltz frames these seminal pieces in his theoretical development by explaining the context in which they were written and, building on the broader aims of these theories, explains the elusive nature of power balancing in today's international system.

Kenneth N. Waltz is Senior Research Associate at the Institute of War and Peace Studies at Columbia University. He is Emeritus Professor at University of California at Berkeley. He is a past president of the American Political Science Association.

D0488044

REALISM AND INTERNATIONAL POLITICS

Kenneth N. Waltz

Routledge
Taylor & Francis Group

NEW YORK AND LONDON

First published 2008
by Routledge
711 Third Avenue, New York, NY 10017

Simultaneously published in the UK
by Routledge
2 Park Square, Milton Park, Abingdon, Oxon OX14 4RN

*Routledge is an imprint of the Taylor & Francis Group,
an informa business*

·   © 2008 Taylor & Francis

Typeset in Galliard by RefineCatch Limited, Bungay, Suffolk

Library of Congress Cataloging in Publication Data
Waltz, Kenneth Neal.
Realism and international politics / Kenneth N. Waltz. – 1st ed.
    p. cm.
ISBN 978–0–415–95477–8 (hardbook : alk. paper) – ISBN 978–0–415–95478–5
(paperbook : alk. paper) 1. International relations – Philosophy. 2. Realism.
3. State, The. 4. World politics. 5. War. I. Title.
JZ1307.W35 2008
327.101–dc22   2007041766

ISBN10: 0–415–95477–0 (hbk)
ISBN10: 0–415–95478–9 (pbk)

ISBN13: 978–0–415–95477–8 (hbk)
ISBN13: 978–0–415–95478–5 (pbk)

CONTENTS

INTRODUCTION

The essays in this volume reflect the thought of a lifetime. Rather than write a general introduction, I deemed it more useful to preface each essay with a brief account of the reason for writing it and the purpose it was intended to serve. I have omitted a few essays, some that were largely excerpts from books and a few other short pieces. I have not tried to eliminate the occasional repetition from one essay to another. To do so would have left awkward and puzzling logical and narrative gaps in some of the essays.

The book is organized under four headings:

I. Essays on theory. From theory all else follows.
II. Essays on international politics. Theory explains and may at times anticipate or predict outcomes.
III. Essays on military affairs. Theory depicts international politics as a self-help system and, *in extremis*, military capabilities are the means by which states acting alone or with others try to protect themselves.
IV. Essays on policy. A political theory, if it is any good, not only explains international outcomes but also provides clues to situations and actions that may produce more of the desired and fewer of the undesired ones.

Part I: Theory

1. *Kant, Liberalism, and War, 1962.*   As a PhD dissertation *Man, the State, and War* was heavy with Spinoza and Kant. To make the dissertation accessible to a wider range of readers I reduced the Spinoza and Kant pages to a minimum. The paper, presented at the American Political Science Association meetings in St. Louis, shows that Kant, the father of political liberalism, was a thoroughgoing realist as well. It also shows that the association of Kant with the recently popular democratic peace thesis is mostly misplaced.

2. *Conflict in World Politics, 1971.*   In writing the concluding chapter of an edited volume, I wanted to do justice to the authors of its essays without simply summarizing what they had said. This desire led me to ask questions

about how the meaning and significance of conflict varies with its context. Some of the ideas eventually found their way into *Theory of International Politics*.

3. *Reflections on* Theory of International Politics, *1986*.   Since I wrote books about theory, I was less inclined to write articles on the subject. Robert O. Keohane, however, suggested the intriguing idea of producing a book in which I would confront some of my plentiful critics. Here is the essay that does so.

4. *The Origins of War in Neorealist Theory, 1988*.   Writing the paper for a conference, I misunderstood the charge. The sponsors wanted mainly a summary of what I had already written. In the final version of the essay originality is at a minimum. I reprint it here because to my surprise it is quite often cited.

5. *Realist thought and Neorealist Theory, 1990*.   The first paragraph of the essay explains its genesis and alludes to my deep debt to William T.R. Fox. It begins by drawing lessons from the first successful effort to develop a social-science theory and ends by summarizing the difference between classical and structural realism.

6 and 7. *Evaluating Theories, 1997*, and *Thoughts about Assaying Theories, 2003*.   One who is writing about theory does well to ask several basic questions at the outset. What is a theory? How can a theory be developed and constructed? How can theories be tested? The social-science literature and the philosophy-of-science literature as well are weak on the first two questions. *Theory of International Politics* grapples with both of them. The third, difficulties of testing, I examine in the following two essays. The essays expose the error of political scientists' conviction that the testing of theories can be done only by seeking to disprove them.

Part II: International politics

8. *The Stability of a Bipolar World, 1964*.   To my great benefit I was invited by Tom Schelling to spend the year 1963–64 at Harvard's Center for International Affairs. Among the ideas then in the air, two were prominent: (1) The United States should increase its military involvement in what used to be called Indochina; (2) Multipolarity was both more peaceful and more durable than bipolarity. Thus, Walter Lippmann's widely read and rightly respected columns depicted the bipolar world as being perpetually in the process of rapidly passing away. I offered my contrary thoughts in a talk at the Harvard–MIT Arms Control Seminar attended mainly by social and natural scientists from both universities. My argument that bipolarity promises peace more reliably than multipolarity and is also quite durable was vehemently

contested—witness commentaries published in *Daedalus* along with my piece. That bipolarity is a more peaceful condition of the world than multipolarity is now widely accepted, and bipolarity did, as I expected, last through the twentieth century—at least nearly so.

9. *Contention and Management in International Relations, 1965.* When I agreed to write this review article, was I shying away from the completion of my second book, as my wife feared? Probably so. To write a thoughtful review essay takes a lot of time, but the books of Inis Claude and F.H. Hinsley were important books written by eminent scholars. They were worth the time spent.

10. *International Structure, National Force, and the Balance of World Power, 1967.* My enduring devotion to Columbia, along with a desire to place our Vietnamese venture in a wider political context, led me to say "yes" when the student editors of the *Journal of International Affairs* asked me for a contribution. Later, invited to give a lecture at the National War College, I repeated much of what I had written, thus prompting an intensely negative reaction from my largely military audience. A lively discussion followed my presentation. Subsequently I was asked if the transcript of the talk could be published by the College's journal. That it appeared as the lead article in a 1969 issue is a testimonial to what was then the defense establishment's openness to critics of our foreign and military policies.

11. *The Myth of National Interdependence, 1970.* When Ray Vernon presented a paper on interdependence to a faculty seminar at Harvard, I was the lonely political scientist in attendance. I dissented from some of the ideas discussed and was, I felt, silently dismissed as one who lacked economic understanding. Thinking about the subject a few days later, I dictated a memorandum to Vernon and to two other economists who had been present—Hollis Chenery and Charles P. Kindleberger. Vernon sent me a note saying that he had dictated a response into a "dead tape" for which he apologized. Chenery failed to respond. Charlie Kindleberger wrote a note whose opening line remains in my memory: "There is something in what you say, but not much."

Not long after, Charlie phoned to ask me to give a lecture to his class at the Sloan School of Management and then turn the lecture into an essay for his forthcoming book, *The International Corporation.* I made two main points: (1) The inequality of states *is* low interdependence, a proposition that remains ill understood; (2) Although interdependence as *sensitivity* to price variations is important economically, interdependence as relative national *vulnerability* is crucial politically. The importance of the distinction between interdependence as sensitivity and as vulnerability is now widely recognized. It was, for example, adopted by Keohane and Nye in their *Power and Interdependence.*

12 and 13. *The Emerging Structure of International Politics, 1993*, and *Structural Realism after the Cold War, 2000*. World War II destroyed the multipolar structure of international politics that had lasted for three centuries. Students of international politics gradually came to understand the profound implications of the new bipolar balance. Subsequently, the demise of the Soviet Union left only one pole standing. Twice in one century, a new international-political order was born. What changes in behavior and outcome should we expect unipolarity to bring? The two essays that follow attempt to answer the question.

14. *Globalization and Governance, 1999*. I accepted an invitation to give a keynote address at a conference in Siena on the idea of globalization. Since I had done little work on international economics since my 1970 essay, it was time to revisit the subject. I presented the paper again on the occasion of receiving the American Political Science Association's James Madison Award for Distinguished Scholarly Contribution to Political Science. I wondered whether it was the globalization or the Americanization of international politics in the absence of a power to balance the United States, and whether it was the tightening of economic interdependence or the enhanced role of military power, that characterized the new world order. Read on. . . .

15. *The Continuity of International Politics, 2002*. The wanton destruction of Minoru Yamasaki's "Twin Towers," and the glancing blow struck at the Pentagon, were traumatic events. The spectacle of terrorists attacking commercial and military targets prompted many voices to proclaim that international politics had been transformed. Transformed? Or did the response to the attack demonstrate the continuity of international politics and the resilience of the nation state? The following essay answers the question.

Part III: Military affairs

16. *Reason, Will, and Weapons, 1959*. For at least two decades after atomic bombs fell on Hiroshima and Nagasaki, the big problem of policy was how to cope with their awesome power. In the late 1950s and early 1960s, a popular answer was by adopting policies of disarmament. I wondered.

17. *Toward Nuclear Peace, 1983*. I was asked to write a paper for a conference jointly sponsored by the Central Intelligence Agency and the Department of Defense on the political effects of nuclear weapons. Having finished the manuscript for *Theory of International Politics*, and feeling that I had not thought hard enough about the effects of nuclear weapons on international politics, I accepted the invitation. The result was published as a government document in 1979 and revised and published as Adelphi Paper number 171 in 1981. I concluded, more strongly than I had expected to, that nuclear

weapons have many merits and indeed that they have served as the only reliable deterrent the world has ever known.

18. *Nuclear Myths and Political Realities, 1990.* I presented the verbal version of this essay as my inaugural address when I became president of the American Political Science Association. It won the Heinz Eulau Prize as the best essay in the *Review* for the year 1990. The essay clears away the elaborations and complications that had clouded the simple and sound conception of deterrence that Bernard Brodie presented at the dawn of the nuclear age.

19. *A Reply (to Critics of Sagan and Waltz), 1995.* Scott Sagan suggested that he and I set forth our contrasting ideas about the implications of nuclear weapons in a single book. The book sparked controversy and led to the writing of essays, some on Scott's side, some on mine. The critical essays and our replies to them were published in a special issue of *Security Studies.* My response follows.

Part IV: Policy

20. *The Politics of Peace, 1967.* For two reasons I strongly opposed our war in Indochina before it started. One reason was that in the competition between the United States and the Soviet Union, Indochina counted little. Winning or losing there would not tilt the world balance. The second reason was that, having read everything that Mao Zedong wrote that was available in English, and having followed the course of guerrilla wars in the Philippines, in Malaya, and in Indochina, I believed that defeating the Vietcong, in addition to being unimportant, would be immensely difficult, if not impossible.

21. *America's European Policy in Global Perspective, 1974.* Henry Kissinger announced that 1974 would be the year of Europe. James Murray of Winthrop Publishing enlisted me and others to write essays for the occasion, which incidentally never arrived. Professor Wolfram Hanrieder organized a series of lectures at Utah State in the beautifully located town of Logan. Here is mine.

22. *Another Gap?, 1981.* The bomber gap and the missile gap had passed into history. In each case there was a gap, but it was in America's and not in the Soviet Union's favor. The new gap, however, was said to be more comprehensive. President Ronald Reagan warned that the Soviet Union was surpassing the United States at every level, tactical and strategic, conventional and nuclear. Many people at home and abroad believed him. One wonders how people could be so wrong so often in their assessment of the balance of military power. The following essay describes the folly.

23. *America as a Model for the World?, 1991.* George Quester asked me to participate in a plenary session at the APSA meetings. My comments were published in an essay that warned strongly of the dangers to others and to ourselves of the gross imbalance of power in America's favor that then and now marks international politics. Ironically the belief that governmental power, unchecked, is easily abused is deeply ingrained in the American psyche. Yet Americans find it hard to believe that the same reasoning applies internationally.

The following essays help one to understand international politics, to figure out what to expect when the distribution of power changes, and to glean guidance for the making of foreign policies. These are among the main aims of theory. The origins of international-political theory are found in ancient Greece where Thucydides laid bare the behavior to be expected when political units contend in an anarchic arena, as states still do. Athens was the most powerful state in its arena, as the United States is today. Athens overreached, and by its own actions sealed its doom. The United States, the one great power in modern history to enjoy a position almost free of security worries, has by its rash actions reduced its economic and military superiority, but without destroying its dominant position.

Structural theory contemplates a world in which two or more states contend. What then is the relevance of the theory when only one state is left in the contest? One can say, "very little." Structural theory becomes a theory about the future, for as Michael Mastanduno has said: In the end, "power will check power."[1] When will the end come? To say what will happen is easier than to say when it will happen.

Yet when a theory says, as realist theory does, that balances recurrently form, one wants to know when the next one is likely to appear. With the demise of the Soviet Union, the world of two great powers became a world of one. The United States is now the world's dominant power. Historically, dominant powers have behaved badly. Moreover, their external behavior bears little relation to their internal political composition—autocratic, liberal-democratic, and totalitarian regimes have all conformed to the pattern. The recent behavior of the United States confirms this. In twenty years, dating from 1983, the United States invaded weak countries six times: Lebanon, Grenada, Panama, Iraq, Afghanistan, and Iraq again. No one could say that all, or even most, of these acts of war were necessities of state.

In a world of four or more states, balance-seeking countries can choose from a number of potential partners. In a world of two great powers, each automatically balances the other, and the behaviors of both are moderated. In a world of one, a balance is lacking. The puzzle, especially given America's blustery binges, is why other states have not balanced against it. The puzzle has few pieces, and they are easily fitted together.

First, balancing is hard to do. Balancing is costly, and the right time to balance is hard to calculate. Moreover, to jump on the bandwagon of an emerging power is tempting. Not only is bandwagoning cheaper than balancing, but one may also hope to score some gains. Thus to cite only a twentieth century example, Britain, France, Italy, and the Soviet Union failed to form a coalition to oppose Hitler's Germany through the 1930s, and a balance was not completed until Germany invaded Russia and Japan struck the United States after World War II had already begun.

Second, economically, technologically, and militarily the gap in capabilities between the United States and others is wide, and the Bush administration's announced policy was to make it wider still. The United States now spends more on its military forces than all of the other states in the world combined. For other states to try to catch up is a formidable task.

Third, the technology of modern warfare makes catching up all the more difficult. In the old days, allies by combining their forces were able to enhance their military might. With nuclear weapons, if two or more states combine their second-strike nuclear forces, what do they have? A second strike force. As Charles de Gaulle noted long ago, nuclear weapons do not add up. Nuclear weapons negate alliances at the strategic level. This is also pretty much the case with highly advanced systems of communication, target acquisition, logistics, and weapons delivery.

Fourth, after the Cold War American apologists claimed that other countries would not balance against the United States. A nice liberal country, however powerful, would supposedly pose no threat to others. Few foreigners believed this at the time and fewer do now. In China in the year 2004 I asked a professor of international politics why Chinese officials and scholars were not more critical of American foreign policy. He gave a simple answer: "we're scared." The United States, more than any other country, has the ability to impose penalties and also the ability to dispense favors. Thus when France and Germany opposed America's most recent invasion of Iraq, they muted their opposition and failed to sustain it. Why make the giant mad when you cannot alter its actions?

Fifth, throughout modern history the big struggles among states always ended with enough Great Powers standing to enable them to constitute a new balance of power. But when the Cold War ended, only one Great Power remained. The materials for building a new balance were lacking. And since the combined strength of the weak fails to make a coalition strong, one has to wait for a single country to become powerful enough to counter the United States. The only country that may do this in the short run is China. Having increased its military spending by more than 17 percent in 2001 and by double digits since then, and having sustained its roughly 10 percent growth rate, China looks like becoming a worthy competitor and one with good reason to compete. China is deadly serious about bringing Taiwan back into the mainland fold. Dispatching two aircraft carrier battle groups toward the China–Taiwan strait, as the United States did early in 1996, was a reminder of

America's ability to intervene in order to blunt China's threats to use force against Taiwan should it decide to proclaim its sovereignty.

I ended an essay that appeared in *International Security* in 1993 with the thought that the checks and balances of internal politics might moderate America's external behavior, but I added that "I would not bet on it." May one hope that the bloody nose now being suffered in Iraq will at last calm the United States down? It probably will, but not for long. The predicted Vietnam effect lasted only a short time. The concentration of power is a powerful predictor of a state's behavior.

Note

1 Michael Mastanduno, "Preserving the Unipolar Moment: Realist Theories and U.S. Grand Strategy after the Cold War," *International Security*, vol. 21, no. 4, Spring 1997, p. 88.

Part I

THEORY

1

KANT, LIBERALISM, AND WAR

Many liberals of the nineteenth century, and their predecessors of the middle eighteenth, thought the natural condition of men to be one of harmony. Dissension and strife do not inhere in man and society; they arise instead from mistaken belief, inadequate knowledge, and defective governance. With the evils defined, the remedies become clear: educate men and their governors, strip away political abuses. This is one theme in the history of liberal thought. Urged by humane philosophers and supported by pacifistic economists, its appeal in Western society is immense and enduring.

There is in liberal thought another theme as well, which is often obscured though it goes back to the earliest philosophers who can fairly be called liberal. Montesquieu, Adam Smith, and Kant made no easy assumptions about the rationality and goodness of man. Among men in nature and states in a world of states, they found not harmony and peace but hostility and war to be the natural condition.

The two liberal traditions are partly contradictory. Kant is often improperly placed in the first of them, which helps to account for many of the misinterpretations of his political philosophy. His essay *Eternal Peace* is seen as one of a succession of peace plans going back to Dante and Dubois in the early fourteenth century, encompassing the French monk Crucé and the abbé St. Pierre, and culminating in the League and the United Nations. Some emphasize the plan, that is, international organization; others the importance of its being based on republican or democratic governments. In his guise as a philosopher urging the peaceful proclivities of democracy, Kant has even infiltrated the State Department. Giving full credit to the analysis of Kant, George V. Allen, an assistant secretary, once said: "The United Nations, with all its virtues, has not yet been able to achieve freedom from fear. The reason is easy to understand. Its second most powerful member is not a democracy."[1]

Some have accepted such an interpretation not to applaud Kant's commanding vision and high moral purpose but rather to decry his political naiveté and simple-minded optimism. Kant's supposed conviction that a Europe of republics would be peaceful, Crane Brinton finds to be a pathetic relic of the Enlightenment.[2] The statement exposes one of the problems of interpretation.

Kant is a child of the Enlightenment; he is also the father of a critical philosophy that goes beyond it. Sometimes he writes as though peace were inevitably coming; at other times, as though *Realpolitik* were the mode of the present and the future. One who cannot ignore the latter aspect may label it a Germanic aberration, as Gooch did in his work on Germany and the French Revolution.[3] While Kant may be seen as a backsliding liberal, he may also be considered a theorist of power politics who hid his Machiavellian ideas by hanging 'round them the fashionable garments of liberalism. Since he explained and in a sense accepted the practice of power politics in the relations of states, since he wrote of nature's plan and man's predetermined destiny, this interpretation too becomes plausible, the more so if his *Rechtsstaat* is taken to be a thinly disguised despotism with the sovereign supposedly limited by law but actually free of any human constraint.[4]

It is little trouble to collate passages that would support in turn each of the preceding interpretations of Kant, but the whole man would thereby elude us. There is a unity in his thought that is hard to grasp. His manner of thinking is foreign to social-science fashions, his mode of analysis rigorous and yet subtle, his style difficult but clear, his writing crabbed and still, as Goethe said, sometimes slyly ironic and even eloquent.

I

"A true political philosophy . . . cannot advance a step without first paying homage to the principles of morals. . . ."[5] It is incumbent upon us to take Kant at his word and begin by briefly discussing his moral philosophy. Kant was neither an empiricist nor an idealist. Empiricism he criticizes as leading to "merely contingent" knowledge; idealism as exceeding the bounds of reason. Man is a member of two worlds: the phenomenal and the noumenal. In the first, he is a creature of the senses, of impulse and desire. Utility or happiness as a standard of morals or legislation is mere caprice, for the object of action is taken from the realm of contingency. There can be no certainty nor universality of agreement. If your happiness is not mine, a government that presumes to tell either of us what objects we should seek and how we should seek them exceeds the bounds of permissible legislation. It undertakes to do what all men could not possibly have assented to.[6] This is the kernel of all liberalism, rigorously defined. It is expressed, for example, by Lord Acton in his argument that liberty is the only end of government that can be generally pursued without producing tyranny. In Kant's words: "No one may force anyone to be happy according to his manner of imagining the well-being of other men; instead, everyone may seek his happiness in the way that seems good to him as long as he does not infringe on the freedom of others to pursue a similar purpose, when such freedom may coexist with the freedom of every other man according to a possible and general law."[7] Where others have grounded the injunction more pragmatically, Kant roots the limitation in a profound analysis of the nature of reason.

4

By his possession of reason, man is distinguished from all mere animals. Man's reasoning abilities are, however, circumscribed. He can know that noumena, things-in-themselves, exist; he cannot know their content. The imperative, which is the basis of morality and of legislation, is then necessarily without content. "Act according to a Maxim which can be adopted at the same time as a Universal Law."[8] My act is proper if everyone could, without contradiction and conflict, claim the right to act similarly. Men would always act in accordance with the categorical imperative if they were wholly creatures of reason. They are not. From the sensual nature of man conflict and violence arise. The contradiction between his condition and his potential gives the right to compel others to enter with him into a civil society in which his rights are secured, and with them the possibility of moral behavior.[9] The criterion of legislation is abstract in order that it may be, within the limits of reason, of general validity. The purpose of legislation is negative: to "hinder hindrances" to freedom so that each may enjoy his antecedently existing rights unmolested.

Each man is an end in himself. The rights of one man before the law are the same as the rights of another. Kant is sharply critical of all practice contrary to this dictum. In the state of nature men have possessions; in the civil state their possessions are secured to them by law and become property. Men have equal rights to property but in varying amounts depending on their situation and abilities. There can, by right, be no nobility of birth but only gradations of rank according to merit. Great inequalities of wealth may, however, limit or even destroy equality of opportunity, as Kant himself remarks. The remedy, negative and typically liberal, is to arrange the laws so as to lessen the perpetuation of family lands by inheritance.[10] To take another example and one that will incline our analysis toward the problem of war, Kant steadfastly opposed the impressment of subjects into military service. The practice was widespread. Karl Alexander, nephew of Frederick the Great, sold his regiments to England for the American War. At the bidding of his English mistress, he finally sold his principality to Prussia for cash and retired to England. In England impressment of sailors was regarded as an undeniable prerogative of the Crown, and the brutal and inefficient practice not eliminated until it was made unnecessary by the Continuous Service Scheme adopted in 1853.[11] In the face of such practices, Kant writes:

> A State is not to be regarded as a property or patrimony like the soil on which it may be settled. It is a society of men, over which no one but itself has the right to rule . . . and to incorporate it as a graft in another State is to destroy its existence as a moral person; it is to reduce it to a thing, and thereby to contradict the idea of the original compact without which a right over a people is inconceivable.

Subjects are not, like the vegetables the farmer uproots and carts off to market, objects that the ruler can dispose of according to his whim.

In many states the ruler does so treat them. Where war does not require of the ruler the least sacrifice of his pleasures he may "resolve for war from insignificant reasons, as if it were but a hunting expedition; and, as regards its propriety, he may leave the justification of it without concern to the diplomatic body, who are always too ready to give their services for that purpose."[12]

The practices of governments contradict the principles of right. How are the required limitations to be secured? The answer has two parts: first, the institutions that are appropriate, and then how they may come to exist. Only in a republic can it be hoped that the principles of right will prevail. In such a state the executive is made up of one or a few; separated from it is an assembly representing the self-dependent citizens, men of property, profession, or craft. The executive presents its proposed legislation, the assembly chants its ayes and nays. The question put to it is not, for example, is a 10 percent tax on bread supportable as compared to a tax of 5 percent? The question, in the manner of Rousseau, is simply this: Does the proposed law accord with the general will? Is it one that everyone, though he would have preferred the lower tax, could conceivably have agreed to? If it is such, then the idea of the original contract is preserved. Still, what if the assembly says "nay" and the executive refuses to listen?

Kant's philosophy, including his political philosophy, moves forward by resolving a series of antinomies or tensions. The enjoyment, as distinct from the possession, of rights depends on the state. However imperfect the state may be, it is greatly preferable to anarchy. On such grounds as these, revolution is absolutely enjoined. Yet one may, as Kant did, view with sympathy revolutions that according to the principles of right would stand condemned. There is no contradiction. He writes, one might say, sometimes noumenally and sometimes phenomenally, or, more accurately, with both aspects of human affairs clearly in his mind. Careful analysis and the clear specification of standards square easily in Kant's philosophy with caution, flexibility, and moderation in the judgment of human behavior.

The other institutional arrangement that is essential to proper governance is freedom of expression. Kant takes *Sapere Aude!* as the motto of the Enlightenment, and one of the most frequently quoted of his statements is that "the liberty of the press is the sole palladium of the rights of the people."[13] One hears a distinct reverberation from the Philosophes' Shield of Evidence or an echo, to take a German formulation, of Schlözer's dictum that statistics and despotism cannot coexist. In his own and his subjects' interest, the ruler ought to permit the widest freedom of expression; but again, if he does not, there is nothing that can rightfully be done about it.

At such points as these some have concluded that Kant's political theory is a defense of despotism coupled with a hope that the despot will rule by law. He does, it is true, reflect the widespread ideas of his time. But they were ideas shared by many who were liberals as well as by others. Only a government secure in its power, Hegel once wrote, can permit the conscientious objector to live by his scruples. Across the North Sea one finds Lord Hardinge, Secretary at War in Wellington's Cabinet, describing the army as:

> a protection rather than any detriment to Liberty. We permitted a licentiousness which under any other constitution might be fatal to the public peace. Meetings were held and language was used which no other empire would permit and which nothing but the confidence of the Crown in the Standing Army would justify even our Government in permitting.

Neither Hegel nor Hardinge were liberals, but they reflect the idea that Kant emphasizes: A government that, while limited, is strong in its sphere can permit a freedom to its subjects that would otherwise endanger the state. Thus Kant, with obvious reference to Frederick the Great, applauds the strength of the Prussian state upon which the individual's liberty depends.[14]

So long at least as the state "runs a danger of being suddenly swallowed up by other States," it must be powerful externally as well as internally. In international relations the difficulties multiply. The republican form is preferable, partly because republics are more peacefully inclined; but despotisms are stronger—and no one would expect or wish to bring the state into jeopardy by decreasing its strength.[15] Standing armies are dangerous, arms races themselves being a cause of war, but in the absence of an outside agency affording protection, each state must look to the effectiveness of its army.[16] A freely flowing commerce is a means of promoting peace, but a state must control imports, in the interests of its subjects "and not for the advantage of strangers and the encouragement of the industry of others, because the State without the prosperity of the people would not possess sufficient power to resist external enemies or to maintain itself as a commonwealth."[17] Not only standing armies but also, indeed more so, the disparity of economic capacities may represent danger, occasion fear, and give rise to war.

Kant's concern with the strength and thus the safety of the state is part of his perception of the necessities of power politics. Among states in the world, as among individuals in the state of nature, there is constantly either violence or the threat of violence. States, like "lawless savages," are with each other "naturally in a nonjuridical condition."[18] There is no law above them; there is no judge among them; there is no legal process by which states can pursue their rights. They can do so only by war, and, as Kant points out, neither war nor the treaty of peace following it, can settle the question of right. A treaty of peace can end only a particular war; a pretext for new hostilities can always be found. "Nor can such a pretext under these circumstances be regarded as unjust; for in this state of society every nation is the judge of its own cause."[19] More surely than those who extract and emphasize merely Kant's republican aspirations and peaceful hopes, Khrushchev speaks as though he had read Kant correctly. "War," in Khrushchev's peculiar yet apt phrase, "is not fatalistically inevitable."[20]

Kant does set forth the "shoulds" and "oughts" of state behavior.[21] He does not expect them to be followed in a state of nature, for, as he says, "philosophically or diplomatically composed codes have not, nor could have, the slightest legal force, since the States as such stand under no common legal constraint. . . ."[22] His intention clearly is that the "oughts" be taken as the basis for the juridical order that must one day be established among states, just as the rights of the individual, though not viable in a state of nature, provided the basis for the civil state.

This is the culminating problem of Kant's philosophy. Men need the protection of law before they have any chance of leading the moral life to which their reason commands them. The civil state is not sufficient. Peace among, as well as within, states is essential to the development of uniquely human capacities. "So act as to treat humanity, whether in thine own person or in that of any other, in every case as an end withal, never as means only."[23] This is the form of the imperative that is most appropriate here. The constant hostility of states and the pressures of recurring war make its fulfillment impossible. How can the problem be solved?

II

As is well known, Kant proclaims the *Rechtsstaat*, or republic, as preeminently the peaceful form of the state. In a republic the unambiguous test of right is applied to every piece of legislation, and every act of the executive will in turn follow the universally established law.[24] Such a state could not undertake an aggressive war, for its sole purpose, a purpose guaranteed by its structure, is to further the moral life of its subjects by enacting and administering positive, general law.[25] There may be reasons for a republic to fight, but they are not internally generated. Kant records, as had Hume, the couplet from Pope's *Essay on Man*:

> For Forms of Government let fools contest; Whate'er is best administered is best.

And, just as with Hume, he cites the thought in order to disagree with it. The point for both of them is that as the context of action varies, similar causes have different effects. Notice what Kant has done. With no comforting illusions about man, he seeks in the state, and among states as will be seen in a moment, the structure that will turn men's "unsocial sociability," their conflict and violence, toward a constructive result.[26]

How are the appropriate structures to come into being, nationally and in the world at large? Kant sees in history, indeed in the very horrors of war, "a deep-seated, maybe far-seeing, attempt on the part of supreme wisdom, if not to found, yet to prepare the way for a rule of law governing the freedom of states, and thus bring about their unity in a system established on a moral basis."[27] Aha! one may say, an overriding determinism, an uncritical teleology, an Hegelian world-spirit marching with benign purpose, a sterile optimism. Kant succumbs to none of these. He is neither determinist, uncritical, nor rosy-faced with hope. A universal plan of nature, unknowable in detail but dimly discernible in outline, must be assumed; it cannot be known. He is moving at the outermost rim of reason to establish the necessity of an act of faith and its compatibility with his own critical philosophy. We can discern in nature "a design to bring forth concord out of the discord of men. . . ." This must be so if Kant's moral theory is correct, for only in concord can man follow the categorical imperative. But, he warns:

> human reason, when dealing with the relation of effects to their causes, must keep within the limits of possible experience; and to speak of Providence as knowable by us in this relation would be putting on Icarian wings with presumptuous rashness in order to approach the mystery of His unfathomable purposes.[28]

His argument, both of limits and of possibilities, is established in the *Pure Reason* and elaborated in the *Practical Reason*. Along with its relation to moral philosophy, his reasoning is great with political implications.

The activities of bees and beavers, guided by instinct, produce regular patterns and predictable results. Citizens of a purely rational world, on the other hand, would act according to a preconcerted plan. Because men behave in neither of these ways, "no regular systematic history of mankind" appears to be possible. But if we take progress not as a final cause but as a postulate of the practical reason, "the cheerless gloom of chance" is illuminated by "the guiding light of reason."[29] In the economic world of Adam Smith, men scratch and claw, each seeking his profit. The result is the greater good of all. If we look at the world and see discrete events, we are overwhelmed by the chaos: each event without cause and all events without meaning. But if we look at the aggregate of events with a proper organizing principle in our minds, we may see in the chaos, order; in the welter of events, a plan of nature. Newton, as Darwin said, did not explain why there is a gravitational force but that there is such a force. The cause, as Kant would put it, located in the bodies, is inaccessible to our reason; but the rules by which it operates can be discerned.[30] And so it is that out of the "universal violence" of the state of nature and "the necessity arising therefrom" comes the resolution of a people "to subject themselves to national law. . . ."[31] The juridical union itself is "a condition of [legal] equality . . . determined by the action and reaction of free wills limiting one another. . . ."[32] And:

> even if a people were not compelled by internal discord to submit to the coercion of public laws, war as an external influence would effect

this. For, according to the arrangement of nature already indicated, every people finds another pressing upon it in its neighborhood and it must form itself internally into a State in order to be equipped as a power so as to defend itself.[33]

Men and states seek their ends little knowing that they are by their actions producing a result that may have been no part of their intentions. Smith's invisible hand is at work in the realm of politics. The "planless aggregate" of human actions can be represented as "constituting a system," though the demonstrations of Kant in the realm of the political are necessarily vaguer, crasser, and less certain than are those of Smith.[34]

There is a sense of progress but not a naive optimism, for as we advance Kant sees that the dangers and difficulties also grow. The practical reason pronounces its irresistible veto: "There shall be no war."[35] Yet without war in the past, men now would be feeble types sheltering in caves and feeding on nuts and berries. The development as conceived by Kant is dialectic:

> By the expenditure of all the resources of the commonwealth in military preparations against each other, by the devastations occasioned by war, and still more by the necessity of holding themselves continually in readiness for it, the full development of the capacities of mankind are undoubtedly retarded in their progress; but, on the other hand, the very evils which thus arise, compel men to find out means against them. A law of equilibrium is thus discovered for the regulation of the really wholesome antagonism of contiguous States as it springs up out of their freedom; and a united power, giving emphasis to this law, is constituted, whereby there is introduced a universal condition of public security among the nations.[36]

Kant mentions, by way of suggestion, some of the ways in which peace may come out of war. The strength of a state is directly related to its general prosperity and well-being, and these in turn to the amount of liberty enjoyed by its subjects. "If the citizen is hindered in seeking his prosperity in any way suitable to himself that is consistent with the liberty of others, the activity of business is checked generally; and thereby the powers of the whole State are again weakened." Since states are in close competition, the sovereign, to avoid weakening his state, must grant a greater liberty to his subjects. Meanwhile the growing intensity of the competition among states leads them to spend larger amounts of money, even in time of peace, in military preparation. Prices rise, the national debt mounts, and finally the states are so weakened by this competition and by actual war that the sovereign is forced to give in peacefully to the people and place in their hands the power to choose between war and peace.[37] The attempt to win in the competition of states leads the sovereign to make some concessions; the impossibility of winning leads to the final concession, at which point, presumably, the republican form becomes the pattern of government throughout the world.

The manner of approach is immensely impressive. Its execution is accomplished with modesty, perception, and political sensibility. This is not to say that the vision is without flaw, the plan without blemish. Kant, if read from one point of view, can be taken as a study in the futility of the unsoundly based "ought." This was clear in his analysis of the individual in a state of nature where, he argued, the moral obligations, the "oughts" that apply to every rational being, cannot possibly be fulfilled. Prior to the establishment of a pacific federation, the "oughts" in international law turn out to mean as little as those applied to man in the state of nature. When the state of nature gives way to the civil state, the "oughts" applied to moral man take on a practical meaning. Those that apply to states can be taken seriously only if the environment of the state is similarly improved. For he says: "Every people, for the sake of its own security, thus may and ought to demand from any other that it shall enter along with it into a constitution, similar to the civil constitution, in which the right of each shall be secured."[38] The civil state is necessary for two reasons, because men are imperfect and because even good men may fall into dispute and require a legally established mediator. The universal law-state would seem to be necessary for a similar pair of reasons.

Yet in spite of a number of statements such as the one just quoted, Kant will not accept the "legal state of Society" on a grand scale, the world constitution "similar to the civil constitution," as a solution to the problem. Every time he uses such phrases he quickly adds qualifications that materially change their meaning. His "universal International State, or Union of Nations," turns out to be "a voluntary combination of different States that would be *dissoluble* at any time, and not such a union as is embodied in the United States of America, founded upon a political constitution, and therefore indissoluble."[39] In such a voluntary organization, Kant says, the settlement of disputes among states can be conducted according to a civil process instead of by war. And yet he has also said in the clearest terms that against the evils of war and the general insecurity of states "there is no possible remedy but a system of international right founded upon public laws conjoined with power, to which every State must submit,—according to the analogy of the civil or political right of individuals in any one State."[40] The seeming contradiction calls for some explanation.

III

Why does Kant, after having constructed an argument internally consistent, turn to the conclusion that not government but a voluntary organization is the solution to the problem of war? He gives two reasons. The first is partly a logical proposition resting on his definition of terms. States already have a legal constitution; it would be illogical to place them under another.

Individuals in a condition of nature have a right to compel others to join with them to form a state. The right of a state to demand that other states submit to the rule of law is not comparably strong. As a matter of right, no state can interfere with the internal arrangements of another. Kant, in contrast to Mazzini and Woodrow Wilson, is a non-interventionist liberal.[41] One suspects that his second reason for shying away from a world state is more important. He fears that such a state, once achieved, would be a greater evil than the wars it is designed to eliminate. It could so easily become a terrible despotism, stifle liberty, kill initiative, and in the end lapse into anarchy.[42]

States in the world are like individuals in the state of nature. They are neither perfectly good nor are they controlled by law. Consequently conflict and violence among them are inevitable. This statement does not lead Kant to the conclusion that a world state is the answer. Distrusting that solution, he casts about for another. The other possibility open to him is that all states so improve that they will act according to maxims that could be universally followed without conflict. While he fears the former solution, he is too cautious and critical to place his faith entirely in the latter. Instead he attempts to combine them. It is the aim of his political philosophy to establish the hope that states may improve enough and learn enough from the suffering and devastation of war to make possible a rule of law among them that is not backed by power but is voluntarily observed. The first factor is the internal improvement of states; the second, the external rule of law. But the second, being voluntary, is dependent on the perfection with which the first is realized. The "power" to enforce the law is derived not from external sanction but from internal perfection.

Can one sensibly expect all states gradually to conform to a pattern that, once universally established, would provide the basis for perpetual peace? At one point Kant says: "Seek ye first the kingdom of pure practical reason and its righteousness, and then will your object, the benefit of perpetual peace, be added unto you."[43] This is a strange injunction to come from Kant, for he has pointed out, as we have several times noted, that it is only in the civil state that man has the possibility of living the moral life. The civil state made changes in man's behavior possible; it was not the other way around. And this is also the view that Kant takes of the relation between the internal and external affairs of states. In the 7th Proposition of his "Principle of the Political Order," for example, he avers that without the proper ordering of the external relations of states, the internal establishment of the perfect civil constitution is impossible.

For the moment, however, let us assume that, without profound change in their external relations, all states have become republics. Kant's conclusion is that at this point perpetual peace is established, at least approximately. The international rule of law is realized, for the law is voluntarily agreed upon and voluntarily obeyed. This whole system of voluntary universal law rests upon an equilibrium of forces that is the culmination of world history.

To show that the equilibrium, once realized, is bound to collapse, one need only refer to Kant's own analysis. He points out that in a state of nature, where each state must define its rights and prosecute them with its own power, no one country can be secure against any other. "Lesion of a less powerful country may be involved merely in the condition of a more powerful neighbor prior to any action at all; and in the State of Nature an attack under such circumstances would be warrantable." This is a logical justification of the right of preventive war. From it Kant derives the principle of the balance of power.[44] How, one may ask, does the final equilibrium of the voluntary federation among states differ from the equilibrium sometimes attained by balance-of-power politics, an equilibrium that Kant properly labelled precarious? It should be clear by now that it differs in only one of the two respects that Kant believes to be essential. He ridicules the balance of power by comparing it with "the house described by Swift, which was built by an architect so perfectly in accordance with all the laws of equilibrium that when a sparrow lighted upon it it immediately fell." Yet the same doubt would seem to apply to Kant's hope for a pacific world secured "not by the weakening of all the separate powers of the States, but by an equilibrium which is brought forth and guaranteed through their rivalry with each other."[45] It is, in Kant's impeccable logic, necessary to supersede the state of nature among states and establish the rule of law. It is, by the same logic, impossible for a voluntary international federation effectively to guarantee the peace. If equilibrium depends on spontaneous agreement or if equilibrium depends on a balance of forces, the federation of Kant is either way doomed to be transitory and shifting. Just as the house designed by a Laputian would collapse under the weight of a sparrow, so Kant's structure falls to the ground whenever one major state chooses to forsake the international federation and flout its universal law.

The difficulty is made all the clearer by noting how, in a republic, the general will pronounces on the question of war and peace. The unambiguous test of right is again applied to a proposed act of the executive. The question is, as with domestic legislation, abstractly put. The answer to it must be a simple yes or no. Since the point is important and generally overlooked, I quote the relevant passage:

> If, for example, a proportioned war-tax were imposed on all the subjects, they are not entitled ... to say that it is unjust because somehow, according to their opinion, the war was unnecessary. For they are not entitled to judge of this; whereas, because it is at least always possible that the war was inevitable and the tax indispensable, it must be regarded as rightful in the judgment of the subject.[46]

IV

Kant has held out a hope for perpetual peace, which upon closer scrutiny seems to disappear. Has he deluded himself with a false optimism, which has then been transferred to many of his interpreters? To answer the question we have to complete the circle and return to a consideration of his moral philosophy.

It is, Kant writes in the *Metaphysics of Morals*, "absolutely impossible to make out by experience with complete certainty a single case in which" an act was purely moral. However:

> whether this or that takes place is not at all the question; but that reason of itself, independent on [sic] all experience, ordains what ought to take place, that accordingly actions of which perhaps the world has hitherto never given an example, the feasibility even of which might be very much doubted by one who founds everything on experience, are nevertheless inflexibly commanded by reason. . . .[47]

A moral act may never have been performed; yet moral behavior is a "necessary" or "practical" goal of mankind. When Kant uses such adjectives he means that the action described is the only action in accordance with man's noumenal nature, that its performance is a duty. Kant demonstrates that the categorical imperative exists and that to follow it is not impossible; he does not imply that men will live according to it. From the moral duty inherent in man's noumenal nature arise other of Kant's postulates. He accords to man in the form of practical reason, or will, what he has denied to him in the form of pure reason. If we are ever to fulfill the moral law, we must assume the existence of progress, an immortal soul, a God.[48]

Kant approaches the problem of war in similar fashion. Perpetual peace is a particular reading of the postulate of progress, for if a condition of peace is not possible, then the prospect of one day realizing the ideal of moral behavior disappears. It is a partial and erroneous interpretation of Kant to say that he thought the realization of "necessary" or "practical" goals something that would occur in anyone's lifetime. Kant's analysis makes the conclusion that a universal rule of law can be achieved almost incomprehensible, but even this conclusion makes sense in his way of thinking; for to say that we can only "comprehend the incomprehensibility" of something is simply to face up to the inherent limitations of reason.[49]

The conclusion that follows from considering Kant's political philosophy in the context of his moral philosophy is borne out by many of his more purely political statements. In the *Philosophy of Law*, after one of his many iterations of the proposition that only in a universal state can man find security, he raises the argument that if the state is extended over too large an area it becomes physically incapable of protecting its members. "Hence," he says:

> the *Perpetual Peace*, which is the ultimate end of all the Right of Nations, becomes in fact an impracticable idea. The political principles, however, which aim at such an end, and which enjoin the

14

formation of such unions among the States as may promote a continuous approximation to a Perpetual Peace are not impracticable. . . .[50]

As he has demonstrated the possibility of moral behavior, so he must establish the possibility of perpetual peace. The second is the precondition of the first, and nothing that is impossible can be imperatively commanded. Peace is possible. This Kant has sought to prove. Its achievement remains an improbability:

> Now, as a matter of fact, the morally practical Reason utters within us its irrevocable *Veto: "There shall be no War."* . . . Hence the question no longer is as to whether Perpetual Peace is a real thing or not a real thing, or as to whether we may not be deceiving ourselves when we adopt the former alternative, but we must *act* on the supposition of its being real. . . . And although the realization of this purpose may always remain but a pious wish, yet we do certainly not deceive ourselves in adopting the maxim of action that will guide us in working incessantly for it; for it is a duty to do this.[51]

V

Kant shares the major tenets of liberalism: the source of the individual's rights lies outside of the state; his freedom may be limited only when its exercise interferes with the rights of others; such limitation must be by known general laws before which all men stand equal; men's capacities are greater than is shown by their present accomplishments; and, finally, their potential will unfold in time, with education being one of the important means of progress. But Kant sees in combination what others have often separated—the defects, or as he says, the evil of men and the possibility of their living good lives, the strength of the state and the liberty of its subjects, progress amidst ever greater difficulties, the approach to peace as wars become fiercer and more frequent. He has, as many liberals do not, an appreciation of politics as struggle, an idea of possible equilibrium not as simple and automatic harmony but always as something perilously achieved out of conflict.

Let the philosophers scribble as they will, writes Kant at the beginning of "Eternal Peace." There is no danger, for rulers will not listen. This has been taken as criticism of states and condemnation of their rulers. But to the philosopher's advice rulers cannot listen, as Kant well knew. He was not engaged in the puerile task of telling men of affairs to stop behaving badly. Nor could he have been, for the dependence of behavior upon condition is one of his major theses. Taken as a King's Mirror, Kant's "Eternal Peace" is lost in futility. But so to take it requires a very un-Kantian interpretation. In describing what the states and the world will have to do and to become if moral behavior is to be possible, Kant makes understandable and in a sense excuses the failures of men and their rulers to achieve moral rectitude.

Many liberals of Kant's time and after have looked upon war as annoyance or aberration, as something, one might say, that lies outside of history. Kant, in contrast, at once condemns war and demonstrates that its occurrence is expected rather than accidental. In the end we are left not with a confident foretelling of "the end of wars and the reign of international law"[52] but with a deeper appreciation of the causes of war and the immense difficulty of doing anything about them.

Notes

1 George V. Allen, "Perpetual Peace Through World-Wide Federation," *Department of State Bulletin*, Vol. 20 (June 19, 1949), pp. 801–802.
2 Crane Brinton, *A Decade of Revolution, 1789–1799* (New York, 1934), p. 261.
3 G. P. Gooch, *Germany and the French Revolution* (London, 1920), p. 271.
4 For a recent example, see the lead review of *The Times Literary Supplement*, January 23, 1959.
5 Kant, *Eternal Peace and other International Essays*, tr. W. Hastie (Boston, 1914), p. 118. This book contains: pp. 1–25, "The Natural Principle of the Political Order Considered in Connection with the Idea of a Universal Cosmopolitan History"; pp. 27–54, "The Principles of Political Right Considered in Connection with the Relation of Theory to Practice in Natural Law"; pp. 55–66, "The Principle of Progress Considered in Connection with the Relation of Theory to Practice in International Law"; pp. 67–168, "Eternal Peace, A Philosophical Essay."
6 See *Fundamental Principles of the Metaphysic of Morals*, esp. sec. 2; and in general, *Critical Examination of Practical Reason*. Both are in Thomas Kingsmill Abbott, tr., *Kant's Critique of Practical Reason and Other Works on the Theory of Ethics*, 6th ed. (London, 1909). For the political parts of the argument, see "Principles of Political Right."
7 Acton, "Nationality," *The History of Freedom and Other Essays* (London, 1907), pp. 270–300; Kant, "Theory and Practice: Concerning the Common Saying: This May Be True in Theory But Does Not Apply to Practice," tr. Carl J. Friedrich, *The Philosophy of Kant* (New York, 1949), p. 416.
8 *The Philosophy of Law*, tr. W. Hastie (Edinburgh, 1887), p. 34.
9 Ibid., pp. 77–78, 157.
10 "Principles of Political Right," pp. 34–39.
11 Gooch, *Germany and the French Revolution*, p. 12; Christopher Lloyd, *The Nation and the Navy* (London, 1954), pp. 131, 209.
12 "Eternal Peace," pp. 70, 78; *Philosophy of Law*, p. 217.
13 "What is Enlightenment?" tr. Friedrich, *Philosophy of Kant*; "Principles of Political Right," p. 50.
14 Alfred Vagts, *A History of Militarism* (New York, 1937), pp. 167–168; "What is Enlightenment?" p. 139.
15 "Eternal Peace," p. 108.
16 Ibid., p. 71. In a way that long remains typical of liberals, Kant, in effect, criticizes the army that has nobility as officers and rabble for its soldiers. He would prefer not the nation-in-arms but an army of citizen-soldiers periodically and voluntarily rehearsing their military duties.
17 Ibid., pp. 98–99; "Principles of Political Right," pp. 42–43.

18 *Philosophy of Law*, p. 214; cf. pp. 223–224: "Further, it may be said that the expression 'an unjust enemy in the state of Nature' is *pleonastic*; for the state of Nature is itself a state of injustice."
19 "Eternal Peace," p. 83; cf. p. 76.
20 *Report of the Central Committee of the Communist Party of the Soviet Union to the 20th Party Congress*. Cf. *Kant's Critique of Teleological Judgement*, tr. James C. Meredith (Oxford, 1928), p. 96. Referring to "a system of all states that are in danger of acting injuriously to one another", Kant says: "In its absence, and with the obstacles that ambition, love of power, and avarice, especially on the part of those who hold the reins of authority, put in the way even of the possibility of such a scheme, *war* is inevitable."
21 *Philosophy of Law*, pp. 219–225; "Eternal Peace," pp. 69–75.
22 "Eternal Peace," p. 83.
23 *Metaphysic of Morals*, p. 47.
24 *Philosophy of Law*, pp. 210–211.
25 "Principle of Progress," p. 64: Each republic "unable to injure any other by violence, must maintain itself by right alone; and it may hope on real grounds that the others being constituted like itself will then come, on occasions of need, to its aid."
26 "That politics may be reduced to a science," *Hume's Political Discourses* (London, n.d.), pp. 229–243; Kant, "Eternal Peace," p. 80n.
27 *Teleological Judgement*, p. 96.
28 "Eternal Peace," p. 91.
29 "Principle of the Political Order," pp. 3–5.
30 Charles Darwin, *The Origin of Species* (London, 1928), p. 455.
31 "Principle of the Political Order," pp. 15–17; "Principle of Progress," p. 62.
32 "Principles of Political Right," pp. 34–35.
33 "Eternal Peace," p. 95.
34 "Principle of the Political Order," p. 22.
35 *Philosophy of Law*, p. 230.
36 "Principle of the Political Order," p. 17; cf. p. 23: "Applying the same method of study everywhere, both to the internal civil constitutions and laws of the States and to their external relations to each other, we see how in both relations the good they contained served for a certain period to elevate and glorify particular nations, and with themselves, their arts and sciences,—until the defects attaching to their institutions came in time to cause their overthrow."
37 Ibid., p. 20; "Principle of Progress," p. 63.
38 "Eternal Peace," p. 81.
39 *Philosophy of Law*, p. 225.
40 "Principle of Progress," p. 65. Cf. "Eternal Peace," pp. 122–123; and *Philosophy of Law*, pp. 163–164, where Kant emphasizes that the federation must have the function of determining according to law, wherever there is a significant conflict, which interpretation of right should prevail.
41 "Eternal Peace," p. 81; and see above, n. 9. For differences among liberals on this question, see Waltz, *Man, the State, and War* (New York, 1959), ch. 4.
42 "Principle of Progress," pp. 62–63; "Eternal Peace," pp. 97–98.
43 "Eternal Peace," p. 114.
44 *Philosophy of Law*, p. 218, where in addition to what is quoted above, he writes: "This international relation is the foundation of the Right of Equilibrium, or of the 'balance of Power,' among all states that are in active contiguity to each other."
45 "Principle of Progress," p. 65; "Eternal Peace," p. 98.

46 "Principles of Political Right," p. 41n.
47 *Metaphysic of Morals*, pp. 23–24.
48 We must, for example, "postulate the *existence of God*, as the necessary condition of the possibility of the *summum bonum*. . . ." *Practical Reason*, p. 221.
49 *Metaphysic of Morals*, p. 84. This is a difficult problem. To put peace in the infinite future would be to demonstrate its impossibility. Kant must therefore think of sequences in the phenomenal world that are not infinite but do continue without end. This abstruse statement of the problem may help to make clear the philosophic context of Kant's political thought. For this resolution of the problem, I am indebted to S. Körner's superb little book, *Kant* (Penguin, 1955), pp. 163–174.
50 *Philosophy of Law*, p. 224; cf. "Principle of the Political Order," p. 13.
51 *Philosophy of Law*, pp. 229–230.
52 Edwin D. Mead's introduction to the book cited above, n. 5.

2

CONFLICT IN WORLD POLITICS

At least one form of conflict, war, has for centuries been the central concern of those who brood over the fate of men and nations. Yet few students of international relations have developed theories of conflict worth mentioning. Sociologists, psychologists, social psychologists, anthropologists, and economists have dealt with the problem of conflict mainly at the level of tensions within and among individuals and groups. Even at this level, theorists have seldom established criteria for distinguishing conflict from other phenomena.

Conflict is an elusive concept. Its chameleon quality is usually explained by pointing out that conflicts are so complex as always to be mixed in character, compounded of cooperation, competition, and contention in ever-changing and unspecifiable proportions. To be sure, this statement has some validity; but it could be applied to any set of continuing interactions. Successive exchanges between parties certainly may, and often do, yield not only changes in issues and interests but also changes in the ways that the parties relate to each other. The importance of developing some scheme for identifying and classifying conflicts in international relations is enhanced, moreover, by realizing that without one we can hardly say which of the endless differences among states actually constitute examples of conflict. Without some formula for discrimination, conflict becomes synonymous with international relations.

What is conflict?

Depending on perspective and definition, one may see conflict absolutely everywhere or almost nowhere. We have to ask which of an infinite number of collisions, which of the many instances in which contrary forces contend, we will in fact label "conflicts."

In order to develop means of identifying conflict, let us begin with a simple case. Pat and Mike have an argument, and finally Pat hits Mike on the nose. Is this a conflict? The answer is not so simple, for it depends upon what we choose to take as a focus. For which unit do we take the action as being significant—that is, as entailing a cost or providing a benefit? If we focus on Pat, we may conclude that she is *resolving* a conflict; in striking the blow she is

19

lessening an inner tension.[1] At the level of the event, however, we can obviously say that the parties are in conflict. Some incompatibility has brought them to blows. The conflict is in the interaction.

Finally, the term "conflict" may be applied to struggles of wider effect—struggles that have important consequences for some larger organization. If the antagonists are placed within some wider order, then the blows exchanged can be evaluated in terms of their positive or negative effects for that order. Conflicts that promise damage, not only to the contenders but also to the system they are part of, are the most terrible and profound—whether of ego and id, of husband and wife, of sections, classes, and races within a country, or of world-shaking wars.

Strife may contribute to the creation and maintenance of an order, or it may become the means of its destruction. The tension of ego and id enlivens the individual, but the tension, if deepened, may drive him to self-destruction. Whether the unit observed is the person, the pair, the state, or the world of states, a distinction must be made between tensions and collisions that have little or no effect on the system within which they occur and those that contribute to the system's development, maintenance, or disruption. The distinction is difficult to make. Whether tension and struggle internal to the system will drive a person to suicide, dissolve a marriage, tear a country apart in civil war, or destroy an international order, depends not only on the units in contention and the intensity of their strife but also on the strength and resilience of the organizational framework.

Nevertheless, explanation of conflict usually proceeds by looking at the condition of each party. The cause of the conflict is found in the properties of the separate units, as these typical questions suggest: Why did one party commit aggression? Why did the other party resist? The content of conflict, the aims and issues involved, are important; but from the answers to such questions one cannot know how content was transformed into conflict. The mechanisms for transforming the internal properties of parties into conflict between them lie not at their individual levels of organization but at a level of organization that comprehends both of them. Thus it was not Pat or Mike who produced the violent interaction but both of them together. In the absence of one, the other's tensions may have found release in his destroying an object or destroying himself. At the level of the unit, the conflict is seen as internal. When and how internal conflict finds external expression, if it does, cannot be explained in terms of either antagonist. To attempt explanation in unit terms is to commit an "ecological" fallacy—to reach conclusions about events at one level by drawing inferences from events, attributes, and interactions at a different level.[2] Attempted explanation at the unit level leads to the infinite proliferation of variables because at this level no one variable, or set of variables, is sufficient to produce the observed result. We must take the unit view and the organizational view simultaneously and ask what effects different organizational conditions may have on the processes of conflict and the prospects for its resolution.

20

The participants' perceptions of issues and causes will often diverge from the observer's. From the participants' standpoint, the struggle may not be interesting in terms of its generating or wrecking an order. The parties in conflict may care only about their own fates. To them the interesting and important questions then lie at the level of events, issues, motivations, actions intensity of feeling, degree of bitterness, strength of will, amount of cost, magnitude of gain. The parties may see themselves only as actors—as personalities, so to speak, and not as parts of a system. At the same time, from the standpoint of the system, the contention among parts may appear to be only an uninteresting series of collisions. Fortunately, wars that shake the world order, or even a regional order, are rare. The systemic unimportance of most wars encourages students to treat wars as events to be understood simply in terms of the attributes and interactions of the contending units. Even so, from the standpoint of the observer, conflict among units cannot be understood without including the organizational perspective.

This statement leads us to the important but difficult question of applying organizational concepts to international relations. Differentiation is a precondition of conflict, and differentiation implies organization, at least in the sense that the different parts stand in a specifiable relation to each other. We can use the term "organization" to cover this preinstitutional condition if we think of an organization simply as a constraint.[3] Because states constrain and limit each other, international relations can be viewed in rudimentary organizational terms. Each state arrives at policies and decides upon actions according to its own internal processes, but its decisions are shaped by the very presence of other states as well as by interactions with them. To make it clear that "organization" need not refer to concrete institutions, and in international relations ordinarily does not refer to them, we shall use the word "structure" and mean by it the relevant environment of states. Sometimes this will be a merely local or regional environment, but more often global structural effects will also come into play. Like a firm operating in a market, a state experiences structural effects whether or not the structure is correctly perceived; and, again like a firm, if the structure is correctly perceived, the strategy of a state can be more intelligently fashioned. Although states are independent, their perceptions of each other and their interactions create a structure to which they tend to adjust. As a consequence of their experience with one another, much of their action becomes habitual.

International structure and national behavior

One may look at conflict in terms of each of the units involved, in terms of the interactions of units, or in terms of an actual or postulated organization that overarches the units. The first perspective is appropriate only when the units are disconnected or near to being so. The second perspective is always insufficient for the reasons given above. The third perspective is ordinarily the appropriate one in cases of international conflict. If conflicts are viewed in terms of the effects of the environment on them and in terms of their effects on the environment, then the classification of conflicts will hinge on major differences in the structure of international politics. The following table sets forth such distinctions, indicates the modes of behavior typical within the different structures, and distributes our 21 cases of conflict in an appropriate fashion among categories.[4]

STRUCTURE	TYPICAL MODES OF BEHAVIOR
A. *Loose association of states* US and USSR US and China USSR and China Argentina and Chile[a] India and Pakistan[a] Malaysia, Philippines, Indonesia Somalia, Ethiopia, Kenya	*Regression*
B. *Close association of states: Opposition* East and West Germany North and South Korea Israel and the Arab Countries[a] South Vietnam Nigeria and Biafra USSR and Czechoslovakia US and Dominican Republic US and Southeast Asia[a]	*Resolute contention*
C. *Close association of states: Cooperation* France and Germany[a] US and Japan US and Canada Portugal and South Africa Great Britain and France Nuclear proliferation[a]	*Integration*
D. *Nonassociation of states*	*Withdrawal*

Note: [a] The parts of three pairs fall into different categories. These essays were originally grouped for comparative purposes according to characteristics other than structure.

Before taking up each category separately, a few words should be said about the table's right-hand column. It derives from Kurt Singer's profound work on the theory of conflict. He has suggested that in response to situations of conflict:

four and only four basic types of meaningful behavior appear to be possible: renouncing one's objective by staying behind the barrier [regression]; attempting to remove or modify the barrier [integration]; leaving the

22

whole obstructed field [withdrawal]; or resolving to destroy the barrier [resolute contention].

Singer argues persuasively that his classification is complete:

every conflict-solution involves two pairs of opposites, which allow for four and only four combinations: subjective and objective, positive and negative. The subject's attitude may be active or passive; and it may acknowledge the objective incompatibility or repudiate it.[5]

Both regression and withdrawal (*A* and *D*) are passive or negative approaches; both integration and fighting (*C* and *B*) are active or positive. Both in regressing and in fighting (*A* and *B*), the parties accept the presence of an objective incompatibility; both in seeking to integrate and in trying to withdraw (*C* and *D*), they refuse to accept their antagonism. "So long as we cling to the criteria of active and passive, positive and negative attitudes," Singer concludes, "the quadruplet of types can claim completeness and finality."[6]

Singer was writing of conflict in general, from psychic disturbance to war among states. When his categories of conflict are applied to international relations, his claim to completeness is validated. The four types of behavior cover both the strategies of states fending for themselves in an anarchic arena and the strategies of states who try to escape from that arena. *A* and *B* represent the traditional view of international politics, with states sometimes maneuvering to avoid war and at other times fighting fiercely. In *A* and *C*, states seek to avoid violence either by leaving each other alone or by making cooperative arrangements. In *A*, states concentrate their attention on their own fates, a tendency that is carried to an extreme in *D*. In *B*, *C*, and *D*, states seek to alter the organization of their affairs profoundly, though by radically different means in one category as compared to another; and if their aims are realized, international politics is brought to an end within the circle of states involved.

To link behavior with structure requires a careful examination of each category. This examination we now undertake.

Loose association of states: regression

Domestically, the force of a government is exercised in the name of right and justice; internationally, the force of a state is employed for the stake of its own protection and advantage. Rebels challenge a government's claim to authority; they question the rightfulness and justice of its rule. Wars among states cannot settle questions of authority and justice; they can only determine the allocation of gains and losses among contenders and settle for a time the question of who is the stronger. Domestically and internationally, relations of superordination and subordination are established; but internationally these are relations of strength, not of authority. The power of the strong may deter the weak from asserting their claims, not because the weak recognize a kind of rightfulness of rule on the part of the strong, but simply because it is not sensible to tangle with them. Conversely, the weak may enjoy considerable freedom of action and gain some tangible advantage if they are so far removed in their capabilities from the strong that the latter are not much bothered by their actions or much concerned by marginal increases in their capabilities.

In the unalloyed anarchy of international relations, each state provides the means for its self-preservation as best it can. Elements of conflict in the competition of states outweigh those of cooperation. When faced with the possibility of cooperative endeavor by which mutual gains may be scored, each state must ask how those gains will be divided. They are compelled to ask not "Will both of us gain?" but "Who will gain more?" If an expected gain is to be divided, say, in the ratio of two to one, one state may use its disproportionate gain to implement a policy intended to damage or destroy the other. Even the prospect of large absolute gains for both parties does not elicit their cooperation so long as each fears how the other will use its increased capabilities. Notice that the impediments to collaboration may not lie in the character and the immediate intention of either party. Instead, the condition of insecurity—at the least, the uncertainty of each about the other's future intentions and actions—works strongly against their cooperation.

The fate of each state depends on its responses to what other states do. Will these responses lead them to integrate their activities in order to improve their well-being, to contend resolutely, or to draw apart and watch each other with wariness and suspicion? The answer depends not only on the extent to which their fates are linked in terms of security but also on how closely they are entangled in other than military ways.

States are closely interdependent if they depend on each other for services and supplies that they cannot easily, if at all, provide for themselves. Out of a condition of mutual dependence is born the desire of each party to control whatever it is dependent upon. In such a condition, states cannot afford simply to leave each other alone. They have strong incentives to make one of two choices: either to use force in order to gain control or to build institutions in order to secure the benefits of cooperation. Their close interdependence leads them either to strive for dominance or to contrive institutions for the regulation of their intertwined affairs. In their daily lives, however, the states of category *A* are not closely entangled, whether one thinks of entanglement in terms of trade and investment or of cultural exchanges and tourism. Because these states are only loosely connected, they can afford to leave each other alone.

States of category *A* accept each other's continued existence, whether or not reluctantly. They seek neither to destroy the structure of their relations nor to change it drastically; rather, they contend for advantage within it. They do not use their political power to create enduring institutions and peaceful patterns of intercourse, but instead to maneuver and manipulate, to threaten and punish. They appear as both antagonists and partners, sometimes skirmishing in a test of wills, sometimes probing to expose weaknesses, sometimes moving toward agreement on specific issues, sometimes simply drawing apart. In the course of their conflicts, they may go to the brink in a sudden flaring of temper or testing of wills and then draw back. The option of drawing back is available, as is the possibility of occasional skirmishing and even of open warfare. But the structure, a loose one, is not broken either when the parties separate and become quiescent or when they confront each other directly. Their confrontations tend to be inconclusive. Their strategies are grounded on the principle that it is better to yield than to risk mutual destruction. The policy dilemma for states in this type of conflict is that both sides are unwilling to resolve differences completely and establish new patterns of coexistence, yet neither side is prepared to destroy the other.

In their relations with each other, the United States and the Soviet Union provide a nearly perfect example of this pattern. Some of their interests coincide: the prevention of nuclear war, the control of other states' weapons, the mutual limitation of defense budgets for the sake of their domestic economies. At the same time, they differ on a number of issues, notably in Europe, Southeast Asia, and the Middle East. Neither side is prepared to risk military weakness, but none of their disputes can be pushed to the point of war. Mutual opposition may require rather than preclude the adjustment of differences, and yet first steps toward agreement do not easily lead further. Instead, they mingle with other acts and events that keep the tension quite high. In the United States, for example, the 1963 test-ban treaty was described as possibly a first big step toward wider disarmament agreements. In almost the same breath it was also said that the United States could not lower her guard because the Soviet Union's aims had not changed.[7] Each country appears to the other as the only power in the world that can do it grievous harm, and each must worry about the other's use of this capability. Their mutual worry limits both the building up of tensions and the abatement of conflict. Incentives to collaborate, and temptations to fight, are limited by the framework of their action. The result is an ebb and flow of tensions as dramatic agreements are made (test ban, nonproliferation treaty) and as specific crises occur (Berlin, Cuba, the Middle East, Vietnam).

In each case within category *A*, the weaker party has been forced by its weakness to use military force cautiously, to cast about for allies, to resort to ideological warfare, or to readjust its aims. The conflicts between Somalia and Ethiopia/Kenya, and between Pakistan and India, are cases in point. Somalia and Pakistan, both considerably weaker than their adversaries, seek territorial gains at the expense of their neighbors in order to be united with a greater number of their compatriots. Neither of them can destroy its adversary, nor wishes to do so, but their ultimate objectives limit their cooperation. As a consequence, relations between Somalia and Ethiopia/Kenya and between

Pakistan and India tend to be dormant when international and domestic conditions prevent the weaker party from pursuing adventurous policies. When the situation is temporarily altered, violence flares up, as in the brief war of 1965 between Pakistan and India and in the sporadic Somali guerrilla campaign that lasted from 1960 to 1967.

More than other cases in this category, Sino-Soviet and Sino-American relations are marked by intense antagonism; but the general patterns are similar. Territorial issues are a major irritant (Taiwan and the Sino-Soviet border area), although these issues are clearly not the sole causes of conflict. As the weaker party, China is unable to press its designs very far against either the United States or the Soviet Union and presents no important military threat to them. The strong parties are not prepared either to use major military force or to work to strengthen their relations with the weak one. Consequently the typical ebb-and-flow pattern prevails: China moves toward the brink over border incidents with the Soviet Union or in response to American actions in East or Southeast Asia, while at the same time the Chinese talk sporadically with one of the superpowers in Warsaw or in Peking or Moscow.

In category A, regression is the dominant mode. Adventurous powers are forced to mold their intentions to contingencies, to let present goals await future opportunities, and to draw back from dangerous confrontations. As Singer suggests, regressive strategy represents the approach of a peasant—patient, shrewd, and persistent. This is a strategy of "dropping and drifting," but the weaker party is "secure in the knowledge that those who yield will . . . conquer in the end."[8] The policies of China, Pakistan, Somalia, Chile, of all of the Malay states, and even of the Soviet Union can often be viewed in these terms.

Close association of states: resolute contention

In category A, the opposition of states raises the specter of possible warfare, but because opposition centers on particular issues, compromises and trade-offs can always be attempted. And even when states are fighting, they intermittently bargain and cajole.

In category B, the parties contend not simply over the difficult issue of who shall gain or lose. They struggle instead with the calamitous question: Who shall dominate whom? The answer to that question can satisfy only one of the parties. Politics, or political form, becomes the stake around which the conflict revolves. One of the parties in contention, and perhaps both of them, seeks to destroy the structure of their relations by undoing the other regime and, in some cases, by displacing its people. Structural struggles spawn strategies of resolute contention; at least one party decides that he will persist in the struggle even should this mean his own destruction. Bargaining becomes impossible, and the conflict becomes the communication.

As the cases of category B suggest, great-power interventions, civil wars, and contention among the dissimilar parts of states that were once united are characteristic instances of this type of struggle. In great-power interventions, conflict is resolved through the adjustment of goals by one party; the weaker state gives way in the face of the threats or the force of the stronger. In civil wars and in the struggle between the parts of a divided state, resolution comes, if it comes at all, through military triumph. Either these conflicts end definitely and abruptly as a result of military action, or they continue in crisis as long as the goal of destruction remains a part of the policy of one of the parties.

The Nigerian civil war was a typical conflict over structure. The conflict could not be resolved through compromise because the conflict involved nothing less than the question of whether one state or two would occupy the area known as Nigeria. As long as Biafra continued to exist, the aims of the Federal Government were thwarted. The defeat of Biafra transferred Ibo-Nigerian relations to another framework. In the Arab–Israeli conflict, the Israelis have managed to perpetuate their existence, but they have not managed to alter the aim of their Arab neighbors to destroy Israel. Their intense confrontation has furthered the integration of Israel and has produced some coherence among deeply divided Arab states. Unless at least one side drastically alters its definition of acceptable political arrangements, intense conflict will continue indefinitely.

·Conflict within South Vietnam and between the two Germanies and the two Koreas turns on political and ideological differences, in contrast to the strong religious and ethnic divisions in the Middle East. In the German case, the prospect that force will be used to achieve reunification has receded in recent years. The most hopeful possibility in cases of this type is that, as the parties develop separate and viable regimes, the issue politics of category *A* will replace the structural struggles of category *B*. The parties may then discover, as the two Germanies show signs of doing, that they can cooperate on some matters without turning every issue into a test of the legitimacy of regimes. In the Korean case, close kinship has not led to reestablishment of social and economic contacts across a hostile frontier. The very intensity of hostility has promoted the tight political integration of both Koreas, a development that vividly illustrates the maxim that organizations are created by their enemies.[9] The political success of the two Koreas has at once lessened their need for each other and made them capable of vying fiercely for mastery.

At whatever level of intensity, the parties to these conflicts share a dissatisfaction with the status quo. They see their basic goals as being incompatible and define the question between them as being, who shall ultimately prevail?

The three cases of great-power intervention are like the others of this category in that the struggle is over the structure, but different in that the parties are of grossly unequal power. These interventions represent forceful attempts to alter conditions within particular states or regions in order to bring client states into conformity with the superpowers' notions of proper political arrangements. In each instance, the superpower demonstrated concern over the integrity of its alliance system and, more profoundly, betrayed a fear that failure to maintain control in one area would weaken its control and lessen the credibility of its commitments elsewhere. In the Dominican Republic and in Czechoslovakia, solutions were swiftly and decisively achieved in central areas of the superpowers' concerns. In Southeast Asia, the United States sought to reinforce her position at the periphery of her sphere of interest rather than at the core. She was unable to change conditions quickly and was also unwilling to yield. Prolonged conflict resulted. In South Vietnam, the American problem has not been merely to dissuade a government from taking certain actions and to compel it to perform others. Instead, America's self-appointed task has been to promote the establishment of a preferred political order, an immense undertaking that requires far more than military means. American aims, if achieved, would maintain the conditions for continued struggle among the new parts of the old Indochina. Any major part of Indochina that achieves strength will want to reunify the whole. That is the nature of structural struggles. The might of the superpowers allows them to determine the size and the intensity of such conflicts, but not always the outcome.

In structural strife, when the conflict is among unequals the stronger parties face difficult tasks. They wish to retain control or to maintain their friends in power, and such ends are difficult to achieve. In structural strife, when the conflict is among equals the struggles have continued interminably.

Close association of states: integration

What can bring two parties closer together than to be locked into a prolonged death-grip? The states of category *B* are closely associated; they are united in their antagonism. The states of category *C* are also closely associated, but in cooperative rather than hostile spirit. If states believe that violent conflict would destroy their common good, they may try to promote closer integration through the establishment of durable institutions and reliable patterns of behavior. What makes it possible for trust to replace hostility in the relations of sovereign states so that they may begin to benefit jointly from peaceful and cooperative endeavors? This question can best be answered by considering the change in the quality of the relations of western European states that took place after 1945. For centuries before that date, European great-power politics tended toward the model of a zero-sum game. One state viewed another's loss as its own gain and was constrained to do so by the very conditions of their mutual existence. Faced with the temptation to cooperate in order to secure joint benefits, each state became wary and was inclined to draw back. Category *A* described the condition of their precarious peacetime existence, a condition that made regression more appropriate than integration. When, on occasion, some European states did move toward cooperation, they did so in order to oppose other states more strongly. The fear that some states would contend resolutely in a structural struggle for dominance overwhelmed the possibilities of European integration. European states could not break the alternation from loose association and regressive behavior to close association and resolute contention as long as each state feared the damaging blows that other states could strike.

The emergence of the Russian and American superpowers created a situation that permitted wider ranging and more effective cooperation among the states of western Europe. They became consumers of security, to use an expression common in the days of the League of Nations. For the first time in modern history, the determinants of war and peace lay outside the arena of European states, and the means of their preservation were provided by others. These new circumstances made possible the famous "upgrading of the common interest," a phrase which conveys the thought that all should work together to improve everyone's lot rather than being obsessively concerned with the precise division of benefits. Not all impediments to cooperation were removed, but one important one was—the fear that the greater advantage of one would be translated into military force to be used against the others. Living in the superpowers' shadow, Britain, France, Germany, and Italy quickly saw that war among them would be fruitless and soon began to believe it impossible.

Once the possibility of war among states disappears, all of them can more freely run the risk of suffering a relative loss. Enterprises can be engaged in that are expected to benefit some parties more than others, partly in the hope for the latter that in other activities the balance of benefits will be reversed and partly in the belief that the overall enterprise itself is valuable. Economic gains may be granted by one state to another in exchange for expected political advantages, including the benefit of strengthening the structure of European cooperation. The removal of worries about security among the states of western Europe does not mean the termination of conflict; it does produce a change in its content. Hard bargaining within the EEC (by France over agricultural policies, for example) indicates that governments do not lose interest in who will gain more and who will gain less. Conflicts of interest remain, but not the expectation that someone will use force to resolve them.

International conditions permitted western European nations to work to upgrade their common interests. The self-interest of each nation encouraged it to join in, as is evident even in the policy of the most reluctant participant, Great Britain. Mutuality of involvement, and the intertwining of affairs, have drawn these states into common endeavors. They cannot easily, if at all, choose to leave each other alone. Because they cannot, the experience of conflict over interests and over purposes leads to efforts to create an apparatus that will reduce conflict or contain it. Politics—negotiation, log-rolling, compromise—becomes the means of achieving preferred arrangements. To manage conflict, a closer integration of activities is sought. The organization by which integration is to be promoted then becomes the object of struggle. How shall it be constructed, and what shall its purposes be? Once these become the most important questions, international relations begin to look like domestic politics.

Saying this makes it clear that some of the cases placed in category *C* may belong in category *A*, or may come to belong there. What placement is appropriate depends on how two questions are answered. Do the parties regard the framework of their relations as being so important that they are willing to compromise on particular military and economic issues in order to preserve and strengthen it? Are the parties free simply to leave each other alone? If the answers are first "yes" and then "no," category *C* is appropriate.

Contiguity, involvement in each other's affairs, mutual confidence built on common experiences—such factors lessen the possibility and the desirability of turning from cooperation and constructive competition and moving instead toward opposition and sharp contention on issues. The high interdependence of some states, as in the case of western Europe, locks them into a cooperative system, and so may the dependence of one state on another, as in the case of the United States and Canada. The close but asymmetric intermingling of their affairs affords the United States many ways of exerting influence.[10] The United States does not have to substitute force for persuasion. The imbalance of capabilities makes it unnecessary to do so. Each party, moreover, recognizes that its interests are better served by negotiating differences than by openly quarreling over them.

A state's perception of its own strength affects its definition of interest. In the six cases of category *C*, three types of weakness have encouraged behavior aimed at strengthening the structure:

1. The parties perceive themselves to be weak in relation to the great powers (West European states).
2. The parties fear potential weakness in relation to adversaries (Portugal and South Africa).
3. A marked difference in capabilities exists between the parties (US and Canada, US and Japan, the superpowers and potential nuclear states).

The nonproliferation treaty nicely shows how, on a particular issue, two countries may try to create a structure distinct from the general structure of their relations. Overall, American–Soviet relations fall into category *A*. The nonproliferation treaty appears, then, as a case of cooperation on a single issue born out of the desire of duopolists to preserve favored positions, a motivation clearly expressed by William C. Foster in 1965 when he was director of the Arms Control and Disarmament Agency:

> *When we consider the cost to us of trying to stop the spread of nuclear weapons, we should not lose sight of the fact that widespread nuclear proliferation would mean a substantial erosion in the margin of power*

which our great wealth and industrial base have long given us relative to much of the rest of the world.[11]

In order to maintain their advantages, strong states may wish to regulate the activities of weak states.

The case of the nonproliferation treaty also shows how different the same structure may look from the standpoint of different states. States that are reluctant to foreswear becoming nuclear powers indefinitely will see American–Soviet regulation not as a limited experiment in institution-building but instead as a simple case of contention. Disarmament efforts have been sponsored mainly by the United States and the Soviet Union. Not surprisingly, they have attempted primarily to regulate other people's armaments. "This has resulted," as a Japanese scholar points out, "in formulating regulations governing non-existent armaments—nuclear weapons of non-nuclear countries rather than governing existing armaments—nuclear weapons of nuclear powers."[12] Self-interest and common interest do not always diverge; the United States and the Soviet Union have tried to persuade other states to believe that a system of regulation will benefit all. Whether the treaty results in a durable system for effective regulation of course remains to be seen.

Nonassociation of states: withdrawal

Category *D* is important, and yet it is devoid of cases. The explanation is obvious. "Conflict can occur," as Lewis Coser has said, "only in the interaction between subject and object; it always presupposes a relationship."[13] If effectively pursued, withdrawal strategies eliminate contact. The conflict of the parties may be deeply felt, but if the connection between them is broken, the conflict cannot find violent expression. There is then no case to write about.

In the absence of cases, we can nevertheless say a few words about withdrawal strategies both in aspiration and in reality. The ideal of most anarchists rests on the thought that lessening contacts reduces the possibility of conflict. They have dreamt of small communities of like-minded men living at peace with other such communities because all of them would be nearly self-sufficient and thus little involved in each other's business. The League of Nations' policy of plebiscites, which offered minority ethnic groups the chance to separate themselves from uncongenial nations, was in effect a strategy of preventing conflict by disentangling peoples. National strategies of withdrawal are usually pursued by countries that are especially weak or especially strong. The classic neutralist policies of Switzerland, Sweden, and Belgium, the aspirations of presently underdeveloped countries to remain "unaligned," Britain's traditional aloofness toward continental affairs, American isolationism—all of these fall into the category of withdrawal strategies. The possibility of withdrawing increases with distance. Withdrawal is an option available to the

31

United States in Southeast Asia, but not to Israel, Czechoslovakia, Biafra, and North and South Vietnam. The effects of withdrawal strategies are found not in cases of conflict but in instances of conflict resolution, of which more will shortly be said.

Situations and strategies

In each category of the table, a mode of behavior tends to dominate: regression, resolute contention, integration, or withdrawal. Rarely, however, does one of the four modes entirely prevail in the policies adopted by states. Several reasons for the mixture of modes are prominent.

First, the leaders of a state may fully understand the situation they face and may adopt corresponding policies. These leaders may, however, be displeased with the results of their policies and feel inclined to forsake or modify them. The two Koreas and the two Germanies, for example, seek to absorb each other in order to reunify their countries. But through a policy of resolute contention in which the legitimacy of the present structure is denied, a new order is inadvertently created. Each side develops new political, economic, and military ties with a different circle of states. A policy of withdrawal ensues that lessens contact between the two sides and decreases the likelihood of destructive conflict as well. Thus, a policy of resolute contention may foster the opponent's integration into a new order. The desire of the Brandt government to increase contacts with East Germany is based partly on the realization that by resolutely denying the legitimacy of the present structure, the West German government has actually strengthened it.

Second, even if the structure of its relations with others should strongly press a state to adopt a particular strategy, the leaders of the state may fail to understand just what the situation requires. Moreover, the pressures of global and regional structures may push in opposite directions. The complexity of most conflicts makes their placement in one category or another uncertain. We usually find mixed cases, not pure ones. The problem of proper placement becomes still more difficult when the policies of states produce changes, as in the German manner just mentioned, that move a case from one category to another or cause it to fluctuate among them. Even if situation determined strategy uniquely, the difficulties of defining situations precisely would still make for perplexity of choice among strategies.

Third, and most important in practice, the structural factor is only one causal force operating among many. Leaders may well appreciate the strength of the constraints upon them, but they may squirm at the thought of accepting them. China, for example, has pursued a strategy of regression in her actions, but a policy of resolute contention in her many defiant proclamations. The regressive strategy indicates her clear perception of limits; bold statements presumably express the frustrations felt. The vastly superior power of an opponent is a strong argument for adopting strategies of regression or withdrawal. Put starkly, if the superior power presses hard, the weak party should simply surrender. The Dubcek and Balaguer regimes quickly did so; Vietcong and Biafran leaders pursued policies of resolute contention instead. Structural constraints are barriers, but men can try to jump over them. Structure shapes and limits choices; it establishes behavioral tendencies without determining behavior.

Resolution of conflict

Any one of the four modes of behavior, if formulated in an appropriate strategy and effectively carried through, resolves the conflict: actively, by integrating the parties through common institutions and procedures or by the conquest and absorption of one by the other; passively, by lessening their interactions or by breaking relations completely.

Active resolution seeks to manage conflict, or to end it, by strategies that increase conflict in the short run. The entanglement of states, in their economic affairs, in their physical fears, and in their ideological differences, draws them into conflict and violence. Many of the bitterest and bloodiest wars have been fought by peoples who were closely involved in each other's affairs and who, being most like each other, became obsessed with differences in interests and creeds that outsiders could not even understand.

Strategies of integration seek to promote closer mutual involvement. If successful, such strategies multiply the possibilities of conflict. These strategies are pursued, however, in the expectation that the experience of conflict will itself encourage the parties to seek means of regulation and management. To follow the integrative imperative means not to lessen tensions but to strengthen the order that contains them. The strategy is active and constructive; to the extent that it is successful, it takes the "international" out of international relations by subjecting the interactions of nations to a common control.

The imperative of resolute contention requires that one party struggle to prevail over its opponent, to break his will. The strategy is active, but destructive. The integration of the parties is once again the objective, but here by establishing a relation of dominator and dominated. The victor establishes a new imperium that places once independent states under his own protection and control. However achieved, integration ends international conflict by abolishing international relations.

Not conflict, but the insistence that conflicts be resolved, leads to the use of force. One way to manage a conflict is to refrain from using force in an attempt to resolve it. Using force may produce a settlement to the user's satisfaction; it may help to bring a more adequate organization into being; or it may end in mutual damage and destruction. One may decide to leave the benefits of integration aside in order to avoid risking the calamities of war. Passive modes of resolution avoid this risk. The parties potentially in conflict try to move backward to a looser organization, a simpler order, in which states interact less frequently and in less important ways, gain more autonomy, and become less interdependent. By regression, states reduce their contacts without ending them in the hope that yielding on issues will become easier. The final strategy for the passive resolution of conflict is withdrawal. If states had no relations, they could fight no wars.

As Georg Simmel has said in effect: no conflict, no movement.[14] In individual and in domestic political terms, the modern western mind associates movement with progress. Active strategies draw the parties together. They intensify conflict, and they offer the prospect of increased benefits through the development and management of collective enterprises. But in the relations of states the possibility of promoting progress through conflictive processes carries high costs. In order to evaluate active and passive strategies, we should look at the effects of those processes.

If force may be used by some states to weaken or destroy others, then all states live in fear and are likely to exaggerate the evil intentions and the dangers involved. The possibility that conflict will be conducted by force leads to competition in the arts and the instruments of force. Competition produces a tendency toward the sameness of the competitors, with those who are unable to keep up simply falling by the wayside. Thus Bismarck's startling victories over Austria in 1866 and France in 1870 quickly led the major continental powers (and Japan) to imitate the Prussian military staff system, and the failure of Britain and the United States to follow the pattern simply indicated that they were outside of the immediate arena of competition. Contending states imitate the military innovations contrived by the country of greatest capability and ingenuity. And so the weapons of major contenders, and even their strategies, begin to look much the same all over the world.

The effects of competition are not confined narrowly to the military realm. Something that might be called socialization to the international political system also occurs. Immediately after their revolution, for example, Bolsheviks appeared on the international scene as the hippies of their day. By his manner of speaking, his dress, and his lifestyle, the hippy dramatically says, "I will not be socialized to *this* system." So the Bolsheviks in the early years of their power preached international revolution and flaunted the conventions of diplomacy. The attitude was well expressed by Trotsky, who, when asked what he would do as foreign minister, replied, "I will issue some revolutionary proclamations to the peoples and then close up the joint."[15] In a competitive arena, however, one party may need the assistance of others. Refusal to play the political game may risk one's own destruction. The pressures of competition were rapidly felt and reflected in the Soviet Union's diplomacy. Thus Lenin, sending foreign minister Chicherin to the Genoa Conference of 1922, bade him farewell with this caution: "Avoid big words."[16] Chicherin, who personified the carefully tailored traditional diplomat rather than the simply uniformed revolutionary, was to refrain from inflammatory rhetoric for the sake of working deals. These he successfully completed with that other pariah power and ideological enemy, Germany.

The close juxtaposition of states promotes their sameness through the disadvantages that arise from a failure to conform to accepted and successful practices. In the Darwinian view, the contending parties are carried to ever higher levels of accomplishment. But in international politics we may well wish that we could forego some of the movement in exchange for a reduction of conflict through the regression of states. And not only that. One may identify conflict with movement, and movement with progress, and applaud the gradual conformity of states to the patterns set by the most highly developed ones. Or one may view such conformity as a denial of national individuality and deplore the reduction of variety.

It has often been argued that benefits would accrue from passive strategies, not only in terms of the relations of states, but also in terms of those states themselves. Viewed internationally, withdrawal is a negative policy, its imperatives being "do less," "become passive," "acquiesce," "retreat." Viewed internally, the aims of the policy may be positive: to perfect the society, to develop the economy, to strengthen the political order—in short, to become less involved in others' affairs in order to tend to one's own. Plato believed, and he has been echoed by a long line of utopian writers, that only the isolated state could realize its own individuality. Rousseau saw and deplored the homogenization of European culture that was developing from the close interplay of European states and their peoples. American isolationists prized and sought to preserve their nation's detachment from Europe so that a new world could be fashioned free of contamination from the old one. And many now deplore the Coca-Cola-ization of the world. These examples strongly support the argument that only the isolated state can preserve its distinctive personality and have the chance to develop that personality according to its own inner character.

Active strategies promise peace through the more adequate organization of closely interconnected activities. Passive strategies promise peace through lessening the contacts among contenders. Either way, international conflict is ultimately ended only by abolishing international relations. Kant's vision of perpetual peace through a voluntary union of republics competes with Rousseau's utopia of an isolated Corsica. Neither condition is attainable—hence the ubiquity of conflict and the recurrence of war among states.

Acknowledgments

I am indebted to Ellyn J. Hessler, whose unpublished paper on conflict was very helpful in the writing of this essay, and to Helen E. Waltz, who suggested a number of substantive, organizational, and stylistic improvements.

Notes

1 Cf. Lewis Coser, *The Functions of Social Conflict* (New York: Free Press, 1956), pp. 39–40.
2 For definitions and illustrations of ecological fallacies, see W. S. Robinson "Ecological Correlations and the Behavior of Individuals," *American Sociological Review*, XV (June 1950), pp. 351–357, and Erwin K. Scheuch, "Cross-National Comparisons Using Aggregate Data: Some Substantive and Methodological Problems," in Richard L. Merritt and Stein Rokkan eds., *Comparing Nations: The Use of Quantitative Data in Cross National Research* (New Haven: Yale University Press, 1966), pp. 131–167.
3 W. Ross Ashby, *An Introduction to Cybernetics* (New York: Wiley, 1956), p. 131.
4 Although this book contains 22 separate essays, only 21 cases appear in the table. The discrepancy is accounted for by the fact that two essays were devoted to the Soviet–American case.
5 Kurt Singer, "The Resolution of Conflict," *Social Research*, 6 (1949), 241. See also his "The Meaning of Conflict," *Australasian Journal of Philosophy*, 27 (December 1949) and *The Idea of Conflict* (Melbourne University Press, 1949).
6 Singer, "The Resolution of Conflict," p. 242.
7 Cf. Kenneth N. Waltz, "The Stability of a Bipolar World," *Daedaelus*, 93 (Summer 1964), 903–904.
8 Singer, "The Resolution of Conflict," p. 231.
9 Kenneth E. Boulding, *Conflict and Defense* (New York: Harper & Row, 1962), p. 162.
10 In 1965, for example, US residents owned 44 percent of the total capital invested in Canadian manufacturing firms. M. Watkins et al., Report of the Task Force on the Structure of Canadian Industry, *Foreign Ownership and the Structure of Canadian Industry* (Ottawa: The Queen's Printer, 1968), pp. 199–200.
11 William C. Foster, "Arms Control and Disarmament," *Foreign Affairs*, 43 (July 1965), p. 591.
12 Hisashi Maeda, *The Nature of Disarmament Problems in the Nuclear Age*, unpublished ms. (Honolulu: East-West Center, 1970), p. i.
13 Lewis Coser, *The Functions of Social Conflict*, p. 59.
14 Georg Simmel, *Conflict and the Web of Group Affiliation*, translated by Kurt H. Wolff and Reinhardt Bendix (New York: Free Press, 1955), pp. 14–16.
15 Leon Trotsky, quoted in Theodore H. Von Laue, "Soviet Diplomacy: G. V. Chicherin, Peoples' Commissar for Foreign Affairs 1918–1930," in Gordon A. Craig and Felix Gilbert eds., *The Diplomats 1919–1939*, 1 (New York: Atheneum, 1963), p. 235.
16 V. I. Lenin, quoted in Barrington Moore Jr., *Soviet Politics: The Dilemma of Power* (Cambridge, MA: Harvard University Press, 1950), p. 204.

3

REFLECTIONS ON *THEORY OF INTERNATIONAL POLITICS*

A Response to My Critics

Richard Ashley says that older realists, despite some limitations, set a high standard of political reasoning from which I and other neorealists have regressed. Robert Keohane says that I merely reformulated realism and made it more systematic without developing "new ways of seeing" international relations (1983: 515). Ashley and Robert Cox are highly critical of structural approaches. John Ruggie complains that having started down the structural path, I failed to follow the path to its end (1983, part V; reprinted above). Facing a variety of criticisms, perhaps I can best begin by saying what I tried to accomplish in *Theory of International Politics.*[1] My aim was to do the following:

1. Develop a more rigorous theory of international politics than earlier realists had done.
2. Show how one can distinguish unit-level from structural elements and then make connections between them.
3. Demonstrate the inadequacy of the prevalent inside-out pattern of thinking that has dominated the study of international politics.
4. Show how state behavior differs, and how expected outcomes vary, as systems change.
5. Suggest some ways in which the theory can be tested and provide some examples of its practical application, largely to economic and military problems.

Structures and units

Anyone who believes that a systemic theory is required for an adequate understanding of international politics has to distinguish between structural and unit levels. In making the distinction, whether certain components belong at one level or the other is not immediately apparent. By my definition, national political structures are spare, and international-political structures even sparer. The second term of the definition—"specification of the functions of formally differentiated units"—appears in domestic but not in international structures as I conceive of them. This leaves only the first and third terms, the ordering principle of the system—anarchy—and the distribution of capabilities across its units—the states. Ruggie argues impressively, but in the end unconvincingly, for restoring the second term. He tries to show that because I omitted it, both a dimension of change and a determinant of change are missing from my model (p. 148). He seeks to capture both the dimension and the determinant by subtly redefining "differentiation."

Ruggie draws a distinction between differentiation meaning "that which denotes *differences* rather than that which denotes *separateness*" (p. 142). The sociologically "proper" definition of differentiation tells us on what basis the segmentation of an anarchic realm is determined. The second component of international-political structure is thus rescued from oblivion. He then argues that "dynamic density," as defined by Durkheim, should have been included in my model as well, since variations in density may be determinants of systemic transformation.

In our discourse, saying who was more faithful to Durkheim is less important than finding the theoretically most tenable and practically most useful definition of structure. Durkheim is nevertheless an able guide to the elusive prey. He distinguishes between societies of mechanical and of organic solidarity, corresponding respectively to the anarchic order of international politics and the hierarchic order of domestic politics. Durkheim describes a mechanical society as "a multitude of little centres, distinctive and alike" (1893:257). They have their own needs and interests, but they do not interact through their special characteristics in such a way as to become entangled in one another's affairs and dependent on one another's efforts. Each unit does for itself roughly what all of the others are doing. Their lives are characterized by a duplication of effort rather than by a division of labor that would produce their integration. Interactions and exchanges among segments are variable and sporadic. Exchange of products, even if more or less regular, gives rise only to "simple relations of *mutualism* having nothing in common with the division of labor" (1893:282).[2] Like units interact only marginally because of their pervasive resemblance. The more nearly units are alike, the less they can gain by cooperating with one another.

The segments of a mechanical society may grow or may shrink. They may range in size from the clans of what anthropologists call segmentary lineage societies, to villages and cities, to such extensive territorial organizations as nations. The distinction between types of society is not one of size. A society may attain great size, but so long as it is composed of similar segments its unity remains mechanical. Because the parts remain little dependent on one another, any of them can be severed from the whole with little effect on the consciousness, happiness, health, and well-being of the remaining parts (1893:148–149, 261).

A mechanical society rests on the similarity of the units that compose it; an organic society is based on their differences. An organic society promotes the sharpening of individual talents and skills. Different parts of the society make their particular contributions to its general welfare. Units become closely linked because they do special jobs and then exchange goods and services in order to meet their common requirements. The division of labor increases efficiency and promotes the general prosperity. More important still, the division of labor makes for social solidarity. As Durkheim says, "when men unite in a contract, it is because, through the division of labor . . . they need each other" (1893:212). The parts of a highly developed society are tightly integrated. Some parts depend on others for services and supplies that they cannot easily, if at all, provide for themselves.[3] Mechanical societies are loosely linked through the resemblance of their members. Organic societies become closely integrated through the differences of their members.

The division of labor renders "societies possible which, without it, would not exist." Social structure is transformed as society progresses from mechanical to organic unity. From differences of structure predictions can be made. Understanding this enabled Durkheim to make one of the most striking predictions to be found in social-science literature. The sexual division of labor, he writes, establishes "a social and moral order *sui generis.*" The division of labor brings unlikes together. Unlike individuals depend on each other precisely because their different activities, the distinct tasks they perform, contribute to their mutual satisfaction and benefit. Unlikes become strongly glued together because they depend on one another's different abilities and skills. It follows that if the division of labor were to lessen, for example if the roles of the sexes became less distinct, marriage would become less stable, and "conjugal society would eventually subsist in sexual relations preeminently ephemeral" (1893:61). The union of likes is brittle because one's own efforts can replace the other's contributions.

The transition from mechanical to organic society proceeds as more and more individuals come "sufficiently in contact to be able to act and react upon one another. If we agree to call this relation and the active [social and economic] commerce resulting from it dynamic or moral density, we can say that the progress of the division of labor is in direct ratio to the moral or dynamic density of society" (1893:257). Durkheim's view seems much in accord with Ruggie's interpretation. Dynamic density acts as a force that may transform mechanical societies or produce a transition from an anarchic to a hierarchic order. In Ruggie's words, *"the principles on the basis of which the constituent units are separated* from one another" have changed (p. 142, his italics). But for Durkheim this is only because the units themselves have become different. They are no longer similar segments weakly united by their resemblance. They have instead become dissimilar parts of a society strongly united by their differences. Durkheim's transformation of society is not rooted in differentiation defined as a principle of separation; it is rooted in the differences of the parts.

How do simple societies become complex ones? Simple and complex societies are organized according to opposite principles. Complex societies grow out of simple societies and must overcome them. In Durkheim's view, the "segmental arrangement is an insurmountable obstacle to the division of labor" (1893:256; cf. 182–185); a structural transformation, the replacement of one principle of order by another, is nothing short of a revolution in social life. How might such a revolution be produced and conducted? Revolution breaks out when the "growth and condensation of societies . . . *necessitate* a greater division of labor*." Population grows; the struggle for existence becomes acute; war breaks out and becomes more violent the harder the population presses on the resources available. The more acute the struggle, the greater the social progress. The stronger segments of the old society forge ahead at the expense of the weaker. The "triumphant segmental organs" take on the vaster tasks of society; the losers are left with the lesser ones (1893:262–272). The division of labor develops in the struggle and flourishes within the newly integrated society. Durkheim faces up to what revolutions ordinarily entail—fierce and bloody struggle with risks high and outcomes always uncertain.

A few points require emphasis. First, the social segments of the old society must begin to break down before the division of labor can appear (1893:256). Because the new social type rests on such different principles, "it can develop only in proportion to the effacement" of the preceding society (1893:182). The transformation of the old structure begins, as Durkheim emphasizes, only when the segments of a mechanical society are thrown upon one another, only when their fates become tightly entangled because of the intense pressures of the struggle for survival (1893:266). Dynamic density consists not only in economic transactions but also in social ones. It is "a function of a number of individuals who are actually having not only commerce but also social relations, i.e., who not only exchange services or compete with one another but also live a common life." The paragraph is worth completing. "For, as purely economic relations leave men estranged from one another, there may be continuous relations of that sort without participation in the same collective existence. Business carried on across the frontiers which separate peoples does not abolish these frontiers" (1895:114). The transformation of social structure is not produced by the mere mutualism of international trade.

Second, the change in property relations that Ruggie identifies with the shift from medieval to modern politics is significant. It is not for Durkheim, nor I should think for most systems theorists, a transformation of structure. The change Ruggie identifies does not move international society from a condition in which like units are weakly held together by their similarities to one in which unlike units are united by their differences. Only a structural

REFLECTIONS ON *THEORY OF INTERNATIONAL POLITICS*

transformation can abolish the international imperative—take care of yourself!
—and replace it with the domestic one—specialize!

The redefinition of property relations, however important it may be, cannot produce a transformation of the international system. Dynamic density may have reshaped the structure of property rights, but that took place within different societies, as Ruggie himself says (pp. 148–150). The point is important since it is often thought, wrongly, that any change having widespread repercussions must be a structural change or even a systemic transformation. Ruggie says that he would be surprised if the changes he alludes to—demographic trends, resource constraints, and the like—"do not adversely affect the managerial capacity of bipolarity and, thereby, alter systemic outcomes" (p. 151). So would I. I would be surprised if many different sorts of unit-level changes did not alter systemic outcomes. Ruggie says that I omit such forces. Yet I define a system as consisting of a structure and of interacting units. The question is not one of omission but of the level at which one sees such forces operating. Changes in some or in all of the units will make their relations harder, or easier, to manage. I might add to Ruggie's cogent example a still stronger one: the nuclear revolution in military weaponry. In my view, the two biggest changes in international politics since World War II are the structural shift from multi- to bipolarity and the unit-level change in the extent and rapidity with which some states can hurt others. Surely, the second change, like the first one, has system-wide effects. Wars that might bring nuclear weapons into play have become much harder to start. One must be struck by the fact that over the centuries great powers have fought more wars and minor states have fought fewer. The frequency of war has correlated less closely with the attributes of states than with their international standing. Standing, of course, is a structural characteristic. Yet because of a change in military technology, a change at the unit level, waging war has more and more become the privilege of poor and weak states. A unit-level change has much diminished a structural effect.

Ruggie has described some forces that "adversely affect the managerial capacity of bipolarity." Unfortunately, in doing so he mingles structural and unit levels. Greatly reducing the odds that war will occur among the great and the major powers represents a profound change in the quality of international life, such as only a structural transformation would ordinarily bring. Just what is, and what is not, changed by the nuclear revolution in weaponry? What has changed is this: The international system has become more peaceful, at least at the top. Since the nuclear revolution, states relate to one another differently, yet each state still has to take care of itself as best it can. Nuclear states continue to compete militarily. The continuity of the system, lodged in its structure, accounts for the latter. Nuclear weapons in the hands of some of the states help to account for the former. Nuclear states are loathe to use their most powerful weapons except in the service of peace, that is, for the sake of deterrence. The latter part of Ruggie's otherwise penetrating essay mixes unit and structural matters.

41

Third, Ruggie is right in saying that for me international structure is not fully generative (pp. 135–136; 148–152). A "generative model of structure" should not be expected to generate all that goes on within a system. Ruggie thinks that structure should contain a logic that accounts for its own transformation and believes that Durkheim's dynamic density reflects "structural effects *and* aggregated unit-level processes" (fn. 45). Ruggie compounds unit-level and structural forces, thus illustrating how difficult it is to keep the levels of a system consistently distinct and separate. Careful though Ruggie has been, his attempt to explain more through structure by increasing its content proves to be the first step down the slippery slope toward reduction. I admire Ruggie's fine and rich account of the historical transition from the medieval to the modern state. The account, however, tells us nothing about the structure of international politics. Durkheim did not confound the internal condition of states with their external environment. Durkheim did not think of dynamic density as part of a system's structure. Dynamic density is a unit-level condition that may burst the bonds of the old system and break its structure apart. Far from thinking of unit-level processes as "all product . . . and . . . not at all productive" (p. 151), I, like Durkheim, think of unit-level processes as a source both of changes in systems and of possible changes of systems, hard though it is to imagine the latter. Neither structure nor units determine outcomes. Each affects the other.

In defining structure, what then are the criteria of inclusion and exclusion? Since not much goes into the definition of structure, a negative injunction is appropriate. Asking whether something is important cannot tell us whether it should be included or excluded. If all that is important for a system were in its structure, then we could ignore the units of the system. We would be saying that structures are determinant, even while knowing that politics is a problematic and uncertain arena of action. Ruggie widens the criteria of inclusion by arguing that property relations, because they affect the way states relate to one another, should be included. His reasoning makes the criteria of inclusion infinitely expansible. Nuclear weapons, as I have said, strongly affect how states relate to one another. So do national ideologies. Surely totalitarian and democratic states relate to one another differently than did the old monarchic states. And one could go on and on.

Still, one might ask why the distribution of capabilities across states should be included in the definition of structure and not other characteristics of states that could be cast in distributional terms. The simple answer is that an international-political system is one of self-help. In a self-help system, states are differently placed by their power. States are self-regarding units. State behavior varies more with differences of power than with differences in ideology, in internal structure of property relations, or in governmental form. In self-help systems, the pressures of competition weigh more heavily than ideological preferences or internal political pressures.

In effect, Ruggie is saying that power does not tell us enough about the placement of states in the system. He is right, but he draws the wrong conclusion. Structures never tell us all that we want to know. Instead they tell us a small number of big and important things. They focus our attention on those components and forces that usually continue for long periods. Clean and simple definitions of structure save us from the pernicious practice of summoning new systems into being in response to every salient change within a system. They direct our attention to the units and to unit-level forces when the particularity of outcomes leads us to search for more idiosyncratic causes than are found in structures.

The world of states is older than any state in it. Thinking only of the modern state system, conventionally dated from 1648, today's states are hardly recognizable when compared with their originals even where their names survive from a distant time. Through all of the changes of boundaries, of social, economic, and political form, of economic and military activity, the substance and style of international politics remain strikingly constant. We can look farther afield, for example, to the China of the warring states era or to the India of Kautilya, and see that where political entities of whatever sort compete freely, substantive and stylistic characteristics are similar. Ruggie would elevate qualities of the units shared by some or by all of them to the level of structure. When the units of an anarchic system develop new qualities through changes of "property rights," of "social formation," and of "state/society relations" (pp. 149–152), or presumably through changes in the quality of weaponry, or whatever, he would have us say that the system has been transformed. Structures would then no longer show us a purely positional picture of society. Ruggie would lower the level of abstraction by adding to structures more information about the characteristics of units and of unit-level processes. Structure, properly defined, is transposable (cf. Nadel 1957: 104–109). If we follow Ruggie's advice, structure will no longer apply to different realms, even where the arrangement of their parts is similar. We shall also lose another advantage of structural approaches. Elegant definitions of structure enable one to fashion an explanatory system having only a few variables. If we add more variables, the explanatory system becomes more complicated, as one sees in Ruggie's essay. Especially in its last part, theoretical acuity gives way to rich and dense description.

Prediction, power, and the testing of theories

With Robert Keohane I have only a few disagreements, largely on questions of emphasis. Contrary to his statement, I do not differ with him over rationality, except semantically. I prefer to state the rationality assumption differently. My preference is based partly on fear that "rationality" carries the wrong connotations. Since making foreign policy is such a complicated business, one cannot expect of political leaders the nicely calculated decisions that the word "rationality" suggests. More significantly, my preference is based on the importance I accord, and Keohane denies, to the process of selection that takes place in competitive systems. In structural-functional logic, behaviors are selected for their consequences (Stinchcombe 1968:85). I fail to understand why Keohane thinks that selection does not work if the death rate of a system's units is low (p. 173). Selection does take place more swiftly and surely when death rates are high, as in a sector of the economy populated by small economic units. In oligopolistic sectors, the survival rate of firms is higher. Their fortunes nevertheless rise and fall. The market shapes behavior by rewarding some firms and penalizing others. Selection lessens the importance of the rationality assumption, but because selection works less well in oligopolistic than in competitive sectors, we need to know more about oligopolistic firms and are able to predict less surely from market theory alone.

In the international-political system, states wax and wane even as their death rates remain low. In the international-political system, great powers come and go, although not with great frequency. We should keep the notion of "selection" in a position of central importance. Even though constrained by a system's structure, a unit of the system can behave as it pleases. It will, however, fare badly if some of the other parties are making reasonably intelligent decisions. That some states imitate the successful practices of others indicates that the international arena is a competitive one in which the less skillful must expect to pay the price of their ineptitude. The situation provides enough incentive to cause most of the actors to behave sensibly. Actors become "sensitive to costs" to use Shai Feldman's apt phrase, which for convenience can be called an assumption of rationality (1982).

Keohane is surely right to emphasize, as I did, that with the aid of a rationality assumption one still cannot, from national interest alone, predict what the policy of a country might be. Any theory of international politics requires also a theory of domestic politics, since states affect the system's structure even as it affects them. This is why Snyder and Diesing in their excellent study explore information processing and decisionmaking (1977). To do so is fully in accord with, rather than a departure from, realist assumptions. Realist theory by itself can handle some, but not all, of the problems that concern us. Just as market theory at times requires a theory of the firm, so international-political theory at times needs a theory of the state. Yet some successful predictions can be made without paying attention to states. We do not always need to hop quickly from structure to states when looking for explanations. For example, contrary to the expectations of such an experienced statesman as President Franklin D. Roosevelt, realist theorists would surely have predicted the collapse of the allied coalition upon the morrow of victory. Whether alliances cohere or collapse depends more on external situations than on internal characteristics of allies, as their contrasting wartime and peacetime behaviors indicate. The prediction follows from balance-of-power theory. The absence of constraints on American policy for three decades following the war, seen in the light of the same theory, was hardly the anomaly that Keohane takes it to be. Overweening power gives a state the opportunity to act beyond its narrowly defined interests *and* provides incentives for others to try to catch up. Predictions can be made when we can answer this question with some confidence: How would we expect any state so placed to act? In 1950, the People's Republic of China intervened in the Korean War, to the surprise of General MacArthur among others. Yet *any* Chinese government seeing the forces of a great power approaching the Yalu border would almost surely have moved militarily if it were able to. Keohane wrongly emphasizes the failure of realist predictions while rightly emphasizing the limitations of the theory when standing alone (pp. 182–183).

Even when we have failed to predict, theory still helps us to understand and explain some things about the behavior of states. States who lost their great-power status in the course of the Second World War no longer behave as they used to. We tend to think of their postwar preoccupation with self, of their inclination to take a free or at least a cheap ride by spending disproportionately little on defense, of their pusillanimous behavior in the oil crisis following the Middle Eastern War of 1973, as deriving from their political attributes. Instead, such behavior follows mainly from the new structure of international politics. Not unexpectedly, the English historian A. J. P. Taylor assigned structural effects to the unit level and saw them as cause. "For years after the second world war," he wrote, "I continued to believe that there would be another German bid for European supremacy and that we must take precautions against it. Events have proved me totally wrong. I tried to learn lessons from history, which is always a mistake. The Germans have changed their national character" (June 4, 1976, p. 742). More perceptively, Roy Macridis saw the importance of changed position. "To speculate about a Franco-German war in the 1950s or 1960s," he wrote, "is just as boring as it would have been to contemplate a war between Sparta and Athens under the Roman Empire" (1971:143). If their national characters, and ours, have changed since the war, it is largely because their and our international positions have become profoundly different.

Not only have some states sunk in the international rankings while others have risen but also a great power now is one of two instead of five or more, as was true earlier. The United States and the Soviet Union behave differently from such countries as Germany and Japan because the latter are no longer great powers. The behavior of the United States and of the Soviet Union is also different from the behavior of earlier great powers. A great power that is one among many learns how to manipulate allies as well as adversaries. Great powers have to accommodate some of their number in order to gain strength vis-à-vis others. In dealing with near equals, they design their policies to influence the actions of others. In a crowded field, those who play the great-power game well flourish; those who do not risk falling by the wayside. The situation of the United States and of the Soviet Union is markedly different. Their field is not crowded. The most telling illustration of the difference is seen in the mutual dependence of allies before and during World War II and in the relative independence of the two alliance leaders since, along with the dependence of their associates on them.

Keohane raises the question of properly defining power and holds my definition to be insufficient. He is right. To define power in terms of who affects whom more strongly, is, I think, a move in the right direction; but I did not carry the definition very far. Although power is a key concept in realist theory, its proper definition remains a matter of controversy. On the fungibility of power, however, Keohane and I differ. Obviously, power is not as fungible as money. Not much is. But power is much more fungible than Keohane allows. As ever, the distinction between strong and weak states is important. The stronger the state, the greater the variety of its capabilities. Power may be only slightly fungible for weak states, but it is highly so for strong ones. Did, for example, America's failure to respond to economic pressures with economic or military force show that the United States was unable to translate its capabilities into effective power, as some thought during the oil embargo of the early 1970s, or did it indicate that the United States, more nearly self-sufficient than most countries, was not pressed hard enough to make the effort seem worthwhile? Moreover, in many of the examples Keohane adduces as evidence that Canada, a weak state, prevailed over the United States, a strong one, I suspect that American officials hardly cared about the outcomes or even noticed what they might be. The United States has more levers to pull than other states do, but need not always pull them.

Keohane rightly criticizes some realists for assuming that states seek to maximize power (pp. 173–174). He wrongly associates me with them because I point out that a balance-of-power system works whether we find states seeking only the minimum of power needed for security or whether some of them strive for domination. Because the belief that states do or should try to maximize power is quite widespread among realists, I emphasized the error in a paragraph containing these sentences: "Only if survival is assured, can states safely seek such other goals as tranquility, profit, and power. Because power is a means and not an end, states prefer to join the weaker of two coalitions. They cannot let power, a possibly useful means, become the end they pursue" (p. 127).

How one should test theories is the only question on which Keohane and I are far apart. In my simple, and perhaps simplistic, recipe for the testing of theories, given in chapter 1 of *Theory of International Politics*, I may have sounded like a "naïve falsificationist." I should like to correct the impression.

In criticizing my comments on testing, Keohane says that I find it difficult to "state precisely the conditions under which coalitions will change" (p. 172). I think it is *impossible* to do that. Because of the impossibility of precise specification, balance-of-power theory, like most theories in the social sciences, is difficult to test. We should therefore apply a variety of tests. Keohane is bothered by my urging that we seek to confirm theories as well as to falsify them. I do indeed depart from Karl Popper, who insists that only efforts to falsify theories count as legitimate tests. That may be a suitable way to go about testing, but it is not the only way. Errol Harris argues that among natural scientists it is a little used method.[4] Attempts to falsify theories are as problematic as attempts to confirm them. Because of the interdependence of theory and fact, we can find no Popperian critical experiment, the negative results of which would send a theory crashing to the ground. The background knowledge against which to test a theory is as problematic as the theory itself. Popper understood the problem but passed over it in various ways. In science there are no ultimate, or certainly true, statements. Therefore, no test is conclusive; in principle we should test theories ad infinitum. One way to avoid an infinite regress is to require not tests but testability. Another way is simply to limit tests on the ground that we are not trying to prove a theory true, but only to disprove a hypothesis (cf. Popper 1935:47–50, 105, 278). Popper's famous example of falsification is the one black swan that disproves the thousands of instances seeming to confirm the proposition that all swans are white. But if the positive statement—this is a black swan—is not proved, the hypothesis is not shown conclusively wrong. As Harris puts it: "We already know that there is and can be no external body of fact—external, that is, to all theory" (1970:353). As Popper once said:

> Science does not rest upon solid bedrock. The bold structure of its theories rises, as it were, above a swamp. It is like a building erected on piles. The piles are driven down from above into the swamp, but not down to any natural or "given" base; and if we stop driving the piles deeper, it is not because we have reached firm ground. We simply stop when we are satisfied that the piles are firm enough to carry the structure, at least for the time being (1935:111).

A theory may help us to understand and explain phenomena and events yet not be a useful instrument for prediction. Darwin's theory of evolution predicted nothing. It did help mightily to explain a changing world. That theories are not merely instruments for prediction opens the way for confirming tests. The inconclusive status of falsification invites us to try other means. Keohane chides me for advocating efforts to confirm theories and at the same time admitting that confirming instances can always be found (p. 172). Because they can be, I insisted on the importance of making tests difficult. This strikes me as being wise counsel since the lower the prior probability of a new piece of evidence, the higher the increased confirmation. Moreover, sound testing does not require one to examine "a universe of cases," as Keohane would have it (p. 172). A small number of cases well studied may be worth hundreds cursorily treated. Insofar as the accumulation of a number of cases is "mere repetition . . . it does not serve to enlighten." Each observation, as Harris has written, is valuable only if it "supplies new information, offers a fresh clue to the form of the total structure" (1970:348). One experiment well designed, one demonstration well conducted, one case carefully examined, may add more to one's confidence in a theory than hundreds of instances looked at hastily.

Testing theories is difficult; interpreting the results of tests is a subtle task. Since results are always problematic, some part of the scientific community has to decide whether enough of an empirical warrant exists to give a theory credibility. Theories gain credibility in a variety of ways—by unsuccessfully attempting to falsify, by successfully attempting to verify, by demonstrating that outcomes are produced in the way the theory contemplates, and by the intellectual force of the theory itself.

Keohane laments realism's lack of a theory of peaceful change, and he calls for more emphasis on norms, institutions, and non-state actors. The structure of a self-help system is defined in terms of its principal actors. The definition does not exclude other components, but merely sets the context of their existence. Empirical and theoretical work often proceeds without consideration of how the structure of the system affects institutions and actions within it. Some states sometimes want to work together to secure the benefits of cooperation. Cooperative projects in the present may lead to more cooperation in the future. But self-help systems do make the cooperation of parties difficult. As Gilpin puts it, "the traditional insights of realism . . . helps us to explain . . . the ongoing retreat from an interdependent world" (p. 312). Rules, institutions, and patterns of cooperation, when they develop in self-help systems, are all limited in extent and modified from what they might otherwise be.

Whether Keohane's conclusion, that *Theory of International Politics* offers nothing new, is valid depends on one's view of the old (p. 175). The behavioral mode of thinking is deeply ingrained in students of international politics. Whether by liberals, Marxists, realists, or behavioralists, the attempt has usually been to explain outcomes through the varying attributes of the acting units. System and structure have become fairly common terms in political science discourse. Only in the most general way, however, had systemic approaches been used to show how a structure shapes and shoves the units of a system. The effects on units of changes in structure had not been identified and examined. I developed a way of thinking that had not been widely familiar. Ashley is partly right: In certain important ways I did break with earlier realist thinking. Keohane is partly right: There is more continuity between earlier realists and me than Ashley noticed. Earlier realists thought of international anarchy simply as setting problems for statesmen different from those to be coped with internally and as altering standards of appropriate behavior. While earlier realists talked about the anarchy of international politics as marking their field of inquiry, they continued to explain international political outcomes in terms of the aims and policies, the actions and interactions, of states and of non-state actors. This remained the dominant pattern of explanation even for those political scientists who began to use the terminology of systems theory.

"Problem-solving" theory

I find Richard K. Ashley difficult to deal with. Reading his essay is like entering a maze. I never know quite where I am or how to get out. He is sometimes elusive, shifting from one view to another. In one essay, he quotes me as saying that "the behavior of states and statesmen . . . is indeterminate." He then correctly observes "that there is room for practical action: *Practical realism has partial autonomy*" (1981:220, 222). In another essay, neorealists, apparently including me, are said to "grant to the 'international political system absolute predominance over the parts' " (p. 288). In the earlier essay, he lumps Morgenthau and me pretty much together and tars us with the same brush. In the later essay, he finds more virtue in Morgenthau and less in me. Some of Ashley's comments bewilder me. Like John Herz, I often fail to recognize myself in what he writes about me (Herz 1981:237). In preceding pages, I attended to some of Ashley's complaints. Others are covered in Robert Gilpin's spirited response to Ashley's indictment of neorealism. I shall avoid repetition.

In Ashley's alternative model of international politics, the balance-of-power regime "*produces* sovereign states, who as a condition of their sovereignty, embody the regime" (above, p. 294, his italics). What can this mean? It may mean that states as we know them behave in certain ways because self-help systems strongly encourage some modes of behavior and discourage others. States develop along certain lines and acquire certain characteristics in order to survive and flourish in the system. In a different regime states would be different and would behave differently. But that seems unlikely to be his meaning because it would bring Ashley into agreement with me on a fundamental proposition. Yet I can see only one other way to interpret the sentence: namely, that the balance-of-power regime antedates the units that engage in the balancing! I find this baffling, yet it does seem to be his meaning. Thus a major charge he brings against me is that I understand international structure:

> not as a deep, internal relation prior to and constitutive of social actors but as an external joining of states-as-actors who have precisely the boundaries, ends, and self-understandings that theorists accord them on the basis of unexamined common sense. In turn—and here is the coup—Waltz grants the structure a life of its own independent of the parts, the states-as-actors; and he shows in countless ways how this structure limits and disposes action on the part of states such that, on balance, the structure is reproduced and actors are drawn into conformity with its requisites. But how is the independence of the structural whole established? It is not established independent of the parts taken together, for it is never anything more than the logical consequence of the parts taken together (p. 287).

This is a pretty fair summary, requiring only a few qualifications. The main one is this: The structure is not "independent of the parts, the states as actors," but constantly interacts with them. Neither the structure nor the units determine, as Ashley seemed to realize in 1981 and had forgotten by 1984.

The root of our differences is exposed in Robert Cox's nice distinction between problem-solving theory and critical theory. Critical theory deals with the "continuing process of historical change" (1981:128; reprinted above, p. 209). Both Cox and Ashley seem to think that my big mistake was to concentrate on the first kind of theory instead of on the second. I have no quarrel with Cox's concern with counter and latent structures, with historical inquiry, and with speculation about possible futures. Ashley and Cox would transcend the world as it is; meanwhile we have to live in it. At the end of his essay Cox speculates about emerging world orders. The likelihood of their realization will vary not only with changing production processes and social forces, which he emphasizes, but also with distributions of capability across states, which I emphasize.

Next to my whole enterprise being misconceived, what bothers Cox and Ashley most is my assumption that states are the units of international politics. They see this as enshrining the state, as freezing the system, and as making it static and eternal. Even though I made abundantly clear that I take the state to be a unit by assumption, Ashley says this: "For despite its statism, neorealism can produce no theory of the state capable of satisfying the state-as-actor premises of its political theory" (p. 279). I have not tried, but surely some neorealist is capable of producing a theory of the state. It would reveal, among other things, one that we already know: The state in fact is not a unitary and purposive actor. I assumed it to be such only for the purpose of constructing a theory. In reality, as I put it: "States pursue many goals, which are often vaguely formulated and inconsistent. They fluctuate with the changing currents of domestic politics, are prey to the vagaries of a shifting cast of political leaders, and are influenced by the outcomes of bureaucratic struggles" (p. 118).

Because I concentrated on "problem-solving" theory and left "critical theory" aside, I had to introduce theoretical concepts. Neither Cox nor Ashley likes the assumption that states are the units of the system. Yet if one is to develop a problem-solving theory about anything, assumptions of this sort have to be made. The alternative is simply to eschew such theories altogether. Would we then know more or less about the social and the natural worlds? In developing a structural theory of international politics, I was most influenced by economists and anthropologists; specifically by microeconomic or market theory and by Emile Durkheim. Obviously, economists in assuming that firms act as maximizing units know that firms in fact do not conform closely to the conception. They know further that forms and modes of economic organization change over the years. The distinction between an assumption and a statement striving for descriptive accuracy should be easy to grasp.

Cox's and Ashley's main objection seems to be that I did not write a theory of domestic politics. Ashley notices that I allow for considerable variety among states but complains that the variety is not a concern of my theory (p. 266). That is so, but only because I essayed an international-political theory and not a domestic one. Not everything need go into one book and not everything can go into one theory.[5] Realizing that I did not write a theory of the state, Ashley and Cox cannot from a theoretical assumption rightly infer what notions I might entertain about the historical origins and development of states and about their possible fates. I find it hard to believe that anyone would think that states will remain fixed in their present condition. But Ashley seems to believe that I hold that odd view. He infers what I believe about states from what I did *not* say about them. In the book he criticizes I abstracted "from every attribute of states except their capabilities" (p. 94). The behavior and practice of states and of statesmen are omitted from international-political theory not because of their unimportance but because their exclusion from the system's structure requires a distinct theory dealing with the politics and policies of states. I see something problematic about this only for those who think that domestic and international politics must be combined in one theory. Someone may one day fashion a unified theory of internal and external politics. Critical theory apparently aspires to do so, but I read in Ashley and Cox only what such a theory might do rather than what the theory is. The theoretical separation of domestic and international politics need not bother us unduly. Economists get along quite well with separate theories of markets and firms. Students of international politics will do well to concentrate on separate theories of internal and external politics until someone figures out a way to unite them.

Ashley accuses me of excluding history from the study of international politics and of immunizing a part of my theory from falsifying tests. In his words: "Despite neorealism's much ballyhooed emphasis on the role of hard falsifying tests as the measure of theoretical progress, neorealism immunizes its statist commitments from any form of falsification" (p. 270). To exclude history from a problem-solving theory is hardly to enjoin the historical study of politics. How can one incorporate history into the type of theory I constructed? Neither Ashley nor Cox gives an answer, but again apparently I should simply not have done what I did but something quite different. Nor does a theoretical assumption about states enjoin anyone from studying them empirically or from theorizing about them. Ashley finds in neorealism "*a historicism of stasis. . . . a historicism that freezes the political institutions of the current world order*" (p. 289). How can any theory have these effects? Ashley has a higher regard for the power of theories than I have. A theory applies only so long as the conditions it contemplates endure in their essentials. If the anarchy of international politics were to give way to a world hierarchy, a theory of international politics would become a theory about the past. Ashley thinks I am reluctant to contemplate "a hierarchy centering power within the grasp of a singular hegemon" because such a concentration would overturn the "fundamental organizing principle of international politics" (p. 277). How could he know this was my reason without asking me? It is true that some of Ashley's neorealists like hegemony better than I do, but that simply illustrates Gilpin's statement that we are a mixed bunch. The influence behind my preference is partly Immanuel Kant and partly Reinhold Niebuhr. Kant feared that a world government would stifle liberty, become a terrible despotism, and in the end collapse into chaos. Niebuhr drew the conclusion from his dim view of human nature that domestically and internationally the ends of security and decency are served better by balanced than by concentrated power. I distrust hegemonic power, whoever may wield it, because it is so easily misused.

Ashley offers an alternative to a neorealist model (pp. 294–297). It looks quite a bit like mine, except that it is wrapped in a capitalist blanket. Does he mean to imply that "a balance-of-power regime" would not exist in, say, a world of socialist states? If this is his meaning, I flatly disagree. Or does he mean that "a balance-of-power regime" would exist but with some differences in the attributes and behaviors of states? No doubt there would be some differences, but not ones of much systemic importance. Balance-of-power politics in much the form that we know it has been practiced over the millennia by many different types of political units, from ancient China and India, to the Greek and Italian city states, and unto our own day.

Critical theory seeks to interpret the world historically and philosophically. Problem-solving theory seeks to understand and explain it. Ashley's critical essay reveals to me no clue about how to write an improved theory of the latter sort. I am sorry that it does not.

Conclusion

Systems theory is frequently criticized for being static. It is in one sense but not in others. Self-ordered systems, as Michael Polanyi wrote, are subject to dual control, that is, "control in accordance with the laws that apply to its elements in themselves, and . . . control in accordance with the laws of the powers that control the comprehensive entity formed by these elements" (1968:1311). The latter are the constraints of the system, with the organization of the parts affecting the way the parts function. International-political systems exhibit dual control. Behaviors and outcomes change as interactions among a system's units become sparser or denser, as alliances shift, as nations adapt their policies to one another. These are changes within the system, and often systems dynamics are identified with, and limited to, such changes. What really matters, it seems, are changes in the behavior of states and in their alignments. That is the whole of the story only if *dynamic* is defined as energy in motion. This is the dynamic of the units. Another part of the story is revealed if *dynamics* are thought of as in physics—the action of forces on bodies in motion or at rest. These are the dynamics of the system. Structural changes alter a system's dynamics. Systemic effects cannot be reconstructed from the system's interacting parts since the parts behave differently because they are parts of a system. The constraints and incentives of a system, its dynamics, change if its structure changes or is transformed. To explain outcomes, we have to look at a system's dynamics and not just at the characteristics and the strategies of the units.

Self-help systems are transformed if their organizing principle shifts from anarchy to hierarchy. Establishing a world government would do this. Either all states pooling their sovereignty or some states conquering the others would transform the system. Self-help systems change through consequential variation in the distribution of capabilities among their members. States can more readily change their system than transform it. States fighting wars have immediate offensive or defensive aims. If the aim is to reduce the number of great powers significantly through conquest, then from a system's perspective the aim is to change the system. The result may be produced aside from the intentions of states. The victors in World War II thought of themselves as fighting a defensive war. In doing so, they nevertheless fought a war that changed the system from one of multipolarity to one of bipolarity. Shortly after helping to produce that change, the United States began to promote another one by encouraging Western European countries to unite. From the unit's perspective, one easily understands why. A united Western Europe would be a bulwark against the Soviet Union. From a system's perspective, the aim is an odd one. Why should one of two great powers wish to move the system from bipolarity to tripolarity?

By rewarding behavior that conforms with systemic requirements and punishing behavior that does not, a system's structure works against transformation. This is fortunate only if we are content with the system we have or if we are pessimistic about the costs and consequences of transformation. Changes in, and transformation of, systems originate not in the structure of a system but in its parts. Through selection, structures promote the continuity of systems in form; through variation, unit-level forces contain the possibilities of systemic change. The possibilities of rising in the international system, and the costs and benefits of doing so, vary as systems change; but states decide whether making the effort to advance is worthwhile. Japan has the capability of raising herself to great-power rank, but has lacked the inclination to do so. Systems change, or are transformed, depending on the resources and aims of their units and on the fates that befall them.

Structures condition behaviors and outcomes, yet explanations of behaviors and outcomes are indeterminate because both unit-level and structural causes are in play. Systems are stable if they endure for long periods. They are impressively stable if they survive the disruption of large-scale wars. The bipolar world has been both stable and peaceful—if peace is defined as the low incidence of war among great and major powers, that is, among those states most immediately affected by the structure of global politics. The bothersome limitations of systemic explanations arise from the problem of weighing unit-level and structural causes. To what extent is an effect to be ascribed to one level or the other? One may believe, as I do, that both bipolarity and nuclear weapons promote peace. But one cannot say for sure whether the structural or the unit-level cause is the stronger. The difficulty of sorting causes out is a serious, and seemingly inescapable, limitation of systems theories of international politics.

Structures shape and shove. They do not determine behaviors and outcomes, not only because unit-level and structural causes interact, but also because the shaping and shoving of structures may be successfully resisted. We attribute such success to Bismarck when we describe him as a diplomatic virtuoso. The unification of Germany, fashioned in the fighting of three short wars, shifted the balance of power in the center of Europe. Could that be done without igniting a general war? Given the structure of European politics, few would have thought so before the event. Later, in 1879, Bismarck forged a long-term alliance with Austria-Hungary. Given the structure of European politics, one would have predicted that an alliance made by two great powers would cause a counteralliance to form. Indeed, the Franco-Russian Alliance may have become inevitable with Prussia's victory over France in 1871, as Friedrich Engels thought (1890:48–49). The measure of Bismarck's diplomatic virtuosity is that the Alliance was not made until 1894, four years after his political demise. With skill and determination structural constraints can sometimes be countered. Virtuosos transcend the limits of their instruments and break the constraints of systems that bind lesser performers.

Thinking in terms of systems dynamics does not replace unit-level analysis nor end the search for sequences of cause and effect. Thinking in terms of systems dynamics does change the conduct of the search and adds a dimension to it. Structural thought conceives of actions simultaneously taking place within a matrix. Change the matrix—the structure of the system—and expected actions and outcomes are altered. The past causes the present, but the causes are mediated by the present system's structure. The examination of structure tells us how a system does what it does. A structure sets the range of expectations. Like any theory, a structural theory leaves some things aside in order to concentrate on others. Like any theory, a structural theory is limited to making predictions and promoting the understanding of events at a level of generality appropriate to the theory. A structural theory of international politics can fix ranges of outcomes and identify general tendencies, which may be persistent and strong ones but will not be reflected in all particular outcomes. We cannot hope to predict specific outcomes, but if our theory is good, we will see the kind of behavior and record the range of outcomes the theory leads us to expect. From the dynamics of the system we can infer general properties of behavior and outcomes within a system and expected changes in those properties as systems change.

Notes

1 This essay has benefited from critical readings by my wife, from correspondence and conversation over the years with Barry Buzan, Robert Keohane, and Glenn Snyder, and from searching and suggestive comments by Vinod Aggarwal.

2 States gain from trade because of their dissimilarities. Durkheim dwells on the resemblance of the units of a mechanical society. This may be confusing. One needs to remember that like units are not identical. They may differ considerably in resource endowment and economic development. Functionally, however, they are like units.

3 Cf. Park: "People live together on the whole, not because they are alike but because they are useful to one another" (1952:80). See also March and Simon: "the greater the *specialization by subprograms* (process specialization), the greater the *interdependence among organizational subunits*" (1958: 159).

4 Excellent examples of test by confirmation, mainly from Newton, Lavoisier, and Harvey, are found on pp. 161–178 of Harrris (1970).

5 In a book about foreign policy I concerned myself at length with the effects of internal structural differences on the external policies and behavior of the United States and Britain (1967).

4

THE ORIGINS OF WAR IN NEOREALIST THEORY

Like most historians, many students of international politics have been skeptical about the possibility of creating a theory that might help one to understand and explain the international events that interest us. Thus Morgenthau, foremost among traditional realists, was fond of repeating Blaise Pascal's remark that "the history of the world would have been different had Cleopatra's nose been a bit shorter" and then asking "How do you systemize that?"[1] His appreciation of the role of the accidental and the occurrence of the unexpected in politics dampened his theoretical ambition.

The response of neorealists is that, although difficulties abound, some of the obstacles that seem most daunting lie in misapprehensions about theory. Theory obviously cannot explain the accidental or account for unexpected events; it deals in regularities and repetitions and is possible only if these can be identified. A further difficulty is found in the failure of realists to conceive of international politics as a distinct domain about which theories can be fashioned. Morgenthau, for example, insisted on "the autonomy of politics," but he failed to apply the concept to international politics. A theory is a depiction of the organization of a domain and of the connections among its parts. A theory indicates that some factors are more important than others and specifies relations among them. In reality, everything is related to everything else, and one domain cannot be separated from others. But theory isolates one realm from all others in order to deal with it intellectually. By defining the structure of international political systems, neorealism establishes the autonomy of international politics and thus makes a theory about it possible.[2]

In developing a theory of international politics, neorealism retains the main tenets of *realpolitik*, but means and ends are viewed differently, as are causes and effects. Morgenthau, for example, thought of the "rational" statesman as ever striving to accumulate more and more power. He viewed power as an end in itself. Although he acknowledged that nations at times act out of considerations other than power, Morgenthau insisted that, when they do so, their actions are not "of a political nature."[3] In contrast, neorealism sees power as a possibly useful means, with states running risks if they have either too little or too much of it. Excessive weakness may invite an attack that greater strength would have dissuaded an adversary from launching. Excessive strength may prompt other states to increase their arms and pool their efforts against the dominant state. Because power is a possibly useful means, sensible statesmen try to have an appropriate amount of it. In crucial situations, however, the ultimate concern of states is not for power but for security. This revision is an important one.

An even more important revision is found in a shift of causal relations. The infinite materials of any realm can be organized in endlessly different ways. Realism thinks of causes as moving in only one direction, from the interactions of individuals and states to the outcomes that their acts and interactions produce. Morgenthau recognized that, when there is competition for scarce goods and no one to serve as arbiter, a struggle for power will ensue among the competitors and that consequently the struggle for power can be explained without reference to the evil born in men. The struggle for power arises simply because men want things, not because of the evil in their desires. He labeled man's desire for scarce goods as one of the two roots of conflict, but, even while discussing it, he seemed to pull toward the "other root of conflict and concomitant evil"—"the *animus dominandi*, the desire for power." He often considered that man's drive for power is more basic than the chance conditions under which struggles for power occur. This attitude is seen in his statement that "in a world where power counts, no nation pursuing a rational policy has a choice between renouncing and wanting power; *and, if it could*, the lust for power for the individual's sake would still confront us with its less spectacular yet no less pressing moral defects."[4]

Students of international politics have typically inferred outcomes from salient attributes of the actors producing them. Thus Marxists, like liberals, have linked the outbreak of war or the prevalence of peace to the internal qualities of states. Governmental forms, economic systems, social institutions, political ideologies—these are but a few examples of where the causes of war have been found. Yet, although causes are specifically assigned, we know that states with widely divergent economic institutions, social customs, and political ideologies have all fought wars. More striking still, many different sorts of organizations fight wars, whether those organizations be tribes, petty principalities, empires, nations, or street gangs. If an identified condition seems to have caused a given war, one must wonder why wars occur repeatedly even though their causes vary. Variations in the characteristics of the states are not linked directly to the outcomes that their behaviors produce, nor are variations in their patterns of interaction. Many historians, for example, have claimed that World War I was caused by the interaction of two opposed and closely balanced coalitions. But then many have claimed that World War II was caused by the failure of some states to combine forces in an effort to right an imbalance of power created by an existing alliance.

Neorealism contends that international politics can be understood only if the effects of structure are added to the unit-level explanations of traditional realism. By emphasizing how structures affect actions and outcomes, neorealism rejects the assumption that man's innate lust for power constitutes a sufficient cause of war in the absence of any other. It reconceives the causal link between interacting units and international outcomes. According to the logic of international politics, one must believe that some causes of international outcomes are the result of interactions at the unit level, and, since variations in presumed causes do not correspond very closely to variations in observed outcomes, one must also assume that others are located at the structural level. Causes at the level of units interact with those at the level of structure, and, because they do so, explanation at the unit level alone is bound to be misleading. If an approach allows the consideration of both unit-level and structural-level causes, then it can cope with both the changes and the continuities that occur in a system.

Structural realism presents a systemic portrait of international politics depicting component units according to the manner of their arrangement. For the purpose of developing a theory, states are cast as unitary actors wanting at least to survive, and are taken to be the system's constituent units. The essential structural quality of the system is anarchy—the absence of a central monopoly of legitimate force. Changes of structure and hence of system occur with variations in the number of great powers. The range of expected outcomes is inferred from the assumed motivation of the units and the structure of the system in which they act.

A systems theory of international politics deals with forces at the international, and not at the national, level. With both systems-level and unit-level forces in play, how can one construct a theory of international politics without simultaneously constructing a theory of foreign policy? An international-political theory does not imply or require a theory of foreign policy any more than a market theory implies or requires a theory of the firm. Systems theories, whether political or economic, are theories that explain how the organization of a realm acts as a constraining and disposing force on the interacting units within it. Such theories tell us about the forces to which the units are subjected. From them, we can draw some inferences about the expected behavior and fate of the units: namely, how they will have to compete with and adjust to one another if they are to survive and flourish. To the extent that the dynamics of a system limit the freedom of its units, their behavior and the outcomes of their behavior become predictable. How do we expect firms to respond to differently structured markets, and states to differently structured international-political systems? These theoretical questions require us to take firms as firms, and states as states, without paying attention to differences among them. The questions are then answered by reference to the placement of the units in their system and not by reference to the internal qualities of the units. Systems theories explain why different units behave similarly and, despite their variations, produce outcomes that fall within expected ranges. Conversely, theories at the unit level tell us why different units behave differently despite their similar placement in a system. A theory about foreign policy is a theory at the national level. It leads to expectations about the responses that dissimilar polities will make to external pressures. A theory of international politics bears on the foreign policies of nations although it claims to explain only certain aspects of them. It can tell us what international conditions national policies have to cope with.

From the vantage point of neorealist theory, competition and conflict among states stem directly from the twin facts of life under conditions of anarchy: States in an anarchic order must provide for their own security, and threats or seeming threats to their security abound. Preoccupation with identifying dangers and counteracting them become a way of life. Relations remain tense; the actors are usually suspicious and often hostile even though by nature they may not be given to suspicion and hostility. Individually, states may only be doing what they can to bolster their security. Their individual intentions aside, collectively their actions yield arms races and alliances. The uneasy state of affairs is exacerbated by the familiar "security dilemma," wherein measures that enhance one state's security typically diminish that of others.[5] In an anarchic domain, the source of one's own comfort is the source of another's worry. Hence a state that is amassing instruments of war, even for its own defense, is cast by others as a threat requiring response. The response itself then serves to confirm the first state's belief that it had reason to worry. Similarly an alliance that in the interest of defense moves to increase cohesion among its members and add to its ranks inadvertently imperils an opposing alliance and provokes countermeasures.

Some states may hunger for power for power's sake. Neorealist theory, however, shows that it is not necessary to assume an innate lust for power in order to account for the sometimes fierce competition that marks the international arena. In an anarchic domain, a state of war exists if all parties lust for power. But so too will a state of war exist if all states seek only to ensure their own safety.

Although neorealist theory does not explain why particular wars are fought, it does explain war's dismal recurrence through the millennia. Neorealists point not to the ambitions or the intrigues that punctuate the outbreak of individual conflicts but instead to the existing structure within which events, whether by design or accident, can precipitate open clashes of arms. The origins of hot wars lie in cold wars, and the origins of cold wars are found in the anarchic ordering of the international arena.

The recurrence of war is explained by the structure of the international system. Theorists explain what historians know: War is normal. Any given war is explained not by looking at the structure of the international-political system but by looking at the particularities within it: the situations, the characters, and the interactions of states. Although particular explanations are found at the unit level, general explanations are also needed. Wars vary in frequency, and in other ways as well. A central question for a structural theory is this: How do changes of the system affect the expected frequency of war?

Keeping wars cold: the structural level

In an anarchic realm, peace is fragile. The prolongation of peace requires that potentially destabilizing developments elicit the interest and the calculated response of some or all of the system's principal actors. In the anarchy of states, the price of inattention or miscalculation is often paid in blood. An important issue for a structural theory to address is whether destabilizing conditions and events are managed better in multipolar or bipolar systems.

In a system of, say, five great powers, the politics of power turns on the diplomacy by which alliances are made, maintained, and disrupted. Flexibility of alignment means both that the country one is wooing may prefer another suitor and that one's present alliance partner may defect. Flexibility of alignment limits a state's options because, ideally, its strategy must please potential allies and satisfy present partners. Alliances are made by states that have some but not all of their interests in common. The common interest is ordinarily a negative one: fear of other states. Divergence comes when positive interests are at issue. In alliances among near equals, strategies are always the product of compromise since the interests of allies and their notions of how to secure them are never identical.

If competing blocs are seen to be closely balanced, and if competition turns on important matters, then to let one's side down risks one's own destruction. In a moment of crisis the weaker or the more adventurous party is likely to determine its side's policy. Its partners can afford neither to let the weaker member be defeated nor to advertise their disunity by failing to back a venture even while deploring its risks.

The prelude to World War I provides striking examples of such a situation. The approximate equality of partners in both the Triple Alliance and Triple Entente made them closely interdependent. This interdependence, combined with the keen competition between the two camps, meant that, although any country could commit its associates, no one country on either side could exercise control. If Austria-Hungary marched, Germany had to follow; the dissolution of the Austro-Hungarian Empire would have left Germany alone in the middle of Europe. If France marched, Russia had to follow; a German victory over France would be a defeat for Russia. And so the vicious circle continued. Because the defeat or the defection of a major ally would have shaken the balance, each state was constrained to adjust its strategy and the use of its forces to the aims and fears of its partners.

In alliances among equals, the defection of one member threatens the security of the others. In alliances among unequals, the contributions of the lesser members are at once wanted and of relatively small importance. In alliances among unequals, alliance leaders need worry little about the faithfulness of their followers, who usually have little choice anyway. Contrast the situation in 1914 with that of the United States and Britain and France in 1956. The United States could dissociate itself from the Suez adventure of its two principal allies and subject one of them to heavy financial pressure. Like Austria-Hungary in 1914, Britain and France tried to commit or at least immobilize their ally by presenting a fait accompli. Enjoying a position of predominance, the United States could continue to focus its attention on the major adversary while disciplining its two allies. Opposing Britain and France endangered neither the United States nor the alliance because the security of Britain and France depended much more heavily on us than our security depended on them. The ability of the United States, and the inability of Germany, to pay a price measured in intra-alliance terms is striking.

In balance-of-power politics old style, flexibility of alignment led to rigidity of strategy or the limitation of freedom of decision. In balance-of-power politics new style, the obverse is true: Rigidity of alignment in a two-power world results in more flexibility of strategy and greater freedom of decision. In a multipolar world, roughly equal parties engaged in cooperative endeavors must look for the common denominator of their policies. They risk finding the lowest one and easily end up in the worst of all possible worlds. In a bipolar world, alliance leaders can design strategies primarily to advance their own interests and to cope with their main adversary and less to satisfy their own allies.

Neither the United States nor the Soviet Union has to seek the approval of other states, but each has to cope with the other. In the great-power politics of a multipolar world, who is a danger to whom and who can be expected to deal with threats and problems are matters of uncertainty. In the great-power politics of a bipolar world, who is a danger to whom is never in doubt. Any event in the world that involves the fortunes of either of the great powers automatically elicits the interest of the other. President Harry S. Truman, at the time of the Korean invasion, could not very well echo Neville Chamberlain's words in the Czechoslovakian crisis by claiming that the Americans knew nothing about the Koreans, a people living far away in the east of Asia. We had to know about them or quickly find out.

In a two-power competition, a loss for one is easily taken to be a gain for the other. As a result, the powers in a bipolar world promptly respond to unsettling events. In a multipolar world, dangers are diffused, responsibilities unclear, and definitions of vital interests easily obscured. Where a number of states are in balance, the skillful foreign policy of a forward power is designed to gain an advantage without antagonizing other states and frightening them into united action. At times in modern Europe, the benefits of possible gains have seemed to outweigh the risks of likely losses. Statesmen have hoped to push an issue to the limit without causing all of the potential opponents to unite. When there are several possible enemies, unity of action among them is difficult to achieve. National leaders could therefore think—or desperately hope, as did Theobald von Bethmann Hollweg and Adolf Hitler before two world wars—that a united opposition would not form.

If interests and ambitions conflict, the absence of crises is more worrisome than their presence. Crises are produced by the determination of a state to

61

resist a change that another state tries to make. As the leaders in a bipolar system, the United States and the Soviet Union are disposed to do the resisting, for in important matters they cannot hope that their allies will do it for them. Political action in the postwar world has reflected this condition. Communist guerrillas operating in Greece prompted the Truman Doctrine. The tightening of Soviet control over the states of Eastern Europe led to the Marshall Plan and the Atlantic Defense Treaty, and these in turn gave rise to the Cominform and the Warsaw Pact. The plan to create a West German government produced the Berlin blockade. During the past four decades, our responses have been geared to the Soviet Union's actions, and theirs to ours.

Miscalculation by some or all of the great powers is a source of danger in a multipolar world; overreaction by either or both of the great powers is a source of danger in a bipolar world. Which is worse: miscalculation or overreaction? Miscalculation is the greater evil because it is more likely to permit an unfolding of events that finally threatens the status quo and brings the powers to war. Overreaction is the lesser evil because at worst it costs only money for unnecessary arms and possibly the fighting of limited wars. The dynamics of a bipolar system, moreover, provide a measure of correction. In a world in which two states united in their mutual antagonism overshadow any others, the benefits of a calculated response stand out most clearly, and the sanctions against irresponsible behavior achieve their greatest force. Thus two states, isolationist by tradition, untutored in the ways of international politics, and famed for impulsive behavior, have shown themselves—not always and everywhere, but always in crucial cases—to be wary, alert, cautious, flexible, and forbearing.

Moreover, the economies of the great powers in a bipolar world are less interdependent than those of the great powers of a multipolar one. The size of great powers tends to increase as their numbers fall, and the larger a state is, the greater the variety of its resources. States of continental size do proportionately less of their business abroad than, for example, Britain, France, and Germany did in their heydays. Never before in modern history have the great powers depended so little on the outside world, and been so uninvolved in one another's economic affairs, as the United States and the Soviet Union have been since the war. The separation of their interests reduces the occasions for dispute and permits them, if they wish, to leave each other alone even though each defines its security interests largely in terms of the other.

Interdependence of parties, diffusion of dangers, confusion of responses: These are the characteristics of great-power politics in a multipolar world. Self-dependence of parties, clarity of dangers, certainty about who has to face them: These are the characteristics of great-power politics in a bipolar world.

Keeping wars cold: the unit level

A major reason for the prolongation of the postwar peace is the destruction of the old multipolar world in World War II and its replacement by a bipolar one.

In a bipolar world, we expect competition to be keen, yet manageable. But to believe that bipolarity alone accounts for the "long peace" between the United States and the Soviet Union is difficult. Given the depth and extent of the distrust felt by both parties, one may easily believe that one or another of the crises that they have experienced would, in earlier times, have drawn them into war. For a fuller explanation of why that did not happen, we must look to that other great force for peace: nuclear weapons.

States continue to coexist in an anarchic order. Self-help is the principle of action in such an order, and the most important way in which states must help themselves is by providing for their own security. Therefore, in weighing the chances of peace, the first questions to ask are questions about the ends for which states use force and about the strategies and weapons they employ. The chances of peace rise if states can achieve their most important ends without actively using force. War becomes less likely as the costs of war rise in relation to the possible gains. Realist theory, old and new alike, draws attention to the crucial role of military technology and strategy among the forces that fix the fate of states and their systems.

Nuclear weapons dissuade states from going to war much more surely than conventional weapons do. In a conventional world, states can believe both that they may win and that, should they lose, the price of defeat will be bearable, although World Wars I and II called the latter belief into question even before atomic bombs were dropped. If the United States and the Soviet Union were now armed only with conventional weapons, the lessons of those wars would be clearly remembered, especially by the Soviet Union, which suffered more in war than the United States. Had the atom never been split, those two nations would still have much to fear from each other. Armed with increasingly destructive conventional weapons, they would be constrained to strive earnestly to avoid war. Yet, in a conventional world, even sad and strong lessons like those of the two world wars have proved exceedingly difficult for states to learn. Throughout modern history, one great power or another has looked as though it might become dangerously strong: for example, France under Louis XIV and Napoleon Bonaparte, and Germany under Wilhelm II and Hitler. In each case, an opposing coalition formed and turned the expansive state back. The lessons of history would seem to be clear: In international politics, success leads to failure. The excessive accumulation of power by one state or coalition of states elicits the opposition of others. The leaders of expansionist states have nevertheless been able to persuade themselves that skillful diplomacy and clever strategy would enable them to transcend the normal processes of balance-of-power politics.

The experience of World War II, bipolarity, and the increased destructiveness of conventional weapons would make World War III more difficult to start than earlier wars were; and the presence of nuclear weapons dramatically increases that difficulty. Nuclear weapons reverse or negate many of the conventional causes of war. Wars can be fought in the face of nuclear weapons, but the higher the stakes and the closer a country comes to winning them, the more surely that country invites retaliation and risks its own destruction. The accumulation of significant power through conquest, even if only conventional weapons are used, is no longer possible in the world of nuclear powers. Those individuals who believe that the Soviet Union's leaders are so bent on world domination that they may be willing to run catastrophic risks for problematic gains fail to understand how governments behave. Do we expect to lose one city or two? Two cities or ten? When these are the pertinent questions, political leaders stop thinking about running risks and start worrying about how to avoid them.

Deterrence is more easily achieved than most military strategists would have us believe. In a conventional world, a country can sensibly attack if it believes that success is probable. In a nuclear world, a country cannot sensibly attack unless it believes that success is assured. A nation will be deterred from attacking even if it believes that there is only a possibility that its adversary will retaliate. Uncertainty of response, not certainty, is required for deterrence because, if retaliation occurs, one risks losing all. As Clausewitz wrote: If war approaches the absolute, it becomes imperative "not to take the first step without thinking what may be the last."[6]

Nuclear weapons make the implications even of victory too horrible to contemplate. The problem that the nuclear powers must solve is how to perpetuate peace when it is not possible to eliminate all of the causes of war. The structure of international politics has not been transformed; it remains anarchic in form. Nuclear states continue to compete militarily. With each state striving to ensure its own security, war remains constantly possible. In the anarchy of states, improving the means of defense and deterrence relative to the means of offense increases the chances of peace. Weapons and strategies that make defense and deterrence easier, and offensive strikes harder to mount, decrease the likelihood of war.[7]

Although the possibility of war remains, the probability of a war involving states with nuclear weapons has been drastically reduced. Over the centuries great powers have fought more wars than minor states, and the frequency of war has correlated more closely with a structural characteristic—their international standing—than with unit-level attributes. Yet, because of a change in military technology, a change at the unit level, waging war has increasingly become the privilege of poor and weak states. Nuclear weapons have banished war from the center of international politics. A unit-level change has dramatically reduced a structural effect.

The probability of major war among states having nuclear weapons approaches zero. But the "real war" may, as James claimed, lie in the preparations for waging it. The logic of a deterrent strategy, if it is followed, also circumscribes the causes of "real wars."[8] In a conventional world, the structure of international politics encourages states to arm competitively. In a nuclear world, deterrent strategies offer the possibility of dampening the competition. Conventional weapons are relative. With conventionl weapons, competing countries must constantly compare their strengths. How secure a country is depends on how it compares to others in the quantity and quality of its weaponry, the suitability of its strategy, the resilience of its society and economy, and the skill of its leaders.

Nuclear weapons are not relative but absolute weapons.[9] They make it possible for a state to limit the size of its strategic forces so long as other states are unable to achieve disarming first-strike capabilities by improving their forces. If no state can launch a disarming attack with high confidence, comparing the size of strategic forces becomes irrelevant. For deterrence, one asks how much is enough, and enough is defined as a second-strike capability. This interpretation does not imply that a deterrent force can deter everything, but rather that, beyond a certain level, additional forces provide no additional security for one party and pose no additional threat to others. The two principal powers in the system have long had second-strike forces, with neither able to launch a disarming strike against the other. That both nevertheless continue to pile weapon upon unneeded weapon is a puzzle whose solution can be found only within the United States and the Soviet Union.

Wars, hot and cold

Wars, hot and cold, originate in the structure of the international political system. Most Americans blame the Soviet Union for creating the Cold War, by the actions that follow necessarily from the nature of its society and government. Revisionist historians, attacking the dominant view, assign blame to the United States. Some American error, or sinister interest, or faulty assumption about Soviet aims, they argue, is what started the Cold War. Either way, the main point is lost. In a bipolar world, each of the two great powers is bound to focus its fears on the other, to distrust its motives, and to impute offensive intentions to defensive measures. The proper question is what, not who, started the Cold War. Although its content and virulence vary as unit-level forces change and interact, the Cold War continues. It is firmly rooted in the structure of postwar international politics, and will last as long as that structure endures.

In any closely competitive system, it may seem that one is either paranoid or a loser. The many Americans who ascribe paranoia to the Soviet Union are saying little about its political elite and much about the international-political system. Yet, in the presence of nuclear weapons, the Cold War has not become a hot one, a raging war among major states. Constraints on fighting big wars have bound the major nuclear states into a system of uneasy peace. Hot wars originate in the structure of international politics. So does the Cold War, with its temperature kept low by the presence of nuclear weapons.

Acknowledgment

The author thanks David Schleicher, who was most helpful in the completion of this article.

Notes

1 Hans J. Morgenthau, "International Relations: Quantitative and Qualitative Approaches," in Norman D. Palmer ed., *A Design for International Relations Research: Scope, Theory, Methods, and Relevance* (Philadelphia, 1970), p. 78.
2 Morgenthau, *Politics among Nations* (New York, 1973; 5th ed.), p. 11. Ludwig Boltzman (trans. Rudolf Weingartner), "Theories as Representations," excerpted in Arthur Danto and Sidney Morgenbesser eds., *Philosophy of Science* (Cleveland, 1960), pp. 245–252. Neorealism is sometimes dubbed structural realism. I use the terms interchangeably and, throughout this article, refer to my own formulation of neorealist theory. See Waltz, *Theory of International Politics* (Reading, MA, 1979); Robert Keohane ed., *Neorealism and its Critics* (New York, 1986).
3 Morgenthau, *Politics among Nations*, p. 27.
4 Idem, Scientific Man vs. Power Politics (Chicago, 1946), pp. 192, 200. Italics added.
5 See John H. Herz, "Idealist Internationalism and the Security Dilemma," *World Politics*, II (1950), pp. 157–180.
6 Karl von Clausewitz, ed. Anatol Rapaport; trans. J. J. Graham, *On War* (Hammondsworth, 1968), V, p. 374.
7 See Malcolm W. Hoag, "On Stability in Deterrent Races," in Morton A. Kaplan ed., *The Revolution in World Politics* (New York, 1962), pp. 388–410; Robert Jervis, "Cooperation under the Security Dilemma," *World Politics*, XXX (1978), pp. 167–214.
8 William James, "The Moral Equivalent of War," in Leon Bramson and George W. Goethals eds., *War: Studies from Psychology, Sociology, and Anthropology* (New York, 1968; rev. ed.), p. 23.
9 Cf. Bernard Brodie, *The Absolute Weapon: Atomic Power and World Order* (New York, 1946), pp. 75–76.

5

REALIST THOUGHT AND NEOREALIST THEORY[1]

Exploring various ways to forward the study of international politics was one of William T. R. Fox's many interests. In 1957, he organized a series of seminars that brought together a number of established scholars, among them Paul Nitze, Hans Morgenthau and Charles Kindleberger, along with such younger scholars as Robert W. Tucker, Morton Kaplan and Martin Wight, to discuss problems in the study of international-political theory and its relation to the behavior of states. A volume edited and co-authored by Bill was the tangible product of the colloquium.[2] As one of the many students and colleagues who benefitted from Bill's ideas, encouragement, and support, I offer this essay as a small contribution toward clarifying some problems in the framing and applying of international-political theory.

I begin by looking at a theoretical breakthrough in a related field: economics. Realists and neorealists represent two of the major theoretical approaches followed by students of international politics in the past half century or so. They encountered problems similar to those the Physiocrats began to solve in France in the middle of the eighteenth century. Students of international politics have had an extraordinarily difficult time casting their subject in theoretical terms. Looking first at an example of comparable difficulties surmounted in a related field may be instructive.

How economic theory became possible

Difficulties common to earlier economists and twentieth-century political scientists are revealed by examining Sir Josiah Child's *A New Discourse*, written mainly in the years 1668 to 1670.[3] Child dealt with a striking question. Why, he wondered, did the prosperity of the Dutch surpass that of the English? In casting about for an answer, he seized on what seemed to be a compelling fact: Namely, that the Dutch rate of interest had been lower than the English rate. The reasoning used to establish the causal role of the rate of interest is correlative and sequential. Child tried to show that the prosperity of various countries varies inversely with prevailing rates of interest. He then established the causal direction by arguing that the expected changes in the level of prosperity followed upon changes in rates of interest.

Child's work is the kind of pre-theoretical effort that provides stimulus to, and material for, later theories. That is its merit. It is, however, the kind of work that can neither provide satisfactory explanations nor lead to the construction of theory. We can profit by noticing why this is so. Child tried to establish a necessary relation between the rate of interest and the level of prosperity. Other economists picked different factors as their favorite causes—the accumulation of bullion, the fertility of the population or the soil, the industry of the people, the level of rents, or whatever. But none was able to show why the relation between the chosen factor or factors and the condition to be accounted for necessarily held. Child, for example, could not supply an answer to this now obvious question: Why doesn't a rise in interest rates attract capital, ultimately lowering its price as with commodities? He could not say whether the association he claimed to have found was causal or coincidental. He could not say whether other factors in play may have caused interest rates and national prosperity to move in opposite directions. Innumerable explanations for the observed relation were available. Pre-physiocratic economists could only cast about for sequences and associations that seemed to pertain within or across countries. They could at best hope to formulate plausible explanations of particular outcomes. They had no way of relating the parts of an economy to one another and to the economy as a whole.

The first step forward was, as it had to be, to invent the concept of an economy as distinct from the society and the polity in which it is embedded. Some will always complain that it is artificial to think of an economy separate from its society and polity. Such critics are right. Yet the critics miss the point Theory is artifice. A theory is an intellectual construction by which we select facts and interpret them. The challenge is to bring theory to bear on facts in ways that permit explanation and prediction. That can only be accomplished by distinguishing between theory and fact. Only if this distinction is made can theory be used to examine and interpret facts.

In the pre-theoretic era of economics, more and more information became available in the form of reported, or purported, facts, and more and more attempts were made to account for them. But differences of explanation remained unreconciled and explanations of particular processes and outcomes did not add up to an understanding of how a national economy works. In a remarkable survey in which the historical development, the sociological setting, and the scientific qualities of economic thought are brought together, Joseph Schumpeter described the best economic literature of that earlier time as having "all the freshness and fruitfulness of direct observation." But, he added, it also "shows all the helplessness of mere observation by itself."[4] Information accumulated, but arguments, even perceptive ones about propositions that might have been developed as theories, did not add up to anything more than ideas about particulars occasioned by current controversies.

Child was better than most economists of his day, although not as good as the best. The most creative economists were frustrated by the condition that Schumpeter described. The seventeenth-century economist Sir William Petty, for example, felt the frustration. Schumpeter described him as creating "for himself theoretical tools with which he tried to force a way through the undergrowth of facts."[5] To eliminate useless and misleading "facts" was an important endeavor, but not a sufficient one. What blocked the progress of economic understanding was neither too little nor too much knowledge but rather the lack of a certain kind of knowledge.

The answers to factual questions pose puzzles that theory may hope to solve and provide materials for theorists to work with. But the work begins only when theoretical questions are posed. Theory cannot be fashioned from the answers to such factual questions as: What follows upon, or is associated with, what? Instead, answers have to be sought to such theoretical questions as these: How does this thing work? How does it all hang together? These questions cannot usefully be asked unless one has some idea of what the "thing" or the "it" might be. Theory becomes possible only if various objects and processes, movements and events, acts and interactions, are viewed as forming a domain that can be studied in its own right. Clearing away useless facts was not enough; something new had to be created. An invention was needed that would permit economic phenomena to be seen as distinct processes, that would permit an economy to be viewed as a realm of affairs marked off from social and political life.

This the Physiocrats first achieved. Francois Quesnay's famous economic table is a picture depicting the circulation of wealth among the productive and unproductive classes of society, but it is a picture of the unseen and the unseeable.[6] Certain cycles are well-known facts of economic life—cycles of sowing and harvesting, of mining, refining, forging, and manufacturing. But such a direct simplification of observable processes is not what Quesnay's table presents. It presents, instead, the essential qualities of an economy in picture form. The Physiocrats were the first to think of an economy as a self-sustaining whole made up of interacting parts and repeated activities. To do so, they had to make radical simplifications—for example, by employing a psychology that saw people simply as seeking the greatest satisfaction from the least effort. They invented the concepts they needed. Their notion of a "social product" can well be described as the intellectual creation of the unobservable and the nonexistent. No one can point to a social product. It is not an identifiable quantity of goods but is instead a concept whose validity can be established only through its role in a theory that yields an improved understanding of the economy.

The Physiocrats developed concepts comprising innumerable particularities and contingencies without examining them. Among these concepts were the durable notions of distribution and circulation. The quaint and crude appearance of some physiocratic ideas should not obscure the radical advance that their theory represented. Economists had found it hard to get a theoretical hold on their subject. In pre-physiocratic economics, as Schumpeter said, "the connecting link of economic causality and an insight into the inner necessities and the general character of economics were missing. It was possible to consider the individual acts of exchange, the phenomenon of money, and the question of protective tariffs as economic problems, but it was impossible to see the total process which unfolds itself in a particular economic period. Before the Physiocrats appeared on the scene, only local symptoms on the economic body, as it were, had been perceived." Only the parts of an economy could be dealt with. It was therefore necessary again in Schumpeter's words, "to derive an explanatory principle from each separate complex of facts—as it were in a gigantic struggle with them—and it was at best possible merely to sense the great general contexts."[7]

International politics: beyond the theoretical pale

What the Physiocrats did for economics is exactly what Raymond Aron and Hans Morgenthau, two of the most theoretically self-conscious traditional realists, believed to be impossible for students of international politics to accomplish. Aron drew a sharp distinction between the study of economics and the study of international politics. The latter he assigned to the category of history, which deals with unique events and situations, and of sociology, which deals with nonlogical actions and searches for general relations among them. In contrast to economics, Aron said international politics suffers from the following difficulties:

- Innumerable factors affect the international system and no distinction can be made between those that are internal and those that are external to it.
- States, the principal international actors, cannot be endowed with a single aim.
- No distinction can be drawn between dependent and independent variables.
- No accounting identities—such as investment equals savings—can be devised.
- No mechanism exists for the restoration of a disrupted equilibrium.
- There is no possibility of prediction and manipulation with identified means leading to specified goals.[8]

Do the reasons cited eliminate the possibility of devising a theory of international politics? If so, then economics would have been similarly hampered. Aron did not relate obvious differences between economics and politics to the requirements of theory construction. He merely identified differences, in the confident belief that because of them no international-political theory is possible.

70

Morgenthau's theoretical stance is similar to Aron's. Morgenthau dealt persuasively with major problems and with issues of enduring importance. He had the knack of singling out salient facts and constructing causal analyses around them. He sought "to paint a picture of foreign policy" that would present its "rational essence," abstracting from personality and prejudice, and, especially in democracies, from the importunities of popular opinion that "impair the rationality of foreign policy."[9] He was engaged, as it were, "in a gigantic struggle" with the facts, seeking "to derive an explanatory principle" from them. Like Petty, he forged concepts that might help him "force a way through the undergrowth of facts," such concepts as "national interest" and "interest defined as power." Like Child, Morgenthau and other realists failed to take the fateful step beyond developing concepts to the fashioning of a recognizable theory.

Morgenthau described his purpose as being "to present a theory of international politics."[10] Elements of a theory are presented, but never a theory. Morgenthau at once believed in "the possibility of developing a rational theory" and remained deeply skeptical about that possibility. Without a concept of the whole, he could only deal with the parts. As is rather commonly done, he confused the problem of explaining foreign policy with the problem of developing a theory of international politics. He then concluded that international political theory is difficult if not impossible to contrive.[11] He was fond of repeating Blaise Pascal's remark that the history of the world would have been different had Cleopatra's nose been a bit shorter, and then asking, "how do you systemize that?"[12] His appreciation of the role of the accidental and the occurrence of the unexpected in politics dampened his theoretical aspirations.

Neorealism's response is that, while difficulties abound, some that seem most daunting lie in misapprehensions about theory. Theory obviously cannot explain the accidental or account for unexpected events. Theories deal in regularities and repetitions and are possible only if these can be identified. As a realist, Morgenthau maintained "the autonomy of politics," but he failed to develop the concept and apply it to international politics.[13] A theory is a depiction of the organization of a domain and of the connections among its parts.[14] A theory indicates that some factors are more important than others and specifies relations among them. In reality, everything is related to everything else, and one domain cannot be separated from others. Theory isolates one realm from all others in order to deal with it intellectually. To isolate a realm is a precondition to developing a theory that will explain what goes on within it. The theoretical ambitions of Morgenthau, as of Aron, were forestalled by his belief that the international political domain cannot be marked off from others for the purpose of constructing a theory.

In summarizing Aron's argument, I have put the first three points in sequence because they are closely interrelated. The single word "complexity" suggests the impediment that concerns him. If "economic, political, and social variables"[15] enter into the international system, as surely they do, if states have not one but many goals, as surely they have, if separating dependent from independent variables and distinguishing effects from causes is an uncertain undertaking, as surely it is—then one can never hope to fashion a theory.

Complexity, however, does not work against theory. Rather, theory is a means of dealing with complexity. Economists can deal with it because they long ago solved Aron's first problem. Given the concept of a market—a bounded economic domain—they have been able to develop further concepts and draw connections among them. Because realists did not solve the first problem, they could not satisfactorily deal with the next two. Men have many motives. If all or very many of them must always be taken into account, economic theory becomes impossible. "Economic man" was therefore created. Men were assumed to be single-minded, economic maximizers. An assumption or a set of assumptions is necessary. In making assumptions about men's (or states') motivations, the world must be drastically simplified; subtleties must be rudely pushed aside, and reality must be grossly distorted. Descriptions strive for accuracy; assumptions are brazenly false. The assumptions on which theories are built are radical simplifications of the world and are useful only because they are such. Any radical simplification conveys a false impression of the world.

Aron's second and third points must be amended. Actors cannot realistically be endowed with a single aim, but we can only know by trying whether or not they can usefully be so endowed for purposes of constructing a theory. Political studies are not different from other studies in the realm of human affairs. We can make bold assumptions about motives, we can guess which few of many factors are salient, we can arbitrarily specify relations of dependence and independence among variables. We may even expect that the more complex and intricate the matters being studied are, the stronger the urge "to be simple-minded" would become.[16]

If international politics is a recalcitrant realm for the theorist, then its special difficulties lie elsewhere than in the first three of Aron's points. Are they perhaps found in the last three? As the fourth of Aron's impediments to theory, I have listed the absence of "accounting identities" or, as others have put it, the lack of a unit of measure and a medium of exchange in which goals can be valued and instruments comparatively priced. Political capability and political effect, whether or not conceived of simply in terms of power, cannot be expressed in units, such as dollars, that would have clear meaning and be applicable to different instruments and ends. Yet one finds in Adam Smith, for example, no numbers that are essential to his theory. Indeed, one finds hardly any numbers at all, and thus no "accounting identities." That supply equals demand or that investment equals savings are general propositions or purported laws that theory may explain. Stating the laws does not depend on counting, weighing, or measuring anything. As Frank Knight well and rightly wrote:

Pure theory, in economics as in any field, is abstract; it deals with forms only, in complete abstraction from content. On the individual side, economic theory takes men with (a) any wants whatever, (b) any resources whatever, and (c) any system of technology whatever, and develops principles of economic behaviour. The validity of its "laws" does not depend on the actual conditions or data, with respect to any of these three elementary phases of economic action.[17]

In politics, not everything can be counted or measured, but some things can be. That may be helpful in the application of theories but has nothing to do with their construction.

The fifth and sixth difficulties discovered by Aron seem to tell us something substantive about politics rather than about its amenability to theory and its status as science. In classical economic theory, no mechanism—that is, no agent or institution—restores a lost equilibrium. Classical and neoclassical economists were microtheorists—market and exchange relations emerge from the exercise of individual choice. The economy is produced by the interaction of persons and firms; it cannot be said to have goals or purposes of its own.[18] Governments may, of course, act to restore a lost equilibrium. So may powerful persons or firms within the economy. But at this point we leave the realm of theory and enter the realm of practice—or "sociology" as Aron uses the term. "Any concrete study of international relations is sociological," he avers.[19] The characteristic attaches to concrete studies and not simply to the study of international politics.

Aron identifies science with the ability to predict and control.[20] Yet theories of evolution predict nothing in particular. Astronomers do predict (although without controlling), but what entitles astronomy to be called a science is not the ability to predict but the ability to specify causes, to state the theories and laws by which the predictions are made. Economic theory is impressive even when economists show themselves to be unreliable in prediction and prescription alike. Since theory abstracts from much of the complication of the world in an effort to explain it, the application of theory in any realm is a perplexing and uncertain matter.

Aron's first three problems can be solved, although in the realm of theory all solutions are tentative. Aron's last three difficulties are not impediments to the construction of theory but rather to its application and testing.

International politics: within the theoretical pale

The new realism, in contrast to the old, begins by proposing a solution to the problem of distinguishing factors internal to international political systems from those that are external. Theory isolates one realm from others in order to deal with it intellectually. By depicting an international-political system as a whole, with structural and unit levels at once distinct and connected, neorealism establishes the autonomy of international politics and thus makes a theory about it possible.[21] Neorealism develops the concept of a system's structure which at once bounds the domain that students of international politics deal with and enables them to see how the structure of the system, and variations in it, affect the interacting units and the outcomes they produce. International structure emerges from the interaction of states and then constrains them from taking certain actions while propelling them toward others.

The concept of structure is based on the fact that units differently juxtaposed and combined behave differently and in interacting produce different outcomes. International structures are defined, first, by the ordering principle of the system, in our case anarchy, and second, by the distribution of capabilities across units. In an anarchic realm, structures are defined in terms of their major units. International structures vary with significant changes in the number of great powers. Great powers are marked off from others by the combined capabilities (or power) they command. When their number changes consequentially, the calculations and behaviors of states, and the outcomes their interactions produce, vary.

The idea that international politics can be thought of as a system with a precisely defined structure is neorealism's fundamental departure from traditional realism. The spareness of the definition of international structure has attracted criticism. Robert Keohane asserts that neorealist theory "can be modified progressively to attain closer correspondence with reality."[22] In the most sensitive and insightful essay on neorealism that I have read, Barry Buzan asks whether the logic of neorealism completely captures "the main features of the international political system." He answers this way:

> The criticisms of Ruggie, Keohane, and others suggest that it does not, because their concerns with factors such as dynamic density, information richness, communication facilities, and such like do not obviously fit into Waltz's ostensibly "systemic" theory.[23]

One wonders whether such factors as these can be seen as concepts that might become elements of a theory? "Dynamic density" would seem to be the most promising candidate. Yet dynamic density is not a part of a theory about one type of society or another. Rather it is a condition that develops in greater or lesser degree within and across societies. If the volume of transactions grows sufficiently, it will disrupt a simple society and transform it into a complex one. Dynamic density is not part of a theory of any society. Rather it is a social force developing in society that under certain circumstances may first disrupt and then transform it.[24] The "such likes" mentioned by Buzan would not fit into any theory. Can one imagine how demographic trends, information richness, and international institutions could be thrown into a theory? No theory can contain the "such likes," but if a theory is any good, it helps us to understand and explain them, to estimate their significance, and to gauge their effects. Moreover, any theory leaves some things unexplained, and no theory enables one to move directly and easily from theory to application. Theories, one must add, are not useful merely because they may help one to understand, explain, and sometimes predict the trend of events. Equally important, they help one to understand how a given system works.

To achieve "closeness of fit" would negate theory. A theory cannot fit the facts or correspond with the events it seeks to explain. The ultimate closeness of fit would be achieved by writing a finely detailed description of the world that interests us. Nevertheless, neorealism continues to be criticized for its omissions. A theory can be written only by leaving out most matters that are of practical interest. To believe that listing the omissions of a theory constitutes a valid criticism is to misconstrue the theoretical enterprise.

The question of omissions arises because I limit the second term that defines structure to the distribution of power across nations. Now and then critics point out that logically many factors other than power, such as governmental form or national ideology, can be cast in distributional terms. Obviously so, but logic alone does not write theories. The question is not what does logic permit, but what does this theory require? Considerations of power dominate considerations of ideology. In a structural theory, states are differently placed by their power and differences in placement help to explain both their behavior and their fates. In any political system, the distribution of the unit's capabilities is a key to explanation. The distribution of power is of special explanatory importance in self-help political systems because the units of the system are not formally differentiated with distinct functions specified as are the parts of hierarchic orders.

Barry Buzan raises questions about the adequacy "of defining structure within the relatively narrow sectoral terms of politics."[25] It may be that a better theory could be devised by differently drawing the borders of the domain to which it will apply, by adding something to the theory, by subtracting something from it, or by altering assumptions and rearranging the relations among a theory's concepts. But doing any or all of these things requires operations entirely different from the mere listing of omissions. Theory, after all, is mostly omissions. What is omitted cannot be added without thoroughly reworking the theory and turning it into a different one. Should one broaden the perspective of international-political theory to include economics? An international political-economic theory would presumably be twice as good as a theory of international politics alone. To fashion such a theory, one would have to show how the international political-economic domain can be marked off from others. One would first have to define its structures and then develop a theory to explain actions and outcomes within it. A political-economic theory would represent a long step toward a general theory of international relations, but no one has shown how to take it.

Those who want to disaggregate power as defined in neorealist theory are either calling for a new theory, while failing to provide one, or are pointing to some of the knotty problems that arise in the testing and application of theory. In the latter case, they, like Aron, confuse difficulties in testing and applying theory with the problem of constructing one.[26] Critics of neorealist theory fail to understand that a theory is not a statement about everything that is important in international-political life, but rather a necessarily slender explanatory construct. Adding elements of practical importance would carry us back from a neorealist theory to a realist approach. The rich variety and wondrous complexity of international life would be reclaimed at the price of extinguishing theory.

Neorealism breaks with realism in four major ways. The first and most important one I have examined at some length. The remaining three I shall treat more briefly. They follow from, and are made possible by, the first one. Neorealism departs from traditional realism in the following additional ways: Neorealism produces a shift in causal relations, offers a different interpretation of power, and treats the unit level differently.

Theory and reality

Causal directions

Constructing theories according to different suppositions alters the appearance of whole fields of inquiry. A new theory draws attention to new objects of inquiry, interchanges causes and effects, and addresses different worlds. When John Hobson cast economics in macrotheoretical terms, he baffled his fellow economists. The London Extension Board would not allow him to offer courses on political economy because an economics professor who had read Hobson's book thought it "equivalent in rationality to an attempt to prove the flatness of the earth."[27] Hobson's figure was apt. Microtheory, the economic orthodoxy of the day, portrayed a world different from the one that Hobson's macrotheory revealed.

Similarly, the neorealist's world looks different from the one that earlier realists had portrayed. For realists, the world addressed is one of interacting states. For neorealists, interacting states can be adequately studied only by distinguishing between structural and unit-level causes and effects. Structure becomes a new object of inquiry, as well as an occasion for argument. In the light of neorealist theory, means and ends are differently viewed, as are causes and effects. Realists think of causes running in one direction, from interacting states to the outcomes their acts and interactions produce. This is clearly seen in Morgenthau's "Six Principles of Political Realism," which form the substance of a chapter headed "A Realist Theory of International Politics."[28] Strikingly, one finds much said about foreign policy and little about international politics. The principles develop as Morgenthau searches for his well-known "rational outline, a map that suggests to us the possible meanings of foreign policy."[29] The principles are about human nature, about interest and power, and about questions of morality. Political realism offers the perspective in which the actions of statesmen are to be understood and judged. Morgenthau's work was in harmony with the developing political science of his day, although at the time this was not seen. Methodological presuppositions shape the conduct of inquiry. The political-science paradigm was becoming deeply entrenched. Its logic is preeminently behavioral. The established paradigm of any field indicates what facts to scrutinize and how they are interconnected. Behavioral logic explains political outcomes through examining the constituent parts of political systems. When Aron and other traditionalists insist that theorists' categories be consonant with actors' motives and perceptions, they are affirming the preeminently behavioral logic that their inquiries follow.[30] The characteristics and the interactions of behavioral units are taken to be the direct causes of political events, whether in the study of national or of international politics. Aron, Morgenthau and other realists tried to understand and explain international outcomes by examining the actions and interactions of the units, the states that populate the international arena, and those who guide their policies. Realism's approach is primarily inductive. Neorealism is more heavily deductive.

Like classical economists before them, realists were unable to account for a major anomaly. Classical theory held that disequilibria would be righted by the working of market forces without need for governmental intervention. Hobson's, and later in fuller form John Maynard Keynes's, macroeconomic theory explained why in the natural course of events recovery from depressions was such a long time coming.[31] A similarly big anomaly in realist theory is seen in the attempt to explain alternations of war and peace. Like most students of international politics, realists infer outcomes from the salient attributes of the actors producing them. Governmental forms, economic systems, social institutions, political ideologies—these are but a few examples of where the causes of war and peace have been found. Yet, although causes are specifically assigned, we know that states with every imaginable variation of economic institution, social custom, and political ideology have fought wars. If an indicated condition seems to have caused a given war, one must wonder what accounts for the repetition of wars even as their causes vary. Variations in the quality of the units are not linked directly to the outcomes their behaviors produce, nor are variations in patterns of interaction. Many, for example, have claimed that World War I was caused by the interaction of two opposed and closely balanced coalitions. But then many have claimed that World War II was caused by the failure of some states to right an imbalance of power by combining to counter an existing alliance. Over the centuries, the texture of international life has remained impressively, or depressingly, uniform even while profound changes were taking place in the composition of states which, according to realists, account for national behavior and international outcomes. Realists cannot explain the disjunction between supposed causes and observed effects. Neorealists can.

Neorealism contends that international politics can be understood only if the effects of structure are added to traditional realism's unit-level explanations. More generally, neorealism reconceives the causal link between interacting units and international outcomes. Neorealist theory shows that causes run not in one direction, from interacting units to outcomes produced, but rather in two directions. One must believe that some causes of international outcomes are located at the level of the interacting units. Since variations in unit-level causes do not correspond to variations in observed outcomes, one has to believe that some causes are located at the structural level of international politics as well. Realists cannot handle causation at a level above states because they fail to conceive of structure as a force that shapes and shoves the units. Causes at the level of units interact with those at the level of the structure and because they do so explanation at the level of units alone is bound to mislead. If one's theory allows for the handling of both unit-level and structure-level causes, then it can cope with both the changes and the continuities that occur in a system.

Power as means and end

For many realists, the desire for power is rooted in the nature of man. Morgenthau recognized that given competition for scarce goods with no one to serve as arbiter, a struggle for power will ensue among the competitors, and that consequently the struggle for power can be explained without reference to the evil born in men. The struggle for power arises because people want things and not necessarily because of the evil in their desires. This he labels one of the two roots of conflict, but even while discussing it he pulls toward the "other root of conflict and concomitant evil"—the *animus dominandi*, the desire for power. He often considers man's drive for power as a datum more basic than the chance conditions under which struggles for power occur.[32]

The reasoning is faithful to Hobbes for whom the three causes of quarrels were competition, diffidence (i.e., distrust), and glory. Competition leads to fighting for gain, diffidence to fighting to keep what has been gained, glory to fighting for reputation. Because some hunger for power, it behooves others to cultivate their appetites.[33] For Morgenthau, as for Hobbes, even if one has plenty of power and is secure in its possession, more power is nevertheless wanted. As Morgenthau put it:

> Since the desire to attain a maximum of power is universal, all nations must always be afraid that their own miscalculations and the power increases of other nations might add up to an inferiority for themselves which they must at all costs try to avoid.[34]

Both Hobbes and Morgenthau see that conflict is in part situationally explained, but both believe that even were it not so, pride, lust, and the quest for glory would cause the war of all against all to continue indefinitely. Ultimately, conflict and war are rooted in human nature.

The preoccupation with the qualities of man is understandable in view of the purposes Hobbes and Morgenthau entertain. Both are interested in understanding the state. Hobbes seeks a logical explanation of its emergence; Morgenthau seeks to explain how it behaves internationally. Morgenthau thought of the "rational" statesman as striving ever to accumulate more and more power. Power is seen as an end in itself. Nations at times may act aside from considerations of power. When they do, Morgenthau insists, their actions are not "of a political nature."[35] The claim that "the desire to attain a maximum of power is universal" among nations is one of Morgenthau's "objective laws that have their roots in human nature."[36] Yet much of the behavior of nations contradicts it. Morgenthau does not explain why other desires fail to moderate or outweigh the fear states may have about miscalculation of their relative power. His opinions about power are congenial to realism. They are easily slipped into because the effort to explain behavior and outcomes by the characteristics of units leads realists to assign to them attributes that seem to accord with behavior and outcomes observed. Unable to conceive of international politics as a self-sustaining system, realists concentrate on the behavior and outcomes that seem to follow from the characteristics they have attributed to men and states. Neorealists, rather than viewing power as an end in itself, see power as a possibly useful means, with states running risks if they have either too little or too much of it. Weakness may invite an attack that greater strength would dissuade an adversary from launching. Excessive strength may prompt other states to increase their arms and pool their efforts. Power is a possibly useful means, and sensible statesmen try to have an appropriate amount of it. In crucial situations, the ultimate concern of states is not for power but for security. This is an important revision of realist theory.

A still more important one is neorealism's use of the concept of power as a defining characteristic of structure. Power in neorealist theory is simply the combined capability of a state. Its distribution across states, and changes in that distribution, help to define structures and changes in them as explained above. Some complaints have been made about the absence of efforts on the part of neorealists to devise objective measures of power. Whatever the difficulties of measurement may be, they are not theoretical difficulties but practical ones encountered when moving from theory to its practical application.

Interacting units

For realists, anarchy is a general condition rather than a distinct structure. Anarchy sets the problem that states have to cope with. Once this is understood, the emphasis of realists shifts to the interacting units. States are unlike one another in form of government, character of rulers, types of ideology, and

79

in many other ways. For both realists and neorealists, differently constituted states behave differently and produce different outcomes. For neorealists, however, states are made functionally similar by the constraints of structure, with the principal differences among them defined according to capabilities. For neorealists, moreover, structure mediates the outcomes that states produce. As internal and external circumstances change, structures and states may bear more or less causal weight. The question of the relative importance of different levels cannot be abstractly or definitively answered. Ambiguity cannot be resolved since structures affect units even as units affect structures. Some have thought that this is a defect of neorealist theory. It is so, however, only if factors at the unit level or at the structural level determine, rather than merely affect, outcomes. Theories cannot remove the uncertainty of politics, but only help us to comprehend it.

Neorealists concentrate their attention on the central, previously unanswered question in the study of international politics: How can the structure of an international-political system be distinguished from its interacting parts? Once that question is answered, attention shifts to the effects of structure on interacting units. Theorists concerned with structural explanations need not ask how variations in units affect outcomes, even though outcomes find their causes at both structural and unit levels. Neorealists see states as like units; each state "is like all other states in being an autonomous political unit." Autonomy is the unit-level counterpart of anarchy at the structural level. A theory of international politics can leave aside variation in the composition of states and in the resources and technology they command because the logic of anarchy does not vary with its content. Realists concentrate on the heterogeneity of states because they believe that differences of behavior and outcomes proceed directly from differences in the composition of units. Noticing that the proposition is faulty, neorealists offer a theory that explains how structures affect behavior and outcomes.

The logic of anarchy obtains whether the system is composed of tribes, nations, oligopolistic firms, or street gangs. Yet systems populated by units of different sorts in some ways perform differently, even though they share the same organizing principle. More needs to be said about the status and role of units in neorealist theory. More also needs to be said about changes in the background conditions against which states operate. Changes in the industrial and military technologies available to states, for example, may change the character of systems but do not change the theory by which their operation is explained. These are subjects for another essay. Here I have been concerned not to deny the many connections between the old and the new realism but to emphasize the most important theoretical changes that neorealism has wrought. I have been all the more concerned to do this since the influence of realist and behavioral logic lingers in the study of international politics, as in political science generally.

Notes

1 I should like to thank David Schleicher for his help on this paper
2 William T. R. Fox, co-author and ed., *Theoretical Aspects of International Relations* (Notre Dame, IN: University of Notre Dame Press, 1959).
3 Josiah Child, *A New Discourse of Trade*, 4th ed. (London: J. Hodges, 1740). See also William Letwin, *Sir Josiah Child, Merchant Economist* (Cambridge, MA: Harvard University Press, 1959).
4 Joseph Schumpeter, *Economic Doctrine and Method: An Historical Sketch*, R. Aris, trans. (New York: Oxford University Press, 1967) p. 24.
5 Ibid., p. 30.
6 François Quesnay was the foremost Physiocrat. His *Tableau Oeconomique* was published in 1758.
7 Schumpeter, op. cit., pp. 42–44, 6.
8 Raymond Aron, "What is a Theory of International Relations?," *Journal of International Affairs* 21, no. 2 (1967) pp. 185–206.
9 Hans J. Motgenthau, *Politics Among Nations*, 5th ed. (New York: Alfred A. Knopf, 1972) p. 7.
10 Ibid., p. 3.
11 Morgenthau, *Truth and Power* (New York: Praeger, 1970) pp. 253–258.
12 Morgenthau, "International Relations: Quantitative and Qualitative Approaches," in Norman Palmer, ed., *A Design for International Relations Research; Scope, Theory, Methods, and Relevance* (Philadelphia: American Academy of Political and Social Science, 1970) p. 78.
13 Morgenthau (1972), op. cit., p. 12.
14 Ludwig Boltzman, "Theories as Representations," excerpt, Rudolph Weingartner, trans., in Arthur Danto and Sidney Morgenbesser eds., *Philosophy of Science* (Cleveland, OH: World, 1960).
15 Aron, op. cit., p. 198.
16 "To be simple-minded" is Anatol Rapoport's first rule for the construction of mathematical models. See his "Lewis F. Richardson's Mathematical Theory of War," *Journal of Conflict Resolution* 1, no. 3 (1957) pp. 275–276.
17 Frank Hyneman Knight, *The Ethics of Competition and Other Essays* (London: George Allen & Unwin, 1936) p. 281.
18 See also James M. Buchanan, "An Individualistic Theory of Political Process," in David Easton ed., *Varieties of Political Theory* (Englewood Cliffs, NJ: Prentice-Hall, 1966) pp. 25–26.
19 Aron, op. cit., p. 198.
20 Ibid., p. 201. See also Morgenthau (1970), op. cit., p. 253.
21 Neorealism is sometimes referred to as structural realism. Throughout this essay I refer to my own formulation of neorealist theory. See esp. chs. 5–6 of *Theory of International Politics* (Reading, MA: Addison-Wesley, 1979).
22 Robert O. Keohane, "Theory of World Politics: Structural Realism and Beyond," in Keohane ed., *Neorealism and Its Critics* (New York: Columbia University Press, 1986) p. 191.
23 Barry Buzan, "Systems, Structures and Units: Reconstructing Waltz's Theory of International Politics," unpublished paper (April 1988) p. 35.
24 John G. Ruggie, "Continuity and Transformation in the World Polity," in Keohane ed. op. cit., pp. 148–152; Waltz, "A Response to my Critics," pp. 323–326. Waltz (1979), op. cit., pp. 126–128.
25 Buzan, op. cit., p. 11.
26 See, for example., Joseph S. Nye, Jr., "Neorealism and Neoliberalism," in

World Politics 40, no. 2 (January 1988), pp. 241–245; Keohane, op. cit., pp. 184–200; Buzan, op. cit., pp. 28–34.

27 John Maynard Keynes, *The General Theory of Employment, Interest, and Money* (London: Macmillan, 1951) pp. 365–366.
28 Morgenthau (1972), op. cit., pp. 4–14.
29 Ibid., p. 5.
30 See Waltz (1979), op. cit., pp. 44, 47, 62.
31 In his *General Theory*. Keynes gives Hobson full credit for setting forth the basic concepts of macroeconomic theory.
32 Morgenthau, *Scientific Man vs. Power Politics* (Chicago: University of Chicago Press, 1946) p. 192.
33 Thomas Hobbes, *Leviathan*.
34 Morgenthau (1972), op. cit., p. 208.
35 Ibid., p. 71.
36 Ibid.
37 On page 95 of *Theory of International Politics*, I slipped into using "sovereignty" for "autonomy." Sovereignty, Ruggie points out, is particular to the modern state. See his "Continuity and Transformation," in Keohane ed., op. cit., pp. 142–148.

6

EVALUATING THEORIES

John Vasquez claims to follow Imre Lakatos but distorts his criteria for judging theories and evaluating research programs. Vasquez claims that facts observed can falsify a theory by showing that its predictions are wrong. He fails to consider the puzzles posed by the interdependence of theory and fact. He places all realists in a single paradigm despite the divergent assumptions of traditional and structural realists. In contrast to Vasquez, I argue that explanation, not prediction, is the ultimate criterion of good theory, that a theory can be validated only by working back and forth between its implications and an uncertain state of affairs that we take to be the reality against which theory is tested, and that the results of tests are always problematic.

Having previously covered the criticisms John Vasquez makes (see especially Waltz 1979, 1986), I respond to his article reluctantly. One is, however, always tempted to try again.

Following Lakatos (1970), albeit shakily, in moving from paradigms to theories to research programs, Vasquez says he places theories in a single paradigm if they "share certain fundamental assumptions" (p. 900). He thereupon lumps old and new realists together in one realist paradigm. This is odd since, as he recognizes, old and new realists work from different basic assumptions. Believing that states strive for ever more power, Hans Morgenthau took power to be an end in itself. In contrast, I built structural theory on the assumption that survival is the goal of states and that power is one of the means to that end. Political scientists generally work from two different paradigms: one behavioral, the other systemic. Old realists see causes as running directly from states to the outcomes their actions produce. New realists see states forming a structure by their interactions and then being strongly affected by the structure their interactions have formed. Old realists account for political outcomes mainly by analyzing differences among states; new realists show why states tend to become like units as they try to coexist in a self-help system, with behaviors and outcomes explained by differences in the positions of states as well as by their internal characteristics (see Waltz 1990). If the term "paradigm" means anything at all, it cannot accommodate such fundamental differences.

Vasquez puts old and new realists in the same pot because he misunderstands realists. He makes odd statements about what paradigms do because he misunderstands paradigms. He believes that paradigms easily generate a family of theories (p. 900). Paradigms are apparently like sausage machines: Turn the crank, and theories come out. Yet no one in any field is able to generate theories easily or even to say how to go about creating them.

Vasquez finds lots of realist theories because he defines theories loosely as "inter-related propositions purporting to explain behavior" (footnote 3). If inter-relating propositions were all it took to make theories, then, of course, we would have many of them. I can, however, think of any number of propositions purporting to explain something that would not qualify as theories by any useful definition of the term. I define theory as a picture, mentally formed, of a bounded realm or domain of activity. A theory depicts the organization of a realm and the connections among its parts. The infinite materials of any realm can be organized in endlessly different ways. Reality is complex; theory is simple. By simplification, theories lay bare the essential elements in play and indicate necessary relations of cause and interdependency—or suggest where to look for them (see Waltz 1979, 1–13). Vasquez, following his definition, finds many theories; I find few.

Vasquez's belief that theories are plentiful and easy to produce reflects the positivist tradition that permeates American political science. At the extreme, positivists believe that reality can be apprehended directly, without benefit of theory. Reality is whatever we directly observe. In a more moderate version of positivism, theory is but one step removed from reality, is arrived at largely by induction, is rather easy to construct, and is fairly easy to test. In their book on interdependence, Keohane and Nye provide a clear example when they "argue that complex interdependence sometimes comes closer to reality than does realism" (1989, p. 23). Yet, if we knew what reality is, theory would serve no purpose. Statements such as "parsimony is a judgment . . . about the nature of the world: it is assumed to be simple," neatly express the idea that theory does little more than mirror reality (King, Keohane, and Verba 1994, p. 20)

Faced with an infinite number of "facts" one must wonder, however, which ones are to be taken as pertinent when trying to explain something. As the molecular biologist Gunther Stent has put it: "Reality is constructed by the mind . . . the recognition of structures is nothing else than the selective destruction of information" (1973, E17). Scientists and philosophers of science refer to facts as being "theory laden" and to theory and fact as being "interdependent." "Every fact," as Goethe nicely put it, "is already a theory." Theory, rather than being a mirror in which reality is reflected, is an instrument to be used in attempting to explain a circumscribed part of a reality of whose true dimensions we can never be sure. The instrument is of no use if it does little more than ape the complexity of the world. To say that a "theory should be just as complicated as all our evidence suggests" (King, Keohane, and Verba 1994, p. 20) amounts to a renunciation of science from Galileo onward.

Because of the interdependence of theory and fact, the construction and testing of theories is a more problematic task than most political scientists have thought. Understanding this, Lakatos rejected "dogmatic falsification" in favor of judging theories by the fruitfulness of the research programs they may spawn. Following Lakatos, Vasquez faults the realist paradigm for what he takes to be the regressive quality of its research program. Forsaking Lakatos, he then adduces evidence that in his view falsifies balance-of-power theory in its structural-realist form. I shall consider both claims.

I disagree with Lakatos on some points, but not on his rejection of the notion that tests can falsify theories. To explain why falsification won't do, I all too briefly mention two problems. First, proving something false requires proving something else true. Yet the facts against which we test theories are themselves problematic. As Lakatos rightly says, in italics, "*theories are not only equally unprovable, . . . they are also equally undisprovable*" (1970, p. 103; cf. Harris 1970, p. 353). Among natural scientists, falsification is a little used method (Bochenski 1965, p. 109; cf. Harris 1970). Social scientists should think about why this is so.

Second, citing Popper (1959), Vasquez insists that "paradigms" should specify the evidence that would disprove them and criticizes realism for not doing so (p. 905). In contrast, Lakatos observes that "*the most admired scientific theories simply fail to forbid any observable state of affairs*" (1970, p. 100, his italics). This is true for many reasons. Lakatos himself points out that we always evaluate theories with a *ceteris paribus* clause implied, and we can never be sure that it holds. To express the same thought in different words, scientific theories deal in idealizations. If the results of scientific experiments are carried to enough decimal points, hypotheses inferred from theories are always proved wrong. As the Nobel laureate in physics Steven Weinberg puts it: "There is no theory that is not contradicted by some experiment" (1992, p. 93). Ernst Nagel (1961, pp. 460–466, 505–509) expressed a similar thought when he pointed out that social-science predictions fail because social scientists do not deal in idealizations. It is because falsification is untenable that Lakatos proposes that we evaluate theories by the fruitfulness of their research programs. Ultimately, he concludes, as others had earlier, that a theory is overthrown only by a better theory (p. 119; cf. Conant 1947, p. 48).

Despite claiming to follow Lakatos's advice to evaluate theories through their research programs, Vasquez emphasizes what he takes to be evidence falsifying balance-of-power theory. According to him, the historian Paul Schroeder (1994) has presented "devastating evidence" against it. One must understand, however, what a theory claims to explain before attempting to test it. Early in his piece, Schroeder (p. 109) draws a picture of neorealism's logic. All of his arrows run in one direction, from the system downward. Realizing that many people have trouble understanding theory, I drew a few pictures myself. Figure 1 depicts one of them (Waltz 1979, p. 40). Structural theory emphasizes that causation runs from structures to states *and* from states to structure. It also explains, among other things, why balances of power recurrently form. Schroeder rejects structural theory because it fails to account for the motives of statesmen. Yet, as William Graham Sumner wrote: "Motives from which men act have nothing at all to do with the consequences of their action" ([1911] 1968, p. 212). I would say "little" rather than "nothing," but the point is clear, and structural theory explains why it holds. What Vasquez takes to be Schroeder's "devastating evidence" turns out to be a melange of irrelevant diplomatic lore. Like Vasquez, Schroeder ignores the basic injunction that theories be judged by what they claim to explain. Moreover, both fail to notice that Morgenthau's understanding of balances of power differs fundamentally from mine. For Morgenthau, balances are intended and must be sought by the statesmen who produce them. For me, balances are produced whether or not intended. Schroeder's "evidence" may apply to Morgenthau's ideas about balances of power; it does not apply to mine. This again shows how misleading it is to place all realists in a single paradigm.

Vasquez and Schroeder note that power is often out of balance. Is structural theory invalidated because the actions of states sometimes fail to bring their system into balance? In answering this question, it is helpful to think of similar problems in economics. Classical economic theory holds that, in the absence of governmental intervention, competitive economies tend toward equilibrium at full employment of the factors of production. Yet one rarely finds an economy in equilibrium. Further, theory leads one to expect that competition will lead to a similarity of products as well as of prices. Illustrating the result, Harold Hotelling (1929) pointed out that autos, furniture, cider, churches, and political parties become much like one another. But a tendency toward the sameness of products may not be apparent at a given moment, for a competitor may successfully outflank its rivals by offering a design that breaks the mold. Do economies in disequilibrium and variations in product design cast doubt on hypotheses inferred from theories of competition? Hardly. Economic theory predicts strong and persistent tendencies rather than particular states or conditions. Similarly, no contradiction exists between saying that international-political systems tend strongly *toward* balance but are seldom *in* balance.

Vasquez's attempt to apply Lakatos's ideas about research programs to balance-of-power theory is as unsuccessful as his attempt to adduce evidence that would falsify it. Lakatos defines a series of theories as progressive "if each new theory has some excess empirical content over its predecessor, that is, if it predicts some novel, hitherto unexpected facts" (1970, p. 116). Newtonian science is a wonderful example of a progressive series of theories, incorporating the same basic assumptions about the universe in theories covering successively more phenomena. Classical economics, able to explain the working of national and of international economies as well, is another example. In international politics, where can one find such a use of fundamental concepts to develop theories covering ever more phenomena? Vasquez claims to find several, but his claim rests sometimes on placing in a single realist program work that belongs in different ones, and sometimes on taking work done when applying a theory as being the creation of a new one.

One cannot judge the fertility of a research program by evaluating work done outside of it. Vasquez takes Randall Schweller's (1994) essay on bandwagoning as work done within the realist paradigm and argues that it provides an example of its degeneration. Schweller, however, sets out to show that the central theory of neorealism is wrong. He rejects neorealism's assumptions about power as a means and survival as the goal of states in favor of Morgenthau's assumption that states seek ever more power. He claims to show that bandwagoning is more common than balancing, believing that if it is, then neorealist theory fails. Schweller and I work within different research programs. The question therefore shifts from the quality of the program to whether his claims about bandwagoning invalidate structural theory.

Structural theory assumes that the dominant goal of states is security, since to pursue whatever other goals they may have, they first must survive. Bandwagoning and balancing by the logic of the theory are opposite responses of security-seeking states to their situations. States concerned for their security value relative gains over absolute ones. At the extremes, however, with very secure or very insecure states, the quest for absolute gains may prevail over the quest for relative ones. Very weak states cannot make themselves secure by their own efforts. Whatever the risks, their main chance may be to jump on a bandwagon pulled by stronger states. Other states may have a choice between joining a stronger state and balancing against it, and they may make the wrong one. States sometimes blunder when trying to respond sensibly to both internal and external pressures. Morgenthau once compared a statesman not believing in the balance of power to a scientist not believing in the law of gravity. Laws can be broken, but breaking them risks punishment. One who violates the law of gravity by stepping from a nineteenth-story window will suffer instant and condign punishment. A state that bandwagons when the situation calls for balancing runs risks, as Mussolini's Italy discovered after it jumped on Hitler's bandwagon, although in international politics punishment may not be swift and sure. By joining the stronger side, Italy became Germany's junior partner, and Mussolini lost control of his policy. Bandwagoning by some states strengthened Germany and encouraged Hitler to further conquest. Only balancing in the middle and later 1930s could have stopped him. Various states, including Italy, paid a great price for their failure to balance earlier. Theory does not direct the policies of states; it does describe their expected consequences.

States' actions are not determined by structure. Rather, as I have said before, structures shape and shove; they encourage states to do some things and to refrain from doing others. Because states coexist in a self-help system, they are free to do any fool thing they care to, but they are likely to be rewarded for behavior that is responsive to structural pressures and punished for behavior that is not.

Vasquez requires that theories predict, since prediction seems to make falsification possible. He therefore seizes upon Schweller's claim that bandwagoning is more common than balancing. Whether this looks like falsifying evidence depends on what is predicted. Like classical economic theory, balance-of-power theory does not say that a system will be in equilibrium most or even much of the time. Instead, it predicts that, willy nilly, balances will form over time. That, Vasquez would no doubt say, is not much of a prediction. Yet Charles Kegley (1993, p. 139) has sensibly remarked that if a multipolar system emerges from the present unipolar one, realism will be vindicated. Seldom in international politics do signs of vindication appear so quickly. Multipolarity is developing before our eyes: To all but the myopic, it can already be seen on the horizon. Moreover, it is emerging in accordance with the balancing imperative.

In the light of structural theory, unipolarity appears as the least stable of international configurations. Unlikely though it is, a dominant power may behave with moderation, restraint, and forbearance. Even if it does, however, weaker states will worry about its future behavior. America's founding fathers warned against the perils of power in the absence of checks and balances. Is unbalanced power less of a danger in international than in national politics? Some countries will not want to bet that it is. As nature abhors a vacuum, so international politics abhors unbalanced power. Faced by unbalanced power, states try to increase their own strength or they ally with others to bring the international distribution of power into balance. The reactions of other states to the drive for dominance of Charles I of Spain, of Louis XIV and Napoleon Bonaparte of France, of Wilhelm II and Adolph Hitler of Germany, illustrate the point.

Will the preponderant power of the United States elicit similar reactions? Unbalanced power, whoever wields it, is a potential danger to others. The powerful state may, and the United States does, think of itself as acting for the sake of peace, justice, and well-being in the world. These terms, however, will be defined to the liking of the powerful, which may conflict with the preferences and interests of others. The powerful state will at times act in ways that appear arbitrary and high-handed to others, who will smart under the unfair treatment they believe they are receiving. Some of the weaker states in the system will therefore act to restore a balance and thus move the system back to bi- or multipolarity. China and Japan are doing so now.

In international politics, overwhelming power repels and leads others to balance against it. Stephen Walt (1987, pp. viii, 5, 21, 263–265) has offered a reformulation of balance-of-power theory, believing that states balance not against power but against threat. Vasquez sees Walt's "refinement" as placing a semantic patch on the original theory in an attempt to rescue it from falsifying evidence. I would agree if I took Walt's reformulation to be the correction of a concept that increases the explanatory power of a defective theory and makes it more precise. Changing the concepts of a theory, however, makes an old theory into a new one that has to be evaluated in its own right. I see "balance of threat" not as the name of a new theory but as part of a description of how makers of foreign policy think when making alliance decisions. Theory is an instrument. The empirical material on which it is to be used is not found in the instrument; it has to be adduced by the person using it. Walt makes this clear when he describes "threat" as one of the "factors that statesmen consider when deciding with whom to ally" (p. 21). In moving from international-political *theory* to foreign-policy *application* one has to consider such matters as statesmen's assessments of threats, but they do not thereby become part of the theory. Forcing more empirical content into a theory would truly amount to a "regressive theory shift." It would turn a general theory into a particular explanation. Vasquez, and Walt, have unfortunately taken the imaginative application of a theory to be the creation of a new one.

Vasquez makes a similar mistake in his appraisal of Christensen's and Snyder's (1990) essay, "Chain Gangs and Passed Bucks." "The authors," according to Vasquez, "find a gap in Waltz's explanation [of European diplomacy preceding World War II] and try to correct it by bringing in a variable from Jervis" (p. 906). However good or bad my brief explanation of what happened in Europe prior to World War II may be (Waltz 1979, pp. 164–170), an explanation is not a theory. A theory does not provide an account of what has happened or of what may happen. Just as a hammer becomes a useful tool when nails and wood are available, so a theory becomes useful in devising an explanation of events when combined with information about them.

The question is not what should be included in an account of foreign policies but what can be included in a theory of international politics. A theory is not a mere collection of variables. If a "gap" is found in a theory, it cannot be plugged by adding a "variable" to it. To add to a theory something that one believes has been omitted requires showing how it can take its place as one element of a coherent and effective theory. If that were easy to do, we would be blessed with a wealth of strong and comprehensive theories.

I conclude by emphasizing a few points about the testing of theories. A theory's ability to explain is more important than its ability to predict. At least Steven Weinberg and many others think so. Believing that scientists will one day come up with a final theory, he writes that even then we will not be able "to predict everything or even very much," but, he adds, we will be able to understand why things "work the way they do" (1992, p. 45; cf. Toulmin 1961, pp. 36–38). Success in explaining, not in predicting, is the ultimate criterion of good theory. Theories of evolution, after all, predict nothing in particular.

Vasquez makes the testing of theories seem easy by adopting a positivist standard: Does the observation made correspond with a theory's prediction? His adoption of such a standard is shown by his crisp assertion that the failure of states to balance "in the period before World War II . . . should be taken as falsifying evidence" (p. 906). Yet what is to be taken as evidence for or against a theory is always in question. Some attempts to balance were made in the prewar years, but a balance formed, so to speak, only in the end. Should delay in completing a balance be taken as evidence contradicting balance-of-power theory? One may not be able to answer the question decisively. Testing theories is an uncertain business. In this case, however, one should certainly remember that the theory being tested explains the process of balancing as well as predicting that balances recurrently form. The theory cannot say how long the process will take.

The title of Errol Harris's (1970) book, *Hypothesis and Perception*, implies a criticism of Popper's claim that a critical test of a hypothesis, if flunked, falsifies a theory once and for all. As Harris suggests, our perceptions count; the results of tests require interpretation. Evaluating a theory requires working back and forth between the implications of the theory and an uncertain state of affairs that we take to be the reality against which the theory is tested. Whether or not events in the 1930s tend to validate or to falsify my version of balance-of-power theory depends as much on how one interprets the theory as on what happened. However, thorough the evaluation of a theory, we can never say for sure that the theory is true. All the more, then, we should test a theory in all of the ways we can think of—by trying to falsify and to confirm it, by seeing whether things work in the way the theory suggests, and by comparing events in arenas of similar structure to see if they follow similar patterns. Weinberg suggests yet another way. "The most important thing for the progress of physics," he writes, "is not the decision that a theory is true, but the decision that it is worth taking seriously" (1992, p. 103). The structural theory set forth in my *Theory of International Politics* at least passes that test.

Acknowledgment

The author is grateful to Karen Ruth Adams for her assistance.

References

Bochenski, J. M. 1965. *The Methods of Contemporary Thought*, trans. Peter Caws. Dordrecht: D. Reidel Publishing.

Christensen, Thomas J., and Jack Snyder. 1990. "Chain Gangs and Passed Bucks: Predicting Alliance Patterns in Multipolarity." *International Organization* 44 (Spring): pp. 137–168.

Conant, James B. 1947. *On Understanding Science.* New Haven, CT: Yale University Press.

Harris, Errol E. 1970. *Hypothesis and Perception.* London: Allen and Unwin.

Hotelling, Harold. 1929. "Stability in Competition." *Economic Journal* 39 (March): pp. 41–57.

Kegley, Charles W., Jr. 1993. "The Neoidealist Moment in International Studies? Realist Myths and the New International Realities." *International Studies Quarterly* 37 (June): pp. 131–146.

Keohane, Robert O., and Joseph S. Nye. 1989. *Power and Interdependence,* 2d ed. New York: Harper Collins.

King, Gary, Robert Keohane, and Sidney Verba. 1994. *Designing Social Inquiry: Scientific Inference in Qualitative Research.* Princeton, NJ: Princeton University Press.

Lakatos, Imre. 1970. "Falsification and the Methodology of Scientific Research Programmes." In *Criticism and the Growth of Knowledge,* ed. Imre Lakatos and Alan Musgrave. Cambridge: Cambridge University Press.

Nagel, Ernst. 1961. *The Structure of Science: Problems in the Logic of Scientific Explanation.* New York: Harcourt, Brace and World.

Popper, Karl R. 1959. *The Logic of Scientific Discovery.* London: Hutchinson.

Schroeder, Paul. 1994. "Historical Reality vs. Neo-Realist Theory." *International Security* 19 (Summer): pp. 108–148.

Schweller, Randall L. 1994. "Bandwagoning for Profit: Bringing the Revisionist State Back In." *International Security* 19 (Summer): pp. 72–107.

Stent, Gunther S. 1973. "Shakespeare and DNA." *New York Times,* January 28, sec. E.

Sumner, William Graham. [1911] 1968. "War." In *War: Studies from Psychology, Sociology, Anthropology,* ed. Leon Bramson and George W. Goethals. New York: Basic Books.

Toulmin, Stephen. 1961. *Foresight and Understanding: An Enquiry into the Aims of Science.* New York: Harper and Row.

Vasquez, John A. 1997. "The Realist Paradigm and Degenerative versus Progressive Research Programs: An Appraisal of Neotraditional Research on Waltz's Balancing Proposition." *American Political Science Review* 91(December): pp. 899–912.

Walt, Stephen M. 1987. *The Origins of Alliances.* Ithaca, NY: Cornell University Press.

Waltz, Kenneth N. 1979. *Theory of International Politics.* New York: McGraw Hill.

Waltz, Kenneth N. 1986. "Reflections on *Theory of International Politics*: Response to My Critics." In *Neorealism and Its Critics,* ed. Robert O. Keohane. New York: Columbia University Press.

Waltz, Kenneth N. 1990. "Realist Thought and Neorealist Theory." *Journal of International Affairs* 44 (Spring/Summer): pp. 21–37.

Waltz, Kenneth N. 1993. "The Emerging Structure of International Politics." *International Security* 17 (Fall): pp. 44–79.

Weinberg, Steven. 1992. *Dreams of a Final Theory.* New York: Pantheon Books.

7

THOUGHTS ABOUT
ASSAYING THEORIES

Students sometimes ask, with a hint of exasperation, why I assign Lakatos in seminars on international-political theory. One easily thinks of a number of reasons to omit him: Philosophy of science is a subject that demands clarity and precision; Lakatos's prose is opaque and vague; reading his well-known essay on "Falsification and Research Programmes" provides no clear guide to the evaluation of theories.[1] One certainly is not told just what to do. Yet the answer to why we should take Lakatos seriously is simple: He demolishes the simplistic notions about testing that have been and remain part of the intellectual stock of most students of political science.

How can we assay theories? Karl Popper gave a pleasingly simple answer. First, make a conjecture, preferably a bold one such as *all swans are white*. Then, search for falsifying instances. Thousands or millions of white swans do not prove that all swans are white, but just one black swan proves the conjecture false. Simply multiplying observations that appear to offer confirmation will not do, because one cannot know of the lurking instance that would defeat the "theory." Popper's idea of the "critical" test rests on a distinction between trying to prove truth and being able to demonstrate falsity. Popper believed that the latter is possible; the former, not.

In 1970, Errol Harris published an insightful but little-known book, *Hypothesis and Perception*.[2] His title suggested that the results of tests require interpretation, and his text developed the argument that seemingly critical tests are at best problematic. Tests attempting to falsify a theory are conducted against background information that in its day is taken for granted. How can we know that the background information is valid? Perhaps the black bird one thought a swan was really a turkey. That nothing is both empirical and certain is a proposition established long ago by David Hume and Immanuel Kant.

If the bold conjecture seems to flunk the critical test, the scientist-observer still has decisions to make about the implications that are to be drawn from the outcome. Lakatos takes the problem up at this point. His dictum is that "*we cannot prove theories and we cannot disprove them either.*"[3] He was right for this reason among others: Facts are no more independent of theories than theories are independent of facts. The validity of theories does not depend on

92

facts that are simply given. Theory and fact are interdependent. As the English astronomer Sir Arthur Stanley Eddington put it, "We should not put over-much confidence in the observational results that are put forward until they have been confirmed by theory."[4] A moment's thought reveals the wisdom of his advice. The earth is the center of the universe, and the sun and other heavenly bodies swirl around it: These beliefs were among the "facts" accepted in antiquity and through the Middle Ages. They were easily "verified" by looking around; they conformed to everyday experience. From Copernicus onward, however, new theories changed old facts.

Are these thoughts relevant for today's political scientists? We have to believe so when we read the following statement in a widely consulted manual on the design of social inquiry: "A theory must be consistent with prior evidence about a research question." To drive the point home the manual's authors quote Stanley Lieberson's pronouncement that a "theory that ignores existing evidence is an oxymoron."[5] Ironically, these thoughts are recorded in a chapter titled "The *Science* in Social Science."[6] The authors' science, however, is of the medieval variety. Theories, they say, may "emerge from detailed observation, but they should be evaluated with new observations." In this positivist perspective, facts are a source of theories and their arbiters as well. A theory is tested by confronting it with "the hard facts of empirical reality."[7] Yet seeming facts exist in infinite number. Which facts are to be taken as providing evidence for or against a theory? Because of the interdependence of theory and fact, one cannot give a simple answer. As Goethe put it, "The highest wisdom is to realize that every fact is already a theory."[8] According to the manual, a theory must indicate what evidence would show the theory wrong. According to Lakatos, a theory cannot specify the observations that would overthrow it.[9] According to the manual, there is an asymmetry between proving something true and proving something false. Theories are to be tested by trying to falsify them. Yet according to Lakatos, "some of the most interesting experiments result . . . in confirmation rather than falsification."[10] Steven Weinberg, Nobel laureate in physics, adds that there "is no theory that is not contradicted by some experiment."[11]

Despite all of the difficulties of testing, we need to evaluate theories in order to get rid of the wrong ones. With this thought, both Popper and Lakatos agree. They differ on how to do the evaluation. If, as Lakatos says, no theory can be shown to be either true or false, what are we to do? Rather than solving the problem of testing theory, Lakatos resorts to a displacement. Since no theory can be proved or disproved, he counsels trying to evaluate a series of theories, which he calls "a research programme." He deftly moves from a problem we cannot solve to one we supposedly can. If variations and elaborations of a theory uncover novel facts, research programs gain credence. A research program is based on and takes care to protect the "hard core" of the original theory. Auxiliary hypotheses provide the protection; they explain why seeming anomalies do not count.

Newtonian science provides the model for Lakatos's idea of a research program. A series of theories based on the same concepts and explaining ever more earthly and heavenly phenomena appeared to find confirmation by continuing to turn up novel facts. To Lakatos, the hard core of Newtonian science is the law of gravity and the three laws of dynamics. (Or, we may wonder, might it be the mental picture of the world in which space and time are absolute and the speed of light is relative?) Lakatos's rule is to stick with a research program as long as it produces "novel facts." The accumulation of anomalies (phenomena not accounted for by the theories) may cast the hard core into doubt, but since theories can be neither falsified nor verified, a theory can be overthrown only by a better one.[12]

In the social sciences, unfortunately, theories are scarce and research programs hard to find. The best example of a social science research program is the elaboration of classical and neoclassical economic theories over a period of more than 150 years, stretching from Adam Smith to John Maynard Keynes. Over the decades, anomalies accumulated and auxiliary hypotheses could no longer defend the hard core. The crucial anomaly was the recurrence of depressions, prolonged to the extent that it became hard to believe that the natural workings of a competitive economy would restore the natural equilibrium of the economy. Hobson showed that economic equilibria can be sustained at a level lower than full employment of the factors of production. When Keynes cast Hobson's ideas in the form of a general theory, macroeconomic theory gained and microeconomic theory lost credence.[13]

Yet one wonders how well the displacement from testing a theory to evaluating a series of theories serves. For a number of reasons, I would say, "not very." First, a research program is not fashioned by the creator of the initiatory theory but by the creator's successors. The original theory may be a good one, but the successor theories weak and defective. If the program should run off the tracks, we would still want to know how good the original theory may be. Second, the problem of evaluating a theory endures, whether or not the theory spawns a succession of theories. Third—an acute problem in the social sciences in applying the "novel facts" test—how are we to decide which facts are to be accepted as novel ones? Some will claim that their theories revealed one or two; others will say, we knew that all along. Fourth, if assaying a theory in itself is not possible, then how can anyone know whether launching a research program is worthwhile? In the end we may be left with Weinberg's thought that the "most important thing . . . is not the decision that a theory is true, but the decision that it is worth taking seriously."[14]

Given the problems of Lakatos's methodology of scientific research programs, why, I ask again, should students of politics pay attention to it? We should do so for one big reason: Lakatos's assaults crush the crassly positivist ideas about how to evaluate theories that are accepted by most political scientists. He demolishes the notion that one can test theories by pitting them against facts. As he puts it, "no finite sample can ever *disprove* a universal probabilistic theory."[15] One should think hard about why this is true. Paying more attention to Lakatos will help.

In this volume, Colin Elman and Miriam Fendius Elman and the contributors ask whether the field of international relations has made any progress in its efforts to develop theories. The book proceeds from the premise that the work of Imre Lakatos provides useful ways of answering this question. The Elmans review Lakatos's methodology of scientific research programs. The authors of the various chapters then use Lakatosian criteria to assess the contribution of different types of research to the improvement of theory in our field.

Notes

1 Imre Lakatos, "Falsification and the Methodology of Scientific Research Programmes," in Imre Lakatos and Alan Musgrave eds., *Criticism and the Growth of Knowledge: Proceedings of the International Colloquium in the Philosophy of Science*, London, 1965, vol. 4 (Cambridge: Cambridge University Press, 1970), pp. 91–196.
2 Errol Harris, *Hypothesis and Perception* (London: Allen and Unwin, 1970).
3 Lakatos, "Falsification and the Methodology of Scientific Research Programmes," p. 100 (emphasis in original).
4 Sir Arthur Stanley Eddington, *New Pathways in Science* (New York: Macmillan, 1935), p. 211.
5 Gary King, Robert O. Keohane, and Sidney Verba, *Designing Social Inquiry: Scientific Inference in Qualitative Research* (Princeton, NJ: Princeton University Press, 1994), p. 19.
6 Ibid., chap. 1.
7 Gary King, Robert O. Keohane, and Sidney Verba, "The Importance of Research Design in Political Science," *American Political Science Review*, Vol. 89, No. 2 (June 1995), pp. 475–476.
8 Johann Wolfgang von Goethe, *Wisdom and Experience*, selections by Ludwig Curtius, trans. and ed. with an introduction by Hermann J. Weigand (New York: Pantheon, 1949), p. 94.
9 King, Keohane, and Verba, *Designing Social Inquiry*, p. 19. Lakatos puts his point this way: "*exactly the most admired scientific theories simply fail to forbid any observable state of affairs.*" Lakatos and Musgrave, *Criticism and the Growth of Knowledge*, p. 100 (emphasis in original).
10 Lakatos, "Falsification and the Methodology of Research Programmes," p. 115. Harris argues that among natural scientists, falsification is a seldom used method. Efforts to confirm theories are much more common. For examples from the work of eminent scientists, see Harris, *Hypothesis and Perception*, pp. 161–178.
11 Steven Weinberg, *Dreams of a Final Theory* (New York: Pantheon Books, 1992), p. 93.
12 Lakatos and Musgrave, *Criticism and the Growth of Knowledge*, p. 119.
13 John A. Hobson, *Imperialism: A Study* (London: Allen and Unwin, 1938; originally published 1902); John Maynard Keynes, *The General Theory of Employment, Interest, and Money* (New York: Harcourt, Brace, n.d.).
14 Weinberg, *Dreams of a Final Theory*, p. 103.
15 Lakatos and Musgrave, *Criticism and the Growth of Knowledge*, p. 102.

Part II

INTERNATIONAL POLITICS

8

THE STABILITY OF A BIPOLAR WORLD

There is a conventional wisdom, accumulated over the centuries, upon which statesmen and students often draw as they face problems in international politics. One part of the conventional wisdom is now often forgotten. Many in Europe, and some in America, have come to regard an alliance as unsatisfactory if the members of it are grossly unequal in power. "Real partnership," one hears said in a variety of ways, "is possible only between equals."[1] If this is true, an addendum should read: Only unreal partnerships among states have lasted beyond the moment of pressing danger. Where states in association have been near equals, some have voluntarily abdicated the leadership to others, or the alliance has become paralyzed by stalemate and indecision, or it has simply dissolved. One may observe that those who are less than equal are often dissatisfied without thereby concluding that equality in all things is good. As Machiavelli and Bismarck well knew, an alliance requires an alliance leader; and leadership can be most easily maintained where the leader is superior in power. Some may think of these two exemplars as unworthy; even so, where the unworthy were wise, their wisdom should be revived.

A second theorem of the conventional wisdom is still widely accepted. It reads: A world of many powers is more stable than a bipolar world, with stability measured by the peacefulness of adjustment within the international system and by the durability of the system itself. While the first element of the conventional wisdom might well be revived, the second should be radically revised.

Pessimism about the possibility of achieving stability in a two-power world was reinforced after the war by contemplation of the character of the two major contenders. The Soviet Union, led by a possibly psychotic Stalin, and the United States, flaccid, isolationist by tradition, and untutored in the ways of international relations, might well have been thought unsuited to the task of finding a route to survival. How could either reconcile itself to coexistence when ideological differences were great and antithetical interests provided constant occasion for conflict? Yet the bipolar world of the postwar period has shown a remarkable stability. Measuring time from the termination of war, 1964 corresponds to 1937. Despite all of the changes in the nineteen years since 1945 that might have shaken the world into another great war, 1964 somehow looks and feels safer than 1937. Is this true only because we now know that 1937 preceded the holocaust by just two years? Or is it the terror of nuclear weapons that has kept the world from major war? Or is the stability of the postwar world intimately related to its bipolar pattern?

Stability within a bipolar system

Within a bipolar world, four factors conjoined encourage the limitation of violence in the relations of states. First, with only two world powers there are no peripheries. The United States is the obsessing danger for the Soviet Union, and the Soviet Union for us, since each can damage the other to an extent that no other state can match. Any event in the world that involves the fortunes of the Soviet Union or the United States automatically elicits the interest of the other. Truman, at the time of the Korean invasion, could not very well echo Chamberlain's words in the Czechoslovakian crisis and claim that the Koreans were a people far away in the east of Asia of whom Americans knew nothing. We had to know about them or quickly find out. In the 1930s, France lay between England and Germany. England could believe, and we could too, that their frontier and ours lay on the Rhine. After World War II, no third power could lie between the United States and the Soviet Union, for none existed. The statement that peace is indivisible was controversial, indeed untrue, when it was made by Litvinov in the 1930s. It became a truism in the 1950s. Any possibility of maintaining a general peace required a willingness to fight small wars. With the competition both serious and intense, a loss to one could easily appear as a gain to the other, a conclusion that follows from the very condition of a two-power competition. Political action has corresponded to this assumption. Communist guerrillas operating in Greece prompted the Truman doctrine. The tightening of Soviet control over the states of Eastern Europe led to the Marshall Plan and the Atlantic Defense Treaty, and these in turn gave rise to the Cominform and the Warsaw Pact. The plan to form a West German government produced the Berlin blockade. Our response in a two-power world was geared to Soviet action, and theirs to ours, which produced an increasingly solid bipolar balance.

Not only are there no peripheries in a bipolar world but also, as a second consideration, the range of factors included in the competition is extended as the intensity of the competition increases. Increased intensity is expressed in a reluctance to accept small territorial losses, as in Korea, the Formosa Strait, and Indochina. Extension of range is apparent wherever one looks. Vice President Nixon hailed the Supreme Court's desegregation decision as our greatest victory in the Cold War. When it became increasingly clear that the Soviet economy was growing at a rate that far exceeded our own, many began to worry that falling behind in the economic race would lead to our losing the Cold War without a shot being fired. Disarmament negotiations have most often been taken as an opportunity for propaganda. As contrasted with the 1930s, there is now constant and effective concern lest military preparation fall below the level necessitated by the military efforts of the major antagonist. Changes between the wars affected different states differently, with adjustment to the varying ambitions and abilities of states dependent on cumbrous mechanisms of compensation and realignment. In a multipower balance, who is a danger to whom is often a most obscure matter: The incentive to regard all disequilibrating changes with concern and respond to them with whatever effort may be required is consequently weakened. In our present world changes may affect each of the two powers differently, and this means all the more that few changes in the national realm or in the world at large are likely to be thought irrelevant. Policy proceeds by imitation, with occasional attempts to outflank.

The third distinguishing factor in the bipolar balance, as we have thus far known it, is the nearly constant presence of pressure and the recurrence of crises. It would be folly to assert that repeated threats and recurring crises necessarily decrease danger and promote stability. It may be equally wrong to assert the opposite, as Khrushchev seems to appreciate. "They frighten us with war," he told the Bulgarians in May of 1962, "and we frighten them back bit by bit. They threaten us with nuclear arms and we tell them: 'Listen, now only fools can do this, because we have them too, and they are not smaller than yours but, we think, even better than yours. So why do you do foolish things and frighten us?' This is the situation, and this is why we consider the situation to be good."[2] Crises, born of a condition in which interests and ambitions conflict, are produced by the determination of one state to effect a change that another state chooses to resist. With the Berlin blockade, for example, as with Russia's emplacement of missiles in Cuba, the United States decided that to resist the change the Soviet Union sought to bring about was worth the cost of turning its action into a crisis. If the condition of conflict remains, the absence of crises becomes more disturbing than their recurrence. Rather a large crisis now than a small war later is an axiom that should precede the statement, often made, that to fight small wars in the present may be the means of avoiding large wars later.

Admittedly, crises also occur in a multipower world, but the dangers are diffused, responsibilities unclear, and definition of vital interests easily obscured. The skillful foreign policy, where many states are in balance, is designed to gain an advantage over one state without antagonizing others and frightening them into united action. Often in modern Europe, possible gains have seemed greater than likely losses. Statesmen could thus hope in crises to push an issue to the limit without causing all the potential opponents to unite. When possible enemies are several in number, unity of action among states is difficult to secure. One could therefore think—or hope desperately, as did Bethmann Hollweg and Adolph Hitler—that no united opposition would form.

In a bipolar world, on the other hand, attention is focused on crises by both of the major competitors, and especially by the defensive state. To move piecemeal and reap gains serially is difficult, for within a world in confusion there is one great certainty, namely, the knowledge of who will oppose whom. One's motto may still be, "push to the limit," but *limit* must be emphasized as heavily as *push*. Caution, moderation, and the management of crisis come to be of great and obvious importance.

Many argue, nonetheless, that caution in crises, and resulting bipolar stability, is accounted for by the existence of nuclear weapons, with the number of states involved comparatively inconsequent. That this is a doubtful deduction can be indicated by a consideration of how nuclear weapons may affect reactions to crises. In the postwar world, bipolarity preceded the construction of two opposing atomic weapons systems. The United States, with some success, substituted technological superiority for expenditure on a conventional military system as a deterrent to the Soviet Union during the years when we had first an atomic monopoly and then a decisive edge in quantity and quality of weapons. American military policy was not a matter of necessity but of preference based on a calculation of advantage. Some increase in expenditure and a different allocation of monies would have enabled the United States to deter the Soviet Union by posing credibly the threat that any Soviet attempt, say, to overwhelm West Germany would bring the United States into a large-scale conventional war.[a] For the Soviet Union, war against separate European states would have promised large gains; given the bipolar balance, no such war could be undertaken without the clear prospect of American entry. The Russians' appreciation of the situation is perhaps best illustrated by the structure of their military forces. The Soviet Union has concentrated heavily on medium-range bombers and missiles and, to our surprise, has built relatively few intercontinental weapons. The country of possibly aggressive intent has assumed a posture of passive deterrence vis-à-vis her major adversary, whom she quite sensibly does not want to fight. Against European and other lesser states, the Soviet Union has a considerable offensive capability.[b] Hence nuclear capabilities merely reinforce a condition that would exist in their absence: Without nuclear technology both the United States and the Soviet Union have the ability to develop weapons of considerable destructive power. Even had the atom never been split, each would lose heavily if it were to engage in a major war against the other.

If number of states is less important than the existence of nuclear power, then one must ask whether the world balance would continue to be stable were three or more states able to raise themselves to comparable levels of nuclear potency. For many reasons one doubts that the equilibrium would be so secure. Worries about accidents and triggering are widespread, but a still greater danger might well arise. The existence of a number of nuclear states would increase the temptation for the more virile of them to maneuver, with defensive states paralyzed by the possession of military forces the use of which would mean their own destruction. One would be back in the 1930s, with the addition of a new dimension of strength which would increase the pressures upon status quo powers to make piecemeal concessions.

Because bipolarity preceded a two-power nuclear competition, because in the absence of nuclear weapons destructive power would still be great, because the existence of a number of nuclear states would increase the range of difficult political choices, and finally, as will be discussed below, because nuclear weapons must first be seen as a product of great national capabilities rather than as their cause, one is led to the conclusion that nuclear weapons cannot by themselves be used to explain the stability—or the instability—of international systems.

Taken together, these three factors—the absence of peripheries, the range and intensity of competition, and the persistence of pressure and crisis—are among the most important characteristics of the period since World War II. The first three points combine to produce an intense competition in a wide arena with a great variety of means employed. The constancy of effort of the two major contenders, combined with a fourth factor, their preponderant power, have made for a remarkable ability to comprehend and absorb within the bipolar balance the revolutionary political, military, and economic changes that have occurred. The Soviet Union moved forward and was checked. Empires dissolved, and numerous new states appeared in the world. Strategic nuclear weapons systems came into the possession of four separate countries. Tactical nuclear weapons were developed and to some extent dispersed. The manned bomber gave way to the missile. Vulnerable missiles were hardened, made mobile, and hidden. A revolution in military technology occurred on an average of once every five years and at an accelerating pace.[3] Two "losses" of China, each a qualified loss but both traumatic, were accommodated without disastrously distorting—or even greatly affecting—the balance between America and Russia.

The effects of American–Soviet preponderance are complex. Its likely continuation and even its present existence are subjects of controversy. The stability of a system has to be defined in terms of its durability, as well as of the peacefulness of adjustment within it. In the pages that follow, some of the effects of preponderance will be indicated while the durability of the system is examined.

The end of the bipolar era?

In a bipolar world, by definition each of two states or two blocs overshadows all others. It may seem that to write in 1964 of bipolarity is merely to express nostalgia for an era already ending. Richard Rosecrance, referring to the period since the war, describes the world as "tripolar."[4] Walter Lippmann, in a number of columns written in late 1963 and early 1964, assesses the recent initiatives of France and Communist China, their ability to move contrary to the desires of the United States and the Soviet Union, as marking the end of the postwar world in which the two superpowers closely controlled the actions of even their major associates.^{c} Hedley Bull, in a paper prepared for the Council on Foreign Relations in the fall of 1963, tentatively reaches the conclusion that between now and 1975 "the system of polarization of power will cease to be recognizable: that other states will count for so much in world politics that the two present great powers will find it difficult, even when cooperating, to dominate them."[5]

If power is identical with the ability to control, then those who are free are also strong; and the freedom of the weak would have to be taken as an indication of the weakness of those who have great material strength. But the weak and disorganized are often less amenable to control than those who are wealthy and well disciplined.^{d} The powerful, out of their strength, influence and limit each other; the wealthy are hobbled by what they have to lose. The weak, on the other hand, bedevil the strong; the poor can more easily ignore their own interests. Such patterns endure and pervade the relations of men and of groups. United States Steel enjoys less freedom to vary the price of its products than do smaller producers. The United States government finds it easier to persuade large corporations and the great labor unions to cooperate in an anti-inflationary policy than to secure the compliance of small firms and independent unions. The political party in opposition is freer to speak irresponsibly than is the government. Power corrupts *and* renders its possessors responsible; the possession of wealth liberates *and* enslaves. That similar patterns are displayed in international relations is hardly surprising. It is not unusual to find that minor states have a considerable nuisance value in relation to states greatly their superiors in power. A Chiang Kai-shek, a Syngman Rhee, or a Mossadegh is often more difficult to deal with than rulers of states more nearly one's equal in power.

The influence and control of the two great powers has stopped short of domination in most places throughout the postwar period. The power of the United States and of the Soviet Union has been predominant but not absolute. To describe the world as bipolar does not mean that either power can exert a positive control everywhere in the world, but that each has global interests which it can care for unaided, though help may often be desirable. To say that bipolarity has, until recently, meant more than this is to misinterpret the history of the postwar world. Secretary Dulles, in the middle 1950s, inveighed against neutralism and described it as immoral. His judgment corresponded to a conviction frequently expressed in Communist statements. P. E. Vyshinsky, in a 1948 issue of *Problems of Philosophy*, declared that "the only determining criterion of revolutionary proletarian internationalism is: are you for or against the U.S.S.R., the motherland of the world proletariat?... The defense of the U.S.S.R., as of the socialist motherland of the world proletariat, is the holy duty of every honest man everywhere and not only of the citizens of the U.S.S.R."[6] The rejection of neutralism as an honorable position for other countries to take is another example of intensity of competition leading to an extension of its range. By coming to terms with neutralism, as both the United States and the Soviet Union have done, the superpowers have shown even their inability to extend their wills without limit.

Bearing in mind the above considerations, can we say whether the recent independent action of France and Communist China does in fact indicate the waning of bipolarity, or does it mean merely the loosening of bipolar blocs, with a bipolar relation between the United States and the Soviet Union continuing to dominate? By the assessment of those who themselves value increased independence, the latter would seem to be the case. The Earl of Home, when he was Secretary of State for Foreign Affairs, thought he saw developing from the increased power of the Soviet Union and the United States a nuclear stalemate that would provide for the middle states a greater opportunity to maneuver.[7] De Gaulle, in a press conference famous for other reasons, included the statement that uncertainty about their use "does not in the least prevent the American nuclear weapons, which are the most powerful of all, from remaining the essential guarantee of world peace."[8] Communist China's calculation of international political and military forces may be highly similar. "Whatever happens," Chou En-lai has said recently, "the fraternal Chinese and Soviet peoples will stand together in any storm that breaks out in the world arena."[9] Ideological disputes between China and Russia are bitter; their policies conflict. But interests are more durable than the alliances in which they sometimes find expression. Even though the bonds of alliance are broken, the interest of the Soviet Union could not easily accommodate the destruction of China if that were to mean that Western power would be poised on the Siberian border.

That strategic stability produces or at least permits tactical instability is now a cliché of military analysis. The axiom, transferred to the political realm, remains true. Lesser states have often found their opportunity to exist in the interstices of the balance of power. The French and Chinese, in acting contrary to the wishes of their principal partners, have certainly caused them some pain. Diplomatic flurries have resulted and some changes have been produced, yet in a more important respect, France and China have demonstrated not their power but their impotence: their inability to affect the dominant relation in the world. The solidity of the bipolar balance permits middle states to act with impunity precisely because they know that their divergent actions will not measurably affect the strength of the Soviet Union or the United States, upon which their own security continues to rest. The decisions of Britain, France, and China to build nuclear establishments are further advertisements of weakness. Because American or Soviet military might provides adequate protection, the middle powers need not participate in a military division of labor in a way that would contribute maximally to the military strength of their major associates.

The United States is inclined to exaggerate the amount of strength it can gain from maintaining a system of united alliances as opposed to bilateral arrangements. The exaggeration arises apparently from vague notions about the transferability of strength. Actually, as one should expect, the contribution of each ally is notable only where it believes that its interests require it to make an effort. In resisting the invasion of North Korean and, later, Chinese troops, roughly 90 percent of the non-Korean forces were provided by the United States.[10] In South Vietnam at the present time the United States is the only foreign country engaged. British and French military units in West Germany, under strength and ill-equipped, are of little use. Western Europe remains, to use the terminology of the 1930s, a direct consumer of security. The only really significant interest of the United States, as is nicely conveyed by Arnold Wolfers' dubbing us "the hub power,"[11] is that each country that may be threatened by Soviet encroachment be politically stable and thus able to resist subversion, be self-dependent and thus less of an expense to us, and be able at the outset of a possible military action to put up some kind of a defense.

On these points, the American interest in Western Europe is precisely the same as its interest in the economically underdeveloped countries. In the case of the European countries, however, losses are harder to sustain and there are advantages clearly to be gained by the United States where our interests and theirs overlap. It would be difficult to argue that the foreign-aid programs undertaken by Britain, France, and West Germany transcend a national purpose or have been enlarged in response to our insisting upon their duty to share the military and economic responsibilities that the United States has assumed. The protection of persons, property, and the pound sterling required Britain to resist Communist guerrillas in Malaya, which was after all still her dependency. In such a case, the bearing of a heavy burden by another country serves its interests and ours simultaneously. If anything, the possibility of a transfer of strength has decreased in the past fifteen years, along with a decline in usable military power in Britain. Britain had in her army 633,242 men in 1948; by 1962 she had 209,500, with further reductions anticipated. The comparable figures for France are 465,000 and 706,000.[12] France, with a system of conscription for a comparatively long term and at relatively low pay, has maintained military forces impressively large when measured as a percentage of her population.[e] As France takes the first steps along the route followed by England, her military planning runs parallel to the earlier English calculations; she will seek to cope with the pressures of large money requirements by making similar adjustments. According to present French plans, the total of men under arms is to be reduced by 40 percent.[f]

To compensate for the loss of *influence* that once came from making a military contribution outside their own borders, the one country has tried and the other is now attempting to build nuclear establishments that supposedly promise them some measure of *independence*. The British effort remains dependent on American assistance, and the French effort to build an effective nuclear weapons system is in its infancy. The independence of recent French policy cannot have been grounded on a nuclear force that barely exists. It is, rather, a product of intelligence and political will exercised by President de Gaulle in a world in which bipolar stalemate provides the weak some opportunity to act. Independence of action by France and by the People's Republic of China is at once a product of loosening alliances—the lesser dependence of principals upon their associates—and a protest against it.

In the wake of the war, the countries of Western Europe derived a considerable influence from their weakness and our inability to let them succumb to internal difficulties or external pressures without thereby disadvantaging ourselves in relation to Russia. We were less free then because they were so dependent upon our support. The Soviet challenge made it important to recreate strength in Western Europe, a purpose that could best be achieved cooperatively. From about 1960 onward, the dependence of each of the nuclear giants upon its associates lessened. The earlier postwar pattern was one of interdependence with consequent influence for junior partners. More recently a lesser interdependence has permitted and produced assertions of independence, which must be understood in part as efforts to recapture influence once enjoyed.

The durability of the bipolar world

Bipolarity as a descriptive term remains appropriate as long as there is a great gap between the power of the two leading countries and the power of the next most considerable states. When one looks in this light at Communist China, he is likely to be mesmerized by the magic of numbers. Surely 750 million Chinese must enable their Communist government to do some things very damaging to the United States or the Soviet Union, or to both of them. When one considers the West European states, he may be struck by their rapid movement from economic and military dependence upon the United States to positions of some independence. It is natural to ask whether this is part of a trend that will continue, or simply a movement from nearly zero on the scale of independence to a threshold that can hardly be passed. It is easy to think that the trend will continue until, again in the words of Hedley Bull, "over the next decade the Soviet Union and the United States will find themselves still the principal powers in opposed systems of alliances, but, like Britain and Germany 1907–1914, aware that their allies are not irrevocably committed to their cause and able to cooperate themselves against their lesser allies on particular issues."[13] But this is an analogy that can mislead. The allies of Britain and of Germany were of an order of power, as measured by a combination of territory, population, and economic capability, similar to that of their principals. That many important changes have occurred in the past fifteen years is obvious. That the changes that have occurred and others that are likely will lift any present state to the level of Soviet or American capabilities is all but impossible.

In 1962, the gross national product of the Soviet Union was $260 billion, of the United States $555 billion, of West Germany $84 billion, and of Communist China roughly $50 billion. If one projects from these figures, the following picture emerges: The Soviet Union, at an assumed growth rate of 5 percent, will have in the year 2004 a gross national product of $2,080 billion; the United States, at a growth rate of 3 percent, will have by 2000 a gross national product of $2,220 billion; West Germany, if it grows at a sustained rate of 6 percent yearly, will have by 1998 a gross national product of $672 billion; and Communist China, projected at 7 percent, will have a gross national product in 2002 of $800 billion.[g] The growth rates assumed are unlikely to be those that actually prevail. The rates chosen are those that will narrow the gap between the greatest and the middle powers to the largest extent presently imaginable. Even on these bases, it becomes clear that the Soviet Union and the United States to the end of the millenium will remain the preponderant powers in the world unless two or more of the middle powers combine in a way that gives them the ability to concert their political and military actions on a sustained and reliable basis.

The gap that exists can be described in other ways which are more fragmentary but perhaps give a still sharper picture. The United States has been spending on its military establishment yearly an amount that is two-thirds or more of the entire West German or British or French gross national product. In 1962, the Europe of the Six plus Great Britain spent on defense less than a quarter of the military expenditure of the United States.[14] The United States spends more on military research and development than any of the three largest of the West European countries spends on its entire military establishment.

The country that would develop its own resources, military and other, in order to play an independent role in the world, faces a dreadful problem. It is understandably tempting for such countries to believe that by developing nuclear weapons systems, they can noticeably close the gap between themselves and the superpowers. The assumption that nuclear weapons will serve as the great equalizers appeared early and shows an impressive persistence. "The small country," Jacob Viner wrote in 1946, "will again be more than a cipher or a mere pawn in power-politics, provided it is big enough to produce atomic bombs."[15] Stanley Hoffmann, writing in the present year, reflects a similar thought in the following words: "True, the French nuclear program is expensive; but it is also true that conventional rearmament is not cheaper, and that a division of labor that would leave all nuclear weapons in United States hands and specialize Europe in conventional forces would earmark Europe for permanent dependence (both military and political) in the cold war and permanent decline in the international competition."[16]

It is difficult to know just what is meant by saying that "conventional rearmament is not cheaper" than a nuclear program, but it is clear that nuclear programs are very expensive indeed.[h] France and Britain now spend about 7 percent of their gross national products on defense. If this were increased to

108

the American level of approximately 10 percent, or even if it were doubled, the defense spending of each country would remain comparatively small. The inability to spend large sums, taken together with the costs of research, development, production, and maintenance, leads one to the conclusion that the French government is betting that Kahn's revolution in military technology every five years will no longer take place. The French might then hope that Polaris submarines, with their missiles, would remain invulnerable. It is doubtful that they are truly invulnerable even now.

The point is a complicated one. By confusing the tracking mechanism of a hunter-killer submarine, an easy accomplishment, one submarine can escape from another. A Soviet submarine, however, may be able to meet and quietly destroy a French submarine as it comes out of port. It is unlikely that the French would in such an event say anything at all; surely they would not wish to draw attention to the loss of what might be one-third of their strategic nuclear system.[i] To prevent this, France could choose to operate her submarine fleet entirely from the Mediterranean, a sea from which the Soviet Union is militarily excluded. But limiting the direction from which missiles may come will make it easier for the Soviet Union to defend against them. Khrushchev's claim that the Soviet Union's rockets can hit a fly in the sky, which strikes Americans as an irrelevant boast, has an important implication for the country that would build a small nuclear force.[17] Missile defenses, almost useless against large numbers, may be highly successful against the approach of only a few missiles. Furthermore, a single command and control system can easily be obliterated. Middle powers will have to concentrate on a single system or a very small number of systems, and thus deny to themselves the invulnerability gained by the United States from dispersion of the weapons of any one system and the existence of multiple systems. Were military innovation to cease, a force such as that projected by France could gradually be built up to a level of military significance. If, however, a future French Polaris force should begin to look dangerous to the Soviet Union, the increased French capability would itself become an incentive for Russia to move faster. And if Russia does, so must we too. Far short of America or Russia using nuclear weapons for the surgical excision of any country's embryonic nuclear capability, the opportunity to develop a nuclear force to a level of usefulness exists, if it is present at all, only on sufferance of the two nuclear giants.

To look upon nuclear weapons systems as the great equalizers is to see them as causes of the increased power of states. It is more accurate and more useful to look upon them as the products of great scientific and economic capability. The railway age brought a great increase in military mobility, which the elder von Moltke brilliantly exploited in the wars for German unification. So long, however, as war power took the form of great masses of men and material, railways were not able to deliver the whole force of a nation to a front or concentrate it upon a point. Even in transporting a portion of a country's military power, railways were not able to cross the front. Thus in 1914,

German armies *marched* through Belgium.[18] In World War II, the wedding of high explosives and air transport still did not make it possible to aggregate a nation's whole power and deliver it suddenly and decisively to designated military targets. World War II was won slowly and largely on the ground. Nuclear technology produced a change decisive in one respect. The power of a nation can now be distilled. Like the French chef who boils down a pig for three days until he has a pint of liquid that represents the very essence of pig, the country that produces nuclear warheads and the requisite delivery systems is distilling the power of a whole nation. But the power has to be there before it can be distilled. The stills of such countries as Britain, France, and Communist China are simply not large enough.

Nuclear weapons systems are not the great equalizers, but they are, rather, in all of their complexity and with all of their tremendous cost, outward signs of the Soviet and American ability to outstrip all others. If other countries should nevertheless be able to build nuclear systems capable of doing great damage on second strike to any attacker, they would then, as the Soviet Union and United States now do, participate in a nuclear stand-off. Competition would shift to other means, which to some extent has already happened, and traditional criteria of power, including economic and military capability, would once again take on their old significance.

This is not to say that nuclear diffusion makes no difference. It is useful to consider briefly some of the possibilities. (1) A threat by Britain, France, or Communist China to use nuclear force in order to deter a conventional attack launched by a great nuclear power is a threat to do limited damage to the invading state at the risk of one's own annihilation. It is a radically different way of assuming the deterrent-defensive posture of Switzerland and should be interpreted as a move to bow out of the great-power picture. In part the desire for an independent nuclear deterrent derives, as the late Hugh Gaitskell put it, "from doubts about the readiness of the United States Government and the American citizens to risk the destruction of their cities on behalf of Europe."[19] The nuclear superiority enjoyed by America in the early 1950s created in Europe a fear that the United States would too easily succumb to a temptation to retaliate massively. The arrival of strategic stability has produced the opposite worry. In the words of a senior British general: "McNamara is practically telling the Soviets that the worst they need expect from an attack on West Germany is a conventional counterattack."[20] Behind the difference on strategy lies a divergence of interest. A policy of strategic nuclear threat makes the United States the primary target. A policy of controlled response would shift some of the danger as well as additional burdens to Europe. The countries of Europe, separate or united, have an incentive to adopt destabilizing military programs. Where Britain has led, France now follows. While it is understandable that lesser powers should, by threatening or using nuclear weapons, want to be able to decide when the United States or the Soviet Union should risk their own destruction, it is also easy to see that both the United States and the

Soviet Union would resist such an outcome. The more badly a country may want to be able to trigger someone else's force, the more difficult it becomes to do so, which is another way of saying that the Soviet Union and the United States have something close to invulnerable second-strike systems.

(2) If a middle power were engaged in a conventional military action against a state of comparable or lesser size, the Soviet Union or the United States might threaten a nuclear strike in order to bring about a withdrawal. It is sometimes thought that the possession of a small nuclear force by the middle power would make such a threat ineffective. In the Suez adventure, for example, military action by Britain and France called forth Soviet rocket threats against them. Against states having no strategic nuclear forces, such threats would be more readily credited, and thus more likely to exert pressure successfully against the conventional action itself. A small military action, however, is not worth and does not require nuclear interference by a great power, for it can be stopped in other ways. The onus of threatening to use nuclear weapons first, in order to interdict conventional interference, is then placed upon the smaller power. Such a threat would not be credible.

Both the first and second uses presuppose the adequacy of the small country's nuclear threat when directed against the United States or the Soviet Union. A capability that is small compared to America's or Russia's may be adequate to its task; a certain minimum, doubtfully achievable in the foreseeable future, is nevertheless required. When Hedley Bull says that the French ambition is "to become strong enough to choose deliberately to act alone,"[21] he may have in mind the second use mentioned above, or the one following, which is seldom discussed.

(3) As the United States and the Soviet Union have opened up a gap in military power between themselves and all others, so Britain, France, the People's Republic of China, and states who may follow them can differentiate themselves from nonnuclear nations. Great Britain has placed nuclear weapons in the Middle and Far East. Let us suppose Indonesia were to move militarily against Malaysia. A British threat to use nuclear weapons could conceivably follow, which might cause Indonesia to stop short or might persuade the United States to offer the support of the Seventh Fleet and American Marines in order to avoid the use of nuclear weapons.

The effects of nuclear diffusion are necessarily uncertain, but one point can sensibly be made: Building a small nuclear force is an unpromising way of seeking to maintain the integrity of one's state, even though it may enable that state to act positively against equal or lesser powers.

There can be approximate equality among states even where there is considerable disparity in the material bases of their power. Whether or not effective power is fashioned from the material available depends upon adequacy of national organization, wisdom of policy, and intensity of effort. In the 1920s, France sought to maintain a greater military strength than Germany in order to compensate for a lesser French productivity and smaller population. Where the material differences are relatively small or where countries of immensely larger capacity are quiescent, it may be possible to "mobilize" a nation in peacetime in order to build on a lesser material base a superior military strength. Germany and Japan in the 1930s began to play the game from which France was withdrawing. The Soviet Union, since the war, has been able to challenge the United States in many parts of the world by spending a disproportionately large share of her smaller income on military means. There is in the West a quiet nightmare that the People's Republic of China may follow such a path, that it may mobilize the nation in order to increase production rapidly while simultaneously acquiring a large and modern military capability. It is doubtful that she can do either, and surely not both, and surely not the second without the first, as the data previously given clearly indicate. As for France and Great Britain, it strains the imagination to the breaking point to believe that in a world in which scientific and technological progress has been rapid, either of them will be able to maintain the pace.[j] Unable to spend on anywhere near the American or Russian level for work in research, development, and production, middle powers will, once they have gained an initial advantage, constantly find themselves falling behind. France and Britain are in the second-ranking powers' customary position of imitating, with a time lag, the more advanced weapons systems of their wealthier competitors.[k]

From the above analysis, it is clear that the time when other states can compete at the highest levels of power by a superiority of effort in mobilizing their resources lies far in the future. Unless some states combine or others dissolve in chaos, the world will remain bipolar until the end of the present century.

Some dissenting opinions

The fact remains that many students of international relations have continued to judge bipolarity unstable as compared to the probable stability of a multipower world. Why have they been so confident that the existence of a number of powers, moving in response to constantly recurring variations in national power and purpose, would promote the desired stability? According to Professors Morgenthau and Kaplan, the uncertainty that results from flexibility of alignment generates a healthy caution in the foreign policy of every country.[22] Concomitantly, Professor Morgenthau believes that in the present bipolar world, "the flexibility of the balance of power and, with it, its restraining influence upon the power aspirations of the main protagonists on the international scene have disappeared."[23] One may agree with his conclusion and yet draw from his analysis another one unstated by him: The inflexibility of a bipolar world, with the appetite for power of each major competitor at once whetted and checked by the other, may promote a greater stability than flexible balances of power among a larger number of states.

What are the grounds for coming to a diametrically different conclusion?

The presumed double instability of a bipolar world, that it easily erodes or explodes, is to a great extent based upon its assumed bloc character. A bloc improperly managed may indeed fall apart. The leader of each bloc must be concerned at once with alliance management, for the defection of an allied state might be fatal to its partners, and with the aims and capabilities of the opposing bloc. The system is more complex than is a multipower balance, which in part accounts for its fragility.[1] The situation preceding World War I provides a striking example. The dissolution of the Austro-Hungarian Empire would have left Germany alone in the center of Europe. The approximate equality of alliance partners, or their relation of true interdependence, plus the closeness of competition between the two camps, meant that while any country could commit its associates, no one country on either side could exercise control. By contrast, in 1956 the United States could dissociate itself from the Suez adventure of its two principal allies and even subject them to pressure. Great Britain, like Austria in 1914, tried to commit, or at least immobilize, its alliance partner by presenting him with a fait accompli. Enjoying a position of predominance, the United States could, as Germany could not, focus its attention on the major adversary while disciplining its ally. The situations are in other respects different, but the ability of the United States, in contrast to Germany, to pay a price measured in intra-alliance terms is striking.

It is important, then, to distinguish sharply a bipolarity of blocs from a bipolarity of countries. Fénelon thought that of all conditions of balance the opposition of two states was the happiest. Morgenthau dismisses this judgment with the comment that the benefits Fénelon had hoped for had not accrued in our world since the war, which depends, one might think, on what benefits had otherwise been expected.[m]

The conclusion that a multipower balance is relatively stable is reached by overestimating the system's flexibility, and then dwelling too fondly upon its effects.[n] A constant shuffling of alliances would be as dangerous as an unwillingness to make new combinations. Neither too slow nor too fast: The point is a fine one, made finer still by observing that the rules should be followed not merely out of an immediate interest of the state but also for the sake of preserving the international system. The old balance-of-power system here looks suspiciously like the new collective-security system of the League of Nations and the United Nations. Either system depends for its maintenance and functioning upon a "neutrality of alignment" at the moment of serious threat. To preserve the system, the powerful states must overcome the constraints of previous ties and the pressures of both ideological preferences and conflicting present interests in order to confront the state that threatens the system.[24]

In the history of the modern state system, flexibility of alignment has been conspicuously absent just when, in the interest of stability, it was most highly desirable.[25] A comparison of flexibility within a multipower world with the ability of the two present superpowers to compensate for changes by their internal efforts is requisite, for comparison changes the balance of optimism and pessimism as customarily applied to the two different systems. In the world of the 1930s, with a European grouping of three, the Western democracies, out of lassitude, political inhibition, and ideological distaste, refrained from acting or from combining with others at the advantageous moment. War provided the pressure that forced the world's states into two opposing coalitions. In peacetime the bipolar world displays a clarity of relations that is ordinarily found only in war. Raymond Aron has pointed out that the international "système depend de ce que sont, concrètement, les deux pôles, non pas seulement du fait qu'ils sont deux."[26] Modifying Aron's judgment and reversing that of many others, we would say that in a bipolar world, as compared to one of many powers, the international system is more likely to dominate. External pressures, if clear and great enough, force the external combination or the internal effort that interest requires. The political character of the alliance partner is then most easily overlooked and the extent to which foreign policy is determined by ideology is decreased.

The number of great states in the world has always been so limited that two acting in concert or, more common historically, one state driving for hegemony could reasonably conclude that the balance would be altered by their actions. In the relations of states since the Treaty of Westphalia, there have never been more than eight great powers, the number that existed, if one is generous in admitting doubtful members to the club, on the eve of the First World War. Given paucity of members, states cannot rely on an equilibrating tendency of the system. Each state must instead look to its own means, gauge the likelihood of encountering opposition, and estimate the chances of successful cooperation. The advantages of an international system with more than two members can at best be small. A careful evaluation of the factors elaborated above indicates that the disadvantages far outweigh them.

Conclusions that bear upon policy

If the preceding explanations are correct, they are also of practical importance. Fixation upon the advantages of flexibility in a multipower balance has often gone hand in hand with an intense anxiety associated with bipolarity: the fear that a downward slide or a sudden technological breakthrough by one great state or the other would decisively alter the balance between them. Either occurrence could bring catastrophic war, which for the disadvantaged would be a war of desperation, or world domination from one center with or without preceding war. The fear is pervasive, and in American writings most frequently rests on the assumption that, internally dissolute and tired of the struggle, we will award the palm to the Soviet Union. Sometimes this anxiety finds a more sophisticated expression, which turns less upon internal derangements. In this view, the United States, as the defensive power in the world, is inherently disadvantaged, for the aggressive power will necessarily gain if the competition continues long enough. But a conclusion derived from an incomplete proposition is misleading. One must add that the aggressive state may lose even though the state seeking to uphold the status quo never takes the offensive. The Soviet Union controls no nation now, except possibly Cuba, that was not part of its immediate postwar gains. It has lost control in Yugoslavia and the control it once seemed to have in China. The United States, since the time it began to behave as a defensive power, has seen some states slip from commitment to neutralism, but only North Vietnam and Cuba have come under Communist control. One would prefer no losses at all, but losses of this magnitude can easily be absorbed. On balance, one might argue that the United States has gained, though such a judgment depends on the base line from which measurement is made as well as upon how gains and losses are defined.

That the United States and the Soviet Union weigh losses and gains according to their effect upon the bipolar balance is crucial, but there are many changes in Africa, or Asia, or Latin America that are not likely to be to the advantage of either the Soviet Union or the United States. This judgment can be spelled out in a number of ways. The doctrine of containment, for example, should be amended to read: Defend, or insulate so that one loss need not lead to another. The habits of the Cold War are so ingrained and the dangers of a bipolar world so invigorating that the defensive country is easily led to overreact. In Southeast Asia, since no gain for Communist China is likely to benefit the Soviet Union, American concern should be confined to maintaining its reputation and avoiding distant repercussions. If one goes further and asks how great a gain will accrue to the People's Republic of China if it extends its territorial control marginally, the answer, in any of the areas open to it, must be "very little." Neutralization moves by President de Gaulle, if they can obscure the responsibility for unwanted events, may in fact be helpful. It is important to realize that the bipolar world is continuing lest we worry unnecessarily and define the irrelevant gesture or even the helpful suggestion of lesser powers as troublesome.

A 5 percent growth rate sustained for three years would add to the American gross national product an amount greater than the entire gross national product of Britain or France or West Germany. Even so, the accretion of power the Soviet Union would enjoy by adding, say, West Germany's capabilities to her own would be immensely important; and one such gain might easily lead to others. Most gains from outside, however, can add relatively little to the strengths of the Soviet Union or the United States. There are, then, few single losses that would be crucial, which is a statement that points to a tension within our argument. Bipolarity encourages each giant to focus upon crises, while rendering most of them of relative inconsequence. We might instead put it this way: Crisis is of concern only where giving way would lead to an accumulation of losses for one and gains for the other. In an age characterized by rapidity of change, in many respects time is slowed down—as is illustrated by the process of "losing" Indochina that has gone on for nineteen years without a conclusive result. Since only a succession of gains could be decisive, there is time for the losing state to contrive a countering action should it be necessary to do so.

Intensity and breadth of competition and recurrence of crises limn a picture of constant conflict verging on violence. At the same time, the relative simplicity of relations within a bipolar world, the great pressures that are generated, and the constant possibility of catastrophe produce a conservatism on the part of the two greatest powers. The Soviet Union and the United States may feel more comfortable dealing *à deux* than in contemplating a future world in which they vie for existence and possible advantage with other superpowers. While there is naturally worry about an increase of tensions to intolerable levels, there is also a fear that the tensions themselves will lead America and Russia to seek agreements designed to bring a relaxation that will be achieved at the expense of lesser powers. The French general, Paul Stehlin, commenting on American opposition to Nth-country nuclear forces, which he interprets as part of an American–Russian effort to maintain a bipolar world, asks wistfully: "Does Europe have less political maturity than the Big Two credit each other with?" With some bitterness he criticizes America for placing "more faith in the ability of the Russians to control their tremendous stockpiles of offensive weapons than they do in my country's capacity to use with wisdom and moderation the modest armaments it is working so hard to develop for purely deterrent purposes."[27]

Worries and fears on any such grounds are exaggerated. The Soviet Union and the United States influence each other more than any of the states living in their penumbra can possibly hope to do. In the world of the present, as of the recent past, a condition of mutual opposition may require rather than preclude the adjustment of differences. Yet first steps toward agreement have not led to second and third steps. Instead they have been mingled with other acts and events that have kept the level of tension quite high. The test ban was described in the United States as possibly a first great step toward wider agreement that would increase the chances of maintaining peace. In almost the same breath it was said that we cannot lower our guard, for Soviet aims have not changed.[28] Larger acts than agreement to halt testing under the sea and above the ground are required to alter a situation that congealed long ago. The Soviet Union and the United States remain for the foreseeable future the two countries that can irreparably damage each other. So long as both possess the capability, each must worry that the other might use it. The worry describes the boundaries that have so far limited both the building up of tensions and the abatement of competition.

Where weapons of horrible destructive power exist, stability necessarily appears as an important end. It will not, however, be everyone's highest value. One who accepts the analysis of bipolarity and the conclusions we have drawn may nevertheless prefer a world of many powers. The unity and self-dependence of Europe may, for example, rank higher as goals than international

116

stability. Or, one may think of European unity as a means of melding American power with the strength of a united Europe in order to achieve Western hegemony. Unipolarity may be preferable, for those peoples who then become dominant, to a competition between two polar states. It may even promise a greater stability. The question is too complicated to take up at the moment, but some words of caution are in order.

The United States has consistently favored the unification of Europe, for adding the strength of a united Europe to the existing power of America would be sufficient to establish a world hegemony. But there is a confusion in American rhetoric that accurately reflects a confusion in thought. We have wanted a Europe united and strong and thus able to share our burdens with us, but a Europe at the same time docile and pliant so that it would agree on which burdens are to be assumed and how duties should be shared. The enchanting dream of Western hegemony has many implications, some of them possibly unpleasant. A Europe of the Seven, or even the Six, could, given time to put its combined resources to work, become a third power in the world on the largest scale. President de Gaulle has entertained the fear that such a Europe, if it were to be born under Anglo-Saxon auspices, would serve as an instrument of American foreign policy. One may have doubts of what would necessarily follow.[29] De Gaulle is a useful instructor. If we find the weak troublesome, will the strong be more easily controlled? A united Europe would represent a great change in the world; because the change would be great, its effects are difficult to foresee. If Europe were to be stable, strong, and cooperative, one might be delighted; but surely it would be dangerous to predict that a new Europe would rapidly find internal stability and develop political maturity. It would be more dangerous still to assume that the old American and the new European state would find their policies always in harmony. It is seemingly a safe assumption that a clear and pressing interest of a new state of Europe would be to stand firm against any Soviet attempts to move forward. But interests must be taken in relation to situations. In a world of three great powers, identical interests may logically lead and in the past have led to dangerously disparate policies. European history of the twentieth century makes optimism difficult. Nor could one be serene about America's reaction. Typically, Americans have insufficiently valued the prize of power. The yearning for a Europe united and thus strong enough to oppose the Soviet Union unaided is but one example. The pressures of bipolarity have helped to produce responsibility of action. A relaxation of those pressures will change the situation to one in which it will no longer be clear who will oppose whom. Two considerations then should give one pause: the necessarily unpredictable quality of the third power and the greater instability of a multipower world.

A system of small numbers can always be disrupted by the actions of a Hitler and the reactions of a Chamberlain. Since this is true, it may seem that we are in the uncomfortable position of relying on the moderation, courage, and rationality of men holding crucial positions of power. Given the vagaries of men and the unpredictability of the individual's reaction to events, one may at this point feel that one's only recourse is to lapse into prayer. We can, nonetheless, take comfort from the thought that, like other men, those who are elevated to·power and direct the activities of great states are not wholly free agents. Beyond the residuum of necessary hope that men will respond sensibly lies the possibility of estimating the pressures that encourage and constrain them to do so. In a world in which two states united in their mutual antagonism far overshadow any other, the incentives to a calculated response stand out most clearly, and the sanctions against irresponsible behavior achieve their greatest force. Not only how the leaders will think but also who they may be will be affected by the presence of pressures and the clarity of challenges. One may lament Churchill's failure to gain control of the British government in the 1930s, for he knew what actions were required to maintain a balance-of-power system. Churchill did come to power, it is interesting to note, as the world began to assume the bipolar form familiar in wartime. If a people representing one pole of the world now indulges itself by selecting inept rulers, it runs clearly discernible risks. Leaders of the United States and the Soviet Union are presumably chosen with an eye to the tasks they will have to perform. Other countries can enjoy, if they wish, the luxury of selecting leaders who will most please their peoples by the way in which internal affairs are managed. The United States and the Soviet Union cannot.

It is not that one entertains the utopian hope that all future Premiers of the Soviet Union and Presidents of the United States will combine in their persons a complicated set of nearly perfect virtues, but rather that the pressures of a bipolar world will strongly encourage them to act in ways better than their characters might otherwise lead one to expect. It is not that one possesses a serene confidence in the peacefulness, or even the survival of the world, but rather that cautious optimism may be justified as long as the pressures to which each must respond are so clearly present. Either country may go beserk or succumb to inanation and debility. That necessities are clear increases the chances that they will be met, but there can be no guarantees. Dangers from abroad may unify a state and spur its people to heroic action. Or, as with France facing Hitler's Germany, external pressures may divide the leaders, confuse the public, and increase their willingness to give way. It may also happen that the difficulties of adjustment and the necessity for calculated action simply become too great. The clarity with which the necessities of action can now be seen may be blotted out by the blinding flash of nuclear explosions. The fear that this may happen has reinforced the factors and processes described in the preceding pages.

By making the two strongest states still more powerful and the emergence of third powers more difficult, nuclear weapons have helped to consolidate a condition of bipolarity. It is to a great extent due to its bipolar structure that the world since the war has enjoyed a stability seldom known where three or more powers have sought to cooperate with each other or have competed for existence.

Notes

[a] The point has been made by Raymond Aron, among others. "Even if it had not had the bomb, would the United States have tolerated the expansion of the Soviet empire as far as the Atlantic? And would Stalin have been ready to face the risk of general war?" Raymond Aron, *The Century of Total War* (Boston: Beacon Press, 1955), p. 151.

[b] Hanson W. Baldwin, from information supplied by Strategic Air Command headquarters, estimates that Russian intercontinental missiles are one-fourth to one-fifth as numerous as ours, though Russian warheads are larger. The Russians have one-sixth to one-twelfth the number of our long-range heavy bombs, with ours having a greater capability (*New York Times*, November 21, 1963). In medium-range ballistic missiles Russia has been superior. A report of the Institute of Strategic Studies estimated that as of October, 1962, Russia had 700 such missiles, the West a total of 250 (*New York Times*, November 9, 1962). British sources tend to place Russian capabilities in the medium range higher than do American estimates. Cf. P. M. S. Blackett, "The Real Road to Disarmament: The Military Background to the Geneva Talks," *New Statesman* (March 2, 1962), pp. 295–300, with Hanson W. Baldwin, *New York Times*, November 26, 1961.

[c] See, for example, Walter Lippmann, "NATO Crisis—and Solution: Don't Blame De Gaulle," *Boston Globe*, December 5, 1963, p. 26: "The paramount theme of this decade, as we know it thus far, is that we are emerging from a two-power world and entering one where there are many powers."

[d] Cf. Georg Simmel, "The Sociology of Conflict, II," *The American Journal of Sociology*, IX (March, 1904), p. 675: "when one opposes a diffused crowd of enemies, one may oftener gain isolated victories, but it is very hard to arrive at decisive results which definitely fix the relationships of the contestants."

[e] In 1960, 1.5% of total population for France; 1.01% for the United Kingdom; 1.39% for the United States. M. R. D. Foot, *Men in Uniform* (London: Weidenfeld and Nicolson, for the Institute for Strategic Studies, 1961), pp. 162, 163.

[f] The reduction is figured from the level of military manpower in 1960. Ministre des Armées, Pierre Messmer, "Notre Politique Militaire," *Revue de Défense Nationale* (May, 1963), p. 754.

[g] To complete the picture, Britain in 1962 had a gross national product of $79 billion and France of $72 billion. Gross national product figures for all of the countries mentioned, except China, are from the *New York Times*, January 26, 1964, E8. The figure of $50 billion for China in 1962, though it is a figure that is widely given, is necessarily a crude estimate. As a close and convenient approximation, I have taken 3%, 5%, 6%, and 7% as doubling in 24, 14, 12, and 10 years, respectively.

[h] Albert Wohlstetter has estimated that the first one hundred Polaris missiles manufactured and operated for five peacetime years will cost three to five times as much as the cost of the first one hundred B-47s ("Nuclear Sharing: NATO and the N+1 Country," *Foreign Affairs*, XXXIX [April, 1981], 364).

[i] France plans to have three nuclear submarines of sixteen missiles each, the first to

be operating in 1969, the others following at two-year intervals (Messmer, "Notre Politique Militaire," p. 747).

j It is not wholly absurd for British and French governments to proclaim, as they frequently do, that an embryonic capability brings an immediate increase of strength; for further expenditures are not likely to bring much of an additional payoff. Cf. President de Gaulle's message to his minister-delegate at Reggane upon the explosion of France's first atomic device: "Hurrah for France! From this morning she is stronger and prouder!" Leonard Beaton and John Maddox, *The Spread of Nuclear Weapons* (London: Chatto & Windus, 1962), p. 91.

k The experiences of Chinese Communists prior to 1949 and of the People's Republic of China since that date suggest that attempts to outflank may bring a greater success than efforts to imitate! Or, applying an economist's term to military matters, would-be Nth-countries would do well to ask, where do we have a comparative advantage?

l Morton A. Kaplan, *System and Process in International Politics* (New York: Wiley, 1957), p. 37; and "Bipolarity in a Revolutionary Age," in Kaplan ed., *The Revolution in World Politics* (New York: Wiley, 1962), p. 254. The difficulties and dangers found in a bipolar world by Kaplan are those detected by Hans J. Morgenthau in a system of opposing alliances. It is of direct importance in assessing the stability of international systems to note that Morgenthau finds "the opposition of two alliances . . . the most frequent configuration within the system of the balance of power" (*Politics Among Nations* [3d ed.; New York: Knopf, 1961, part 4], p. 189). Kaplan, in turn, writes that "the most likely transformation of the 'balance of power' system is to a bipolar system" (*System and Process*, p. 36).

m Kaplan, though he treats the case almost as being trivial, adds a statement that is at least suggestive: "The tight bipolar system is stable only when both bloc actors are hierarchically organized" (*System and Process*, p. 43).

n Kaplan, e.g., by the fourth and sixth of his rules of a balance-of-power system, requires a state to oppose any threatening state and to be willing to ally with any other (*System and Process*, p. 23).

References

1 Henry Kissinger, "Strains on the Alliance," *Foreign Affairs*, XLI (January, 1963), 284. Cf. Max Kohnstamm, "The European Tide," *Dædalus*, XCIII (Winter, 1964), pp. 100–102; McGeorge Bundy's speech to the Economic Club of Chicago, *New York Times*, December 7, 1961; John F. Kennedy, "Address at Independence Hall," Philadelphia, July 4, 1962, *Public Papers of the Presidents of the United States* (Washington, DC: Government Printing Office, 1963), pp. 537–539.

2 Quoted in V. D. Sokolovskii ed., *Soviet Military Strategy*, Herbert S. Dinerstein, Leon Gouré, and Thomas W. Wolfe, translators and English editors (Englewood Cliffs: Prentice-Hall, 1963), p. 43.

3 Herman Kahn, *On Thermonuclear War* (Princeton: Princeton University Press, 1960), p. 315.

4 Richard N. Rosecrance, *Action and Reaction in World Politics* (Boston: Little, Brown, 1963), pp. 210–211.

5 Hedley Bull, "Atlantic Military Problems: A Preliminary Essay." Prepared for

the Council on Foreign Relations meeting of November 20, 1963, p. 21. Quoted with permission of the author.

6 P. E. Vyshinsky, "Communism and the Motherland," as quoted in *The Kremlin Speaks* (Department of State publication, 4264, October, 1951), pp. 6, 7.

7 National Union of Conservative and Unionist Associations, *Official Report*, 81st Annual Conference, Llandudno (October 10–13, 1962), p. 93.

8 Ambassade de France, Speeches and Press Conferences, No. 185 (January 14, 1963), p. 9.

9 In a statement taped in Peking before his African trip in January of 1964, *New York Times*, February 4, 1964, p. 2. Cf. the message sent by Communist China's leaders to Premier Khrushchev upon the occasion of his seventieth birthday. After referring to differences between them, it is stated that: "In the event of a major world crisis, the two parties, our two peoples will undoubtedly stand together against our common enemy," *New York Times*, April 17, 1964, p. 3.

10 Leland M. Goodrich, "Korea: Collective Measures Against Aggression," *International Conciliation*, No. 494 (October, 1953), p. 164.

11 "Stresses and Strains in 'Going It With Others,' " in Arnold Wolfers ed., *Alliance Policy in the Cold War* (Baltimore: Johns Hopkins Press, 1959), p. 7.

12 *The Statesman's Year-Book*, S. H. Steinberg ed. (London: Macmillan, 1948), p. 50. Ibid. (1951), p. 991. Ibid. (1963), pp. 103, 104, 1003. The figures for Great Britain exclude the women's services, Territorial Army, and colonial troops. Those for France exclude the gendarmes.

13 Bull, "Atlantic Military Problems," p. 24.

14 Alastair Buchan and Philip Windsor, *Arms and Stability in Europe* (New York: Praeger, 1963), p. 205.

15 Jacob Viner, "The Implications of the Atomic Bomb for International Relations," *Proceedings of the American Philosophical Society*, XC (1946), p. 55.

16 Stanley Hoffmann, "Cursing de Gaulle Is Not a Policy," *The Reporter*, XXX (January 30, 1964), p. 40.

17 Cf. Malcolm W. Hoag, "On Stability in Deterrent Races," in Morton A. Kaplan ed., *The Revolution in World Politics* (New York: Wiley, 1962), pp. 408, 409.

18 Cf. a forthcoming book by Victor Basiuk, Institute of War and Peace Studies, Columbia University.

19 *House of Commons, Parliamentary Debates* (March 1, 1960), cols. 1136–1138. Compare Hugh Gaitskell, *The Challenge of Co-Existence* (London: Methuen, 1957), pp. 45–46.

20 Quoted by Eldon Griffiths, "The Revolt of Europe," *The Saturday Evening Post*, CCLXIII (March 9, 1963), p. 19.

21 Bull, "Atlantic Military Problems," p. 29.

22 Hans J. Morgenthau, *Politics Among Nations* (3d ed.; New York: Knopf, 1961), part 4. Morton A. Kaplan, *System and Process in International Politics* (New York: Wiley, 1957), pp. 22–36. I shall refer only to Morgenthau and Kaplan, for their writings are widely known and represent the majority opinion of students in the field.

23 Morgenthau, *Politics Among Nations*, p. 350. Cf. Kaplan, *System and Process*, pp. 36–43; and Kaplan, "Bipolarity in a Revolutionary Age," in Kaplan ed., *The Revolution in World Politics* (New York: Wiley, 1962), pp. 251–266.

121

24 The point is nicely made in an unpublished paper by Wolfram F. Hanrieder, "Actor Objectives and International Systems" (Center of International Studies, Princeton University, February, 1964), pp. 43–44.

25 For a sharp questioning of "the myth of flexibility," see George Liska's review article "Continuity and Change in International Systems," *World Politics*, XVI (October, 1963), pp. 122–123.

26 Raymond Aron, *Paix et Guerre entre les Nations* (Paris: Calmann–Lévy, 1962), p. 156.

27 Gen. Paul Stehlin, "The Evolution of Western Defense," *Foreign Affairs*, XLII (October, 1963), pp. 81, 77.

28 See, for example, Secretary Rusk's statement before the Senate Foreign Relations Committee, *New York Times*, August 13, 1963.

29 Ambassade de France, Speeches and Press Conferences, No. 175 (May 15, 1962), p. 6.

9

CONTENTION AND MANAGEMENT IN INTERNATIONAL RELATIONS

F. H. Hinsley, *Power and the Pursuit of Peace: Theory and Practice in the History of Relations Between States,* Cambridge, Cambridge University Press, 1963, 416 pp., $6.95.
Inis L. Claude, Jr., *Power and International Relations,* New York, Random House, 1962, 310 pp., $4.50.

The idea that peaceful adjustment of the relations of states may result from contention among them Claude believes to be hopelessly outmoded. The presence of nuclear weapons means that any equilibrium of states, however stable it may seem, is not nearly stable enough. The task of the theorist and the statesman alike is to introduce order from above, to replace the "invisible hand" by which adjustments are contrived in systems of self-regulation with something a little more substantial. Here the juxaposition of our two authors enlivens the subject. F. H. Hinsley considers the notion of spontaneous equilibrium to be a liberating idea. He applies the eighteenth century's beautiful system of natural harmony to the world of the present and is delighted with the result. Though large-scale war would now be devastating, we need not worry. Nuclear power is absolute and nuclear states, competent to control the instruments of power at their disposal, deter each other absolutely.

The character of an international system depends upon the number of great states that exist, the capabilities with which they are endowed, the ambitions they may entertain, and the nature of relations among them. Variations in these factors, which are central in any theory of international politics, determine the stability of the international equilibrium and at the same time make the managerial task more or less pressing. Because of the assumptions that each author adopts, both of the books under review are unevenly developed. In neither of them is sufficient effort made to weigh the importance of all of the factors and to establish relations of cause and interdependence among them.

I Modern states and nuclear weapons

Hinsley places great emphasis upon the peaceful proclivities of the modern state. In earlier periods, a portion of the populace sometimes goaded its government to war. Since late in the nineteenth century, he observes, this has no longer been the case. In all states, totalitarian and democratic alike, the opinions of the people, dedicated to peace, have constituted an impediment to war which the ruler bent upon war has had to overcome before he could commit his armies to battle. Hinsley places even greater emphasis on "administrative" barriers than he does on popular restraints. "Contrary to a cherished belief of internationalists . . . states as organizations, as cabinets, as civil services with civil service committees, as comprehensively competent but also immensely complicated structures of power, were less and less the causes or the instigators of violence and war, if ever they had been, and were becoming more and more disposed to shift to avoid these things, even as they were becoming more and more capable of doing so" (p. 288). The judgment is judiciously illustrated by citing the case of Baldwin's Britain between the two wars, but Hinsley also applies it to Hitler's Germany and to Stalin's Russia. He has echoed, apparently unconsciously, the earlier opinion of Max Weber, and applied it to a different purpose. He who seizes control of a state by revolutionary force or military occupation, Weber had reasoned, is confronted by a bureaucratic apparatus that is immensely difficult to move. "The question is always who controls the existing bureaucratic machinery." The answer, he suggested, is that "such control is possible only in a very limited degree to persons who are not technical specialists. Generally speaking, the trained permanent official is more likely to get his way in the long run than his nominal superior, the Cabinet minister, who is not a specialist."[1] The "political master," no matter how he has come to power, "finds himself in the position of the 'dilettante' who stands opposite the expert. . . ." Weber concluded that modern bureaucracy "makes 'revolution,' in the sense of the forceful creation of entirely new formations of authority, technically more and more impossible. . . ."[2] But, as has often been suggested and as Hitler's career has illustrated, the charismatic leader playing upon mass irrationality, employing instruments of terror, and displaying a contempt for the expert may well subvert the bureaucracy and bend it to his will.[3] If, as Hinsley asserts, the checks upon Stalin's and Hitler's "uses of power were still immensely greater than those which all earlier despots had faced" (p. 285), so were the means available to them for overcoming these checks. Even if the modern state as such is peaceful, evil men are able to make war. While Hinsley has drawn attention to important tendencies that are often overlooked, in the end he reaches an unduly optimistic conclusion.

The conclusion is required for the case he is making. If the political leader is the instrument of his peacefully inclined people and is restrained by a corps of cautious bureaucrats, we can count on leaders to behave intelligently, whether or not they are wise. The intelligent policy for a nuclear state is always to refrain from using force.

The second great source of restraints Hinsley finds in the existence of nuclear weapons. Nuclear weapons, he writes, "constitute for the first time a true deterrent, one that will never have to be relied upon so long as it exists—and this is likely to be for ever" (p. 347). Countless commentators have worried about the escalation of violence from the conventional to the nuclear level, about nuclear war coming by accident, about the irrationality of states-men compounded by the possible rationality of an irrational policy, about nuclear war by preemption, about the delicacy of the balance of terror and the dangers of nuclear diffusion. Hinsley dismisses all of such worries. We need not be concerned about the destabilizing effects of nuclear diffusion, for the possession of great power will render its holders responsible (p. 355), which is possibly true but surely not self-evidently so. Nor is he concerned that innovations in weaponry may have destabilizing effects. If nuclear weapons are absolute, then among those states that have them differences of strength are inconsequential. To increase the destructive power of nuclear weapons beyond their "present awesome limits, as opposed to improving the means of delivering them to their targets, is a pointless operation." Apparently it is also pointless to worry about improvement of delivery systems or means of defend-ing against them, for Hinsley immediately goes on to say: "Pass beyond this Great Power barrier, as states will do in future in increasing numbers, and you are a Great Power; and although some Great Powers are more powerful than others, all inhabit a territory in which the only defeat that can be inflicted by one upon another is a diplomatic defeat in a war of nerves—and in which all are or will become aware of this fact" (pp. 354–355). There is nothing between the holocaust, of which nuclear states will be sufficiently wary, and diplomatic maneuver, which is a harmless sport.

The thought that has occurred to others Hinsley apparently considers to be trivial: That if the powers in possession of sophisticated systems of nuclear weapons find themselves stalemated at the strategic level, the very condition of stalemate may tempt them to pursue whatever objectives they may have in other ways. Some states will exhaust their capabilities if they choose to build strategic nuclear systems and thus be disadvantaged if military competition should turn in part upon other means. Differences in power among nuclear states would still matter; the possibility of using force to secure the ends of the state would continue to exist. Hinsley offers little evidence to support his contrary opinions. The evidence he does offer turns out to be appallingly wrong. Anxious "to evade the technical deterrent," governments, he says, listened "to theorists who misguidedly urged the development of tactical atomic weapons. . . ." Because of the danger that the tactical use of nuclear weapons may lead to all-out nuclear war, they were quickly "persuaded . . . to retrace their steps" (p. 348). One may then wonder why Secretary McNamara announced in November of 1963 that the tactical nuclear strength of the

Alliance "has been increased, on the ground in Europe, by more than 60% in the last two years."[4]

Finally, wedding his notions about the state to his misunderstanding of nuclear deterrence, Hinsley argues that precautions "taken against accidents with the nuclear weapons—against those accidents that might arise from faulty radar, the mad second-lieutenant or the thoughtless Prime Minister—have become so complex that the procedure for reaching a decision to use the weapons is already too complicated to be operated even in the retaliatory role to which the weapons have been confined." This is a daring conclusion to have reached by "reading between the lines of newspaper accounts . . ." (p. 348). The checks, as he notices, are designed to make the system proof against accidents. They are also, as he chooses not to emphasize, designed to assure that the ultimate decision to use them will remain in the hands of the head of the government. Only if one believes that the logic of deterrence is invincible and the state omnicompetent does it follow that a system designed to ensure that only calculated use can be made of nuclear weapons should make any use of them at all impossible.

II International equilibrium

In more general terms, Hinsley is persuaded that in some eras the international balance is relatively even and that peace is a product of the equilibrium's stability. In other periods, marked by an imbalance of states, violence and war inevitably occur. In most of the nineteenth century, the international equilibrium was stable; therefore, war was rare, and those wars that did occur were limited. From the 1890s to the end of the Second World War, a time of transition, the relations of states were characterized by extreme imbalance among them. But nowhere does he make clear why in the 1930s, for example, with half a dozen great powers in the world, shifts in the alignment of nations did not bring balance out of national disparities in power, nor indeed does he make clear what the imbalance was. Winston Churchill has described the failure of the Western democracies in the middle 1930s as being a failure to use wisely a superiority of power that lay in their hands. This is obviously not the imbalance Hinsley has in mind. Under what international conditions will the greatest efforts to achieve a satisfactory balance be elicited and be most likely to succeed? Hinsley gives little help to anyone seeking an answer. How the possibilities of adjustment are affected by variations in the number of powers that exist and the extent of differences in strength among them does not interest him. Reflecting on the causes of wars, he finds their origins in the uneven development of states, which necessarily produces imbalances among them.[5]

He seems to be optimistic about the chances of peace only where equilibrium is tantamount to fixity, which will exist when states happen to achieve parallel development of industry, technology, and political organization. While this is an important factor, other conditions are important as well. Because his analysis is elliptic, he slips into the habit of simply assuming that when peace has prevailed, equilibrium has been achieved. Peace among major states has prevailed since the Second World War as "the new balance . . . has been completing itself among them" (p. 350). Why did peace prevail before the balance was completed? He argues that "since 1946 war by design and war by miscalculation have both been ruled out because the Great Powers have become acutely aware of the fatal consequences for themselves of using [nuclear] weapons, and—except in retaliation against their use—have determined not to use them" (p. 348). But until sometime in the early 1950s the Soviet Union did not possess nuclear weapons systems. Deterrence in the years immediately following the war must have depended upon other means, and peace between the most powerful states must have rested on other conditions.

Hinsley is confident that the present international equilibrium will endure. His state of mind is interesting; what would be more interesting still—a careful specification of the factors upon which his confidence is based—is often lacking. He proclaims in his subtitle that the marriage of theory and practice will be consummated in the pages of his book. In fact, he does not even have them living in sin. He seeks to make "a first effort" to raise the study of international relations "to a more scientific level" (p. 6). His method, advertised as being interdisciplinary, is in fact almost wholly historical, and the amalgamation of "findings" scarcely detectable. Part I, "A History of Internationalist Theories," reads very much like the writings of the rationalist seekers of peace of a generation or more ago, of men like F. M. Stawell and A. C. F. Beales—with this major difference: Where they were optimists to the point of utopianism, Hinsley's writing is suffused with an ironic and effective skepticism. Theories penned in the seventeenth century are, he says, still accepted despite their earlier demolition by Jean Jacques Rousseau and by others. But the theories he has in mind are largely theories of international organization in forms which, despite his assertion, are no longer widely accepted by students of international relations. Part III is a consideration of international relations and organizations in the twentieth century. Just as early in the book he deftly dispatches some corpses, here, with a brevity that would be pleasing if the analyses and judgments were not already thoroughly familiar, he underscores the weakness of the League and the United Nations and reviews the causes of two world wars.

Hinsley's bow to theory and to science appears merely as a nod to current fashion, for early in the book one learns that old theories are obsolete, and one reads nowhere in his pages of new ones to replace them. The promised effort to delineate theory and illuminate practice by carefully identifying important factors and rigorously examining their relations of cause and interdependence gives way to a combination of common sense and history. His impressive knowledge of history is brilliantly deployed in Part II, wherein he interprets the diplomacy of the modern state system. Without a serviceable theory or a detailed and reliable knowledge of the present interrelations of policy and power, his attempt to describe the bases of the current balance and estimate its stability gains little from previous chapters. In the end, even one who agrees with his specific conclusions will be made uneasy by the ground upon which he rests them.

Equilibrium is an important problem for both authors, though neither of them deals with it well. Hinsley is so sure of a happy international outcome that he does not examine carefully enough the conditions that may underlie it. Claude is so certain that contention among states will destroy them that he fails to ask whether variations within a laissez-faire system may not alter both the importance and the possibility of accomplishing managerial tasks. He declares, without analyzing the proposition, that "a balance of power system requires that effective power be diffused among a substantial number of major states" (p. 90). Yet he concludes at once that the world is bipolar and that "the balance of power system exists by default" (p. 93), which is enough to make one despair. His low expectation of stability in a bipolar world results from focusing upon one means of adjustment only: the opportunity of nations to change partners according to the stately rhythm of an eighteenth-century minuet as variations occur in the fortunes and forces of each of them. Overlooking other important means of adjustment, he assumes that the one means presently unavailable is in fact indispensable. Two states are too few to permit adjustments to take place, and were there a larger number of states, the international equilibrium would anyway be unreliable.

Claude distrusts the "invisible hand" that supposedly contrives order among freely contending units. He has not sufficiently appreciated that the "invisible hand" is a metaphor intended to suggest that harmony in competition is a possible result of contention rather than itself being a cause of the outcome (pp. 88–89). But is the economist's metaphor of the "invisible hand" one that applies at all in the realm of politics? "We may," according to Bertrand de Jouvenel, "hold the view that economic activities tend to combine harmoniously: we can not hold it in the case of political activities."[6] Though many students of politics concur in the judgment, its acceptance is not justified. There are two questions involved, and both of them are important. First, is it possible for a competitive political system to be self-equilibrating? Second, with specific reference to international relations, can we live with the harmony that the contention of states may produce? A condition comparable to one that is described as harmonious within an economy will be widely deplored as dangerously discordant and destructively unstable if it prevails among states in the world. An economic system is said to be functioning satisfactorily if equilibrium at a high level of factor employment prevails. Harmony is taken to be not only consistent with, but in part dependent upon, the periodic disappearance of some of the constituent units of the system, only to have them replaced by others. In a system of economic competition, it is desirable that the inefficient be driven to the wall. Each firm seeks to promote its own interests, but the constructive result of competition transcends the interests of the separate units. Firms that are proficient survive, while others, less skillfully managed, go bankrupt. The disappearance of the relatively inefficient, forced by the operation of the system itself, is a condition of the good performance of the economy. If the efficient who are too small and too weak to stand up to their stronger competitors also disappear, that is merely unfortunate.

Both the economic and international political systems of competition involve possibly destructive conflict. In international politics, if an aggressive state becomes strong or a strong state becomes aggressive, the weak will presumably suffer. In the international system, few states lose their lives; in a free economy, many firms do. In the economic realm, harmony is defined in terms of the overall result achieved, while the units of the system are constantly in jeopardy. Although the constructive purpose of the contention of economic units is quite easily seen, it is difficult to argue that states collectively are better off because of the competition they engage in. In the age of Social Darwinism, the invigoration of states that was thought to result from competition among them was often applauded. The triumph of the strong was an indication of virtue; if the weak succumbed, it was because of their vices. In international politics, discord is said to prevail because we are no longer content that the international system be perpetuated but are necessarily obsessed with the fate of the units that make up the system. Differences in the incidence of destruction and "death" do not account for the reluctance to refer to international politics as a harmonious realm, while economic systems of competition are often so described. Instead, one may conclude, the standards of performance now applied to international political systems are higher, or at least widely different. As John Maynard Keynes once remarked, those who believe that unhampered processes of natural selection lead to progress have not counted the costs of the struggle.[7] In international politics, we often count nothing but the costs of the struggle.

In describing harmony and discord in economic and political activities, de Jouvenel has distinguished between types of activities that do or do not "combine harmoniously," and has thereby drawn attention to some important differences between economic and political life. He has unfortunately obscured the equally important distinction between regulated and unregulated competition. Economic systems of free enterprise are ordinarily hedged about in ways that channel men's energies constructively. One may think of anti-trust laws, pure food and drug standards, securities and exchange regulations, laws against shooting a competitor, and rules forbidding false claims in advertising. Much the same can be said of political competition within a well-ordered state. The loss of an election may destroy the political career of a candidate; the loss of successive elections may result in the disappearance of a party. In England, the Liberal Party has flickered on the verge of extinction. Some may shed a nostalgic tear, but grief has been limited by the emergence of the Labour Party and its ability to perpetuate a condition of political competition. And the competition is, perforce, carried on without violence.

In the relations of states, with competition unregulated, war will occasionally occur. Though in one of its aspects war is a means of adjustment within the international system, the occurrence of war has often mistakenly been taken to indicate that the system itself has broken down. At times, as during much of the eighteenth and nineteenth centuries, war was tolerable, since, being circumscribed, it was of limited destructive effect. The costs of war now appear to be frighteningly high. Since the most impressive of large and complicated self-regulatory systems have operated only within a contrived order, Claude would seem to be on firm ground in asserting that "the management of power is the real issue" (p. 7). He is saying that with power internationally uncontrolled it is unreasonable to expect that the peaceful adjustment of the relations of states will be produced by the independent policy of each of them without the operation of war as a means of regulation. This would be to ask for much more from the international political system than has ever been expected in domestic economics or politics. But in describing expectations this way, it is at once implicitly assumed that war and the risk of war are more painful to bear than the costs of constructing and sustaining systems of management would be and that managerial functions are now very badly performed.

III International society and international management

Power, which Claude defines as "essentially military capability" (p. 6), is a means sometimes used in an effort to accomplish a purpose. Management requires both a manager and an entity susceptible to being managed. It is difficult to understand what is meant by the management of power, even power defined as military force, for power and force are not entities. Military forces can be managed, though often with difficulty even by the state whose instruments they supposedly are. The management of power in international relations requires at a minimum controlling the military forces that are at each state's disposal. International management may in some sense be required, yet it is not clear that if the requirement were fulfilled we would be any better off. We know the evils of the system we have lived with and can only imagine those that would exist in a noticeably different world. There is a frightful danger of war among states coexisting in anarchy. Except by an uninteresting process of definition—effective management of power would mean the absence of organized violence—it does not follow that more management necessarily means a lesser possibility of war.

Claude has posed the international problem in Hobbesian terms: If life is to be preserved, power must be managed—in this case, the military forces disposed of by states who are in close association without really forming a society. By the logic of Hobbes, men give up their freedom to get all they can in exchange for the security of what they may already possess, but the dominant end of men—self-preservation—remains as the motive power of their actions. Decisions of the sovereign that bring the existence of a man or the security of a group of men into jeopardy will naturally be resisted.[8] The relation of ruler to ruled then resolves itself into a question of power. Claude, like Hobbes, isolates one big fear, the fear of death, and proposes one big remedy, central control. If the remedy were successfully applied, the result would be purely Hobbesian: A relation between the governors and the governed, based on force and utility, wherein the superior do what they can, the inferior suffer what they must, and quiet prevails so long as resistance can be contained or the inferior are sufficiently pleased with the benefits they receive to remain acquiescent.

A tolerable world is often said to be one in which the pressing danger of war is absent and still the freedom of states is preserved. Freedom entails self-dependence. But the self-dependence of states means that each state must develop and maintain the power upon which its security rests. Each state's quest for security must then render all states insecure. The dilemmas of international politics are cruel, and every imagined escape from them poses difficulties and dangers as great as those that now exist. States cannot entrust the management of power to a central agency unless that agency is competent to protect its client states. The more powerful the clients and the more the power of each of them appears to be a threat to the others, the greater must be the power that is lodged in the hands of the manager. The establishment of a manager of power would then invite the states to use their own power in a struggle to control the central agency.

In a society of states with little coherence, weak attempts to manage international affairs from the center have little influence over the activities of the separate states, especially those of great power. Thus Claude finds that a collective security system, where the most powerful states requiring management also serve as the managers, resolves itself into a balance-of-power system with which it is substantially identical (pp. 123–133); and Hinsley dismisses the thought that international organization can accomplish anything of importance. For the most part, both of them eschew the notion that the Third World chorus chanting in the General Assembly words sometimes intended to moderate the policies of the great powers can have a useful effect. To manage power, power is required.

If important political functions must be centrally performed and if there is practically no society upon which agencies of central control can be erected, then a manager possessed of great power is at once badly needed and impossible to find. It is now often argued that the sharp horns of the Hobbesian dilemma are being blunted by the growing interdependence of states. According to Claude, for example, "the affairs of nations have become and bid fair to become more and more tightly interwoven" (p. 276). Interdependence that locks national interests so closely together that separation is self-evidently destructive of all good things may increase the chances of peace. Short of that threshold, the new form of the old argument that war will not occur because it does not pay brings little comfort. If interdependence is growing at a pace that exceeds the development of central control, then interdependence may increase the occasions for war.

It is, one should add, not even clear that the interdependence of states has increased overall. The present relation of the underdeveloped countries to the states that constitute the Development Assistance Committee is less close than was the old imperial tie. For most states, foreign trade as a percentage of national income is smaller now than it was fifty or sixty years ago. In 1913, imports and exports combined represented almost 60 percent of Great Britain's national income, more than 40 percent of Germany's and France's, almost 30 percent of Italy's, and almost 14 percent of Russia's and America's.[9] Most of the great powers of the day were also great traders; economically they were closely knit together. Germany, for example, in the years preceding the First World War was Britain's second-best customer, both as a source of imports and as a market for exports. The high degree of interdependence in these cases may have been unusual; even exceptional interdependence, far from leading to the unity of great-power contenders, did not prevent them from fighting a bloody war.

It may be argued that because trade has increased in absolute amount while declining in proportion to production, some sectors of national economies have become closely entwined without regard for political boundaries. Undoubtedly so in some cases, but the two greatest powers in the world today, both of them large in extent and industrially developed, trade little with each other or with the rest of the world.[10] Beyond that, where there is interdependence it can now more easily be broken. Technological and other advances make quite easily possible the development of substitutes for most items of import, or, putting it differently, large and economically well-developed countries, the very ones that are crucial in a system of balance, can more quickly move toward an autarkic condition. It is also doubtful that foreign travel and cosmopolitan contact loom any larger now than they did earlier, for one must bear in mind that the number of people influential in government has also increased in the meantime.

The myth of increased interdependence may be important in its own right, but one should also look at the reality. Where there is firm expectation of peace, as there has been among Western European states since the war, interdependence easily grows; where the expectation is lacking, as it has been between the United States and the Soviet Union, interdependence develops more slowly. In speaking of the interdependence of states, the fear of military loss often looms larger than the hope of economic gain. If we do not succeed in living peacefully together, we may all be buried in a common grave. Consciousness of the nuclear danger may sharpen the desire to eliminate it, but it does not provide the means of doing so. Nor are alliances any longer as important to the mightiest of nations as they were to all of the great powers in the late nineteenth and early twentieth centuries. Economically and militarily, the interdependence of states has declined.

It is scarcely relevant to argue that the growing interdependence of global society provides the basis for the establishment of a world management when deep ideological and other cleavages separate those states whose powers the world management would have to contain. Claude asserts that "the proposition that states must, in their own interest, react in some responsible way to the reality of their common interest in the ordering of relationships among themselves" cannot legitimately be questioned (p. 277). But since not all states do react in this way, and no state always does, the proposition *must* be questioned. Since interdependence has developed nowhere near to the point of producing a global community, unless it be a community of fear, international control, if it is to operate, must be based on a mechanistic balance. It may indeed be that neither man's wit nor nature's contrivance is adequate to produce a world reliably at peace. So one must suspect and, being suspicious, proceed to ask if it is possible to combine whatever benign results history has produced with a little human contrivance in order to make a presently supportable peace somewhat more secure. Who will do the contriving? Claude, when he comes to grips with the problem of international management, concentrates on world government, which he has rightly termed "utopia." Since there are important managerial tasks to be accomplished and no present or likely future agency to perform them, his quest should sensibly have become a search for a surrogate of government.

In the absence of an authoritative manager, the performance of management functions is difficult to discern. In a sector of the economy, one may prefer that many firms roughly equal in size compete with each other, within rules laid down by the government. Where there is no single agency to make rules and enforce them, smaller numbers of units and greater imbalances between the few strong and the many weak may be preferable. When two states overshadow in power all others, can they not manage to get along both with each other and with the rest of the world somewhat as oligopolists manage their markets, make serious and often successful efforts to avoid destructive price wars among themselves, and buy out or ignore the smaller firms whose efforts can do little more than annoy them?[11] From this perspective, two adversary-partners, the Soviet Union and the United States, deter each other and, with a reluctance born of mutual suspicion, impose a measure of control—or seek to manage—situations of danger whose unfavorable outcomes would grossly damage both of them.

Any one of several firms that dominate a field will have more to say about all of the matters that affect it than will one wheat farmer among thousands. Oligopolists may prefer duopoly while differing as to which two of several firms should survive. Duopolists may prefer monopoly or conceivably wish that worries about the management of markets were shared by a wider circle of firms. The possibilities are not fewer but more numerous in international relations than in a constricted segment of the economy precisely because there is no single authority who can impose from above limitations upon the transformation of the system. The principal entities that constitute the international system are also its managers. They try to cope with the affairs of each day; they may also seek to affect the nature and direction of change.

If the international system cannot be transcended, it may be useful to ask if it can be transformed. Direction can be imparted in ways that may be useful, though they fall short of the governmental type of control that the presence of a legally competent manager would provide. If the amount and type of direction and the degree of self-regulation existing in a bipolar world are insufficient, is there the possibility of changes in the international system which states that presently exist can hope to produce? An imbalance of international forces may lead to the opportunity of one state to dominate, singly or in combination with others—that is, to use its own power to control the use of power by other states. At times this has been the half-articulated dream of American policy. Robert W. Tucker has discerned it in the threat of massive retaliation, the message conveyed being: Cross the line we have drawn—or, in more general terms, violate the rules we have laid down—and you will be erased.[12] More recently, Senator J. William Fulbright and other artificers of an Atlantic imperium have aspired to a condition of world hegemony that would provide the material basis for managing the world without having achieved world government in form. "If the West goes on to realize its fullest possible strength in an Atlantic partnership, it can," the Senator has recently written, "bring about a decisive shift in the world balance of power and permanently foreclose the possibility of significant Communist expansion."[13] More recently still, President Johnson has described the purpose of American military strength as being "to put an end to conflict."[14]

If one believed that a world in which a single state or grouping of states enjoys hegemony would promise a greater stability than one in which two or more powers contend, he might then favor efforts to construct an Atlantic imperium. There are questions to be answered, some of which theoretical analysis can hope to illuminate. A few can be briefly suggested. To construct an Atlantic imperium without first achieving political unity in Western Europe would require the United States to bring European states separately, successively, and reliably under its influence. Efforts to do so might themselves provoke European states to seek political union more diligently. Should the unity of Europe ensue, for this reason or for others, one might then hope, as many Americans have, that a Western European State would reliably cooperate with the United States and that Western hegemony would then be assured.

There are other ways to contrive changes that would affect both the conditions of international equilibrium and the possibilities of world management. One of them has just been suggested. If hegemony is undesirable, an equilibrium of states the best we can hope for, and a condition of bipolarity incompatible with the operation of a balance of power, would then a world *à trois* be preferable? If it would be, then it is apparent, without repeating what has already been said, that some actions can be taken by the United States to widen the circle of great powers.

IV Conclusion

The theoretical enterprise, if it is to be forwarded, must rest on a broader view of possibilities and a more thorough and systematic analysis of conditions than either author has undertaken. While men of affairs have wondered what a new international order, if there is to be one, will look like and have sought to affect the outcome, few theorists have analyzed the good or bad results that could be expected to ensue from one transformation or another of the international system. It is disappointing that neither Claude nor Hinsley has done this. Both of them trench into most of the ground that a theory of international relations must cover. In neither book, however, does one find a careful consideration of the different degrees of stability or the various possibilities of establishing international control that are likely to result from variations in the nature and number of major states in the world. One would have expected from Hinsley a better-informed and more thorough analysis of the factors upon which a peaceful equilibrium may rest and a systematic consideration of how changes in these factors would be expected to affect the prospects of peace. From Claude one would have hoped for a more imaginative identification of the different possibilities of managing, coping, and contriving in international politics under conditions where no single, formal, adequately equipped managerial agency can exist Many of the interesting and important questions have been left aside by both authors.

Since the relation between theory and practice is one of their major concerns, the omissions are serious ones. They have arisen directly from the perspectives and methods of the authors. Hinsley believes that serviceable international principles and a pervading sense of collectivity will not be revived "until men have assimilated the lessons of the past fifty years of international struggle on a world scale . . ." (p. 271). The truth of the statement, if any, must rest on a psychological theory of politics, which is nowhere adumbrated. Claude explicitly rejects the present possibility of a general theory of international politics and argues that "human wisdom tends to consist of assembled snippets," that theory-building should be thought of "as a process marked by eclecticism and revisionism, rather than as a kind of creative spasm . . ." (p. 273).[15] But without a wider theory, how can one know which snippet will be of strategic theoretical importance or figure out how one factor should be related to another, weighed in importance, and assessed for effect in the decisions that leaders of states must constantly make? Only with theoretical conceptions more widely drawn and more systematically developed than either author has done can ends be compared and empirical investigations undertaken, models experimented with mentally, common sense adduced, and the sociology of international relations usefully studied.

Notes

1 Max Weber, *The Theory of Social and Economic Organization*, trans, by A. M. Henderson and Talcott Parsons, ed. by Talcott Parsons (New York 1947), p. 338.
2 *From Max Weber: Essays in Sociology*, trans, and ed. by H. H. Gerth and C. Wright Mills (London 1947), pp. 232, 230.
3 The point is nicely made by Frederic S. Burin, "Bureaucracy and National Socialism: A Reconsideration of Weberian Theory," in Robert K. Merton, Alisa P. Gray, Barbara Hockey, Hanan C. Selvin, eds., *Reader in Bureaucracy* (Glencoe, IL., 1952), pp. 33–47.
4 Secretary of Defense McNamara, speech to the Economic Club of New York, November 18, 1963; quoted in William W. Kaufmann, *The McNamara Strategy* (New York 1964), p. 310.
5 Cf. F. H. Hinsley, "The Development of the European States System Since the Eighteenth Century," in *Transactions of the Royal Historical Society*, 5th Series, II (London 1961), p. 79. His conclusion is essentially the same as Halévy's, and his analysis has the same merits and defects. See Elie Halévy, *The World Crisis of 1914–1918* (Oxford 1930).
6 Bertrand de Jouvenel, "On the Nature of Political Science," *American Political Science Review*, LV (December 1961), p. 776.
7 J. M. Keynes, "The End of Laissez-faire—II," *New Republic*, XLVIII (September 1, 1926), p. 37.
8 "If the sovereign command a man, though justly condemned, to kill, wound, or maim himself; or not to resist those that assault him; or to abstain from the use of food, air, medicine, or any other thing, without which he cannot live; yet hath that man the liberty to disobey.... When therefore our refusal to obey, frustrates the end for which the sovereignty was ordained; then there is no liberty to refuse: otherwise there is." Further: "If a monarch, or sovereign assembly, grant a liberty to all, or any of his subjects, which grant standing, he is disabled to provide for their safety, the grant is void...." (Thomas Hobbes, *Leviathan*, ed. by Michael Oakeshott [Oxford, n.d.], ch. 21, pp. 142, 144.)
9 Karl W. Deutsch and Alexander Eckstein, "National Industrialization and the Declining Share of the International Economic Sector, 1890-1959," *World Politics*, XIII (January 1961), Table 2, 275.
10 For 1957, imports and exports as a percentage of national income: United States, 9.2 percent; Soviet Union, 4.9 percent (ibid.).
11 Cf. Roger D. Masters, "A Multi-Bloc Model of the International System," *American Political Science Review*, LV (December 1961), pp. 789–790.
12 Robert W. Tucker, *The Just War: A Study in Contemporary American Doctrine* (Baltimore 1960), pp. 190–193.
13 J. William Fulbright, *Prospects for the West* (Cambridge, MA., 1963), p. 27.
14 "Excerpts from Speech to Coast Guard," *New York Times*, June 4, 1964.
15 The distinction is unwarranted. Contrast Thomas S. Kuhn's profound examination of accumulation, crisis, and spasmodic creativity in the natural sciences, in *The Structure of Scientific Revolutions* (Chicago 1962), esp. see pp. 9, 10, 13.

10

INTERNATIONAL STRUCTURE, NATIONAL FORCE, AND THE BALANCE OF WORLD POWER

Balance of power is the hoariest concept in the field of international relations. Elaborated in a variety of analyses and loaded with different meanings, it has often been praised or condemned, but has seldom been wholly rejected. In a fascinating historical account of balance-of-power concepts, Martin Wight has distinguished nine meanings of the term.[1] For purposes of theoretical analysis a tenth meaning, cast in causal terms, should be added.

Balance-of-power theory assumes that the desire for survival supplies the basic motivation of states, indicates the responses that the constraints of the system encourage, and describes the expected outcome. Beyond the survival motive, the aims of states may be wondrously varied; they may range from the ambition to conquer the world to the desire merely to be left alone. But the minimum responses of states, which are necessary to the dynamics of balance, derive from the condition of national coexistence where no external guarantee of survival exists. Perception of the peril that lies in unbalanced power encourages the behavior required for the maintenance of a balance-of-power system.

Because of the present narrow concentration of awesome power, the question arises whether the affairs of the world can any longer be conducted or understood according to the balance-of-power concept, the main theoretical prop of those traditionally called realists. Even many who share the realist concern with power question its present relevance. They do so for two reasons.

It is, in the first place, widely accepted that balance-of-power politics requires the presence of three or more states. Political thought is so historically conditioned that the balance of power as it is usually defined merely reflects the experience of the modern era. In Europe for a period of three centuries, from the Treaty of Westphalia to the Second World War, five or more great powers sometimes sought to coexist peacefully and at other times competed for mastery. The idea thus became fixed that a balance of power can exist only where the participants approximate the customary number. But something more than habit is involved. Also mixed into ideas about necessary numbers is the notion that flexibility in the alignment of states is a require-ment of balance-of-power politics. The existence of only two states at the summit of power precludes the possibility of international maneuver and national realignment as ways of compensating for changes in the strength of either of them. Excessive concentration of power negates the possibility of playing the politics of balance.

Second, war or the threat of war, another essential means of adjustment, is said to be of only limited utility in the nuclear age. In balances of power, of course, more is placed on the scales than mere military force. Military force has, however, served not only as the *ultima ratio* of international politics but indeed as the first and the constant one. To reduce force to being the *ultima ratio* of politics implies, as Ortega y Gasset once noted, "the previous submis-sion of force to methods of reason."[2] Insufficient social cohesion exists among states and the instruments of international control are too weak to relegate power to the status of simply the *ultima ratio*. Power cannot be separated from the purposes of those who possess it; in international politics power has appeared primarily as the power to do harm.[3] To interdict the use of force by the threat of force, to oppose force with force, to annex territory by force, to influence the policies of other states by the threat or application of force—such uses of force have always been present at least as possibilities in the relations of states. The threat to use military forces and their occasional com-mitment to battle have helped to regulate the relations of states, and the preponderance of power in the hands of the major states has set them apart from the others. But, it is now often said, nuclear weapons, the "best" weapons of the most powerful states, are the least usable. At the extreme, some commentators assert that military force has become obsolete. Others, more cautious in their claims, believe that the inflated cost of using military force has seriously distorted both the balance between the militarily strong states and the imbalance between the strong and the weak ones. National military power, though not rendered wholly obsolete by nuclear weapons, nevertheless must be heavily discounted. The power of the two nuclear giants, it would seem, is then seriously impaired.[4]

A weird picture of the political world is thus drawn. The constraints of balance-of-power politics still operate: Each state by its own efforts fends for its rights and seeks to maintain its existence. At the same time, the operation of balance-of-power politics is strangely truncated; for one essential means of adjustment is absent, and the operation of the other is severely restricted. In the nineteenth-century liberals' vision of a world without power, force was to be banished internationally by the growing perfection of states and their con-sequent acceptance of each other as equals in dignity. The liberal utopia has reappeared in odd form. The limitation of power—or in extreme formula-tions, its abolition—is said to derive from the nuclear armament of some states; for nuclear armament makes at once for gross inequality in the power of states and for substantial equality among all states through the inability of the most powerful to use force effectively. Those who love paradox are under-standably enchanted. To examine the ground upon which the supposed paradox rests is one of the main aims of this essay.

I

The first reason for believing that balance-of-power politics has ended is easy to deal with, for only its relevance, not its truth, is in question.

If the balance-of-power game is really played hard it eventuates in two par-ticipants, whether states or groupings of them. If two groupings of states have hardened or if the relation of major antagonism in the world is simply between two nations, the balance-of-power model no longer applies, according to the conventional definition. This conclusion is reached by placing heavy emphasis on the process of balancing (by realignments of states) rather than on altering power (which may depend on the efforts of each state).[5] In a two-power world, emphasis must shift from the international process of balancing to the prospect of altering power by the internal efforts of each participant.

Admittedly, the old balance-of-power model cannot be applied without modification to a world in which two states far exceed all others in the force at their disposal. Balance-of-power analysis, however, remains highly useful if the observer shifts his perspective from a concentration upon international man-euver as a mode of adjustment to an examination of national power as a means of control and national effort as a way of compensating for incipient disequi-libria of power. With this shift in perspective, balance-of-power politics does not disappear; but the meaning of politics changes in a manner that can only be briefly suggested here.

In a world of three or more powers the possibility of making and breaking alliances exists. The substance of balance-of-power politics is found in the diplomacy by which alliances are made, maintained, or disrupted. Flexibility of alignment then makes for rigidity in national strategies: A state's strategy must satisfy its partner lest that partner defect from the alliance. A comparable situ-ation is found where political parties compete for votes by forming and reforming electoral coalitions of different economic, ethnic, religious, and regional groups. The strategies (or policies) of the parties are made so as to attract and hold voters. If it is to be an electoral success, a party's policy cannot simply be the policy that its leaders may think would be best for the country. Policy must at least partly be made for the sake of party management. Simi-larly in an alliance of approximately equal states, strategy is at least partly made for the sake of the alliance's cohesion. The alliance diplomacy of Europe in the years before World War I is rich in examples of this. Because the defection or defeat of a major state would have shaken the balance of power, each state was constrained to adjust its strategy and the deployment of its forces to the aims and fears of its partners. This is in sharp contrast to the current situation in NATO, where de Gaulle's disenchantment, for example, can only have mild repercussions. Though concessions to allies will sometimes be made, neither the Soviet Union nor the United States alters its strategy or changes its military dispositions simply to accommodate associated states. Both superpowers can make long-range plans and carry out their policies as best they see fit, for they need not accede to the demands of third parties. That America's strategy is not made for the sake of de Gaulle helps to explain his partial defection.

Disregarding the views of an ally makes sense only if military cooperation is relatively unimportant. This is the case in NATO, which in fact if not in form consists of unilateral guarantees by the United States to its European allies. The United States, with a preponderance of nuclear weapons and as many men in uniform as all of the Western European states combined,[6] may be able to protect her allies; they cannot possibly protect her. Because of the vast differences in the capacities of member states, the approximately equal sharing of burdens found in earlier alliance systems is no longer conceivable. The gross inequality between the two superpowers and the members of their respective alliances makes any realignment of the latter fairly insignificant. The leader's strategy can therefore be flexible. In balance-of-power politics, old style, flexibility of alignment made for rigidity of strategy or the limitation of freedom of decision. In balance-of-power politics, new style, the obverse is true: Rigidity of alignment in a two-power world makes for flexibility of strategy or the enlargement of freedom of decision.

Those who discern the demise of balance-of-power politics mistakenly identify the existence of balances of power with a particular mode of adjustment and the political means of effecting it. Balances of power tend to form so long as states desire to maintain their political identities and so long as they must rely on their own devices in striving to do so. With shrinking numbers, political practices and methods will differ; but the number of states required for the existence and perpetuation of balance-of-power politics is simply two or more, not, as is usually averred, some number larger than two.

II

The reduction in the number of major states calls for a shift in conceptual perspective. Internal effort has replaced external realignment as a means of maintaining an approximate balance of power. But the operation of a balance of power, as previously noted, has entailed the occasional use of national force as a means of international control and adjustment. Great-power status was traditionally conferred on states that could use force most handily. Is the use of force in a nuclear world so severely inhibited that balance-of-power analysis has lost most if not all of its meaning?

Four reasons are usually given in support of an affirmative answer. First, because the nuclear might of one superpower balances that of the other, their effective power is reduced to zero. Their best and most distinctive forces, the nuclear ones, are least usable. In the widely echoed words of John Herz, absolute power equals absolute impotence.[7] Second, the fear of escalation strongly inhibits even the use of conventional forces, especially by the United States or the Soviet Union. Nuclear powers must fear escalation more than other states do, for in any war that rose to the nuclear level they would be primary targets. They may, of course, still choose to commit their armies to battle, but the risks of doing so, as they themselves must realize, are higher than in the past. Third, in the nuclear age enormous military power no longer ensures effective control. The Soviet Union has not been able to control her Asian and European satellites. The United States has found it difficult to use military force for constructive purposes even against weak opponents in Southeast Asia. Political rewards have not been proportionate to the strength of the states that are militarily most powerful. Finally, the weak states of the world, having become politically aware and active, have turned world opinion into a serious restraint upon the use of force, whether in nuclear or conventional form. These four factors, it is argued, work singly and in combination to make the use of force more costly and in general to depreciate its value.

Never have great powers disposed of larger national products, and seldom in peacetime have they spent higher percentages of them on their military forces. The money so lavishly expended purchases more explosive power and more varied ways of delivering it than ever before in history. In terms of world distribution, seldom has military force been more narrowly concentrated. If military force is less useful today, the irony of history will have yet another vivid illustration. Has force indeed so depreciated as to warp and seriously weaken the effects of power in international relations? The above arguments make it seem so; they need to be reexamined. The following analysis of the use of force deals with all four arguments, though not by examining them one by one and in the order in which they are stated.

E. H. Carr long ago identified the error of believing "in the efficacy of an international public opinion," and he illustrated and explained the fallacy at length.[8] To think of world opinion as a restraint upon the military actions of states, one must believe that the strong states of the world—or for that matter the weak ones—would have used more military force and used it more often had they not anticipated their condemnation. Unless in a given instance world opinion can be defined, its source identified, and the mode of its operation discerned, such a view is not plausible. To believe in the efficacy of world opinion is to endow a nonexistent agent and an indefinable force with effective restraining power. Not world opinion but national views, shaped into policies and implemented by governments, have accounted for past events in international relations. Changes that would now permit world opinion, whatever that might be, to restrict national policies would have to lie not in the operation of opinion itself but in other changes that have occurred in the world. With "world opinion," as with Adam Smith's "invisible hand," one must ask: What is the reality that the metaphor stands for? It may be that statesmen pay their respects to world opinion because they are already restrained by other considerations.

Are such considerations found, perhaps, in changes that have taken place in the nature and distribution of force itself? If the costs of using military force have lessened its value, then obeisance paid to world opinion is merely a cloak for frustration and a hypocritical show of politeness. That the use of force is unusually costly, however, is a conclusion that rests on a number of errors. One that is commonly committed is to extend to all military force the conclusion that nuclear force is unusable. After listing the changes effected by nuclear weapons, one author, for example, concludes that these changes tend to restrict "the usability and hence the political utility of national military power in various ways."[9] This may represent merely a slip of the pen; if so, it is a telling one. A clearer and more interesting form of the error is found in the argument that the two superpowers, each stalemated by the other's nuclear force, are for important political purposes effectively reduced to the power of middle-range states. The effective equality of states apparently emerges from the very condition of their gross inequality. We read, for example, that "the very change in the nature of the mobilizable potential has made its actual use in emergencies by its unhappy owners quite difficult and self-defeating. As a result, nations endowed with infinitely less can behave in a whole range of issues as if the difference in power did not matter." The conclusion is driven home—or, rather, error is compounded—by the argument that the United States thinks in "cataclysmic terms," lives in dread of all-out war, and bases its military calculations on the forces needed for the ultimate but unlikely crisis rather than on what might be needed in the less spectacular cases that are in fact more likely to occur.[10]

Absolute power equals absolute impotence, at least at the highest levels of force represented by the American and Soviet nuclear armories. At lesser levels of violence many states can compete as though they were substantially equal. The best weapons of the United States and the Soviet Union are useless, and the distinctive advantage of those two states is thus negated. But what about American or Soviet nuclear weapons used against minor nuclear states or against those who are entirely without nuclear weapons? Here again, it is claimed, the "best" weapon of the most powerful states turns out to be the least usable. The nation that is equipped to "retaliate massively" is not likely to find the occasion to use its capability. If amputation of an arm were the only remedy available for an infected finger, one would be tempted to hope for the best and leave the ailment untreated. The state that can move effectively only by committing the full power of its military arsenal is likely to forget the threats it has made and acquiesce in a situation formerly described as intolerable. Instruments that cannot be used to deal with small cases—those that are moderately dangerous and damaging—remain idle until the big case arises. But then the use of major force to defend a vital interest would run the grave risk of retaliation. Under such circumstances, the powerful are frustrated by their very strength; and although the weak do not thereby become strong, they are, it is said, nevertheless able to behave as though they were.

Such arguments are often made and have to be taken seriously. In an obvious sense, part of the contention is valid. When great powers are in a stalemate, lesser states acquire an increased freedom of movement. That this phenomenon is now noticeable tells us nothing new about the strength of the weak or the weakness of the strong. Weak states have often found opportunities for maneuver in the interstices of a balance of power. This is, however, only part of the story. To maintain both the balance and its byproduct requires the continuing efforts of America and Russia. Their instincts for self-preservation call forth such efforts: The objective of both states must be to perpetuate an international stalemate as a minimum basis for the security of each of them—even if this should mean that the two big states do the work while the small ones have the fun. The margins within which the relative strengths of America and Russia may vary without destroying the stalemate are made wide by the existence of second-strike retaliatory forces, but permissible variation is not without limit. In the years of the supposed missile gap in America's disfavor, Khrushchev became unpleasantly frisky, especially over Berlin and Cuba. The usefulness of maintaining American nuclear strength was demonstrated by the unfortunate consequences of its apparent diminution.

Strategic nuclear weapons deter strategic nuclear weapons (though they may also do more than that). Where each state must tend to its own security as best it can, the means adopted by one state must be geared to the efforts of others. The cost of the American nuclear establishment, maintained in peaceful readiness, is functionally comparable to the costs incurred by a government in order to maintain domestic order and provide internal security. Such expenditure is not productive in the sense that spending to build roads is, but it is not unproductive either. Its utility is obvious, and should anyone successfully argue otherwise, the consequences of accepting his argument would quickly demonstrate its falsity. Force is least visible where power is most fully and most adequately present.[11] The better ordered a society and the more competent and respected its government, the less force its policemen are required to employ. Less shooting occurs in present-day Sandusky than did on the western frontier. Similarly in international relations, states supreme in their power have to use force less often. "Non-recourse to force"—as both Eisenhower and Khrushchev seem to have realized—is the doctrine of powerful states. Powerful states need to use force less often than their weaker neighbors because the strong can more often protect their interests or work their wills in other ways—by persuasion and cajolery, by economic bargaining and bribery, by the extension of aid, or finally by posing deterrent threats. Since states with large nuclear armories do not actually "use" them, force is said to be discounted. Such reasoning is fallacious. Possession of power should not be identified with the use of force, and the usefulness of force should not be confused with its usability. To introduce such confusions into the analysis of power is comparable to saying that the police force that seldom if ever employs violence is weak or that a police force is strong only when policemen are swinging their clubs. To vary the image, it is comparable to saying that a man with large assets is not rich if he spends little money or that a man is rich only if he spends a lot of it.

But the argument, which we should not lose sight of, is that just as the miser's money may grossly depreciate in value over the years, so the great powers' military strength has lost much of its usability. If military force is like currency that cannot be spent or money that has lost much of its worth, then is not forbearance in its use merely a way of disguising its depreciated value? Conrad von Hötzendorf, Austrian Chief of Staff prior to the First World War, looked upon military power as though it were a capital sum, useless unless invested. In his view, the investment of military force was ultimately its commitment to battle.[12] It may be permissible to reason in this way, but it makes the result of the reasoning a foregone conclusion. As Robert W. Tucker has noted, those who argue that force has lost its utility do so "in terms of its virtually uncontrolled use." But, he adds, "alter the assumption on which the argument proceeds—consider the functions served by military power so long as it is not overtly employed or employed only with restraint—and precisely the opposite conclusion may be drawn."[13]

In the reasoning of Conrad, military force is most useful at the moment of its employment in war. Depending on a country's situation, it may make much better sense to say that military force is most useful when it deters an attack, that is, when it need not be used in battle at all. When the strongest state militarily is also a status-quo power, nonuse of force is a sign of its strength. Force is most useful, or best serves the interests of such a state, when it need not be used in the actual conduct of warfare. Again, the reasoning is old-fashioned. Throughout a century that ended in 1914, the British navy was powerful enough to scare off all comers, while Britain carried out occasional imperial ventures in odd parts of the world. Only as Britain's power weakened did her military forces have to be used to fight a full-scale war. By being used, her military power had surely become less useful.

Force is cheap, especially for a status-quo power, if its very existence works against its use. What does it mean then to say that the cost of using force has increased while its utility has lessened? It is highly important, indeed useful, to think in "cataclysmic terms," to live in dread of all-out war, and to base military calculations on the forces needed for the ultimate but unlikely crisis. That the United States does so, and that the Soviet Union apparently does too, makes the cataclysm less likely to occur. But not only that. Nuclear weapons deter nuclear weapons; they also serve as a means of limiting escalation. The temptation of one country to employ larger and larger amounts of force is lessened if its opponent has the ability to raise the ante. Conventional force may be used more hesitantly than it would be in the absence of nuclear weapons because it cannot be assumed that escalation will be perfectly regulated. But force can be used with less hesitation by those states able to parry, to thrust, and to threaten at varied levels of military endeavor.

Where power is seen to be balanced, whether or not the balance is nuclear, it may seem that the resultant of opposing forces is zero. But this is misleading. The vectors of national force do not meet at a point, if only because the power of a state does not resolve into a single vector. Military force is divisible, especially for the state that can afford a lot of it. In a nuclear world, contrary to some assertions, the dialectic of inequality does not produce the effective equality of strong and weak states. Lesser states that decide to establish a nuclear arsenal by slighting their conventional forces render themselves unable to meet any threat to themselves other than the ultimate one (and that doubtfully). By way of contrast, the military doctrine of the United States, to which the organization of her forces corresponds, is one of flexible response. Great powers are strong not simply because they have nuclear weapons but also because their immense resources enable them to generate and maintain power of all types, military and other, at different technological levels.

Just as the state that refrains from applying force is said to betray its weakness, so the state that has trouble in exercising control is said to display the defectiveness of its power. In such a conclusion, the elementary error of identifying power with control is evident. Absence of control or failure to press hard to achieve it may indicate either that the would-be controller noticed that, try as he might, he would have insufficient force or inappropriate types of force at his command; or it may indicate that he chose to make less than a maximum effort because imposition of control was not regarded as very important. One student of international relations has remarked that "though the weapons of mass destruction grow more and more ferociously efficient, the revolutionary guerrilla armed with nothing more advanced than an old rifle and a nineteenth-century political doctrine has proved the most effective means yet devised for altering the world power-balance."[14] But the revolutionary guerrilla wins civil wars, not international ones, and no civil war can change the balance of power in the world unless it takes place in the United States or the Soviet Union. Enough of them have occurred since the Second World War to make the truth of this statement clear without need for further analysis. Even in China, the most populous of states, a civil war that led to a change of allegiance in the Cold War did not seriously tilt the world balance.

Two states that enjoy wide margins of power over other states need worry little about changes that occur among the latter. Failure to act may then not betray the frustrations of impotence; instead it may demonstrate the serenity of power. The United States, having chosen to intervene in Vietnam, has limited the use of its military force. Because no realignment of national power in Vietnam could in itself affect the balance of power between the United States and the Soviet Union—or even noticeably alter the imbalance of power between the United States and China—the United States need not have intervened at all. Whether or not it could have safely "passed" in

Southeast Asia, the American government chose not to do so; nor have its costly, long-sustained efforts brought success. If military power can be equated with control, then the United States has indeed demonstrated its weakness. The case is instructive. The People's Republic of China has not moved militarily against any country of Southeast Asia. The United States could successfully counter such a move, one would expect, by opposing military force with military force. What has worried some people and led others to sharpen their statements about the weakness of the powerful is that the United States, hard though it has tried, has been unable to put down insurrection and halt the possible spread of Communist ideology.

Here again old truths need to be brought into focus. As David Hume long ago noted, "force is always on the side of the governed."[15] The governors, being few in number, depend for the exercise of their rule upon the more or less willing assent of their subjects. If sullen disregard is the response to every command, no government can rule. And if a country, because of internal disorder and lack of coherence, is unable to rule itself, no body of foreigners, whatever the military force at its command, can reasonably hope to do so. If Communism is the threat to Southeast Asia, then military forces are not the right means for countering it. If insurrection is the problem, then it can hardly be hoped that an alien army will be able to pacify a country that is unable to govern itself. Foreign troops, though not irrelevant to such problems, can only be of indirect help. Military force, used internationally, is a means of establishing control over a territory, not of exercising control within it. The threat of a nation to use military force, whether nuclear or conventional, is preeminently a means of affecting another state's external behavior, of dissuading a state from launching a career of aggression and of meeting the aggression if dissuasion should fail.

Dissuasion or deterrence is easier to accomplish than "compellence," to use an apt term invented by Thomas C. Schelling.[16] Compellence is more difficult to achieve than deterrence, and its contrivance is a more intricate affair. In Vietnam, the United States faces not merely the task of compelling a particular action but of promoting an effective political order. Those who argue from such a case that force has depreciated in value fail in their analyses to apply their own historical and political knowledge. The master builders of imperial rule, such men as Bugeaud, Galliéni, and Lyautey, played both political and military roles. In like fashion, successful counterrevolutionary efforts have been directed by such men as Templer and Magsaysay, who combined military resources with political instruments.[17] Military forces, whether domestic or foreign, are insufficient for the task of pacification, the more so if a country is rent by faction and if its people are politically engaged and active. To say that militarily strong states are feeble because they cannot easily bring order to minor states is like saying that a pneumatic hammer is weak because it is not suitable for drilling decayed teeth. It is to confuse the purpose of instruments and to confound the means of external power with the agencies of internal governance. Inability to exercise *political* control over others does not indicate *military* weakness. Strong states cannot do everything with their military forces, as Napoleon acutely realized; but they are able to do things that militarily weak states cannot do. The People's Republic of China can no more solve the problems of governance in some Latin American country than the United States can in Southeast Asia. But the United States can intervene with great military force in far quarters of the world while wielding an effective deterrent against escalation. Such action exceeds the capabilities of all but the strongest of states.

Differences in strength do matter, though not for every conceivable purpose. To deduce the weakness of the powerful from this qualifying clause is a misleading use of words. One sees in such a case as Vietnam not the *weakness* of great military power in a nuclear world but instead a clear illustration of the *limits* of military force in the world of the present as always.

III

Only a sketch, intended to be suggestive, can here be offered of the connections between the present structure of the global balance of power, the relations of states, and the use of force internationally.

Unbalanced power is a danger to weak states. It may also be a danger to strong ones. An imbalance of power, by feeding the ambition of some states to extend their control, may tempt them to dangerously adventurous activity. Safety for all states, one may then conclude, depends upon the maintenance of a balance among them. Ideally, in this view, the rough equality of states gives each of them the ability to fend for itself. Equality may then also be viewed as a morally desirable condition. Each of the states within the arena of balance will have at least a modest ability to maintain its integrity. At the same time, inequality violates one's sense of justice and leads to national resentments that are in many ways troublesome. Because inequality is inherent in the state system, however, it cannot be removed. At the pinnacle of power, only a few states coexist as approximate equals; in relation to them, other states are of lesser moment. The bothersome qualities of this inevitable inequality of states should not cause one to overlook its virtues. In an economy, in a polity, or in the world at large, extreme equality is associated with instability. To draw another domestic analogy: Where individualism is extreme, where society is atomistic, and where secondary organizations are lacking, government tends either to break down into anarchy or to become highly centralized and despotic. Under conditions of extreme equality, the prospect of oscillation between those two poles was well described by de Tocqueville; it was illustrated by Hobbes; and its avoidance was earnestly sought by the authors of the *Federalist Papers*. In a collection of equals, any impulse ripples through the whole society. Lack of secondary groups with some cohesion and continuity of commitment, for example, turns elections into auctions with each party in its promises tempted to bid up the others. The presence of social and economic groups, which inevitably will not all be equal, makes for less volatility in society.

Such durable propositions of political theory are lost sight of in the argument, frequently made, that the larger the number of consequential states the more stable the structure of world politics will be.[18] Carried to its logical conclusion, the argument must mean that perfect stability would prevail in a world in which many states exist, all of them approximate equals in power.

The analysis of the present essay leads to a different conclusion. The inequality of states, though not a guarantee of international stability, at least makes stability possible. Within the structure of world politics, the relations of states will be as variable and complex as the movements and patterns of bits of glass within a kaleidoscope. It is not very interesting to ask whether destabilizing events will occur and disruptive relations will form, because the answer must always be yes. More interesting are such questions as these: What is the likely durability of a given political structure, whether international or domestic? How does it affect the relations of states, or of groups and individuals? How do the relations of constituent units and changes within them in turn affect the political structure? Within a state, people use more violence than do governments. In the United States in 1965, 9,814 people were murdered, but only seven were executed.[19] Thus one says (with some exaggeration, since fathers still spank their children) that the state enjoys a monopoly of *legitimate* violence. Too much violence among individuals will jeopardize the political structure. In international relations it is difficult to say that any particular use of violence is illegitimate, but some states have the ability to wield more of it. Because they do, they are able both to moderate others' use of violence and to absorb possibly destabilizing changes that emanate from uses of violence that they do not or cannot control. In the spring of 1966, Secretary McNamara remarked that in the preceding eight years there had been "no less than 164 internationally significant outbreaks of violence. . . ."[20] Of course, not only violence is at issue. To put the point in more general terms, strong structures are able to moderate and absorb destabilizing changes; weak structures succumb to them.

No political structure, whether domestic or international, can guarantee stability. The question that one must ask is not whether a given distribution of power is stable but how stable different distributions of power are likely to be. For a number of reasons, the bipolar world of the past two decades has been highly stable.[21] The two leading states have a common interest in stability: they would at least like to maintain their positions. In one respect, bipolarity is expressed as the reciprocal control of the two strongest states by each other out of their mutual antagonism. What is unpredictable in such a two-party competition is whether one party will try to eliminate the other. Nuclear forces of second-strike capacity induce an added caution. Here again force is useful, and its usefulness is reinforced in proportion as its use is forestalled.

Fear of major war induces caution all around; the Soviet Union and the United States wield the means of inducing that caution.

The constraints of duopolistic competition press in one direction: duopolists eye each other warily, and each is very sensitive to the gains of the other. Working in the opposite direction, however, is the existence of the immense difference in power between the two superpowers and the states of middle or lesser rank. This condition of inequality makes it unlikely that any shifts in the alignment of states would very much help or hurt either of the two leading powers. If few changes can damage the vital interests of either of them, then both can be moderate in their responses. Not being dependent upon allies, the United States and the Soviet Union are free to design strategies in accord with their interests. Since the power actually and potentially at the disposal of each of them far exceeds that of their closest competitors, they are able to control in some measure the possibly destabilizing acts of third parties or to absorb their effects. The Americans and Russians, for example, can acquire the means of defending themselves against the nuclear assaults that the Chinese and French may be able to launch by the mid-1970s. Antiballistic missile systems, useful against missiles launched in small number, are themselves anti-proliferation devices. With considerable expectation of success, states with vast economic, scientific, and technological resources can hope to counter the armaments and actions of others and to reduce their destabilizing effects.[22] The extent of the difference in national capabilities makes the bipolar structure resilient. Defection of allies and national shifts of allegiance do not decisively alter the structure. Because they do not, recalcitrant allies may be treated with indifference; they may even be effectively disciplined. Pressure can be applied to moderate the behavior of third states or to check and contain their activities. The Suez venture of Britain and France was stopped by American financial pressure. Chiang Kai-shek has been kept on a leash by denying him the means of invasion. The prospective loss of foreign aid helped to halt warfare between Pakistan and India, as did the Soviet Union's persuasion. In such ways, the wielding of great power can be useful.

The above examples illustrate hierarchical control operating in a way that often goes unnoticed because the means by which control is exercised are not institutionalized. What management there now is in international relations must be provided, singly and occasionally together, by the duopolists at the top. In certain ways, some of them suggested above, the inequality of states in a bipolar world enables the two most powerful states to develop a rich variety of controls and to follow flexible strategies in using them.

A good many statements about the obsolescence of force, the instability of international politics, and the disappearance of the bipolar order are made because no distinction has been clearly and consistently drawn between international structure, on the one hand, and the relations of states on the other. For more than two decades, power has been narrowly concentrated; and force has been used, not orgiastically as in the world wars of this century, but in a controlled way and for conscious political purposes. Power may be present when force is not used, but force is also used openly. A catalogue of examples would be both complex and lengthy. It would contain such items, on the American side of the ledger, as the garrisoning of Berlin, its supply by airlift during the blockade, the stationing of troops in Europe, the establishment of bases in Japan and elsewhere, the waging of war in Korea and Vietnam, and the "quarantine" of Cuba. Seldom if ever has force been more variously, more persistently, and more widely applied; and seldom has it been more consciously used as an instrument of national policy. Since the war we have seen, not the cancellation of force by nuclear stalemate, but instead the political organization and pervasion of power; not the end of balance of power owing to a reduction in the number of major states, but instead the formation and perpetuation of a balance *à deux.*

Notes

1 Martin Wight, "The Balance of Power," in *Diplomatic Investigations: Essays in the Theory of International Politics,* ed. by Herbert Butterfield and Martin Wight (Cambridge: Harvard University Press, 1966), p. 151.
2 Quoted in Chalmers Johnson, *Revolutionary Change* (Boston: Little, Brown, 1966), p. 13.
3 I do not mean to imply that this exhausts the purposes of power. In this essay, however, I cannot analyze other aspects of power either in themselves or in relation to the power to do harm.
4 The point has been made most extensively by Klaus Knorr and most insistently by Stanley Hoffmann. See Knorr, *On the Uses of Military Power in the Nuclear Age* (Princeton: Princeton University Press, 1966). See also Hoffmann, "Obstinate or Obsolete? The Fate of the Nation-State and the Case of Western Europe," *Daedalus,* Vol. XCV (Summer 1965), especially pp. 897, 907; "Europe's Identity Crisis: Between the Past and America," *Daedalus,* Vol. XCIII (Fall 1964), especially pp. 1287–88; "Nuclear Proliferation and World Politics," in *A World of Nuclear Powers?,* ed. by Alastair Buchan (Englewood Cliffs, NJ: Prentice-Hall, 1966); and two essays in *The State of War* (New York: Praeger, 1965), "Roulette in the Cellar: Notes on Risk in International Relations," especially pp. 140–147, and "Terror in Theory and Practice," especially pp. 233–251.
5 See, for example, Inis L. Claude, Jr., *Power and International Relations* (New York: Random House, 1962), p. 90; and Morton A. Kaplan, *System and Process in International Politics* (New York: John Wiley & Sons, 1957), p. 22.
6 See "The Text of Address by McNamara to American Society of Newspaper Editors," *The New York Times,* May 19, 1966, p. 11.
7 John Herz, *International Politics in the Atomic Age* (New York: Columbia University Press, 1959), pp. 22, 169.
8 Edward Hallett Carr, *The Twenty Years' Crisis, 1919–1939,* 2nd ed. (New York: Harper & Row, 1964), p. 140.
9 Knorr, *On the Uses of Military Power,* p. 87.
10 Hoffmann, "Europe's Identity Crisis," pp. 1279, 1287–1288.
11 Cf. Carr, *The Twenty Years' Crisis,* pp. 103, 129–132.
12 "The sums spent for the war power is money wasted," he maintained, "if the

war power remains unused for obtaining political advantages. In some cases the mere threat will suffice and the war power thus becomes useful, but others can be obtained only through the warlike use of the war power itself, that is, by war undertaken in time; if this moment is missed, the capital is lost. In this sense, war becomes a great financial enterprise of the State." Quoted in Alfred Vagts, *Defense and Diplomacy: The Soldier and the Conduct of Foreign Relations* (New York: King's Crown Press, 1956), p. 361.

13 Robert W. Tucker, "Peace and War," *World Politics*, Vol. XVII (Jan. 1965), p. 324 fn. For a comprehensive and profound examination of the use of force internationally, see Robert Osgood and Robert Tucker, *Force, Order, and Justice.*

14 Coral Bell, "Non-Alignment and the Power Balance," *Survival*, Vol. V (Nov.–Dec. 1963), p. 255.

15 "The soldan of Egypt or the emperor of Rome," he went on to say, "might drive his harmless subjects like brute beasts against their sentiments and inclination. But he must, at least, have led his *mamalukes* or *praetorian bands*, like men, by their opinion." "Of the First Principles of Government," in *Hume's Moral and Political Philosophy*, ed. by Henry D. Aiken (New York: Hafner, 1948), p. 307.

16 Thomas C. Schelling, *Arms and Influence* (New Haven: Yale University Press, 1966), pp. 70–71.

17 The point is well made by Samuel P. Huntington, "Patterns of Violence in World Politics," in *Changing Patterns of Military Politics*, ed. by Samuel P. Huntington (New York: The Free Press of Glencoe, 1962), p. 28.

18 By "structure" I mean the pattern according to which power is distributed; by "stability," the perpetuation of that structure without the occurrence of grossly destructive violence.

19 U.S. Bureau of the Census, *Statistical Abstract of the United States: 1966* (Washington, DC: Government Printing Office, 1966), p. 165.

20 *The New York Times*, May 19, 1966, p. 11.

21 For further examination of the proposition, see Kenneth N. Waltz, "The Stability of a Bipolar World," *Daedalus*, Vol. XCIII (Summer 1964), pp. 881–909. On the possibility of exercising control, see Waltz, "Contention and Management in International Relations," *World Politics*, Vol. XVII (July 1065), pp. 720–744.

22 On the limitations of a small nuclear force, see Waltz, *Foreign Policy and Democratic Politics* (Boston: Little, Brown, 1967), pp. 145–148.

11

THE MYTH OF NATIONAL
INTERDEPENDENCE*

"Peace is indivisible," a slogan of the 1930s, suggests that a small war anywhere means war everywhere unless the small war can somehow be stopped. The domino theory is an old one. Its economic equivalent is found in statements, frequently made, that America cannot exist as an island of affluence in a sea of impoverished nations. From such statements the mistaken conclusion is often drawn that a growing closeness of interdependence would improve the chances of peace.

But close interdependence means closeness of contact and raises the prospect of at least occasional conflict. The fiercest civil wars and the bloodiest international ones have been fought within arenas populated by highly similar people whose affairs had become quite closely knit together. It is hard to get a war going unless the potential participants are somehow closely linked. Interdependent states whose relations remain unregulated must experience conflict and will occasionally fall into violence. If regulation is hard to come by, as it is in the relations of states, then it would seem to follow that a lessening of interdependence is desirable.

Focusing on the international corporation, however, has led many economists to believe that international interdependence is high and is rapidly becoming higher. The thought is forcefully put by the various people who claim that the national state has become an obsolete economic unit. If the interdependence of nations is high and becoming higher, we must expect international difficulties to multiply. I am inclined to be sanguine because I believe that interdependence is low and, if anything, is on the decrease. Those who come to the opposite conclusion apparently do so for two reasons. What interdependence entails is often incorrectly understood. Because this is so, economic developments are looked at aside from their proper context.

The meaning of interdependence

A comparison of the conditions of internal and external interdependence will make it clear that in international relations interdependence is always a marginal affair. The political elements of a state are formally differentiated according to the degrees of their authority, and their distinct functions are specified. Specification of roles and differentiation of functions characterize any state, the more fully so as the state is more highly developed. The parts of a highly developed polity are closely interdependent. Some parts depend on others for services and supplies that they cannot easily, if at all, provide for themselves. Thus Washington depends upon Kansas for its beef and its wheat, and Kansas depends on Washington for protection and regulation. In saying that in such situations interdependence is close, one need not maintain that the one part could not learn to live without the other. One need only say that the cost of breaking the interdependent relation would be high. Where the political and economic division of labor is elaborately developed, high inequality may be found; and yet a mutuality of interest among unequals may be said to prevail.[1]

The domestic order is composed of heterogeneous elements; the international order is composed of homogeneous units. Each state regulates its own affairs and supplies largely out of its own resources the food, clothing, housing, transportation, and amenities consumed and used by its citizens. The international order is characterized by the coaction of like units. Since the functions of all states are highly similar, differentiation among them is principally according to their varied capabilities.

Because the units that populate the international arena are the same in type, interdependence among them is low even if those units are of approximately equal size. Interdependence is further reduced by the immense disparity in the capabilities of states. This last point can be stated as an iron law: high inequality among like units *is* low interdependence.

How interdependent are these not very interdependent states, and what difference does the answer to this question make? In the European-centered great-power politics of the three centuries that ended with World War II, five or more great powers sought to coexist peacefully and at times contended for mastery. Since World War II, only two states have perched at the pinnacle of power. It follows from the law just stated that the interdependence of states is less now than it was earlier. But this deduction will not be accepted unless the force and meaning of the law are made clear. The validity of the proposition can be established by looking at international trade and investment, not simply at a moment in time and as absolute amounts, but by viewing them in relation to the volume of internal business and in comparison with the patterns of previous periods.[2]

Trade: changes in national involvement

Even if the interdependence of nations is in general low, we nevertheless want to know whether it is lower or higher now than in earlier times. In the late nineteenth and early twentieth centuries, the external sector loomed large. Not only was the level of external transactions high in comparison with internal production, but also the internal order was characterized by a low level of governmental activity. Even if the interdependence of nations has increased in the meantime, the progress of internal integration and the increased intervention of governments in their domestic economies means that for most states the internal sector now looms larger than it once did. But it is not even clear that the interdependence of states has increased overall.

Prior to World War I, most of the great powers of the world were also great traders; economically they were closely tied together. In the years preceding World War I, for example, Germany was Britain's second-best customer, both as a source of imports and as a market for exports. Measured in terms of their own economies, the two greatest powers in the world today trade little with each other or with the rest of the world.[3] Most of this change can be accounted for by the fact that the present great powers of the world are geographically much larger than the old ones.[4] Britain, France, Italy, and Japan, it should be noticed, also trade a smaller proportion of their national product now than they once did.[5]

From the recent growth of world trade, however, one might be tempted to conclude that the relative decreases in trade are only temporary and that the interdependence of nations is now tending toward the old level. In the years from 1953 to 1965, both trade in manufactured goods and trade in primary products grew more rapidly than world output in each of the two categories.[6] In the economic data for the first half of this century, however, there is a strong component of war and depression. To a considerable extent we are dealing, in the past two decades, with recovery rates; and the recovery is rooted in the economic resurgence of Western Europe and Japan. In the years from 1926 to 1930 world manufactures grew more rapidly than trade in manufactured goods—about 40% as compared to less than 15%. This was in part because of the faster economic growth of the United States, a relatively self-sufficient country, as compared to the economic growth of West European countries, which are more dependent on imports. Beginning in the 1950s, the rapid growth of Japan and of West European countries has given a corresponding boost to world trade.[7]

As well as considering the decline of trade in relation to GNP and the recent growth of world trade overall, we should ask whether changes in the composition and direction of trade have affected the extent of interdependence. In advanced industrial countries a larger proportion of the national product is now composed of products whose raw-material content is low. This is true not only because the service sector has grown but also because more value is added to raw materials as they are transformed into technologically more complicated goods. The GNP's of advanced countries have thus grown faster than their demand for primary products.[8] In 1953, trade among developed countries accounted for 37.2% of world trade; 12 years later the amount had increased to 46.5%. In 1953, the trade of less-developed with developed countries accounted for 19.3% of world trade; 12 years later the amount had decreased to 14%.[9] The exchange of finished goods for primary products has grown less rapidly than trade in finished goods among industrial countries. A lesser portion of trade now is done out of near necessity, and more of it is merely for profit. The present relation of less-developed to developed countries is less close than was the old imperial tie.

Shifts in the composition of trade, with primary products in decline relative to manufactured goods, change the political as well as the economic significance of trade. Before World War I, as Richard Cooper points out, large differences in comparative costs meant that "trade was socially very profitable" but "less sensitive to small changes in costs, prices, and quality."[10] I would add that trade then, as well as being socially very profitable, was politically very significant. States are mutually dependent if they rely on each other for goods and services that cannot easily be produced at home. That kind of interdependence is difficult (costly) to break. The other kind of interdependence —sensitivity of response to variations in factor prices—may be economically more interesting; it is also politically less important.

Even though trade in relation to production and the proportionate amount of raw materials imported have declined, one might nevertheless imagine a country being heavily dependent on a small quantity of imports. But is this really the case? In the decades during which congressional renewal of the Reciprocal Trade Act was recurrently at issue, it was customary for the friends of free trade to emphasize the extent of American dependence on imported minerals and ores. The Report of the Commission headed by Clarence B. Randall, for example, stated that: "we depend on foreign sources today for over 30 percent of our requirements of copper, lead, and zinc; over 50 percent of our requirements of tungsten, bauxite, and antimony; over 75 percent of our requirements of chrome and manganese; practically all of our nickel requirements; and all our requirements of tin, natural rubber, and jute."[11] Bad economics may make good political strategy; we should, however, notice that the economic case was distorted.

The quantity of imports is not just a function of scarcity; it is also a matter of price. Reliance on imports at a particular time does not necessarily represent dependence, as the following points make clear:

1. The nearness of a country's approach to autarky cannot be measured simply by amounts imported. It is not possession but rather reliability of access that counts. Whether Lorraine was part of France or of Germany, those countries were less sure of the availability of its iron than the United States is of bauxite and nickel from Latin America and Canada.[12]

2. Not only the location of suppliers but also their numbers are important. Wayward political movements or revolutions or wars elsewhere in the world may well shut off some of a country's supplies. The larger a country's trade, in absolute terms, the larger the number of its suppliers is likely to be. The United States, as the world's largest trader, enjoys a multiplicity of sources

of supply. Here as in other matters, there is safety in numbers. Worries are further reduced by remembering that the market for primary products is one that favors the buyer. Manganese, for example, is often cited as an instance of America's dependence on imports; but those imports come from a large number of eager suppliers, Brazil and India among them.[13]

3. Suppose, however, that war engulfed much of the globe and disrupted many or most of the channels of trade. This possibility was a more active worry in the late 1940s and early 1950s than it has been in the 1960s, and the response to it was more than sufficiently effective. In the considerable efforts made to stockpile strategic materials, the problem was not to acquire and store enough of them but rather to prevent domestic producers from unloading unduly large quantities upon the American government. Glenn Snyder, for example, has pointed out that as of June 1964, "about 60 per cent of the stockpile was surplus and subject to disposal . . . more than 80 per cent of the total excess was concentrated in 12 materials—aluminum, chromite, cobalt, copper, lead, manganese, molybdenum, nickel, rubber, tin, tungsten, and zinc."[14] Often domestic interests resisted the government's efforts to dispose of the surplus for fear of reducing prices.

4. The resiliency of the economy is increased, and dependence on imports is lessened, by improved methods for the use and recovery of materials. The electroplating process in tin-plating, introduced in 1949, resulted in a steady drop in imports. In recent years, the secondary recovery of antimony has yielded a larger supply than imports of the metal itself.[15] The ability to make do in the face of adversity is one of the most impressive qualities of large and advanced economies. The synthetic production of rubber provides the most impressive example. The need was not recognized until the fall of Singapore in 1942. The United States was able to develop an entirely new large-scale industry while fighting a global war on two fronts. The worry of primary producers that synthetics will further shrink their markets is more sensible than American worries about access to raw materials.

Large and economically well-developed countries, the very ones that are crucial in world politics, can more quickly move toward an autarkic condition. I am not suggesting that we should forgo imports and rely on our own resources, but merely that we can move in that direction at relatively low cost if we have to. The low cost of disentanglement is a measure of low dependence.

If not dependent on particular items of import, may the economy nevertheless be sensitive to adverse economic movements that originate outside of the national arena? Here also big countries are at an immense advantage. I shall give only a few illustrations of this. If a country exports a large portion of its manufactured output, as advanced countries smaller than the United States and the Soviet Union tend to do, then changes in trade will have major effects on that country's economic growth.[16] Of more relevance to the less-developed countries is the tendency for foreign trade to be most important where incomes are lowest and for the fluctuations in the trade of those countries to be unusually large.[17] Countries of large GNP are doubly protected from such effects. The circle of their customers and suppliers is wider, thus increasing the chances that some external fluctuations will balance off others. And since their trade is relatively small, even sharply adverse foreign developments do not greatly affect the domestic economy. From 1950 to 1956, for example, the year-to-year fluctuation in national income derived from changes in the terms of trade was 2.8% for less-developed countries and 1.5% for developed countries. For the United States, it was only 0.2%.[18]

A small portion of America's trade is a big portion of the trade of many another country. In 1966, for example, 42.5% of Peru's total exports and 18.2% of India's were sent to the United States; but the exports of each of those countries amounted to only 1.2% of total United States imports. The asymmetrical relation also holds for industrial countries. Japan, the United Kingdom, and France sent 30.7%, 12.3%, and 6.0%, respectively, of their total exports to the United States. The respective shares of U.S. imports that these totals represent were 11.8%, 6.8%, and 2.5%.[19] Smaller countries are strongly constrained to make domestic economic decisions with an eye on their external accounts. The United States is much less constrained to do so, and yet our domestic economic decisions will affect other states more than theirs will affect us. The political importance of this condition arises from the asymmetry of the relation.[20] Decisions by the United States, whether or not intended to harm or to bring pressure against another state, can have grave effects.

What looks to some like a thickening web of economic interdependence obscures relations that are best described as a compound of independence and dependence, and that is quite a different thing. But this point can be developed better if we add consideration of foreign investment to the discussion of international trade.

Investment: national and corporate stakes

Statements about whether interdependence is higher or lower now than it used to be easily obscure the fact that recent economic changes within and among nations and the political consequences attendant upon them are changes of kind rather than merely of degree. When the great powers of the world were small in geographic compass, they naturally did a higher proportion of their business abroad. The narrow concentration of power in the present and the fact that the United States and the Soviet Union are little dependent on the rest of the world produce a very different international situation. Since at the same time the size of America's foreign business in terms of world totals is large, its impact on others is considerable.

It may be, however, that the enterprise of international corporations and the recent increase of foreign investments modify these trends and move the world back toward a closer integration. But is this really happening?

When Britain was the world's leading state economically, the portion of her wealth invested abroad far exceeded the portion that now represents America's stake in the world. In 1910, the value of total British investment abroad was 1½ times larger than its national income. In 1966, total American foreign investments, both official and private, were only 18% as large as its national income. In 1910, Britain's return on investment abroad amounted to 8% of national income; in 1966, the comparable figure for the United States was only 1%.[21]

Although, in comparison, the stock of American investment is not high, the rate of its recent growth is impressive. Britain's foreign investment had tripled in the 30 years prior to 1910. From 1958 to 1966, American investment abroad grew at an average rate of 8% yearly, which in 18 years would increase the total fourfold. One should, however, be wary of assuming that such a high rate will continue long enough to raise American investments to the point where they become a much higher percentage of GNP. One may expect continued growth although I rather doubt that it will be as rapid. Not just American technology but also skills in management and marketing enabled American subsidiaries operating in the less-advanced and less-well-organized European environment to earn a higher return on capital invested in Europe than on capital invested at home. As with the opening of mines in Latin America or the drilling of oil wells in the Middle East, businessmen properly and usefully responded to the possibility of increased profits. As we have known since Adam Smith and Ricardo, the effect of everyone's seeking to increase his profits is to drive the profit rate downward. Something of the same sort is happening here. American capital in Europe earned 18% yearly in 1959 as compared to 13% at home. In 1965 return abroad and at home stood at 13% and 15%, respectively.[22] On economic grounds, one would expect a leveling off.

On political grounds, one might entertain the same expectation. Precisely because the operations of American corporations abroad have concentrated in those sectors of the economy that are thought by the host countries to be most significant for economic growth and for their military establishments, political resistance to the encroachment of American firms has occurred and will continue to do so.

But such resistance has been of limited effect. Just as political fragmentation invites imperial control, so low economic capability easily leads to dependence upon another state of higher economic capability. The higher the costs of disentanglement, the higher the degree of dependence; the lagging state will only get weaker if foreign capital and technology are excluded.

The American computer industry can get along without the assistance of French companies, but Machines Bull felt it could not survive without American capital and technology. In 1962, the French government resisted the purchase by General Electric of 20% of Bull's shares. Unable to find another French or European partner, the French government was constrained in 1964 to accept a 50–50 arrangement with General Electric. By the middle 1960s

General Electric's share in the company had grown to approximately two-thirds.[23] General Electric, Control Data, and other American firms may require foreign affiliations in order to compete with IBM. There may be genuine interdependence at the level of the firm. It is a mistake, however, to identify interdependence at that level with the interdependence of states. The attempts of European firms to band together are impeded by the greater attraction of establishing connections with American firms, for they are the ones with the most advanced technology, the most plentiful capital, and the most impressive managerial abilities. When German aviation companies sought ties with firms in other countries, they did not go to Britain or France. Larger benefits were to be gained by association with American companies.

Nor is it easy for foreign firms to catch up. The size of the home market enables American firms to operate on a large scale and to generate resources that can be used abroad to compete with or even to overwhelm native industries. General Motors could have given away every Opel it produced in 1965 and still have made $1 billion in profit.[24] As long as IBM spends yearly on research and development an amount equal to the gross sales of Britain's largest computer company, the American industry is likely to retain its lead. Two-thirds of the world's and two-thirds of Europe's markets in computers have been captured by IBM.[25] The size of its operations enables the company to spend money on a governmental scale. The $5 billion that IBM committed to the development of its model 360 computer was equal to the amount that France planned to spend on her nuclear force in the years from 1965 to 1970.[26]

The disadvantages of foreign firms are paralleled by the difficulties their governments face. In 1962, America's gross expenditure on research and development amounted to $17.5 billion; Britain, France, Belgium, Holland, and Germany together spent $4.3 billion. American expenditure amounted to about 3% of GNP or about $100 per capita, and for the European states named, to about 1½% of their GNPs or about $25 per capita.[27]

Under these conditions, national governments are constrained to permit domestic firms to make arrangements with American companies. The smaller states' opportunities to maneuver are further limited by competition among them. If, say, France follows an effective policy of exclusion, American capital and firms, and the technology these firms carry with them, will locate in neighboring countries. Even one who believes that the economies of those countries would become beholden to America cannot help but notice that they would also be enriched and be enabled to compete more effectively in European markets, including the markets of countries that had excluded American firms.

In 1967, the output of American firms operating abroad amounted to some $120 billion. This product represented, in effect, the world's third largest economy, surpassed only by the Unite States and the Soviet Union.[28] In 1965, residents of the United States owned 44% of the capital invested in Canadian manufacturing firms and those firms accounted for 48% of Canada's export of manufactured goods. In the United Kingdom, American subsidiaries accounted for 7½% of the capital, 10% of the sales, and 17% of the export of manufactured goods.[29] In France, American firms "control" only 5% to 7% of the economy, according to Robert Gilpin, but America's influence is wider than the figures suggest because the companies that Americans do control are strategic ones.[30]

Who is able to regulate these vast undertakings? Most Americans who have considered the question conclude that the American government is not able to do so with very much success. Foreigners more often incline to the opposite view. On the basis of their study, the authors of the Canadian report previously cited draw "the general picture . . . of a tight legal and administrative network capable of being turned to any objective in foreign policy or to meet any future stringency, such as a further deterioration of the American balance of payments position."[31] Rules made under the authority of the Export Control Act of 1949 control not only American exports but also those exports of other countries that contain American components and embody American technical data. Under the Trading with the Enemy Act of 1917, the Office of Foreign Assets Control regulates the exports of American subsidiaries abroad whether or not the commodities they produce incorporate American components or technology. Enforcement can be secured by holding the American parent criminally liable for its subsidiaries' activity.[32]

By an executive order issued in January of 1968, President Johnson made previously voluntary guidelines mandatory. The American government can now control the payments of foreign subsidiaries to their American parents and can regulate companies that are incorporated abroad, that operate under foreign law, and that may in part be foreign owned. Further, by requiring the approval of the Secretary of Commerce for private investments abroad, the American government may, if it chooses, control both the amount and the direction of capital flow.[33]

Whatever the extent of American control over various operations, one may nonetheless believe that with well over $100 billion of assets abroad the vulnerability of American interests to punitive regulation by foreign governments, or even to confiscation, must be proportionate to the size of the stake. Just as the sudden severance of its trade would be a hard blow for the United States to absorb, so would the nearly complete loss of its investments abroad. Surely, if all or much of this capital were suddenly wrenched from us, the American economy itself would be seriously damaged. I would not care to deny that. We do have plenty to lose, and we can emphasize the "plenty" or we can emphasize the possibility of its loss. But if we imagine a situation in which American assets in Canada, Latin America, Europe, and the Middle and Far East are simultaneously confiscated, we are imagining a situation comparable in its impact to a global war. Indeed, short of such a catastrophe, it is hard to see why or how all or most foreign governments would suddenly set upon American capital and enterprises.

Partly, as suggested earlier, the question becomes one of who needs whom more. Confiscation would result in the loss of assets and profits of American firms, and for those few of them whose foreign operations are a major part of their business, that could be fatal. It is widely agreed, however, that physical plant and capital investment have not been as important as the managerial and organizational abilities of American firms and their capacity for technological innovation. Foreign economies would lose capabilities that could not easily be reproduced. Partly, also, the diversity of American investment, both in terms of types of enterprise and of their geographic location, itself provides insurance against sudden and sharp reversals. Nations do not easily bring their policies into concert, and that is a comfort for the nation whose operations are global.

Rhetoric and reality

The American rhetoric of interdependence has taken on some of the qualities of an ideology. The word "interdependence" subtly obscures the inequalities of national capability, pleasingly points to a reciprocal dependence, and strongly suggests that all states are playing the same game.

If interdependence is really close, each state is constrained to treat other states' acts as though they were events within its own borders. A mutuality of dependence leads each state to watch others with wariness and suspicion. Near self-sufficiency and the possession of great capabilities, however, insulate a nation from the world by muting the effects of adverse movements that originate outside of the national arena. One who looks only at the activities of American firms, and at their considerable stake in foreign countries, may then in one misdirected leap reach the conclusion that the size of this stake renders America vulnerable. At the level of the firm, it may be all right to dwell upon the extent of integration. At the level of international politics, it is grossly misleading to do so. It often seems that the approach of international economists would, if applied to domestic economics, cause it all to be written in terms of the firm and not at all in terms of the market. It is necessary to look at the matrix of action rather than simply at the discrete activities that fill it. One who does so reaches a different conclusion.

Someone who has a lot to lose can afford to lose quite a bit of it. This maxim is, of course, a common proposition of oligopolistic economics. That a large and well-placed firm can afford to run at a loss for some years is taken not as a sign of weakness and vulnerability but as being a considerable advantage. Where disparities are great, whether among firms or among states, the largest of them need worry least about the bothersome activities of others. Since in such situations interdependence does not reduce to zero, we can rightly say that all of the parties are vulnerable, but we should hasten to add that some are much less so. Some states, of course, are closely interdependent economically, but neither the United States nor the Soviet Union is among them. In economic terms and from their points of view, the world is loosely coupled.

Finally, as well as the insulation that permits lassitude, the highly skewed distribution of resources gives rise to the possibility of those with the largest share exercising some control. When the point is made that multinational corporations make their decisions on a global basis, one gets the impression that nations no longer matter. But that is grossly misleading. We should not lightly conclude that decentralization of operations means that centers of control are lacking.

From about the middle of the nineteenth century, the quicker transmission of ideas resulted, in the words of R. D. McKenzie, in "centralization of control and decentralization of operation." As he put it, "the modern world is integrated through information collected and distributed from fixed centers of dominance."[34] The complaints of some Europeans strikingly echo these words. One has to ask where most of the threads come together, and the answer is not in London, or Brussels, or Paris, but rather in New York City and Washington.

Decisions are made in terms of whole corporations and not just according to the condition and interest of certain subsidiaries. The picture usually drawn is one of a world in which economic activity has become transnational, with national borders highly permeable and businessmen making their decisions without even bearing them in mind. But most of the largest international corporations are based in America; most of their research and development is done there; most of their top personnel is American. Under these conditions, it is reasonable to suppose that in making corporate decisions the American perspective will be the most prominent one. Similarly, though both American and foreign governments try to regulate the activities of these corporations, the fact that most of them are American based gives a big advantage to the latter government. The advantage is made much stronger by the ability of the American government to grant or withhold a variety of favors, for example, in matters of trade, aid, loans, financial arrangements, and the supply of atomic energy for peaceful purposes. If means for bringing other countries into compliance with preferred American policies are desired, the American government does not have to look far to find them. The customary response of American commentators when the regulatory instruments available to their government are mentioned is to dwell on the ease of evasion. There is something to that response, though it underplays the fact that control— domestically as well as internationally—is often difficult to achieve.

What is really important, however, is to notice that we do not need much control. The size of American operations abroad does give the United States influence in the affairs of other nations, a situation that prevails whether or not we wish it. But the fact that, in relation to our resources, the stake is small means that the exercise of influence and control is less needed. These points can be clearly seen if both the similarity and the difference between America's present and Britain's past positions in the world are kept in mind.

Britain in its heyday had a huge stake in the world, and that stake also loomed large in relation to her own national product. From her immense and far-flung activities, she gained a considerable leverage. Because of the extent to which she depended on the rest of the world, wise and skillful use of that leverage was called for. When the great powers of the day depended on foodstuffs and raw materials imported from abroad much more heavily than the United States and the Soviet Union do now, that very dependence pressed them to make efforts to control the sources of their vital supplies.

Today, the myth of interdependence both obscures the realities of international politics and asserts a false belief about the conditions that may promote peace. The size of the two greatest powers gives them some capacity for control and at the same time insulates them to a considerable extent from the effects of other states' behavior. The inequality of nations produces a condition of equilibrium at a low level of interdependence. In the absence of a system of international regulation, loose coupling and a certain amount of control exerted by large states help to promote the desired stability.

Notes

* I am grateful to the National Science Foundation for supporting my research on this subject, to Harvard's Center for International Affairs at which the research and writing were done, and to Ellyn Hessler, who assisted me on every aspect of this paper.

1 Cf. R. E. Park, *Human Communities: the City and Human Ecology* (Glencoe, IL.: Free Press, 1952), p. 80: "People live together on the whole, not because they are alike, but because they are useful to one another." Cf. also J. G. March and H. A. Simon, *Organizations* (New York: John Wiley & Sons, 1958), p. 159: "The greater the *specialization by subprograms* (process specialization), the greater the *interdependence among organizational subunits.*"

2 I have, of course, had to leave some things out of this paper. To draw a fuller picture would require consideration of monetary and balance of payments problems, short-term capital movements, etc. The conclusions reached would, I believe, be similar to those arrived at by examining international trade and investment.

3 The situation of low economic interdependence along with high political-military interdependence suggests the limits of drawing conclusions from economic conditions alone. I have, however, confined myself to worrying about the international political implications of economic developments.

4 Cf. K. W. Deutsch, C. I. Bliss, and A. Eckstein, "Population, Sovereignty, and the Share of Foreign Trade," *Economic Development and Cultural Change*, Vol. X (July 1962), pp. 353–366; S. Kuznets, "Economic Growth of Small Nations," in E. A. G. Robinson, ed., *Economic Consequences of the Size of Nations* (London: Macmillan, 1960), pp. 14–32; H. B. Chenery, "Patterns of Industrial Growth," *American Economic Review*, Vol. L (September 1960), pp. 624–654; C. P. Kindleberger, *Foreign Trade and the National Economy* (New Haven: Yale University Press, 1962), pp. 32–37.

5 K. W. Deutsch and A. Eckstein, "National Industrialization and the Declining Share of the International Economic Sector, 1890–1959," *World Politics*, Vol. XIII (January 1961), p. 275. Cf. S. Kuznets, *Modern Economic Growth* (New Haven: Yale University Press, 1966), pp. 312–314. Decline is marked for all of the great powers except Germany. The comparison made, however, is

between all of Germany earlier and Western Germany now. The change in the size of the state, of course, affects the level of its foreign trade.

6 M. Z. Cutajar and A. Franks, *The Less Developed Countries in World Trade: A Reference Handbook* (London: Overseas Development Institute, 1967), Table 1, p. 21.

7 A. Maizels, *Industrial Growth and World Trade* (Cambridge: Cambridge University Press, 1963), pp. 79–81.

8 The point is often made. See e.g., R. Nurkse, Wicksell Lectures for 1959, published as *Patterns of Trade and Development* (Stockholm: Almquist & Wiksell, 1959), p. 23.

9 Data taken from Ref. 6, Table 2, p. 22.

10 R. N. Cooper, *The Economics of Interdependence: Economic Policy in the Atlantic Community* (New York: McGraw-Hill, 1968), p. 152. On p. 68, Cooper identifies a "gradual convergence of cost structures among the industrial countries — an evolution which results in narrowing the economic basis on which foreign trade rests."

11 Commission on Foreign Economic Policy, *Report to the President and to the Congress* (Washington, DC: U.S. Government Printing Office, 1954), p. 39.

12 (a) Department of the Interior, Bureau of Mines, *Minerals Yearbook, 1967*, Vol. I (Washington, DC: U.S. Government Printing Office, 1968), p. 36; (b) W. S. Woytinsky and E. S. Woytinsky, *World Population and Production* (New York: Twentieth Century Fund, 1953), Table 335, p. 791.

13 Reference 12a, p. 711. See also P. W. Bidwell, *Raw Materials: A Study of American Policy* (New York: Harper, 1958), p. 192.

14 G. H. Snyder, *Stockpiling Strategic Materials* (San Francisco: Chandler, 1966), p. 247.

15 Reference 12b, pp. 804, 820; cf. Ref. 12a, pp. 187, 1119.

16 Reference 7, pp. 222–224.

17 H. W. Singer, "U.S. Foreign Investment in Underdeveloped Areas: the Distribution of Gains between Investing and Borrowing Countries," *American Economic Review*, Vol. XL (May 1950), p. 473.

18 M. Michaely, *Concentration in International Trade* (Amsterdam: North-Holland, 1962), Table 18, p. 113.

19 Figures computed from data in United Nations Statistical Office, *Yearbook of International Trade Statistics, 1966* (New York: United Nations, 1968). West Germany is the only country for which the difference in proportions is small.

20 The 4 percent of its 1966 GNP that the United States exported amounted to 14.7 percent of the world's total exports. The corresponding figures for the United Kingdom were 15.3 and 6.8 percent. Calculated from (a) U.S. Bureau of the Census, *Statistical Abstract of the United States: 1968;* 89th ed. (Washington, DC: U.S. Government Printing Office, 1968); (b) Central Statistical Office, *Annual Abstract of Statistics, No. 105, 1968* (London, Her Majesty's Stationery Office, 1968); (c) Ref. 19.

21 Computed on the basis of figures on British foreign investment: A. H. Imlah, *Economic Elements in the Pax Britannica* (Cambridge, MA.: Harvard University Press, 1958), pp. 70–75; on British national income, Ref. 12b, p. 385; on U.S. national income and foreign investment, Ref. 20a.

22 W. Guzzardi, Jr., "Why the Climate is Changing for U.S. Investment," *Fortune*, Vol. LXXV (September 1967), p. 117.

23 R. Gilpin, *France in the Age of the Scientific State* (Princeton: Princeton University Press, 1968), p. 50; Ref. 22, p. 116.

24 C. Layton, *Trans-Atlantic Investments* (Boulogne-sur-Seine: Atlantic Institute, 1968), p. 47.
25 Reference 24, p. 98.
26 T. A. Wise, "I.B.M.'s $5,000,000,000 Gamble," *Fortune*, Vol. LXXIV (September 1966), p. 118; Ref. 23, p. 65.
27 Ref. 23, p. 27.
28 E. Littlejohn, "The Influence of Multinational Corporations on International Affairs," paper given at the Ninth Annual Convention of the International Studies Association, March 28–30, 1968 (unpublished), p. 1.
29 M. Watkins et al., Report of the Task Force on the Structure of Canadian Industry, *Foreign Ownership and the Structure of Canadian Industry* (Ottawa: The Queen's Printer, 1968), pp. 199–200.
30 Reference 23, p. 51.
31 Reference 29, p. 339.
32 Reference 29, pp. 313–314, 317–318.
33 Cf. Reference 29, p. 336; Ref. 28, pp. 3–4; A. de Riencourt, *The American Empire* (New York: Dial Press, 1968), pp. 228–290.
34 R. D. McKenzie, "The Concept of Dominance and World-Organization," *American Journal of Sociology*, Vol. XXXIII (July 1927), pp. 34–35.

12

THE EMERGING STRUCTURE OF INTERNATIONAL POLITICS

For more than three hundred years, the drama of modern history has turned on the rise and fall of great powers. In the multipolar era, twelve great powers appeared on the scene at one time or another. At the beginning of World War II, seven remained; at its conclusion, two. Always before, as some states sank, others rose to take their places. World War II broke the pattern; for the first time in a world of sovereign states, bipolarity prevailed.

In a 1964 essay, I predicted that bipolarity would last through the century.[1] On the brow of the next millennium, we must prepare to bid bipolarity adieu and begin to live without its stark simplicities and comforting symmetry. Already in the fall of 1989, Undersecretary of State Lawrence Eagleburger expressed nostalgia for the "remarkably stable and predictable atmosphere of the Cold War," and in the summer of 1990, John Mearsheimer gave strong reasons for expecting worse days to come.[2]

For almost half a century it seemed that World War II was truly "the war to end wars" among the great and major powers of the world. The longest peace yet known rested on two pillars: bipolarity and nuclear weapons. During the war, Nicholas Spykman foresaw a postwar international order no different "from the old," with international society continuing "to operate within the same fundamental power patterns."[3] Realists generally shared his expectation. The behaviors of states, the patterns of their interactions, and the outcomes their interactions produced had been repeated again and again through the centuries despite profound changes in the internal composition of states. Spykman's expectations were historically well grounded and in part borne out. States have continued to compete in economic, military, and other ways. The use of force has been threatened, and numerous wars have been fought on the peripheries. Yet, despite deep ideological and other differences, peace prevailed at the center of international politics. Changes in structure, and in the weaponry available to some of the states, have combined to perpetuate a troubled peace.[4] As the bipolar era draws to a close, we must ask two questions: What structural changes are in prospect? What effects may they have?

The end of bipolarity—and of the Cold War

The conflation of peace and stability is all too common. The occurrence of major wars is often identified with a system's instability.[5] Yet systems that survive major wars thereby demonstrate their stability. The multipolar world was highly stable, but all too war-prone. The bipolar world has been highly peaceful, but unfortunately less stable than its predecessor.

Almost as soon as their wartime alliance ended, the United States and the Soviet Union found themselves locked in a cold war. In a world of two great powers, each is bound to focus its fears on the other, to distrust its intentions, and to impute offensive intentions even to defensive measures. The competition of states becomes keener when their number reduces to two. Neorealist, or structural, theory leads one to believe that the placement of states in the international system accounts for a good deal of their behavior.[6] Through most of the years of the Cold War the United States and the Soviet Union were similarly placed by their power. Their external behaviors therefore should have shown striking similarities. Did they? Yes, more than has usually been realized. The behavior of states can be compared on many counts. Their armament policies and their interventions abroad are two of the most revealing. On the former count, the United States in the early 1960s undertook the largest strategic and conventional peacetime military buildup the world had yet seen. We did so while Khrushchev tried at once to carry through a major reduction in conventional forces and to follow a strategy of minimum deterrence, even though the balance of strategic weapons greatly favored the United States. As one should have expected, the Soviet Union soon followed in America's footsteps, thus restoring the symmetry of great-power behavior. And so it was through most of the years of the Cold War. Advances made by one were quickly followed by the other, with the United States almost always leading the way. Allowing for geographic differences, the overall similarity of their forces was apparent. The ground forces of the Soviet Union were stronger than those of the United States, but in naval forces the balance of advantage was reversed. The Soviet Union's largely coastal navy gradually became more of a blue-water fleet, but one of limited reach. Its navy never had more than half the tonnage of ours. Year after year, NATO countries spent more on defense than the Warsaw Treaty Organization (WTO) countries did, but their troops remained roughly equal in numbers.

The military forces of the United States and the Soviet Union remained in rough balance, and their military doctrines tended to converge. We accused them of favoring war-fighting over deterrent doctrines, while we developed a war-fighting doctrine in the name of deterrence. From the 1960s onward, critics of military policy urged the United States to "reconstitute its usable war-fighting capability." Before he became secretary of defense, Melvin R. Laird wrote that "American strategy must aim at fighting, winning, and recovering," a strategy that requires the ability to wage nuclear war and the willingness to strike first.[7] One can find many military and civilian statements to similar effect over the decades. Especially in the 1970s and 1980s, the United States accused the Soviet Union of striving for military superiority. In turn, the Republican platform of 1980 pledged that a Republican administration would reestablish American strategic superiority. Ronald Reagan as president softened the aspiration, without eliminating it, by making it his goal to establish a "margin of safety" for the United States militarily. Military competition between the two countries produced its expected result: the similarity of forces and doctrines.

Comparison on the second count, interventionist behavior, requires some discussion because our conviction that the United States was the status quo and the Soviet Union the interventionist power distorted our view of reality. The United States as well as the Soviet Union intervened widely in others' affairs and spent a fair amount of time fighting peripheral wars. Most Americans saw little need to explain our actions, assumed to be in pursuit of legitimate national interests and of international justice, and had little difficulty in explaining the Soviet Union's, assumed to be aimed at spreading Communism across the globe by any means available. Americans usually interpreted the Soviet Union's behavior in terms of its presumed intentions. Intentions aside, our and their actions were similar. The United States intervened militarily to defend client states in China, Korea, and Vietnam, and even supported their ambitions to expand. The Soviet Union acted in Afghanistan as the United States did in Vietnam, and intervened directly or indirectly in Angola, Mozambique, and Ethiopia.

David Holloway quotes a Soviet work, *War and the Army*, published in 1977, as follows: "Before the Socialist state and its army stands the task of defending, together with other Socialist states and their armies, the whole Socialist system and not only its own country." Beyond that broad purpose, Soviet forces were to help liberated countries thwart counterrevolution.[8] America assumed similar missions. Defending against or deterring attacks on the United States required only a fraction of the forces we maintained. We mounted such large forces because we extended defensive as well as deterrent forces to cover Western Europe, the Persian Gulf area, Northeast Asia, and other parts of the world from Central America to the Philippine Islands. We identified our security with the security of other democratic states and with the security of many undemocratic states as long as they were not Communist, and indeed even with some Communist ones. The interests we identified with our own were even more widely embracing than those of the Soviet Union. At the conclusion of the Second World War, the Soviet Union began edging outward. In response, one finds Clark Clifford advising President Harry S. Truman as early as 1946 that America's mission was to be not merely the tiresome one of containing the Soviet Union but also the ennobling one of creating and maintaining "world order."[9] We zestfully accepted the task.

Before World War II, both the United States and the Soviet Union had developed ideologies that could easily propel them to unilateral action in the name of international duty: interventionist liberalism in the one country, international Communism in the other. Neither, however, widely exported its ideology earlier. The postwar foreign policies of neither country can be understood apart from the changed structure of international politics, exercising its pressures and providing its opportunities. More than the Soviet Union, the United States acted all over the globe in the name of its own security and the world's well-being. Thus Barry Blechman and Stephen Kaplan found that in the roughly thirty years following 1946, the United States used military means in one way or another to intervene in the affairs of other countries about twice as often as did the Soviet Union.[10]

The Soviet Union's aim was to export its ideology by planting and fostering Communist governments in more and more countries, and America's was to plant and foster democratic ones. President Reagan thought that we should worry about the Soviet Union's establishing a "military beachhead" in Nicaragua "inside our defense perimeters," thus threatening the safe passage of our ships through the Caribbean.[11] Throwing the cloak of national security over our interventions in Central America hardly concealed our rage to rule or to dictate to others how to govern their countries. Vice President George Bush, in February of 1985, set forth what we expected of Nicaragua and the signs of progress we looked for. He mentioned these: "That the Sandinistas bring the Democratic leaders back into the political process; that they hold honest, free and fair elections; that they stop beating up on the church, the unions and the business community and stop censoring the press; that they sever control of the army from the Sandinista party; and that they remove that most insidious form of totalitarian control, the neighborhood spy system called the 'SDC (Sandinista Defense Committee)'."[12] According to a senior official, the Reagan administration "debated whether we had the right to dictate the form of another country's government. The bottom line was yes, that some rights are more fundamental than the right of nations to nonintervention, like the rights of individual people. . . . We don't have the right to subvert a democratic government but we do have the right against an undemocratic one."[13] The difference between the United States and the Soviet Union has been less in their behaviors than in their ideologies. Each sought to make other countries over in its own image. Stalin said of World War II: "This war is not as in the past. Whoever occupies a territory also imposes on it his own social system. Everyone imposes his own system as far as his army can reach. It cannot be otherwise."[14] The effort to impose one's own social system continued into the Cold War, with the aim to be accomplished by peaceful means if possible.

Rooted in the postwar structure of international politics, the Cold War for more than four decades stubbornly refused to evolve into a warm peace. The Cold War could not end until the structure that sustained it began to erode. Bipolarity worked against détente in the 1970s. The changing structure of international politics worked for détente in the 1980s.

Structural change begins in a system's units, and then unit-level and structural causes interact. We know from structural theory that states strive to maintain their positions in the system. Thus, in their twilight years great powers try to arrest or reverse their decline. We need to look only at the twentieth century for examples. In 1914, Austria-Hungary preferred to fight an unpromising war rather than risk the internal disintegration that a greater Serbia would threaten. Britain and France continued to act as though they were great powers, and struggled to bear the expense of doing so, well into the 1950s.[15] At the end of that decade, when many Americans thought that we were losing ground to the Soviet Union, John F. Kennedy appealed to the nation with the slogan, "Let's get the country moving again." And Defense Secretary Dick Cheney resisted a 50 percent cut in defense spending spread throughout the 1990s with the argument that this "would give us the defense budget for a second-class power, the budget of an America in decline."[16]

The political and economic reconstruction attempted by the Soviet Union followed in part from external causes. Gorbachev's expressed wish to see the Soviet Union "enter the new millennium as a great and flourishing state" suggests this.[17] Brezhnev's successors, notably Andropov and Gorbachev, realized that the Soviet Union could no longer support a first-rate military establishment on the basis of a third-rate economy. Economic reorganization, and the reduction of imperial burdens, became an externally imposed necessity, which in turn required internal reforms. For a combination of internal and external reasons, Soviet leaders tried to reverse their country's precipitous fall in international standing but did not succeed.

The rise and fall of great powers

In the fairly near future, say ten to twenty years, three political units may rise to great-power rank: Germany or a West European state, Japan, and China. In a shorter time, the Soviet Union fell from the ranks, making the structure of international politics hard to define in the present and difficult to discern in the future. This section asks how the structure of international politics is likely to change.

The Soviet Union had, and Russia continues to have, impressive military capabilities. But great powers do not gain and retain their rank by excelling in one way or another. Their rank depends on how they score on a combination of the following items: size of population and territory, resource endowment, economic capability, military strength, political stability and competence. The Soviet Union, like Tsarist Russia before it, was a lopsided great power, compensating for economic weakness with political discipline, military strength, and a rich territorial endowment. Nevertheless, great-power status cannot be maintained without a certain economic capability. In a conventional world, one would simply say that the years during which Russia with its many weaknesses will count as a great power are numbered, and that the numbers are pretty small ones. Although Russia has more than enough military capability, technology advances rapidly, and Russia cannot keep pace. In a nuclear world, however, the connection between a country's economic and technological capability, on the one hand, and its military capability, on the other, is loosened.

With conventional weapons, rapid technological change intensifies competition and makes estimating the military strengths of different countries difficult. In 1906, for example, the British *Dreadnought*, with the greater range and firepower of its guns, made older battleships obsolete. With nuclear weapons, however, short of a breakthrough that would give the United States either a first-strike capability or an effective defense, Russia need not keep pace militarily with American technology. As Bernard Brodie put it: "Weapons that do not have to fight their like do not become useless because of the advent of newer and superior types."[18] Since America's nuclear weapons are not able to fight Russia's, the strategies of the two countries are decoupled. Each country can safely follow a deterrent strategy no matter what the other may do.[19] In contrast, the development of either a first-strike capability or an effective strategic defense would carry the world back to conventional times: Weapons would once again be pitted against weapons. All of the parties to the strategic competition would again become concerned over, or obsessed with, the balance of advantage between offensive and defensive forces. Worry about the possibly uneven development of weapons would drive competition to high intensity. A country with a decisive but possibly fleeting offensive advantage would be tempted to strike before another country could find ways of safeguarding its forces. A country with an effective defense, fearing that an adversary might find ways to overcome it, would be tempted to launch a preventive blow. Fortunately, as far ahead as the imagination can reach, no offensive or defensive breakthrough that would negate deterrent forces is in sight.

So long as a country can retaliate after being struck, or appears to be able to do so, its nuclear forces cannot be made obsolete by an adversary's technological advances. With deterrence dominant, a second-strike force need only be a small one, and it is easy to say how large the small force needs to be: large enough to sustain a first strike without losing the ability to retaliate with some tens of warheads. Both the United States and the Soviet Union have long had warheads and delivery systems that far exceed the requirement of deterrence. Moreover, deterrent strategies make large conventional forces irrelevant. They need only be big enough to require an adversary to attack on a scale that reveals the extent of its aggressive intentions. A trip-wire force is the only conventional component that a deterrent nuclear strategy requires.[20]

Nuclear weaponry favors status-quo countries by enabling them to concentrate attention on their economies rather than on their military forces. This is good news for a country in straitened circumstances. By relying on deterrence, Russia can concentrate on turning resources in the military sector of her economy—a favored and presumably rather efficient one—to civilian uses.

Nuclear weaponry widens the range within which national economic capabilities may vary before the boundary between the great and the major
powers is reached. Nuclear weapons alone do not make states into great
powers. Britain and France did not become great powers when they became
nuclear ones. Russia will not remain a great power unless it is able to use its
resources effectively in the long run. While it is trying to do so, its large
population, vast resources, and geographic presence in Europe and Asia compensate for its many weaknesses. Russia's vulnerabilities are low, as is its need
for Third-World intervention forces. The ability of Russia to play a military
role beyond its borders is low, yet nuclear weapons ensure that no state can
challenge it. Short of disintegration, Russia will remain a great power—indeed
a great defensive power, as the Russian and Soviet states were through most of
their history.

How does the weakened condition of Russia affect the structure of international politics? The answer is that bipolarity endures, but in an altered state.
Bipolarity continues because militarily Russia can take care of itself and
because no other great powers have yet emerged. Some of the implications of
bipolarity, however, have changed. Throughout the Cold War, the United
States and the Soviet Union held each other in check. With the waning of
Soviet power, the United States is no longer held in check by any other country or combination of countries. According to Herbert Butterfield, François
Fénelon, a French theologian and political counselor who died in 1715, was
the first person to understand balance of power as a recurring phenomenon
rather than as a particular and ephemeral condition. He believed that a country wielding overwhelming power could not for long be expected to behave
with moderation.[21] Balance-of-power theory leads one to predict that other
countries, alone or in concert, will try to bring American power into balance.
What are the possibilities?

Because nuclear weapons alter the relation between economic capability
and military power, a country with well less than half of the economic capability of the leading producer can easily compete militarily if it adopts a status-quo
policy and a deterrent strategy. Conversely, the leading country cannot use
its economic superiority to establish military dominance, or to gain strategic
advantage, over its great-power rivals.

Can one then say that military force has lost its usefulness or simply become
irrelevant? Hardly. Nuclear weapons do, however, narrow the purposes for
which strategic power can be used. No longer is it useful for taking others'
territory or for defending one's own. Nuclear weapons bend strategic forces
to one end: deterring attacks on a country's vital interests. Partly because
strategic weapons serve that end and no other, peace has held at the center of
international politics through five postwar decades, while wars have often raged
at the periphery. Nuclear weapons have at once secured the vital interests of
states possessing them and upheld the international order.

Nuclear countries can neither gain nor lose much in military conflicts with one another. Winning big, because it risks nuclear retaliation, becomes too dangerous to contemplate. George Ball has labeled the retaliatory threat a "cosmic bluff,"[22] but who will call it? Nothing that might be gained by force is worth risking the destruction of one's cities even if the attacker somehow knew that the attacked would be unlikely to retaliate. Nuclear weaponry solves the credibility problem; put differently, nuclear weapons create their own credibility. The mere possibility of nuclear use causes extreme caution all around. Logic says that once the deterrent threat has failed, carrying it out at the risk of one's own destruction is irrational. But logic proves unpersuasive because a would-be attacker cannot be sure that logic will hold.

Nuclear weapons produced an underlying stillness at the center of international politics that made the sometimes frenzied military preparations of the United States and the Soviet Union pointless, and efforts to devise scenarios for the use of their nuclear weapons bizarre. Representative Helen Delich Bentley remarked in the fall of 1989 that "after having spent more than $1 trillion for defense in the last 10 years, we find ourselves not stronger but greatly weakened."[23] She was right. Our most recent military buildup, beginning with the Carter administration and running through most of Reagan's, was worse than irrelevant because it burned up resources that could have safely been put to constructive use.

If the leaders of a country understand the implications of nuclear weapons, they will see that with them they can enjoy a secure peace at reasonable cost. Because nuclear weapons widen the range of economic capabilities within which great powers and would-be great powers can effectively compete, the door to the great-power club will swing open if the European Community (EC), Germany, China, or Japan knock on it.[24] Whether or not they do so is partly a matter of decision: the decision by Japan and Germany to equip themselves as great powers or, in the case of Western Europe, the collective decision to become a single state. But in political as in other realms, choices are seldom entirely free. Late in the nineteenth century, the United States faced such a decision. Economically it qualified as a great power; militarily it chose not to become one. Some observers thought that the Spanish–American War marked America's coming of age as a great power. But no state lacking the military ability to compete with other great powers has ever been ranked among them. America's ability to do so remained latent. We entered World War I belatedly, and then we depended heavily on the materiel of our allies. In his memoirs, Lloyd George remarked that in the great battles of April to June 1918, American aviators flew French planes. He added that the "light and medium artillery used up to the end of the War by the American Army was supplied by the French. The heaviest artillery was supplied by the British. No field guns of American pattern or manufacture fired a shot in the War. The same thing applies to tanks."[25] At the end of World War II, the United States dismantled its military machine with impressive—or alarming—rapidity, which seemed to portend a retreat from international affairs. Quickly, however, the world's

173

woes pressed upon us, and our leaders saw that without our constructive efforts the world would not become one in which we could safely and comfortably live.

Some countries may strive to become great powers; others may wish to avoid doing so. The choice, however, is a constrained one. Because of the extent of their interests, larger units existing in a contentious arena tend to take on system-wide tasks. As the largest powers in the system, the United States and the Soviet Union found that they had global tasks to perform and global interests to mind.

In discussing the likely emergence of new great powers, I concentrate on Japan as being by population and product the next in line. When Japan surrendered on August 15, 1945, Homer Bigart of the *New York Herald Tribune* wrote that, "Japan, paying for her desperate throw of the dice at Pearl Harbor, passed from the ranks of the major powers at 9:05 a.m. today."[26] In 1957, when Carter, Herz, and Ranney published the third edition of their *Major Foreign Powers*,[27] Japan was not among them. In 1964, projecting national economic growth rates to see what countries might become great powers by the end of the century, I failed even to consider Japan. Yet now Japan is ready to receive the mantle if only it will reach for it.

Much in Japan's institutions and behavior supports the proposition that it will once again take its place among the great powers. In most of the century since winning its Chinese War of 1894–95, Japan has pressed for preeminence in Asia, if not beyond. From the 1970s onward, Japan's productivity and technology have extended its influence worldwide. Mercantilist policies enhance the role of the state, and Japan's policies have certainly been mercantilist. Miyohei Shinohara, former head of the economics section of the Japanese Economic Planning Agency, has succinctly explained Japan's policy:

> The problem of classical thinking undeniably lies in the fact that it is essentially "static" and does not take into account the possibility of a dynamic change in the comparative advantage or disadvantage of industries over a coming 10- or 20-year period. To take the place of such a traditional theory, a new policy concept needs to be developed to deal with the possibility of intertemporal dynamic development.[28]

The concept fits Japan's policy, but is not a new one. Friedrich List argued in the middle of the nineteenth century that a state's trade policy should vary with its stage of economic development. He drew sharp distinctions between exchange value and productive power, between individual and national interests, and between cosmopolitan and national principles. Free trade serves world interests by maximizing exchange value, but whether free trade serves a nation's interest depends on its situation.[29] States with primitive economies should trade their primary products freely and use foreign earnings to begin to industrialize. At that stage, protective tariffs work against the development of manufactures. A state at an intermediate level of development should protect only those infant industries that have a fair chance of achieving a comparative advantage. Such a state should aim not to maximize "value" but to develop its "productive power." Exposed to competition from states that are more advanced economically, a state's industries may die in infancy. Where potential productive power exists, a state should use tariffs to promote its development. List likens nations who slavishly follow "the School's" free-trade theory to "the patient who followed a printed prescription and died of a misprint."[30] To clinch the point that cheap imports work against the development of a nation's industries, he observed that "the worst of all things" would be for American farmers to be given their manufactured goods by England.[31] Exchange value would be maximized at the expense of America's future productive power.[32] At the final stage of development, attained in List's day only by England, free trade is again the sensible policy. "For such a country," he wrote, "the cosmopolitan and the national principle are one and the same thing."[33] With rapid technological change, one must wonder whether the final stage ever arrives. List, however, appeared to believe, as Smith did earlier and Keynes did later, that in a distant day nations would have accumulated all of the riches to which their resources entitled them.[34]

The United States acquiesced in Japan's protectionist policies when Japan was in List's intermediate stage of development, but objected more and more strenuously as its economy became more fully developed. Some Japanese and American voices have joined in urging Japan to loosen its economic policies, although most of the Japanese voices have been muted. A policy report of The Japan Forum on International Relations suggested that the government modify its policies to overcome its mercantilist reputation, to divorce its overseas development assistance from commercial interests that appear self-serving, and to drop "infant industry policies."[35] But will Japan do so? Major changes of policy would be required. Japan's imports of products that it manufactures have, according to Clyde Prestowitz, been "nearly nil." According to Lester Thurow, rather than allowing foreign companies to establish a Japanese market for products of superior technology, the Japanese have welcomed such products "only when they have lost the technological edge."[36]

Japan might take effective steps toward opening her economy, but I doubt it. Shinohara accepts that as "a new major economic power" Japan has an obligation to work "for stable growth of the world economy." But doing so, he adds, does not require Japan to drop policies designed "to nourish infant industries over a span of 5–10 years." A "degree of protection may be justified." In a dynamic world, "competition tends to become brutal," and theories "framed in a surrealistic and hypothetical world when Adam Smith and David Ricardo were predominant are no longer applicable."[37] Whether culturally ingrained or rooted in the structure of government, Japan's economic policy is not likely to take a new direction. Why should more than marginal

175

concessions be made, when the policies Japan has followed have been so successful? If a country has followed one road to success, why should it turn onto another one? The United States may accuse Japan of unfair trade practices, or the United States may instead, as Bruce Scott suggests, recognize that Japan has a strategy of "creating advantages rather than accepting the status quo." Simply put, its "approach may be more competitive than ours."[38]

The likelier course for Japan to follow is to extend its economic policies regionally. Thus the policy announced by Ministry of International Trade and Industry (MITI) Minister Tamura in Bangkok in January of 1987 called for integrating other Asian nations, especially the Association of Southeast Asian Nations (ASEAN), more closely with Japan's economy. The five-year economic plan, released by the Economic Planning Agency in May of 1988, calls, in the words of David Arase, "for the construction of an international division of labor through more imports, more FDI, and more ODA (Foreign Direct Investment and Official Development Assistance)." Japan now uses ODA, not simply to develop new sources of supply and to open new markets, but more broadly "to integrate the Asian-Pacific region under Japanese leadership." The "flying geese" pattern of development and the notion of an "Asian Brain" that manipulates "capital, technology, and trade to construct a regional division of labor tightly coordinated from Tokyo," are made explicit in a major Economic Planning Agency policy study.[39]

Japan's successful management of its economy is being followed by the building of a regional economic bastion. Quite a few Japanese talk and write as though this represents their future. Other leading states have taken notice. The United States made a defensive gesture of despair by putting the "Super-301" retaliation trade-sanction clause in the 1988 Omnibus Trade and Competitive Act to be used as a lever for the opening of Japan's economy more widely to America's—and of course to others'—exports, and the EC strove to achieve economic unity in 1992 partly out of fear that a disunited Europe could not stand up to Japanese and American competition. Economic competition is often as keen as military competition, and since nuclear weapons limit the use of force among great powers at the strategic level, we may expect economic and technological competition among them to become more intense. Thus, as Gorbachev reminded the Central Committee in May of 1986, the Soviet Union is "surrounded not by invincible armies but by superior economies."[40]

One may wonder, however, why less concern for military security should be followed by more concern for the ability of one's country to compete economically. Should one not expect reduced concern for security to go hand-in-hand with reduced concern for one's competitive position? Among many negative answers that can be given to this question, I emphasize four strong ones:

1. Despite changes that constantly take place in the relations of nations, the basic structure of international politics continues to be anarchic. Each state

fends for itself with or without the cooperation of others. The leaders of states and their followers are concerned with their standings, that is, with their positions vis-à-vis one another. Michael Mastanduno has related the results of Robert Reich's asking various groups whether they would prefer that over the next decade Japan's economy grow by 75 percent and America's by 25 percent, or that Japan's economy grow by 10.3 percent and America's by 10 percent. Of six different audiences, only the one made up of economists preferred the former, and they did so unanimously.[41] (Clearly, Friedrich List and Bruce Scott were not present.)

2. One may wonder why, with worries over military security reduced, and with the disappearance of the Soviet Union, concern for relative gains should take precedence over concern for absolute ones. With a 75 percent and 25 percent increase in production respectively, Japan and the United States would both be markedly better off at the end of a decade. With a 10.3 percent and 10 percent gain, both countries would be just about stagnant. On the face of it, the preference of five out of six groups for the latter condition appears to be irrational. But the "face" is merely a mask disguising international-political reality. Friedrich Engels's understanding that economic competition is ultimately more important than military competition is reflected in his remark that industrial espionage was in his day a more serious business, and a business more fiercely conducted, than military espionage. Technical and economic advances accumulate. One technological breakthrough may lead to others. Economic growth rates compound. By projecting adjusted national growth rates of gross domestic product (GDP) from the period 1950 to 1980 into the year 2010 using 1975 international dollars, William Baumol and his associates arrived at an expected GDP per capita of $19,000 for the United States and of $31,000 for Japan. That disparity will result if the United States grows at 1.90 percent yearly and Japan at 4.09 percent. Yet if the United States should raise its average annual rate from 1.90 to 3.05 percent, the two countries would be tied for first place among the sixteen countries for which calculations are shown.[42]

3. Prosperity and military power, although connected, cannot be equated. Yet with the use of military force for consequential advantage negated at least among nuclear powers, the more productive and the more technologically advanced countries have more ways of influencing international outcomes than do the laggards. America's use of economic means to promote its security and other interests throughout the past five decades is sufficient illustration. The reduction of military worries will focus the minds of national leaders on their technological and economic successes and failures.

4. Uncertainty is a synonym for life, and nowhere is uncertainty greater than in international politics. Anarchy places a premium on foresight. If one cannot know what is coming, developing a greater resource base for future use takes precedence over present prosperity. Reflecting Reich's informal finding, a *Newsweek*/Gallup poll of September 1989 showed that 52 percent of Americans thought the economic power of Japan was a greater threat to the

United States than the military power of the Soviet Union.[43] Whatever the limitations on the national use of force, the international political realm continues to be an intensely competitive one. Concern over relative gains continues to be the natural preoccupation of states.[44] If Japan's methods continue to prove successful, other countries will emulate or counter them. Many have argued that, as Richard Barnet has put it, with the "globalization" of the economy, states have "lost the power to manage stable economies within their frontiers."[45] Japan certainly has not and is not likely to do so. To manage "globalization," leading states are likely to strengthen their economic influence over states on which they depend or to which they are closely connected. Since incentives to compete are strong, the likely outcome is a set of great powers forming their own regional bases in Asia, Europe, and America, with Russia as a military power on the economic fringe.[46] Japan will lead the East Asian bloc, now forming; questions about China's and Northeast Asia's roles are as yet unresolved. Western Europe, including the EC, trades increasingly among the countries that the EC comprises, while its global imports and exports are gradually declining.[47] And if the North American Free Trade Agreement (NAFTA) succeeds, the United States will be at the center of the world's largest economic bloc with presently about six trillion dollars in annual trade. Countries and regions that lag in the race will become more and more dependent on others.

National preferences and international pressures

Economically, Japan's power has grown and spread remarkably. But does that indicate a desire to play the role of a great power? Japan's concerted regional activity, its seeking and gaining prominence in such bodies as the IMF and the World Bank, and its obvious pride in economic and technological achievements all indicate that it does. Confidence in economic ability and technical skill leads a country to aspire to a larger political role. "Both Britain and the United States," Yojiro Eguchi of the Nomura Research Institute remarked in 1974, "created and ran international systems with themselves at the top when they were leading creditors." Noting that in ten years Japan's external assets would far exceed America's at their peak, he concluded that "now it is Japan's turn to come up with an international system suited to itself."[48] No country has a better claim than Japan to being a larger partner in managing the world's economy.

Like Japan, Germany has recently shown an inclination to play a more prominent role in the world. President Bush described the Houston meeting of heads of government held in July of 1990 as the first economic summit conference of the "post-postwar era." Chancellor Kohl emerged at the summit as a dominant leader, and Prime Minister Thatcher noted that, "there are three regional groups at this summit, one based on the dollar, one on the yen, one on the Deutschmark."[49] The terms of German unification, which were to have been worked out by the four victors of World War II together with the two Germanies, were instead negotiated by Kohl and Gorbachev at a meeting in the Caucasus. West Germany is the leading state in Europe in both economic and conventional military power. East Germany added a gross domestic product only one sixth as large as West Germany's, but this is far short of its potential. For some years the eastern part of Germany will be a drain on its economy. For Germany's place in the world, how much does that matter? We often underestimate the economic disparities among great powers now, as we did in prenuclear days. To cite a striking example, Japan and the United States in 1940 had GNPs of $9 billion and $100 billion, respectively, and per capita incomes of $126 and $754.[50] In the prenuclear era, a poor country aspiring to a place among the great ones had to discipline its people and harness its resources to its military aims. In the nuclear era, countries with smaller economic bases can more easily achieve great-power status. Although a united Germany's GDP is smaller than Japan's, in one sense Germany is already more of an economic presence globally than Japan, and even rivals the United States. In four of the seven years from 1986 through 1992, Germany's exports were larger than America's, and they were always larger than Japan's. (See Table 1.) Moreover, Germany is in the best position to play a leading role in eastern Europe, Ukraine, and Russia. *Newsweek* quoted a top adviser to Chancellor Kohl as saying, "We *want* to lead. Perhaps in time the United States will take care of places like Central America, and we will handle eastern Europe."[51] Ironically, Japan in Asia and Germany in eastern Europe are likely in the next century to replay roles in some ways similar to those they played earlier.

The effect of national economic capability varies over the centuries. Earlier, enough national productivity to sustain a large military force, however much the people had to stint themselves, could make a state a great power. Now, without a considerable economic capability no state can hope to sustain a world role, as the fate of the Soviet Union has shown. In the mercantilist era, international economics was national politics. During the nineteenth century, the link was weakened, but no longer. Oligopolistic firms care about relative gains and market shares. Similarly, states in today's international politics are

Table 1 Exports in billions of U.S. dollars

	1986	1987	1988	1989	1990	1991	1992
U.S.	227.16	254.12	322.43	363.81	393.59	421.73	447.47
Germany	243.33	294.37	323.32	341.23	410.10	402.84	422.27
Japan	210.76	231.29	264.86	273.93	287.58	314.79	340.00

Source: These data are based on 1975 (Japan), 1980 (Germany), and 1987 (U.S.) prices as indexed by the IMF, *International Financial Statistics*, Vol. XLV, No. 1 (Washington, DC: International Monetary Fund, January 1992), p. 72; and Vol. XLVI, No. 4 (April 1993), p. 58

not merely trying to maximize value in the present but also to secure their future positions. As I have said before, the distinction between high and low politics, once popular among international political economists, is misplaced. In self-help systems, how one has to help oneself varies as circumstances change.

The increased international activity of Japan and Germany reflects the changing structure of international politics. The increase of a country's economic capabilities to the great-power level places it at the center of regional and global affairs. It widens the range of a state's interests and increases their importance. The high volume of a country's external business thrusts it ever more deeply into world affairs. In a self-help system, the possession of most but not all of the capabilities of a great power leaves a state dependent on others and vulnerable to those who have the instruments that the lesser state lacks. Even though one may believe that fears of nuclear blackmail are misplaced, will Japan and Germany be immune to them? In March of 1988, Prime Minister Takeshita called for a defensive capability matching Japan's economic power.[52] Whether or not he intended to, he was saying that Japan should present itself in great-power panoply before the nations of the world. A great power's panoply includes nuclear weapons.

Countries have always competed for wealth and security, and the competition has often led to conflict. Why should the future be different from the past? Given the expectation of conflict, and the necessity of taking care of one's interests, one may wonder how a state with the economic capability of a great power can refrain from arming itself with the weapons that have served so well as the great deterrent.

Since the 1950s, West European countries have feared that the American deterrent would not cover their territories. Since the 1970s, Japan has at times expressed similar worries. The increase of Soviet Far Eastern Forces in the late 1970s led Japan to reexamine its view of the Soviet threat. It is made uneasy now by the near-doubling of China's military budget between 1988 and 1993. Its three-million strong army, undergoing modernization, and the growth of its sea and air power-projection capabilities produce apprehension in all of China's neighbors and add to the sense of instability in a region where issues of sovereignty and territorial disputes abound. The Korean peninsula has more military forces per square kilometer than any other portion of the globe. Taiwan is an unending source of tension. Disputes exist between Japan and Russia over the Kurile Islands, and between Japan and China over the Senkaku Islands. China and Britain have had trouble agreeing on the future of Hong Kong. Cambodia is a troublesome problem for both Vietnam and China. Half a dozen countries lay claim to all or some of the Spratly Islands, strategically located and supposedly rich in oil. The presence of China's ample nuclear forces and the presumed development of North Korea's, combined with the drawdown of American military forces, can hardly be ignored by Japan, the less so since economic conflicts with the United States cast doubt on the reliability of American military guarantees. Reminders of Japan's dependence and vulnerability multiply in large and small ways. In February of 1992, Prime Minister Miyazawa derided America's labor force for its alleged lack of a "work ethic," even though productivity per man-hour is higher in America than it is in Japan. This aroused Senator Ernest F. Hollings, who responded by fliply referring to the atomic bomb as, "Made in America by lazy and illiterate Americans, and tested in Japan."[53] His remark made more Japanese wonder whether they indeed may require a nuclear military capability of their own. Instances in which Japan feels dependent and vulnerable will increase in number. For example, as rumors about North Korea's developing nuclear capabilities gained credence, Japan became acutely aware of its lack of observation satellites. Uncomfortable dependencies and perceived vulnerabilities will lead Japan to acquire greater military capabilities, even though many Japanese may prefer not to.

In recent years, the desire of Japan's leaders to play a militarily more assertive role has become apparent, a natural response to Japan's enhanced economic standing. Again the comparison with America at the turn of the previous century is striking, when presidents wanted to develop America's military forces (and also to annex more countries). Congress served as a brake;[54] in Japan, public opinion now serves the same purpose. Yet the key question is not whether the Japanese people wish their country to become a great power. The key question is whether its people and its leaders will begin to feel that Japan needs the range of capabilities possessed by other countries in its region, and in the world, in order, as Andrew Hanami has put it, to cope defensively and preventively with present and possible future problems and threats.[55] The many American voices that have urged Japan to carry a larger share of her security burden, and the increasing tilt of American public opinion against Japan, have led her leaders to wonder how far they can count on the United States for protection. In the emerging multipolar world, can Japan expect to continue to rent American military forces by paying about 60 percent of their cost, while relying on the American strategic deterrent? The great powers of the world must expect to take care of themselves.

Yoichi Funabashi has praised Japan for fulfilling its international responsibilities in nonmilitary ways. In his view, Japan is a "global civilian power," taking its place in a world in which humane internationalism is replacing the heavily military politics of the Cold War.[56] One wonders. The United States put its security interests above its concern for economic competitiveness throughout the years of the Cold War. It no longer does so. As military worries fall, economic worries rise. Competition continues, and conflict turns increasingly on technological and economic issues. Conflict grows all the more easily out of economic competition because economic comparisons are easier to make than military ones. Militarily, one may wonder who is the stronger but, in a conventional world, will not find out until a war is fought. Economically, however, the consequences of price and quality differentials quickly become apparent. Decreased concern over security translates directly into increased concern over economic competitiveness because the United States is no longer so willing to subordinate the second concern to the first one.

For a country to choose not to become a great power is a structural anomaly. For that reason, the choice is a difficult one to sustain. Sooner or later, usually sooner, the international status of countries has risen in step with their material resources. Countries with great-power economies have become great powers, whether or not reluctantly. Japanese and German reasons for hesitating to take the final step into the great-power arena are obvious and need not be rehearsed. Yet when a country receives less attention and respect and gets its way less often than it feels it should, internal inhibitions about becoming a great power are likely to turn into public criticisms of the government for not taking its proper place in the world. Pride knows no nationality. How long can Japan and Germany live alongside other nuclear states while denying themselves similar capabilities? Conflicts and crises are certain to make them aware of the disadvantages of being without the military instruments that other powers command. Japanese and German nuclear inhibitions arising from World War II will not last indefinitely; one might expect them to expire as generational memories fade. The probability of both countries' becoming nuclear powers in due course is all the higher because they can so easily do so. There is only one nuclear technology, and those who have harnessed the atom for peaceful purposes can quickly move into the nuclear military business. Allocating costs between nuclear and conventional armaments is difficult, the more so since some weapons systems have both conventional and nuclear uses. Everyone agrees, however, that nuclear weaponry accounts for the lesser part of a country's defense budget.

For Germany and Japan the problems of becoming a nuclear power are not economic or technological; they are political. In time, internal inhibitions can be overcome, but other countries will be made uneasy if Germany or Japan become nuclear powers. We have been through this before. Americans treated the prospect of China's becoming a nuclear power as almost unthinkable. Yet China and other countries have become nuclear powers without making the world a more dangerous one. Why should nuclear weapons in German and Japanese hands be especially worrisome? Nuclear weapons have encouraged cautious behavior by their possessors and deterred any of them from threatening others' vital interests. What reasons can there be for expecting Germany and Japan to behave differently? Some countries will fear the effects that may follow if Germany or Japan go nuclear, but who will try to stop them? A preventive strike, launched before any warheads can possibly have been made, would be required. Israel's destruction of Iraq's nuclear facility in June of 1981 set the precedent. Would anyone want to follow it by striking at Germany or Japan? The question answers itself.

Moreover, the internal and external problems of becoming a nuclear power are not as great as they once were. Israel for years denied the existence of its nuclear forces, but no longer bothers to lie about them. One may wonder whether Japan, now stockpiling plutonium, is already a nuclear power or is content to remain some months or moments from becoming one. Consistently since the mid-1950s, the Japanese government has defined all of the weapons of the Self-Defense Forces as conforming to constitutional requirements. Nuclear weapons purely for defense would be deemed constitutional.[57]

Japan has to worry about China, and China has to worry about Japan, while both are enmeshed in the many problems of their region. Yet one often hears this question asked: Why should Japan want nuclear weapons? To argue that it does not misses the point. Any country in Japan's position is bound to become increasingly worried about its security, the more so because China is rapidly becoming a great power in every dimension: internal economy, external trade, and military capability.

From 1965 to 1980, China's annual economic growth rate averaged 6.8 percent and from 1980 to 1990, 9.5 percent. Western economists estimate that China can sustain growth rates between 6 and 9 percent without serious inflationary problems. An economy that grows at 8 percent yearly doubles in size every nine years. The World Bank estimated that China's GDP in 1990 was $364,900 million.[58] Data on China are suspect, but to any periodic visitor the rapidity of its material progress is obvious. If it manages to maintain an effective government and a measure of economic freedom for its industrious people, within a decade it will be in the great-power ranks. Modernizing its three-million-strong army, buying ships and airplanes abroad and building its own as well, China will rapidly gain in power-projection capability. America, with the reduction of its forces, a Cold War-weary people, and numerous neglected problems at home, cannot hope to balance the growing economic and military might of a country of some 1.2 billion people while attending to other security interests. Unless Japan responds to the growing power of China, China will dominate its region and become increasingly influential beyond it.

Although most Japanese now shy away from the thought that their country will once again be a world power, most Chinese do not. Balance-of-power politics in one way or another characterize all self-help systems. Nations have to make choices. They can always choose not to develop counterweights to the dominant power, presently the United States, or not to balance against a rapidly growing one, such as China. India, Pakistan, perhaps North Korea, and China all wield nuclear military force capable of deterring others from threatening their vital interests. Increasingly Japan will be pressed to follow suit and also to increase its conventional abilities to protect its interests abroad.

Two points about nuclear weapons remain. First, some commentators have asserted that Japan and Germany cannot become nuclear powers because they have too little land and too great a concentration of targets on it. Roger Hilsman has claimed that "no nation with territory that is less than continental

183

size can now play the nuclear game." He argues that Japan, Germany, and England have "come to understand this."[59] But direct access to the oceans solves the problem of force vulnerability for all three of the countries mentioned, and target concentration does not matter since it is easy to make enough warheads to cover the targets one cares to, no matter how dispersed they may be. Territorially small countries are no worse off than big ones. Invulnerability of delivery systems, not dispersal of targets, is the crucial consideration.

Second, an argument of a different sort holds that by monopolizing certain technologies, Japan can manipulate the military balance to its advantage. It can substitute economic for military means. Diet member Shintaro Ishihara is one of the authors of *The Japan That Can Say No*, a work that became famous in the United States before it was published in Japan. He advanced the notion that if "Japan sold chips to the Soviet Union and stopped selling them to the United States, this would upset the entire military balance." But because nuclear weapons resist obsolescence, the act he imagines would not have the effects he foresees. Ishihara, nevertheless, asserts more broadly that "economic warfare is the basis for existence in the free world," and believes that in that kind of struggle there "is no hope for the U.S."[60] Countries naturally play their strong suits up and play their weak ones down. Both Stalin and Mao belittled nuclear weaponry when only the United States had it. Neither superiority in the chip business nor a broader technological lead will enable Japan to secure the sources of its oil. Nor will conventional forces, along with economic superiority, substitute for nuclear deterrence.

The case of Western Europe remains. Economically and militarily the possibilities are easily drawn. The achievement of unity would produce an instant great power, complete with second-strike nuclear forces. But politically the European case is complicated. Many believe that the EC has moved so far toward unity that it cannot pull back, at least not very far back. That is probably true, but it is also probably true that it has moved so far toward unity that it can go no farther. The easier steps toward unity come earlier, the harder ones later, and the hardest of all at the end. Economic unity is not easily achieved, but the final decision to form a single, effective political entity that controls foreign and military policies as well as economic ones is the most difficult, made more so because the number of states the EC comprises has now grown to twelve, and an additional four have candidate status. Especially in Britain and France, many believe that their states will never finally surrender their sovereignty. Indeed, the Maastricht Treaty on European Union had trouble securing the assent of Denmark and France, and its economic and social provisions remain controversial in Britain. Common foreign and defense policies are to be concluded only by heavily qualified majorities, and the defense policies "of certain member states" are to be respected.[61] The Community's external policy thereby becomes nearly a cipher. Germans may ultimately find that reunification and the renewed life of a great power are more invigorating than the struggles, complications, and compromises that come during, and would come after, the uniting of Western Europe.

Despite severe difficulties, three factors may enable Western Europe to achieve political unity. The first is Germany, the second is Japan, and the third is the United States. Uneasiness over the political and economic clout of Germany, intensified by the possibility of its becoming a nuclear power, may produce the final push to unification. And West Europeans, including many Germans, doubt their abilities to compete on even terms with Japan and America unless they are able to act as a political as well as an economic unit. Indeed, without political unification, economic unity will always be as impaired as it is now.

If the EC fails to become a single political entity, the emerging world will nevertheless be one of four or five great powers, whether the European one is called Germany or the United States of Europe. The next section asks what differences this will make in the behavior and interaction of states.

Balance of power politics: old style, new style

The many who write of America's decline seem to believe that its fall is imminent. What promised to be the American century will be halved by Japan's remarkable economic resurgence, or so they say. Yet the economic and technological superiority of Japan over the United States is not foreordained. Technologically, Japan and the United States are about on a par; but in economic growth and technological progress the trend favors Japan. We should notice, however, that, with a low birth rate, essentially no immigration, and an aging population, productivity is the only road to growth unless more women can be effectively used in the workforce. And to increase production becomes more difficult as Japan approaches the limit of what present technology offers. Under these circumstances, high growth rates threaten to bring inflation. And since aging populations consume more and save less, Japan and the United States are likelier to converge in their growth rates than to diverge, with Japan moving rapidly to a position of economic superiority. One may expect the economic gap between America and Japan to narrow further, but more slowly, given America's impressive resource base and the tendency of countries to respond energetically to intimations of decline. One must be careful: American voices of doom in the 1950s had little effect on our policies until Sputnik was lofted in 1957. In the 1970s, the Soviet Union did not move to check its declining fortunes but tried, only to fail, in the 1980s. The United States in the 1980s concentrated on competing militarily—and pointlessly— with a moribund Soviet Union. In the 1990s, it will surely heed the economic and technological challenges of Japan.

The structure of international politics is changing not because the United States suffered a serious decline, but because the Soviet Union did so, while Japan, China, and Western Europe continued to progress impressively. For some years to come and for better or worse, the United States will be the leading country economically as well as militarily.

What about Germany? If Germany should become a great power, it would be at the bottom of the list. Japan, with about 60 percent of America's gross domestic product, can easily compete militarily. But can Germany, with about half of Japan's, do so? I believe that it can for two reasons, easily adduced from the second part of this essay. First, offensive and defensive advantage has been transformed by nuclear weapons into deterrent strength easily achieved. Second, an adequate economic base together with the ability to develop an area of operations beyond one's borders is enough to enable a country to vault into the great-power category. Germany is better placed than a British–French combination would be to achieve the second. Many possibilities are open. Germany's beginning to act as a great power may, instead of goading Western Europe to unite, cause Britain and France to do so. But the second possibility is even less likely than the unlikely first one.

Changes spawn uncertainties and create difficulties, especially when the changes are structural ones. Germany, Japan, and Russia will have to relearn their old great-power roles, and the United States will have to learn a role it has never played before: namely, to coexist and interact with other great powers. The United States, once reflexively isolationist, after 1945 became reflexively interventionist, which we like to call "internationalism." Whether isolationist or internationalist, however, our policies have been unilaterally made. The country's involvement became global, but most of the decisions to act abroad were made without much prior consultation with other countries. This was entirely natural: Who pays the piper calls the tune. Decisions are made collectively only among near-equals.

Events have rent the veil of internationalism that cloaked America's postwar policies. Watching the Germans directing Western policy toward the Soviet Union in the summer of 1990, Representative Lee Hamilton remarked that "this is an example of the new multi-polar world that's going to make us learn a new meaning for the word 'consult.' These days it doesn't mean us going to Europe and telling them what to do."[62] In the spring of the same year, the United States tried to shape the charter of a new Bank for Eastern Europe because we would not enjoy there the veto over policies that we had in such organizations as the World Bank and the International Monetary Fund. This prompted a *New York Times* correspondent to remark that for "the first time in the postwar period, Washington is participating in the establishment of a multilateral lending institution that it will not control—reflecting the decline of this country's relative global weight."[63] The old and the new great powers will have to relearn old roles, or learn new ones, and figure out how to enact them on a shifting stage. New roles are hard to learn, and actors may trip when playing on unfamiliar sets. Under the circumstances, predictions about the fates of states and their systems become harder to make.

Units in a self-help system engage in balancing behavior. With two great powers, balancing is done mainly by internal means. Allies have been useful and have therefore been wanted, but they were not essential in the security relations of the big two. Because one of the foundations of the postwar peace—nuclear weapons—will remain, and one—bipolarity—will disappear, we have to compare the problems of balancing in conventional and nuclear worlds. In a bipolar-conventional world, a state has to estimate its strength only in relation to one other. In a multipolar-conventional world, difficulties multiply because a state has to compare its strength with a number of others and also has to estimate the strength of actual and potential coalitions. Moreover, in a conventional world, no one category of weapons dominates. States have to weigh the effectiveness of present weapons, while wondering about the effects that technological change may bring, and they have to prepare to cope with different strategies. "To be sure," Georg Simmel remarked, "the most effective presupposition for preventing struggle, the exact knowledge of the comparative strength of the two parties, is very often only to be obtained by the actual fighting out of the conflict."[64] In a conventional world, miscalculation is hard to avoid.

In a nuclear world one category of weapons is dominant. Comparing the strategic strength of nations is automatically accomplished once all of them have second-strike forces. Even should some states have larger and more varied strategic forces than others, all would effectively be at parity. The only way to move beyond second-strike forces is to create a first-strike capability or to put up an effective strategic defense. Since no one will fail to notice another state's performing either of those near-miracles, war through miscalculation is practically ruled out. Since no one has been able to figure out how to use strategic nuclear weapons other than for deterrence, nuclear weapons eliminate the thorny problems of estimating the present and future strengths of competing states and of trying to anticipate their strategies. And since nuclear states easily generate second-strike forces, they do not need one another's help at the strategic level. Strategically, nuclear weapons make alliances obsolete, just as General de Gaulle used to claim.[65]

Nuclear weapons eliminate neither the use of force nor the importance of balancing behavior. They do limit force at the strategic level to a deterrent role, make estimating the strategic strength of nations a simple task, and make balancing easy to do. Multipolarity abolishes the stark symmetry and pleasing simplicity of bipolarity, but nuclear weapons restore both of those qualities to a considerable extent. Nuclear weapons have yet another beneficial effect on the relations of the nations that have them. Conventional states shy away from cooperating for the achievement of even large absolute gains if their uneven division would enable some to turn their disproportionate gain into a military advantage. Because states with second-strike forces cannot convert economic gain into strategic advantage, an important part of the relative-absolute gains problem is negated. And since nuclear countries cannot make important gains through military conquest without inviting retaliation, the importance of conventional forces is reduced. The elimination of one and the reduction of another military concern means that the relative-absolute gains problem will be rooted much more in worries about how the distribution of gains from joint ventures may affect the economic and technological progress of competing states. Economic competition will provide plentiful sources of conflict, but we should prefer them to military ones.

Balance-of-power theory leads one to expect that states, if they are free to do so, will flock to the weaker side. The stronger, not the weaker side, threatens them, if only by pressing its preferred policies on other states. John Dryden gave the thought poetic expression:

> But when the chosen people grew more strong,
> The rightful cause at length became the wrong.[66]

Though this was written three centuries ago as a comment on Great Britain, according to Anthony Lewis, the Israeli government found that the couplet fit its case closely enough to merit proscription for Arab readers. Even if the powerful state's intentions are wholly benign, less powerful states will, from their different historical experiences, geographic locations, and economic interests, interpret events differently and often prefer different policies. Thus within NATO, Western European countries differed with American interpretations of the Soviet Union's behavior, the nature of the threats it entailed, and the best means of dealing with them.

In a multipolar world, the United States as the strongest power will often find other states edging away from it: Germany moving toward Eastern Europe and Russia, and Russia moving toward Germany and Japan.[67] Yet despite the collapse of the Soviet Union and the dissolution of the WTO, American policy continues to bank on NATO's continued cohesion and influence. In the words of Secretary of State James Baker, NATO "provides one of the indispensable foundations for a stable European security environment."[68] But we must wonder how long NATO will last as an effective organization. As is often said, organizations are created by their enemies. Alliances are organized against a perceived threat. We know from balance-of-power theory as well as from history that war-winning coalitions collapse on the morrow of victory, the more surely if it is a decisive one. Internal and external examples abound. In Britain, large parliamentary majorities make party discipline difficult to maintain. In Poland, Solidarity struggled to prevail; once it did so, it split into various factions. Coalitions formed to counter Napoleon defeated him twice and collapsed both times. Victory in World War II turned wartime allies into peacetime adversaries.

As the Soviet Union began to unravel, Josef Joffe, an astute observer of American and European affairs, saw that the United States would soon be "set to go home." He asked, "who will play the role of protector and pacifier once America is gone?"[69] Europe and Russia may for a time look on NATO, and on

America's presence in Western Europe, as a stabilizing force in a time of rapid change. In an interim period, the continuation of NATO makes sense. In the long run, it does not. The presence of American forces at higher than token levels will become an irritant to European states, whose security is not threatened, and a burden to America acting in a world that is becoming more competitive politically and economically as it becomes less so militarily.

How can an alliance endure in the absence of a worthy opponent? Ironically, the decline of the Soviet Union in Eastern Europe entailed the decline of the United States in the West. Without the shared perception of a severe Soviet threat, NATO would never have been born. The Soviet Union created NATO, and the demise of the Soviet threat "freed" Europe, West as well as East. But freedom entails self-reliance. In this sense, both parts of Europe are now setting forth on the exhilarating but treacherous paths of freedom. In the not-very-long run, they will have to learn to take care of themselves or suffer the consequences. American withdrawal from Europe will be slower than the Soviet Union's. America, with its vast and varied capabilities, can still be useful to other NATO countries, and NATO is made up of willing members. NATO's days are not numbered, but its years are. Some hope that NATO will serve as an instrument for constraining a new Germany. But once the new Germany finds its feet, it will no more want to be constrained by the United States acting through NATO than by any other state.

Conclusion

A number of scholars have written suggestively about the relation between the standing of states and their propensity to fight. A. F. K. Organski and Robert Gilpin argue that peace prevails once one state establishes primacy. The hegemonic state lacks the need to fight, and other states lack the ability.[70] Some states, however, may concert to challenge the superior one, and when leading states decline, other states rise to challenge them. Unrest at home may accompany the decline of states, tempting them to seek foreign wars in order to distract their people. Or they may take one last military fling hoping to recoup their fortunes. Japan, China, and Germany are now the rising states, and Russia the declining one. But even if they wished to, none could use military means for major political or economic purposes. In the presence of nuclear weapons, any challenge to a leading state, and any attempt to reverse a state's decline, has to rely on political and economic means.

John Mueller believes that war among developed states became obsolescent after World War II for reasons that have little to do with nuclear weapons. War has lost its appeal, and "substantial agreement has risen around the twin propositions that prosperity and economic growth should be central national goals and that war is a particularly counterproductive device for achieving these goals."[71] Norman Angell was not wrong, but merely premature, when he concluded that wars would no longer be fought because they do not pay.[72] John

Mearsheimer, however, makes the telling point that, "if any war could have convinced Europeans to forswear conventional war, it should have been World War I, with its vast casualties." But then if Mearsheimer is right in believing that an "equality of power . . . among the major powers" minimizes the likelihood of war, World War I should never have been fought.[73] The opposing alliances were roughly equal in military strength, and their principal members understood this. Yet, as we well know, war is always possible among states armed only with conventional weapons. Some rulers will sooner or later convince themselves that subtle diplomacy will prevent opponents from uniting and that clever strategy will enable them to win a swift victory at an affordable price.

Peace is sometimes linked to the presence of a hegemonic power, sometimes to a balance among powers. To ask which view is right misses the point. It does so for this reason: The response of other countries to one among them seeking or gaining preponderant power is to try to balance against it. Hegemony leads to balance, which is easy to see historically and to understand theoretically. That is now happening, but haltingly so because the United States still has benefits to offer and many other countries have become accustomed to their easy lives with the United States bearing many of their burdens.

The preceding paragraph reflects international-political reality through all of the centuries we can contemplate. But what about the now-widespread notion that because there may be more major democratic states in the future, and fewer authoritarian ones, the Wilsonian vision of a peaceful, stable, and just international order has become the appropriate one? Democratic states, like others, have interests and experience conflicts. The late Pierre Bérégovoy, when he was prime minister of France, said in 1992 that a European power was needed "because it's unhealthy to have a single superpower in the world."[74] He believed this not because the one superpower is undemocratic, but simply because it is super. The stronger get their way—not always, but more often than the weaker. Democratic countries, like others, are concerned with losing or gaining more in the competition among nations, a point richly illustrated by intra-EC politics.

If democracies do not fight democracies, then one can say that conflict among them is at least benign. Unfortunately there are many problems with this view. Few cases in point have existed. When one notes that democracies have indeed sometimes fought other democracies, the proposition dissolves. The American–British War of 1812 was fought by the only two democratic states that existed, and conflict and bitterness between them persisted through the century and beyond. In the 1860s, the northern American democracy fought the southern one. Both parties to the Civil War set themselves up as distinct and democratic countries and the South's belligerence was recognized by other countries. An important part of the explanation for World War I is that Germany was a pluralistic democracy, unable to harness its warring internal interests to a coherent policy that would serve the national interest.[75] One might even venture to say that if a Japanese–American war had occurred in recent years, it would have been said that Japan was not a democracy but rather a one-party state. From Kant onward, it has been implied that democracies do not fight democracies, but only if they are democracies of the right sort. Propositions of this type are constants in the thinking of those who believe that what states are like determines how they behave.

And there is the rub. A relative harmony can, and sometimes does, prevail among nations, but always precariously so. The thawing of the Cold War led to an expectation that the springtime buds of peace will blossom. Instead it has permitted latent conflicts to bloom in the Balkans and elsewhere in Eastern Europe, in parts of what was greater Russia and later the Soviet Union, and in the Middle East. Unity in Western Europe has become more difficult to achieve partly because there is no real threat to unite against.

Yet in placid times, and even in times that are not so placid, the belief that power politics is ending tends to break out. Brent Scowcroft has written recently that balancing "interests off each other" is a "peculiar conception that was appropriate for certain historical circumstances." He foresees instead a world in which all pursue "the same general goals."[76] John Steinbruner envisions a world in which people accept a "configuration of cooperative forces" because militarily "they cannot manage anything else." He adds that an "arrangement that does this" must be open to all who wish to belong.[77] These ideas are among the many versions of the domino theory, so long popular in America. Once the bandwagon starts to roll, it collects the bystanders. Stephen Van Evera believes that if we get through the present difficult patch, meaning mainly that if democracies emerge in Eastern Europe and the former Soviet Union, then "for the first time in history, the world's major countries would all share common political and economic systems and enjoy the absence of ideological conflict." The major causes of war would be "tamed," and "possibilities for wider great power cooperation to prevent war worldwide would be opened."[78] In contrast, this article has used structural theory to peer into the future, to ask what seem to be the strong likelihoods among the unknowns that abound. One of them is that, over time, unbalanced power will be checked by the responses of the weaker who will, rightly or not, feel put upon. This statement, however, implies another possibility. The forbearance of the strong would reduce the worries of the weak and permit them to relax. Fareed Zakaria has pointed out that two countries, when overwhelmingly strong, did not by their high-handed actions cause other powers to unite against them—Great Britain and the United States in their heydays.[79] Both exceptions to the expected balancing behavior of states can easily be explained. Britain could not threaten the major continental powers; its imperial burdens and demographic limitations did not permit it to do so. The United States was held in check by its only great-power rival. What is new in the proclaimed new world order is that the old limitations and restraints now apply weakly to the United States. Yet since foreign-policy behavior can be explained only by a conjunction of external and internal conditions, one may hope that America's internal preoccupations will produce not an isolationist policy, which has become impossible, but a forbearance that will give other countries at long last the chance to deal with their own problems and to make their own mistakes. But I would not bet on it.

Acknowledgments

For their thoughtful comments, I should like to thank Karen Adams, David Arase, Jamais Cascio, James Fearon, Robert Gilpin, Robert Keohane, Sean Lynn-Jones, Robert Powell, and Steve Weber.

Notes

1 Kenneth N. Waltz, "The Stability of a Bipolar World," *Daedalus*, Vol. 93, No. 3 (Summer 1964).
2 Lawrence Eagleburger, quoted in Thomas Friedman, "U.S. Voicing Fears That Gorbachev Will Divide West," *New York Times*, September 16, 1989, pp. 1, 6; John J. Mearsheimer, "Back to the Future: Instability in Europe After the Cold War," *International Security*, Vol. 15, No. 1 (Summer 1990), pp. 5–56.
3 Nicholas J. Spykman, *America's Strategy in World Politics: The United States and the Balance of Power* (New York: Harcourt, Brace and Company, 1942), p. 461.
4 On the causes of multipolar-conventional war and of bipolar-nuclear peace, see esp. Waltz, "Stability," *The Spread of Nuclear Weapons: More May Be Better*, Adelphi Paper No. 171 (London: International Institute for Strategic Studies [IISS], 1981); and Waltz, *Theory of International Politics* (New York: McGraw-Hill, 1979). John Lewis Gaddis and Mearsheimer have offered similar explanations. See Gaddis, "The Long Peace," *International Security*, Vol. 10, No. 4 (Spring 1986), pp. 99–142. Since the reasoning is now familiar, I refrain from summarizing it here.
5 I made this mistake in "The Stability of a Bipolar World," but have since corrected the error.
6 Neorealist, or structural, theory is developed in Waltz, *Theory of International Politics*.
7 Melvin R. Laird, *A House Divided: America's Strategy Gap* (Chicago: Henry Regnery, 1962), pp. 53, 78–79.
8 David Holloway, *The Soviet Union and the Arms Race*, second ed. (New Haven: Yale University Press, 1984), p. 81.
9 Arthur Krock, *Memoirs* (New York: Funk and Wagnalls, 1968), appendix A, p. 480.
10 Barry Blechman and Stephen S. Kaplan, *Force Without War: U.S. Armed Forces as a Political Instrument* (Washington, DC: Brookings, 1978).
11 "Excerpts from Reagan's Speech on Aid for Nicaragua Rebels," *New York Times*, June 25, 1986, p. A12.
12 "Excerpts from Remarks by Vice President George Bush," Press Release, Austin, Texas, February 28, 1985.
13 Quoted in Robert W. Tucker, *Intervention and the Reagan Doctrine* (New York: Council on Religion and International Affairs, 1985), p. 5.
14 Quoted in Josef Joffe, "After Bipolarity: Eastern and Western Europe: Between

Two Ages," in *The Strategic Implications of Change in the Soviet Union*, Adelphi Paper No. 247 (London: IISS, Winter 1989/90), p. 71.

15 *The Economist* apparently believes that Britain and France were great powers well into the 1950s, claiming that the Suez Crisis of 1956 "helped destroy Britain and France as great powers"; June 16, 1990, p. 101.

16 Michael R. Gordon, "Cheney Calls 50% Military Cut a Risk to Superpower Status," *New York Times*, March 17, 1990, p. 4.

17 "Succession in Moscow: First Hours in Power, Gorbachev in His Own Words," *New York Times*, March 12, 1985, p. A16.

18 Bernard Brodie, *War and Politics* (New York: Macmillan, 1973), p. 321.

19 Some Soviet commentators understand this. See, especially, Andrei Kokoshin, "The Future of NATO and the Warsaw Pact Strategy: Paper II," in *The Strategic Implications of Change in the Soviet Union*, Adelphi Paper No. 247 (London: IISS, Winter 1989/90), pp. 60–65.

20 For fuller treatment of this and other strategic questions, see Waltz, "Nuclear Myths and Political Realities," *American Political Science Review*, Vol. 84, No. 3 (September 1990).

21 Herbert Butterfield, "The Balance of Power," in Butterfield and Martin Wight, eds., *Diplomatic Investigations* (London: George Allen and Unwin, 1966), p. 140. Fénelon may have been first, but the idea was in the air. See Daniel Defoe, *A True Collection of the Writings of the Author of the True Born Englishman, Corrected by himself* (London, printed and to be sold by most booksellers in London, Westminster, 1703), p. 356.

22 Quoted by David Garnham, "Extending Deterrence with German Nuclear Weapons," *International Security*, Vol. 10, No. 1 (Summer 1985), p. 97.

23 Helen Delich Bentley, letter to the *New York Times*, November 20, 1989, p. A18.

24 Earlier I said the opposite, arguing that for would-be great powers the military barriers to entry were high. As nuclear technology became widely available, and warheads smaller and thus easier to deliver, second-strike forces came within the reach of many states. See Waltz, "The Stability of a Bipolar World," pp. 895–896.

25 David Lloyd George, *War Memoirs, 1917–1918* (Boston: Little, Brown, 1936), pp. 452–453.

26 Quoted by Richard Severa, "Homer Bigart, Acclaimed Reporter, Dies," in *New York Times*, April 17, 1991, p. C23.

27 Gwendolyn M. Carter, John H. Herz, John C. Ranney, *Major Foreign Powers* (New York: Harcourt, Brace, 1957).

28 Miyohei Shinohara, *Industrial Growth, Trade, and Dynamic Patterns in the Japanese Economy* (Tokyo: University of Tokyo Press), 1982, p. 24. Shinohara says that List was the first to develop "the theory of infant industry protection," but thinks that he would be surprised by Japan's thorough application of it. List, however, did not invent the theory. Instead, he applied it to developing countries and used it to attack economists' belief that free trade serves the interests of all nations. The belief that Japan invented what is sometimes called "strategic trade theory" is widespread. See Bruce R. Scott, "National Strategies: Key to International Competition," in Scott and George C. Lodge, eds., *U.S. Competitiveness in the World Economy* (Boston: Harvard Business School Press, 1985), pp. 95, 138. To give another example, Paul R. Krugman describes as a "new trade theory" what in fact was anticipated by List in every particular. "Introduction: New Thinking about Trade Policy," in Krugman,

ed., *Strategic Trade Policy and the New International Economics* (Cambridge, MA.: MIT Press, 1986).

29 Frederick List, *National System of Political Economy*, trans. G. A. Matile (Philadelphia: Lippincott, 1856), pp. 74, 79, 244, 253.

30 Margaret Hirst, *Life of Friedrich List And Selections from his Writings, 1909* (New York: Augustus M. Kelley, 1965), p. 289. "The School" refers to Adam Smith, David Ricardo, and their followers.

31 Ibid., p. 51n.

32 Cf. Shinohara: "The 'comparative technical progress criterion' pays more attention to the possibility of placing a particular industry in a more advantageous position in the future. . . . The term could be called the 'dynamized comparative cost doctrine'." Shinohara, *Industrial Growth*, p. 25. Cf. also Scott, who wrote that an interdependent world calls for "emphasis on baking relative to distributing the pie"; Scott, "National Strategies," p. 137.

33 List, *National System*, p. 79.

34 On Smith and Keynes, see Robert Heilbroner, "Reflections, Economic Predictions," *New Yorker*, July 8, 1991, pp. 70–77.

35 *Japan Forum on International Relations*, "Japan, the United States and Global Responsibilities," April, 1990, pp. 18–24.

36 Clyde V. Prestowitz, Jr., *Trading Places: How We Allowed Japan to Take the Lead* (New York: Basic Books, 1988), p. 76; Lester G. Thurow, "Global Trade: The Secret of Success" (review of Michael E. Porter's *The Competitive Advantage of Nations*), *New York Times*, Book Review Section, May 27, 1990, p. 7.

37 Shinohara, *Industrial Growth*, pp. 113, 118–119.

38 Scott, "National Strategies," p. 100; cf. p. 131.

39 David Arase, "U.S. and ASEAN Perceptions of Japan's Role in the Asian-Pacific Region," in Harry H. Kendall and Clara Joewono, eds., *ASEAN, Japan, and the United States* (Berkeley: Institute of East Asian Studies, 1990), pp. 270–275.

40 Quoted by Dusko Doder and Louise Branson, *Gorbachev: Heretic in the Kremlin* (New York: Viking, 1990), p. 207.

41 Michael Mastanduno, "Do Relative Gains Matter? America's Response to Japanese Industrial Policy," *International Security*, Vol. 16, No. 1 (Summer 1991), pp. 73–74.

42 William J. Baumol, Sue Anne Batey Blackman, and Edward N. Wolff, *Productivity and American Leadership: The Long View* (Cambridge, MA.: MIT Press, 1989), Table 12.3, p. 259.

43 "The Perceived Threat: A Newsweek Poll," *Newsweek*, October 9, 1989, p. 64.

44 For incisive analysis of the relative-gains problem, see Joseph M. Grieco, "Understanding the Problem of International Cooperation: The Limits of International or Neoliberal Institutionalism and the Future of Realist Theory," in David Baldwin, ed., *Neorealism and Neoliberalism: The Contemporary Debate* (New York: Columbia University Press, 1993); and Robert Powell, "Absolute and Relative Gains in International Relations Theory," *American Political Science Review*, Vol. 85, No. 4 (December 1991) pp. 1303–1320.

45 Richard J. Barnet, "Reflections, Defining the Moment," *New Yorker*, July 16, 1990, p. 56.

46 Krugman among others has argued that the postwar free-trade system is giving way to regional trading blocs. This outcome, he believes, "is as good as we are going to get" and has the advantage that regional pacts "can exclude Japan." Louis Uchitelle, "Blocs Seen as Imperiling Free Trade," *New York*

Times, August 26, 1991, p. Dl. Cf. Steve Weber and John Zysman, "The Risk That Mercantilism Will Define the New Security System," in Wayne Sandholtz, et al., *The Highest Stakes* (New York: Oxford University Press, 1992), pp. 167–196.

47 Wayne Sandholtz and John Zysman, "1992: Recasting the European Bargain," *World Politics*, Vol. 42, No. 1 (October 1989), pp. 122–123.

48 Quoted by Richard Rosecrance and Jennifer Taw, "Japan and the Theory of International Leadership," *World Politics*, Vol. 42, No. 2 (January 1990), p. 207.

49 R. W. Apple, Jr., "A New Balance of Power," *New York Times*, July 12, 1990, p. A1.

50 Figures expressed in current prices. U.S. data from *Historical Statistics of the United States: Colonial Times to 1970*, Part 1 (Washington, DC: U.S. Department of Commerce, Bureau of the Census, 1975), p. 224. Japanese data derived from B. R. Mitchell, *International Historical Statistics: Africa and Asia* (New York: New York University Press, 1982), p. 732; *National Income and Statistics of Various Countries 1938–1947* (Lake Success, NY: Statistical Office of the United Nations, 1948), Appendix III, pp. 246–247; Thelma Liesner, *Economic Statistics 1900–1983: United Kingdom, United States of America, France, Germany, Italy, Japan* (New York: Facts on File, 1985), p. 117.

51 "The New Superpower," *Newsweek*, February 26, 1970, p. 17.

52 Arase, "U.S. and ASEAN Perceptions of Japan's Role in the Asian-Pacific Region."

53 David E. Sanger, "Japan Premier Joins Critics of American's Work Habits," *New York Times*, February 4, 1992, p. A1; "Senator Jokes of Hiroshima Attack," *New York Times*, March 4, 1992, p. A12.

54 Fareed Zakaria, "The Rise of a Great Power: National Strength, State Structure, and American Foreign Policy, 1865–1908" (Harvard University, PhD dissertation), ch. 3.

55 Andrew Hanami, "Japan's Strategy in Europe," unpublished conference paper, October 1992, p. 2.

56 "Japan's Better Example," Editorial, *New York Times*, April 20, 1992, p. A16.

57 Norman D. Levin, "Japan's Defense Policy: The Internal Debate," in Kendall and Joewono, *ASEAN, Japan, and the United States*.

58 World Bank, *World Development Report, 1992: Development and the Environment* (Oxford: Oxford University Press, 1992), pp. 220, 222. Recalculating GDP according to the purchasing power of its currency at home, the IMF concluded that China's GDP in 1992 was $1.66 trillion. The World Bank, applying purchasing-power parity differently, arrived at a figure of $2.6 trillion, a bit higher than Japan's. But one must remember that China's GDP is shared by a huge population. Using the new method, the IMF estimates America's per-capita income at $22,200, Japan's at $19,100, Germany's at $19,500, and China's at $1,450. Steven Greenhouse, "New Tally of World's Economies Catapults China Into Third Place," *New York Times*, May 20, 1993, p. A1.

59 Roger Hilsman, "How Dead Is It?" *New York Newsday*, March 18, 1990, p. 5.

60 Quoted in Flora Lewis, "Japan's Looking Glass," *New York Times*, November 8, 1989, p. A21.

61 Council of the European Communities, Commission of the European Communities, *Treaty on European Union*, as signed in Maastricht on February 7, 1992 (Luxembourg: Office for Official Publications of the European Communities, 1992), Title V, Articles J.8, No. 2; J.3, No. 3; and J.4, Nos. 3 and 4.

62 R. W. Apple, Jr., "As Bush Hails Decision Many See Bonn Gaining," *New York Times*, July 17, 1990, p. A9.
63 Clyde H. Farnsworth, "U.S. Threatens Not to Join Bank for East Europe If Soviets Benefit," *New York Times*, March 15, 1990, p. A1.
64 Georg Simmel, "The Sociology of Conflict," *American Journal of Sociology*, Vol. 9 (January 1904), p. 501.
65 Waltz, "Nuclear Myths and Political Realities."
66 From John Dryden, "Absalom and Acitophel."
67 Karl-Heinz Hornhues, deputy majority leader of the Bundestag, reported that Russian leaders suggested that Germany and Russia form a counterweight to the United States. Marc Fisher, "Germany Says Russia Seeks a Policy Ally," *International Herald Tribune*, February 3, 1993, p. 6.
68 James Baker, "Euro-Atlantic Architecture: From West to East," Address to the Aspen Institute, Berlin, Germany, June 18, 1991, *U.S. Department of State Dispatch*, June 24, 1991, p. 439. For an incisive analysis of the roles and relations of the United States, Western Europe, and the Soviet Union, see Christopher Layne, "Toward German Unification?," *Journal of Contemporary Studies*, Vol. 7, No. 4 (Fall 1984), pp. 7–37.
69 Joffe, "After Bipolarity," pp. 75–76.
70 A. F. K. Organski, *World Politics* (New York: Knopf, 1958); Robert Gilpin, *War and Change in World Politics* (Cambridge: Cambridge University Press, 1981).
71 John Mueller, *Retreat from Doomsday: The Obsolescence of Major War* (New York: Basic Books, 1989), pp. 219, 222.
72 Norman Angell, *The Great Illusion* (London: Heinemann, 1914).
73 Mearsheimer, "Back to the Future," p. 18.
74 Quoted in Flora Lewis, "Europe's Last-Minute Jitters," *New York Times*, April 24, 1992, p. A35.
75 See Waltz, "America as a Model for the World? A Foreign Policy Perspective," *PS*, Vol. XXIV, No. 4 (December 1991), pp. 667–670.
76 Brent Scowcroft, in "Geopolitical Vertigo and the U.S. Role," *New Perspectives Quarterly*, Vol. 9, No. 3 (Summer 1992), pp. 6–9.
77 John Steinbruner, "Defense Budget Priorities," Institute of International Studies, *Currents*, Vol. 1, No. 4 (Supplement), March 30, 1992, p. 3.
78 Stephen Van Evera, "Preserving Peace in the New Era," *Boston Review*, Vol. 17, No. 6 (November/December 1992), p. 4.
79 Fareed Zakaria, "Is Realism Finished?," *The National Interest*, No. 30 (Winter 1992/93), p. 24.

13

STRUCTURAL REALISM
AFTER THE COLD WAR

Some students of international politics believe that realism is obsolete.[1] They argue that, although realism's concepts of anarchy, self-help, and power balancing may have been appropriate to a bygone era, they have been displaced by changed conditions and eclipsed by better ideas. New times call for new thinking. Changing conditions require revised theories or entirely different ones.

True, if the conditions that a theory contemplated have changed, the theory no longer applies. But what sorts of changes would alter the international political system so profoundly that old ways of thinking would no longer be relevant? Changes *of* the system would do it; changes *in* the system would not. Within-system changes take place all the time, some important, some not. Big changes in the means of transportation, communication, and war fighting, for example, strongly affect how states and other agents interact. Such changes occur at the unit level. In modern history, or perhaps in all of history, the introduction of nuclear weaponry was the greatest of such changes. Yet in the nuclear era, international politics remains a self-help arena. Nuclear weapons decisively change how some states provide for their own and possibly for others' security; but nuclear weapons have not altered the anarchic structure of the international political system.

Changes in the structure of the system are distinct from changes at the unit level. Thus, changes in polarity also affect how states provide for their security. Significant changes take place when the number of great powers reduces to two or one. With more than two, states rely for their security both on their own internal efforts and on alliances they may make with others. Competition in multipolar systems is more complicated than competition in bipolar ones because uncertainties about the comparative capabilities of states multiply as numbers grow, and because estimates of the cohesiveness and strength of coalitions are hard to make.

Both changes of weaponry and changes of polarity were big ones with ramifications that spread through the system, yet they did not transform it. If the system were transformed, international politics would no longer be international politics, and the past would no longer serve as a guide to the future. We would begin to call international politics by another name, as some do. The terms "world politics" or "global politics," for example, suggest that politics among self-interested states concerned with their security has been replaced by some other kind of politics or perhaps by no politics at all.

What changes, one may wonder, would turn international politics into something distinctly different? The answer commonly given is that international politics is being transformed and realism is being rendered obsolete as democracy extends its sway, as interdependence tightens its grip, and as institutions smooth the way to peace. I consider these points in successive sections. A fourth section explains why realist theory retains its explanatory power after the Cold War.

Democracy and peace

The end of the Cold War coincided with what many took to be a new democratic wave. The trend toward democracy combined with Michael Doyle's rediscovery of the peaceful behavior of liberal democratic states *inter se* contributes strongly to the belief that war is obsolescent, if not obsolete, among the advanced industrial states of the world.[2]

The democratic peace thesis holds that democracies do not fight democracies. Notice that I say "thesis," not "theory." The belief that democracies constitute a zone of peace rests on a perceived high correlation between governmental form and international outcome. Francis Fukuyama thinks that the correlation is perfect: Never once has a democracy fought another democracy. Jack Levy says that it is "the closest thing we have to an empirical law in the study of international relations."[3] But, if it is true that democracies rest reliably at peace among themselves, we have not a theory but a purported fact begging for an explanation, as facts do. The explanation given generally runs this way: Democracies of the right kind (i.e., liberal ones) are peaceful in relation to one another. This was Immanuel Kant's point. The term he used was *Rechtsstaat* or republic, and his definition of a republic was so restrictive that it was hard to believe that even one of them could come into existence, let alone two or more.[4] And if they did, who can say that they would continue to be of the right sort or continue to be democracies at all? The short and sad life of the Weimar Republic is a reminder. And how does one define what the right sort of democracy is? Some American scholars thought that Wilhelmine Germany was the very model of a modern democratic state with a wide suffrage, honest elections, a legislature that controlled the purse, competitive parties, a free press, and a highly competent bureaucracy.[5] But in the French, British, and American view after August of 1914, Germany turned out not to be a democracy of the right kind. John Owen tried to finesse the problem of definition by arguing that democracies that perceive one another to be liberal democracies will not fight.[6] That rather gives the game away. Liberal democracies have at times prepared for wars against other liberal democracies and have sometimes come close to fighting them. Christopher Layne shows that some wars between democracies were averted not because of the reluctance of democracies to fight each other but for fear of a third party—a good realist reason. How, for example, could Britain and France fight each other over Fashoda in 1898 when Germany lurked in the background? In emphasizing the international political reasons for democracies not fighting each other, Layne gets to the heart of the matter.[7] Conformity of countries to a prescribed political form may eliminate some of the causes of war; it cannot eliminate all of them. The democratic peace thesis will hold only if all of the causes of war lie inside of states.

The causes of war

To explain war is easier than to understand the conditions of peace. If one asks what may cause war, the simple answer is "anything." That is Kant's answer: The natural state is the state of war. Under the conditions of international politics, war recurs; the sure way to abolish war, then, is to abolish international politics.

Over the centuries, liberals have shown a strong desire to get the politics out of politics. The ideal of nineteenth-century liberals was the police state, that is, the state that would confine its activities to catching criminals and enforcing contracts. The ideal of the laissez-faire state finds many counterparts among students of international politics with their yen to get the power out of power politics, the national out of international politics, the dependence out of interdependence, the relative out of relative gains, the politics out of international politics, and the structure out of structural theory.

Proponents of the democratic peace thesis write as though the spread of democracy will negate the effects of anarchy. No causes of conflict and war will any longer be found at the structural level. Francis Fukuyama finds it "perfectly possible to imagine anarchic state systems that are nonetheless peaceful." He sees no reason to associate anarchy with war. Bruce Russett believes that, with enough democracies in the world, it "may be possible in part to supersede the 'realist' principles (anarchy, the security dilemma of states) that have dominated practice . . . since at least the seventeenth century."[8] Thus the structure is removed from structural theory. Democratic states would be so confident of the peace-preserving effects of democracy that they would no longer fear that another state, so long as it remained democratic, would do it wrong. The guarantee of the state's proper external behavior would derive from its admirable internal qualities.

This is a conclusion that Kant would not sustain. German historians at the turn of the nineteenth century wondered whether peacefully inclined states could be planted and expected to grow where dangers from outside pressed daily upon them.[9] Kant a century earlier entertained the same worry. The seventh proposition of his "Principles of the Political Order" avers that establishment of the proper constitution internally requires the proper ordering of the external relations of states. The first duty of the state is to defend itself, and outside of a juridical order none but the state itself can define the actions required. "Lesion of a less powerful country," Kant writes, "may be involved merely in the condition of a more powerful neighbor prior to any action at all; and in the State of Nature an attack under such circumstances would be warrantable."[10] In the state of nature, there is no such thing as an unjust war.

Every student of international politics is aware of the statistical data supporting the democratic peace thesis. Everyone has also known at least since David Hume that we have no reason to believe that the association of events provides a basis for inferring the presence of a causal relation. John Mueller properly speculates that it is not democracy that causes peace but that other conditions cause both democracy and peace.[11] Some of the major democracies—Britain in the nineteenth century and the United States in the twentieth century— have been among the most powerful states of their eras. Powerful states often gain their ends by peaceful means where weaker states either fail or have to resort to war.[12] Thus, the American government deemed the democratically elected Juan Bosch of the Dominican Republic too weak to bring order to his country. The United States toppled his government by sending 23,000 troops within a week, troops whose mere presence made fighting a war unnecessary. Salvador Allende, democratically elected ruler of Chile, was systematically and effectively undermined by the United States, without the open use of force, because its leaders thought that his government was taking a wrong turn. As Henry Kissinger put it: "I don't see why we need to stand by and watch a country go Communist due to the irresponsibility of its own people."[13] That is the way it is with democracies—their people may show bad judgment. "Wayward" democracies are especially tempting objects of intervention by other democracies that wish to save them. American policy may have been wise in both cases, but its actions surely cast doubt on the democratic peace thesis. So do the instances when a democracy did fight another democracy.[14] So do the instances in which democratically elected legislatures have clamored for war, as has happened for example in Pakistan and Jordan.

One can of course say, yes, but the Dominican Republic and Chile were not liberal democracies nor perceived as such by the United States. Once one begins to go down that road, there is no place to stop. The problem is heightened because liberal democracies, as they prepare for a war they may fear, begin to look less liberal and will look less liberal still if they begin to fight one. I am tempted to say that the democratic peace thesis in the form in which its proponents cast it is irrefutable. A liberal democracy at war with another country is unlikely to call it a liberal democracy.

Democracies may live at peace with democracies, but even if all states became democratic, the structure of international politics would remain anarchic. The structure of international politics is not transformed by changes internal to states, however widespread the changes may be. In the absence of an external authority, a state cannot be sure that today's friend will not be tomorrow's enemy. Indeed, democracies have at times behaved as though today's democracy is today's enemy and a present threat to them. In Federalist Paper number six, Alexander Hamilton asked whether the thirteen states of the Confederacy might live peacefully with one another as freely constituted republics. He answered that there have been "almost as many popular as royal wars." He cited the many wars fought by republican Sparta, Athens, Rome, Carthage, Venice, Holland, and Britain. John Quincy Adams, in response to James Monroe's contrary claim, averred "that the government of a Republic was as capable of intriguing with the leaders of a free people as neighboring monarchs."[15] In the latter half of the nineteenth century, as the United States and Britain became more democratic, bitterness grew between them, and the possibility of war was at times seriously entertained on both sides of the Atlantic. France and Britain were among the principal adversaries in the great power politics of the nineteenth century, as they were earlier. Their becoming democracies did not change their behavior toward each other. In 1914, democratic England and France fought democratic Germany, and doubts about the latter's democratic standing merely illustrate the problem of definition. Indeed, the democratic pluralism of Germany was an underlying cause of the war. In response to domestic interests, Germany followed policies bound to frighten both Britain and Russia. And today if a war that a few have feared were fought by the United States and Japan, many Americans would say that Japan was not a democracy after all, but merely a one-party state.

What can we conclude? Democracies rarely fight democracies, we might say, and then add as a word of essential caution that the internal excellence of states is a brittle basis of peace.

Democratic wars

Democracies coexist with undemocratic states. Although democracies seldom fight democracies, they do, as Michael Doyle has noted, fight at least their share of wars against others.[16] Citizens of democratic states tend to think of their countries as good, aside from what they do, simply because they are democratic. Thus former Secretary of State Warren Christopher claimed that "democratic nations rarely start wars or threaten their neighbors."[17] One might suggest that he try his proposition out in Central or South America. Citizens of democratic states also tend to think of undemocratic states as bad, aside from what they do, simply because they are undemocratic. Democracies promote war because they at times decide that the way to preserve peace is to defeat nondemocratic states and make them democratic.

During World War I, Walter Hines Page, American ambassador to England, claimed that there "is no security in any part of the world where people cannot think of a government without a king and never will be." During the Vietnam War, Secretary of State Dean Rusk claimed that the "United States cannot be secure until the total international environment is ideologically safe."[18] Policies aside, the very existence of undemocratic states is a danger to others. American political and intellectual leaders have often taken this view. Liberal interventionism is again on the march. President Bill Clinton and his national security adviser, Anthony Lake, urged the United States to take measures to enhance democracy around the world. The task, one fears, will be taken up by the American military with some enthusiasm. Former Army Chief of Staff General Gordon Sullivan, for example, favored a new military "model," replacing the negative aim of containment with a positive one: "To promote democracy, regional stability, and economic prosperity."[19] Other voices urge us to enter into a "struggle" to ensure that people are governed well." Having apparently solved the problem of justice at home, "the struggle for liberal government becomes a struggle not simply for justice but for survival."[20] As R. H. Tawney said: "Either war is a crusade, or it is a crime."[21] Crusades are frightening because crusaders go to war for righteous causes, which they define for themselves and try to impose on others. One might have hoped that Americans would have learned that they are not very good at causing democracy abroad. But, alas, if the world can be made safe for democracy only by making it democratic, then all means are permitted and to use them becomes a duty. The war fervor of people and their representatives is at times hard to contain. Thus Hans Morgenthau believed that "the democratic selection and responsibility of government officials destroyed international morality as an effective system of restraint."[22]

Since, as Kant believed, war among self-directed states will occasionally break out, peace has to be contrived. For any government, doing so is a difficult task, and all states are at times deficient in accomplishing it, even if they wish to. Democratic leaders may respond to the fervor for war that their citizens sometimes display, or even try to arouse it, and governments are sometimes constrained by electoral calculations to defer preventive measures. Thus British Prime Minister Stanley Baldwin said that if he had called in 1935 for British rearmament against the German threat, his party would have lost the next election.[23] Democratic governments may respond to internal political imperatives when they should be responding to external ones. All governments have their faults, democracies no doubt fewer than others, but that is not good enough to sustain the democratic peace thesis.

That peace may prevail among democratic states is a comforting thought. The obverse of the proposition—that democracy may promote war against undemocratic states—is disturbing. If the latter holds, we cannot even say for sure that the spread of democracy will bring a net decrease in the amount of war in the world.

With a republic established in a strong state, Kant hoped the republican form would gradually take hold in the world. In 1795, America provided the hope. Two hundred years later, remarkably, it still does. Ever since liberals first expressed their views, they have been divided. Some have urged liberal states to work to uplift benighted peoples and bring the benefits of liberty, justice, and prosperity to them. John Stuart Mill, Giuseppe Mazzini, Woodrow Wilson, and Bill Clinton are all interventionist liberals. Other liberals, Kant and Richard Cobden, for example, while agreeing on the benefits that democracy can bring to the world, have emphasized the difficulties and the dangers of actively seeking its propagation.

If the world is now safe for democracy, one has to wonder whether democracy is safe for the world. When democracy is ascendant, a condition that in the twentieth century attended the winning of hot wars and cold ones, the interventionist spirit flourishes. The effect is heightened when one democratic state becomes dominant, as the United States is now. Peace is the noblest cause of war. If the conditions of peace are lacking, then the country with a capability of creating them may be tempted to do so, whether or not by force. The end is noble, but as a matter of *right*, Kant insists, no state can intervene in the internal arrangements of another. As a matter of *fact*, one may notice that intervention, even for worthy ends, often brings more harm than good. The vice to which great powers easily succumb in a multipolar world is inattention; in a bipolar world, overreaction; in a unipolar world, overextension.

Peace is maintained by a delicate balance of internal and external restraints. States having a surplus of power are tempted to use it, and weaker states fear their doing so. The laws of voluntary federations, to use Kant's language, are disregarded at the whim of the stronger, as the United States demonstrated a decade ago by mining Nicaraguan waters and by invading Panama. In both cases, the United States blatantly violated international law. In the first, it denied the jurisdiction of the International Court of Justice, which it had previously accepted. In the second, it flaunted the law embodied in the Charter of the Organization of American States, of which it was a principal sponsor.

If the democratic peace thesis is right, structural realist theory is wrong. One may believe, with Kant, that republics are by and large good states *and* that unbalanced power is a danger no matter who wields it. Inside of, as well as outside of, the circle of democratic states, peace depends on a precarious balance of forces. The causes of war lie not simply in states or in the state system; they are found in both. Kant understood this. Devotees of the democratic peace thesis overlook it.

The weak effects of interdependence

If not democracy alone, may not the spread of democracy combined with the tightening of national interdependence fulfill the prescription for peace offered by nineteenth-century liberals and so often repeated today?[24] To the supposedly peaceful inclination of democracies, interdependence adds the propulsive power of the profit motive. Democratic states may increasingly devote themselves to the pursuit of peace and profits. The trading state is replacing the political-military state, and the power of the market now rivals or surpasses the power of the state, or so some believe.[25]

Before World War I, Norman Angell believed that wars would not be fought because they would not pay, yet Germany and Britain, each other's second-best customers, fought a long and bloody war.[26] Interdependence in some ways promotes peace by multiplying contacts among states and contributing to mutual understanding. It also multiplies the occasions for conflicts that may promote resentment and even war.[27] Close interdependence is a condition in which one party can scarcely move without jostling others; a small push ripples through society. The closer the social bonds, the more extreme the effect becomes, and one cannot sensibly pursue an interest without taking others' interests into account. One country is then inclined to treat another country's acts as events within its own polity and to attempt to control them.

That interdependence promotes war as well as peace has been said often enough. What requires emphasis is that, either way, among the forces that shape international politics, interdependence is a weak one. Interdependence within modern states is much closer than it is across states. The Soviet economy was planned so that its far-flung parts would be not just interdependent but integrated. Huge factories depended for their output on products exchanged with others. Despite the tight integration of the Soviet economy, the state fell apart. Yugoslavia provides another stark illustration. Once external political pressure lessened, internal economic interests were too weak to hold the country together. One must wonder whether economic interdependence is more effect than cause. Internally, interdependence becomes so close that integration is the proper word to describe it. Interdependence becomes integration because internally the expectation that peace will prevail and order will be preserved is high. Externally, goods and capital flow freely where peace among countries appears to be reliably established. Interdependence, like integration, depends on other conditions. It is more a dependent than an independent variable. States, if they can afford to, shy away from becoming excessively dependent on goods and resources that may be denied them in crises and wars. States take measures, such as Japan's managed trade, to avoid excessive dependence on others.[28]

The impulse to protect one's identity—cultural and political as well as economic—from encroachment by others is strong. When it seems that "we will sink or swim together," swimming separately looks attractive to those able to do it. From Plato onward, utopias were set in isolation from neighbors so that people could construct their collective life uncontaminated by contact with others. With zero interdependence, neither conflict nor war is possible. With integration, international becomes national politics.[29] The zone in between is a gray one with the effects of interdependence sometimes good, providing the benefits of divided labor, mutual understanding, and cultural enrichment, and sometimes bad, leading to protectionism, mutual resentment, conflict, and war.

The uneven effects of interdependence, with some parties to it gaining more, others gaining less, are obscured by the substitution of Robert Keohane and Joseph Nye's term "asymmetric interdependence" for relations of dependence and independence among states.[30] Relatively independent states are in a stronger position than relatively dependent ones. If I depend more on you than you depend on me, you have more ways of influencing me and affecting my fate than I have of affecting yours. Interdependence suggests a condition of roughly equal dependence of parties on one another. Omitting the word "dependence" blunts the inequalities that mark the relations of states and makes them all seem to be on the same footing. Much of international, as of national, politics is about inequalities. Separating one "issue area" from others and emphasizing that weak states have advantages in some of them reduces the sense of inequality. Emphasizing the low fungibility of power furthers the effect. If power is not very fungible, weak states may have decisive advantages on some issues. Again, the effects of inequality are blunted. But power, not very fungible for weak states, is very fungible for strong ones. The history of American foreign policy since World War II is replete with examples of how the United States used its superior economic capability to promote its political and security interests.[31]

In a 1970 essay, I described interdependence as an ideology used by Americans to camouflage the great leverage the United States enjoys in international politics by making it seem that strong and weak, rich and poor nations are similarly entangled in a thick web of interdependence.[32] In her recent book, *The Retreat of the State*, Susan Strange reached the same conclusion, but by an odd route. Her argument is that "the progressive integration of the world economy, through international production, has shifted the balance of power away from states and toward world markets." She advances three propositions in support of her argument: (1) power has "shifted upward from weak states to stronger ones" having global or regional reach; (2) power has "shifted sideways from states to markets and thus to non-state authorities deriving power from their market shares"; and (3) some power has "evaporated" with no one exercising it.[33] In international politics, with no central authority, power does sometimes slip away and sometimes moves sideways to markets. When serious slippage occurs, however, stronger states step in to reverse it, and firms of the stronger states control the largest market shares anyway. One may doubt whether markets any more escape the control of major states now than they did in the nineteenth century or earlier—perhaps less so since the competence of states has increased at least in proportion to increases in the size and complications of markets. Anyone, realist or not, might think Strange's first proposition is the important one. Never since the Roman Empire has power been so concentrated in one state. Despite believing that power has moved from states to markets, Strange recognized reality. She observed near the beginning of her book that the "authority—the 'power over' global outcomes enjoyed by American society, and therefore indirectly by the United States government—is still superior to that of any other society or any other government." And near the end, she remarked that the "authority of governments tends to over-rule the caution of markets." If one wondered which government she had in mind, she answered immediately: "The fate of Mexico is decided in Washington more than Wall Street. And the International Monetary Fund (IMF) is obliged to follow the American lead, despite the misgivings of Germany or Japan."[34]

The history of the past two centuries has been one of central governments acquiring more and more power. Alexis de Tocqueville observed during his visit to the United States in 1831 that "the Federal Government scarcely ever interferes in any but foreign affairs; and the governments of the states in reality direct society in America."[35] After World War II, governments in Western Europe disposed of about a quarter of their peoples' income. The proportion now is more than half. At a time when Americans, Britons, Russians, and Chinese were decrying the control of the state over their lives, it was puzzling to be told that states were losing control over their external affairs. Losing control, one wonders, as compared to when? Weak states have lost some of their influence and control over external matters, but strong states have not lost theirs. The patterns are hardly new ones. In the eighteenth and nineteenth centuries, the strongest state with the longest reach intervened all over the globe and built history's most extensive empire. In the twentieth century, the strongest state with the longest reach repeated Britain's interventionist behavior and, since the end of the Cold War, on an ever widening scale, without building an empire. The absence of empire hardly means, however, that the extent of America's influence and control over the actions of others is of lesser moment. The withering away of the power of the state, whether internally or externally, is more of a wish and an illusion than a reality in most of the world.

Under the Pax Britannica, the interdependence of states became unusually close, which to many portended a peaceful and prosperous future. Instead, a prolonged period of war, autarky, and more war followed. The international economic system, constructed under American auspices after World War II and later amended to suit its purposes, may last longer, but then again it may not. The character of international politics changes as national interdependence tightens or loosens. Yet even as relations vary, states have to take care of themselves as best they can in an anarchic environment. Internationally, the twentieth century for the most part was an unhappy one. In its last quarter, the clouds lifted a little, but twenty-five years is a slight base on which to ground optimistic conclusions. Not only are the effects of close interdependence problematic, but so also is its durability.

The limited role of international institutions

One of the charges hurled at realist theory is that it depreciates the importance of institutions. The charge is justified, and the strange case of NATO's (the North Atlantic Treaty Organization's) outliving its purpose shows why realists believe that international institutions are shaped and limited by the states that

206

found and sustain them and have little independent effect. Liberal institution-alists paid scant attention to organizations designed to buttress the security of states until, contrary to expectations inferred from realist theories, NATO not only survived the end of the Cold War but went on to add new members and to promise to embrace still more. Far from invalidating realist theory or casting doubt on it, however, the recent history of NATO illustrates the subordination of international institutions to national purposes.

Explaining international institutions

The nature and purposes of institutions change as structures vary. In the old multipolar world, the core of an alliance consisted of a small number of states of comparable capability. Their contributions to one another's security were of crucial importance because they were of similar size. Because major allies were closely interdependent militarily, the defection of one would have made its partners vulnerable to a competing alliance. The members of opposing alliances before World War I were tightly knit because of their mutual depend-ence. In the new bipolar world, the word "alliance" took on a different mean-ing. One country, the United States or the Soviet Union, provided most of the security for its bloc. The withdrawal of France from NATO's command structure and the defection of China from the Soviet bloc failed even to tilt the central balance. Early in the Cold War, Americans spoke with alarm about the threat of monolithic communism arising from the combined strength of the Soviet Union and China, yet the bloc's disintegration caused scarcely a ripple. American officials did not proclaim that with China's defection, America's defense budget could safely be reduced by 20 or 10 percent or even be reduced at all. Similarly, when France stopped playing its part in NATO's military plans, American officials did not proclaim that defense spending had to be increased for that reason. Properly speaking, NATO and the WTO (Warsaw Treaty Organization) were treaties of guarantee rather than old-style military alliances.[36]

Glenn Snyder has remarked that "alliances have no meaning apart from the adversary threat to which they are a response."[37] I expected NATO to dwindle at the Cold War's end and ultimately to disappear.[38] In a basic sense, the expectation has been borne out. NATO is no longer even a treaty of guarantee because one cannot answer the question, guarantee against whom? Functions vary as structures change, as does the behavior of units. Thus the end of the Cold War quickly changed the behavior of allied countries. In early July of 1990, NATO announced that the alliance would "elaborate new force plans consistent with the revolutionary changes in Europe."[39] By the end of July, without waiting for any such plans, the major European members of NATO unilaterally announced large reductions in their force levels. Even the pretense of continuing to act as an alliance in setting military policy disappeared.

With its old purpose dead, and the individual and collective behavior of its members altered accordingly, how does one explain NATO's survival and expansion? Institutions are hard to create and set in motion, but once created, institutionalists claim, they may take on something of a life of their own; they may begin to act with a measure of autonomy, becoming less dependent on the wills of their sponsors and members. NATO supposedly validates these thoughts.

Organizations, especially big ones with strong traditions, have long lives. The March of Dimes is an example sometimes cited. Having won the war against polio, its mission was accomplished. Nevertheless, it cast about for a new malady to cure or contain. Even though the most appealing ones—cancer, diseases of the heart and lungs, multiple sclerosis, and cystic fibrosis—were already taken, it did find a worthy cause to pursue, the amelioration of birth defects. One can fairly claim that the March of Dimes enjoys continuity as an organization, pursuing an end consonant with its original purpose. How can one make such a claim for NATO?

The question of purpose may not be a very important one; create an organization and it will find something to do.[40] Once created, and the more so once it has become well established, an organization becomes hard to get rid of. A big organization is managed by large numbers of bureaucrats who develop a strong interest in its perpetuation. According to Gunther Hellmann and Reinhard Wolf, in 1993 NATO headquarters was manned by 2,640 officials, most of whom presumably wanted to keep their jobs.[41] The durability of NATO even as the structure of international politics has changed, and the old purpose of the organization has disappeared, is interpreted by institutionalists as evidence strongly arguing for the autonomy and vitality of institutions.

The institutionalist interpretation misses the point. NATO is first of all a treaty made by states. A deeply entrenched international bureaucracy can help to sustain the organization, but states determine its fate. Liberal institutionalists take NATO's seeming vigor as confirmation of the importance of international institutions and as evidence of their resilience. Realists, noticing that as an alliance NATO has lost its major function, see it mainly as a means of maintaining and lengthening America's grip on the foreign and military policies of European states. John Kornblum, U.S. senior deputy to the undersecretary of state for European affairs, neatly described NATO's new role. "The Alliance," he wrote, "provides a vehicle for the application of American power and vision to the security order in Europe."[42] The survival and expansion of NATO tell us much about American power and influence and little about institutions as multilateral entities. The ability of the United States to extend the life of a moribund institution nicely illustrates how international institutions are created and maintained by stronger states to serve their perceived or misperceived interests.

The Bush administration saw, and the Clinton administration continued to see, NATO as the instrument for maintaining America's domination of the foreign and military policies of European states. In 1991, U.S. Undersecretary of State Reginald Bartholomew's letter to the governments of European members of NATO warned against Europe's formulating independent positions on defense. France and Germany had thought that a European security and defense identity might be developed within the EU and that the Western European Union, formed in 1954, could be revived as the instrument for its realization. The Bush administration quickly squelched these ideas. The day after the signing of the Maastricht Treaty in December of 1991, President George Bush could say with satisfaction that "we are pleased that our Allies in the Western European Union . . . decided to strengthen that institution as both NATO's European pillar and the defense component of the European Union."[43]

The European pillar was to be contained within NATO, and its policies were to be made in Washington. Weaker states have trouble fashioning institutions to serve their own ends in their own ways, especially in the security realm. Think of the defeat of the European Defense Community in 1954, despite America's support of it, and the inability of the Western European Union in the more than four decades of its existence to find a significant role independent of the United States. Realism reveals what liberal institutionalist "theory" obscures: Namely, that international institutions serve primarily national rather than international interests.[44] Robert Keohane and Lisa Martin, replying to John Mearsheimer's criticism of liberal institutionalism, ask: How are we "to account for the willingness of major states to invest resources in expanding international institutions if such institutions are lacking in significance?"[45] If the answer were not already obvious, the expansion of NATO would make it so: To serve what powerful states believe to be their interests.

With the administration's Bosnian policy in trouble, Clinton needed to show himself an effective foreign policy leader. With the national heroes Lech Walesa and Vaclav Havel clamoring for their countries' inclusion, foreclosing NATO membership would have handed another issue to the Republican Party in the congressional elections of 1994. To tout NATO's eastward march, President Clinton gave major speeches in Milwaukee, Cleveland, and Detroit, cities with significant numbers of East European voters.[46] Votes and dollars are the life-blood of American politics. New members of NATO will be required to improve their military infrastructure and to buy modern weapons. The American arms industry, expecting to capture its usual large share of a new market, has lobbied heavily in favor of NATO's expansion.[47]

The reasons for expanding NATO are weak. The reasons for opposing expansion are strong.[48] It draws new lines of division in Europe, alienates those left out, and can find no logical stopping place west of Russia. It weakens those Russians most inclined toward liberal democracy and a market economy. It strengthens Russians of the opposite inclination. It reduces hope for further large reductions of nuclear weaponry. It pushes Russia toward China instead of drawing Russia toward Europe and America. NATO, led by America, scarcely considered the plight of its defeated adversary. Throughout modern history, Russia has been rebuffed by the West, isolated and at times surrounded.

209

Many Russians believe that, by expanding, NATO brazenly broke promises it made in 1990 and 1991 that former WTO members would not be allowed to join NATO. With good reason, Russians fear that NATO will not only admit additional old members of the WTO but also former republics of the Soviet Union. In 1997, NATO held naval exercises with Ukraine in the Black Sea, with more joint exercises to come, and announced plans to use a military testing ground in western Ukraine. In June of 1998, Zbigniew Brzezinski went to Kiev with the message that Ukraine should prepare itself to join NATO by the year 2010.[49] The farther NATO intrudes into the Soviet Union's old arena, the more Russia is forced to look to the east rather than to the west.

The expansion of NATO extends its military interests, enlarges its responsibilities, and increases its burdens. Not only do new members require NATO's protection, they also heighten its concern over destabilizing events near their borders. Thus Balkan eruptions become a NATO and not just a European concern. In the absence of European initiative, Americans believe they must lead the way because the credibility of NATO is at stake. Balkan operations in the air and even more so on the ground exacerbate differences of interest among NATO members and strain the alliance. European members marvel at the surveillance and communications capabilities of the United States and stand in awe of the modern military forces at its command. Aware of their weaknesses, Europeans express determination to modernize their forces and to develop their ability to deploy them independently. Europe's reaction to America's Balkan operations duplicates its determination to remedy deficiencies revealed in 1991 during the Gulf War, a determination that produced few results.

Will it be different this time? Perhaps, yet if European states do achieve their goals of creating a 60,000 strong rapid reaction force and enlarging the role of the WEU, the tension between a NATO controlled by the United States and a NATO allowing for independent European action will again be bothersome. In any event, the prospect of militarily bogging down in the Balkans tests the alliance and may indefinitely delay its further expansion. Expansion buys trouble, and mounting troubles may bring expansion to a halt.

European conditions and Russian opposition work against the eastward extension of NATO. Pressing in the opposite direction is the momentum of American expansion. The momentum of expansion has often been hard to break, a thought borne out by the empires of Republican Rome, of Czarist Russia, and of Liberal Britain.

One is often reminded that the United States is not just the dominant power in the world but that it is a *liberal* dominant power. True, the motivations of the artificers of expansion—President Clinton, National Security Adviser Anthony Lake, and others—were to nurture democracy in young, fragile, long-suffering countries. One may wonder, however, why this should be an American rather than a European task and why a military rather than a political-economic organization should be seen as the appropriate means for carrying it out. The task of building democracy is not a military one. The military security of new NATO members is not in jeopardy; their political development and economic well-being are. In 1997, U.S. Assistant Secretary of Defense Franklin D. Kramer told the Czech defense ministry that it was spending too little on defense.[50] Yet investing in defense slows economic growth. By common calculation, defense spending stimulates economic growth about half as much as direct investment in the economy. In Eastern Europe, economic not military security is the problem and entering a military alliance compounds it.

Using the example of NATO to reflect on the relevance of realism after the Cold War leads to some important conclusions. The winner of the Cold War and the sole remaining great power has behaved as unchecked powers have usually done. In the absence of counterweights, a country's internal impulses prevail, whether fueled by liberal or by other urges. The error of realist predictions that the end of the Cold War would mean the end of NATO arose not from a failure of realist theory to comprehend international politics, but from an underestimation of America's folly. The survival and expansion of NATO illustrate not the defects but the limitations of structural explanations. Structures shape and shove; they do not determine the actions of states. A state that is stronger than any other can decide for itself whether to conform its policies to structural pressures and whether to avail itself of the opportunities that structural change offers, with little fear of adverse affects in the short run.

Do liberal institutionalists provide better leverage for explaining NATO's survival and expansion? According to Keohane and Martin, realists insist "that institutions have only marginal effects."[51] On the contrary, realists have noticed that whether institutions have strong or weak effects depends on what states intend. Strong states use institutions, as they interpret laws, in ways that suit them. Thus Susan Strange, in pondering the state's retreat, observes that "international organization is above all a tool of national government, an instrument for the pursuit of national interest by other means."[52]

Interestingly, Keohane and Martin, in their effort to refute Mearsheimer's trenchant criticism of institutional theory, in effect agree with him. Having claimed that his realism is "not well specified," they note that "institutional theory conceptualizes institutions both as independent and dependent variables."[53] Dependent on what?—on "the realities of power and interest." Institutions, it turns out, "make a significant difference in conjunction with power realities."[54] Yes! Liberal institutionalism, as Mearsheimer says, "is no longer a clear alternative to realism, but has, in fact, been swallowed up by it."[55] Indeed, it never was an alternative to realism. Institutionalist theory, as Keohane has stressed, has as its core structural realism, which Keohane and Nye sought "to broaden."[56] The institutional approach starts with structural theory, applies it to the origins and operations of institutions, and unsurprisingly ends with realist conclusions.

Alliances illustrate the weaknesses of institutionalism with special clarity. Institutional theory attributes to institutions causal effects that mostly originate

211

within states. The case of NATO nicely illustrates this shortcoming. Keohane has remarked that "alliances are institutions, and both their durability and strength ... may depend in part on their institutional characteristics."[57] In part, I suppose, but one must wonder in how large a part. The Triple Alliance and the Triple Entente were quite durable. They lasted not because of alliance institutions, there hardly being any, but because the core members of each alliance looked outward and saw a pressing threat to their security. Previous alliances did not lack institutions because states had failed to figure out how to construct bureaucracies. Previous alliances lacked institutions because in the absence of a hegemonic leader, balancing continued within as well as across alliances. NATO lasted as a military alliance as long as the Soviet Union appeared to be a direct threat to its members. It survives and expands now not because of its institutions but mainly because the United States wants it to.

NATO's survival also exposes an interesting aspect of balance-of-power theory. Robert Art has argued forcefully that without NATO and without American troops in Europe, European states will lapse into a "security competition" among themselves.[58] As he emphasizes, this is a realist expectation. In his view, preserving NATO, and maintaining America's leading role in it, are required in order to prevent a security competition that would promote conflict within, and impair the institutions of, the European Union. NATO now is an anomaly; the dampening of intra-alliance tension is the main task left, and it is a task not for the alliance but for its leader. The secondary task of an alliance, intra-alliance management, continues to be performed by the United States even though the primary task, defense against an external enemy, has disappeared. The point is worth pondering, but I need to say here only that it further illustrates the dependence of international institutions on national decisions. Balancing among states is not inevitable. As in Europe, a hegemonic power may suppress it. As a high-level European diplomat put it, "it is not acceptable that the lead nation be European. A European power broker is a hegemonic power. We can agree on U.S. leadership, but not on one of our own."[59] Accepting the leadership of a hegemonic power prevents a balance of power from emerging in Europe, and better the hegemonic power should be at a distance than next door.

Keohane believes that "avoiding military conflict in Europe after the Cold War depends greatly on whether the next decade is characterized by a continuous pattern of institutionalized cooperation."[60] If one accepts the conclusion, the question remains: What or who sustains the "pattern of institutionalized cooperation"? Realists know the answer.

International institutions and national aims

What is true of NATO holds for international institutions generally. The effects that international institutions may have on national decisions are but one step removed from the capabilities and intentions of the major state or states that gave them birth and sustain them. The Bretton Woods system strongly affected individual states and the conduct of international affairs. But when the United States found that the system no longer served its interests, the Nixon shocks of 1971 were administered. International institutions are created by the more powerful states, and the institutions survive in their original form as long as they serve the major interests of their creators, or are thought to do so. "The nature of institutional arrangements," as Stephen Krasner put it, "is better explained by the distribution of national power capabilities than by efforts to solve problems of market failure"[61]—or, I would add, by anything else.

Either international conventions, treaties, and institutions remain close to the underlying distribution of national capabilities or they court failure.[62] Citing examples from the past 350 years, Krasner found that in all of the instances "it was the value of strong states that dictated rules that were applied in a discriminating fashion only to the weak."[63] The sovereignty of nations, a universally recognized international institution, hardly stands in the way of a strong nation that decides to intervene in a weak one. Thus, according to a senior official, the Reagan administration "debated whether we had the right to dictate the form of another country's government. The bottom line was yes, that some rights are more fundamental than the right of nations to nonintervention. . . . We don't have the right to subvert a democracy but we do have the right against an undemocratic one."[64] Most international law is obeyed most of the time, but strong states bend or break laws when they choose to.

Balancing power: not today but tomorrow

With so many of the expectations that realist theory gives rise to confirmed by what happened at and after the end of the Cold War, one may wonder why realism is in bad repute.[65] A key proposition derived from realist theory is that international politics reflects the distribution of national capabilities, a proposition daily borne out. Another key proposition is that the balancing of power by some states against others recurs. Realist theory predicts that balances disrupted will one day be restored. A limitation of the theory, a limitation common to social-science theories, is that it cannot say when. William Wohlforth argues that though restoration will take place, it will be a long time coming.[66] Of necessity, realist theory is better at saying what will happen than in saying when it will happen. Theory cannot say when "tomorrow" will come because international-political theory deals with the pressures of structure on states and not with how states will respond to the pressures. The latter is a task for theories about how national governments respond to pressures on them and take advantage of opportunities that may be present. One does, however, observe balancing tendencies already taking place.

Upon the demise of the Soviet Union, the international-political system became unipolar. In the light of structural theory, unipolarity appears as the least durable of international configurations. This is so for two main reasons.

One is that dominant powers take on too many tasks beyond their own borders, thus weakening themselves in the long run. Ted Robert Gurr, after examining 336 polities, reached the same conclusion that Robert Wesson had reached earlier: "Imperial decay is . . . primarily a result of the misuse of power which follows inevitably from its concentration."[67] The other reason for the short duration of unipolarity is that even if a dominant power behaves with moderation, restraint, and forbearance, weaker states will worry about its future behavior. America's founding fathers warned against the perils of power in the absence of checks and balances. Is unbalanced power less of a danger in international than in national politics? Throughout the Cold War, what the United States and the Soviet Union did, and how they interacted, were dominant factors in international politics. The two countries, however, constrained each other. Now the United States is alone in the world. As nature abhors a vacuum, so international politics abhors unbalanced power. Faced with unbalanced power, some states try to increase their own strength or they ally with others to bring the international distribution of power into balance. The reactions of other states to the drive for dominance of Charles V, Hapsburg ruler of Spain, of Louis XIV and Napoleon I of France, of Wilhelm II and Adolph Hitler of Germany, illustrate the point.

The behavior of dominant powers

Will the preponderant power of the United States elicit similar reactions? Unbalanced power, whoever wields it, is a potential danger to others. The powerful state may, and the United States does, think of itself as acting for the sake of peace, justice, and well-being in the world. These terms, however, are defined to the liking of the powerful, which may conflict with the preferences and interests of others. In international politics, overwhelming power repels and leads others to try to balance against it. With benign intent, the United States has behaved and, until its power is brought into balance, will continue to behave in ways that sometimes frighten others.

For almost half a century, the constancy of the Soviet threat produced a constancy of American policy. Other countries could rely on the United States for protection because protecting them seemed to serve American security interests. Even so, beginning in the 1950s, Western European countries and, beginning in the 1970s, Japan had increasing doubts about the reliability of the American nuclear deterrent. As Soviet strength increased, Western European countries began to wonder whether the United States could be counted on to use its deterrent on their behalf, thus risking its own cities. When President Jimmy Carter moved to reduce American troops in South Korea, and later when the Soviet Union invaded Afghanistan and strengthened its forces in the Far East, Japan developed similar worries.

With the disappearance of the Soviet Union, the United States no longer faces a major threat to its security. As General Colin Powell said when he was chairman of the Joint Chiefs of Staff: "I'm running out of demons. I'm running out of enemies. I'm down to Castro and Kim II Sung."[68] Constancy of threat produces constancy of policy; absence of threat permits policy to become capricious. When few if any vital interests are endangered, a country's policy becomes sporadic and self-willed.

The absence of serious threats to American security gives the United States wide latitude in making foreign policy choices. A dominant power acts internationally only when the spirit moves it. One example is enough to show this. When Yugoslavia's collapse was followed by genocidal war in successor states, the United States failed to respond until Senator Robert Dole moved to make Bosnia's peril an issue in the forthcoming presidential election; and it acted not for the sake of its own security but to maintain its leadership position in Europe. American policy was generated not by external security interests, but by internal political pressure and national ambition.

Aside from specific threats it may pose, unbalanced power leaves weaker states feeling uneasy and gives them reason to strengthen their positions. The United States has a long history of intervening in weak states, often with the intention of bringing democracy to them. American behavior over the past century in Central America provides little evidence of self-restraint in the absence of countervailing power. Contemplating the history of the United States and measuring its capabilities, other countries may well wish for ways to fend off its benign ministrations. Concentrated power invites distrust because it is so easily misused. To understand why some states want to bring power into a semblance of balance is easy, but with power so sharply skewed, what country or group of countries has the material capability and the political will to bring the "unipolar moment" to an end?

Balancing power in a unipolar world

The expectation that following victory in a great war a new balance of power will form is firmly grounded in both history and theory. The last four grand coalitions (two against Napoleon and one in each of the world wars of the twentieth century) collapsed once victory was achieved. Victories in major wars leave the balance of power badly skewed. The winning side emerges as a dominant coalition. The international equilibrium is broken; theory leads one to expect its restoration.

Clearly something has changed. Some believe that the United States is so nice that, despite the dangers of unbalanced power, others do not feel the fear that would spur them to action. Michael Mastanduno, among others, believes this to be so, although he ends his article with the thought that "eventually, power will check power."[69] Others believe that the leaders of states have learned that playing the game of power politics is costly and unnecessary. In fact, the explanation for sluggish balancing is a simple one. In the aftermath of earlier great wars, the materials for constructing a new balance were readily at hand.

Previous wars left a sufficient number of great powers standing to permit a new balance to be rather easily constructed. Theory enables one to say that a new balance of power will form but not to say how long it will take. National and international conditions determine that. Those who refer to the unipolar moment are right. In our perspective, the new balance is emerging slowly; in historical perspectives, it will come in the blink of an eye.

I ended a 1993 article this way: "One may hope that America's internal preoccupations will produce not an isolationist policy, which has become impossible, but a forbearance that will give other countries at long last the chance to deal with their own problems and make their own mistakes. But I would not bet on it."[70] I should think that few would do so now. Charles Kegley has said, sensibly, that if the world becomes multipolar once again, realists will be vindicated.[71] Seldom do signs of vindication appear so promptly.

The candidates for becoming the next great powers, and thus restoring a balance, are the European Union or Germany leading a coalition, China, Japan, and in a more distant future, Russia. The countries of the European Union have been remarkably successful in integrating their national economies. The achievement of a large measure of economic integration without a corresponding political unity is an accomplishment without historical precedent. On questions of foreign and military policy, however, the European Union can act only with the consent of its members, making bold or risky action impossible. The European Union has all the tools—population, resources, technology, and military capabilities—but lacks the organizational ability and the collective will to use them. As Jacques Delors said when he was president of the European Commission: "It will be for the European Council, consisting of heads of state and government . . ., to agree on the essential interests they share and which they will agree to defend and promote together."[72] Policies that must be arrived at by consensus can be carried out only when they are fairly inconsequential. Inaction as Yugoslavia sank into chaos and war signaled that Europe will not act to stop wars even among near neighbors. Western Europe was unable to make its own foreign and military policies when its was an organization of six or nine states living in fear of the Soviet Union. With less pressure and more members, it has even less hope of doing so now. Only when the United States decides on a policy have European countries been able to follow it.

Europe may not remain in its supine position forever, yet signs of fundamental change in matters of foreign and military policy are faint. Now as earlier, European leaders express discontent with Europe's secondary position, chafe at America's making most of the important decisions, and show a desire to direct their own destiny. French leaders often vent their frustration and pine for a world, as Foreign Minister Hubert Védrine recently put it, "of several poles, not just a single one." President Jacques Chirac and Prime Minister Lionel Jospin call for a strengthening of such multilateral institutions as the International Monetary Fund and the United Nations, although how this would diminish America's influence is not explained. More to the point,

Védrine complains that since President John Kennedy, Americans have talked of a European pillar for the alliance, a pillar that is never built.[73] German and British leaders now more often express similar discontent. Europe, however, will not be able to claim a louder voice in alliance affairs unless it builds a platform for giving it expression. If Europeans ever mean to write a tune to go with their libretto, they will have to develop the unity in foreign and military affairs that they are achieving in economic matters. If French and British leaders decided to merge their nuclear forces to form the nucleus of a European military organization, the United States and the world will begin to treat Europe as a major force.

The European Economic Community was formed in 1957 and has grown incrementally to its present proportions. But where is the incremental route to a European foreign and military policy to be found? European leaders have not been able to find it or even have tried very hard to do so. In the absence of radical change, Europe will count for little in international politics for as far ahead as the eye can see, unless Germany, becoming impatient, decides to lead a coalition.

International structure and national responses

Throughout modern history, international politics centered on Europe. Two world wars ended Europe's dominance. Whether Europe will somehow, someday emerge as a great power is a matter for speculation. In the meantime, the all-but-inevitable movement from unipolarity to multipolarity is taking place not in Europe but in Asia. The internal development and the external reaction of China and Japan are steadily raising both countries to the great power level.[74] China will emerge as a great power even without trying very hard so long as it remains politically united and competent. Strategically, China can easily raise its nuclear forces to a level of parity with the United States if it has not already done so.[75] China has five to seven intercontinental missiles (DF-5s) able to hit almost any American target and a dozen or more missiles able to reach the west coast of the United States (DF-4s).[76] Liquid fueled, immobile missiles are vulnerable, but would the United States risk the destruction of, say, Seattle, San Francisco, and San Diego if China happens to have a few more DF-4s than the United States thinks or if it should fail to destroy all of them on the ground? Deterrence is much easier to contrive than most Americans have surmised. Economically, China's growth rate, given its present stage of economic development, can be sustained at 7 to 9 percent for another decade or more. Even during Asia's near economic collapse of the 1990s, China's growth rate remained approximately in that range. A growth rate of 7 to 9 percent doubles a country's economy every ten to eight years.

Unlike China, Japan is obviously reluctant to assume the mantle of a great power. Its reluctance, however, is steadily though slowly waning. Economically, Japan's power has grown and spread remarkably. The growth of a country's economic capability to the great power level places it at the center of regional and global affairs. It widens the range of a state's interests and increases their importance. The high volume of a country's external business thrusts it ever more deeply into world affairs. In a self-help system, the possession of most but not all of the capabilities of a great power leaves a state vulnerable to others that have the instruments that the lesser state lacks. Even though one may believe that fears of nuclear blackmail are misplaced, one must wonder whether Japan will remain immune to them.

Countries have always competed for wealth and security, and the competition has often led to conflict. Historically, states have been sensitive to changing relations of power among them. Japan is made uneasy now by the steady growth of China's military budget. Its nearly 3 million strong army, undergoing modernization, and the gradual growth of its sea- and air-power projection capabilities, produce apprehension in all of China's neighbors and add to the sense of instability in a region where issues of sovereignty and disputes over territory abound. The Korean peninsula has more military forces per square kilometer than any other portion of the globe. Taiwan is an unending source of tension. Disputes exist between Japan and Russia over the Kurile Islands, and between Japan and China over the Senkaku or Diaoyu Islands. Cambodia is a troublesome problem for both Vietnam and China. Half a dozen countries lay claim to all or some of the Spratly Islands, strategically located and supposedly rich in oil. The presence of China's ample nuclear forces, combined with the drawdown of American military forces, can hardly be ignored by Japan, the less so because economic conflicts with the United States cast doubt on the reliability of American military guarantees. Reminders of Japan's dependence and vulnerability multiply in large and small ways. For example, as rumors about North Korea's developing nuclear capabilities gained credence, Japan became acutely aware of its lack of observation satellites. Uncomfortable dependencies and perceived vulnerabilities have led Japan to acquire greater military capabilities, even though many Japanese may prefer not to.

Given the expectation of conflict, and the necessity of taking care of one's interests, one may wonder how any state with the economic capability of a great power can refrain from arming itself with the weapons that have served so well as the great deterrent. For a country to choose not to become a great power is a structural anomaly For that reason, the choice is a difficult one to sustain. Sooner or later, usually sooner, the international status of countries has risen in step with their material resources. Countries with great power economies have become great powers, whether or not reluctantly. Some countries may strive to become great powers; others may wish to avoid doing so. The choice, however, is a constrained one. Because of the extent of their interests, larger units existing in a contentious arena tend to take on systemwide tasks. Profound change in a country's international situation produces radical change in its external behavior. After World War II, the United States broke with its centuries-long tradition of acting unilaterally and refusing to make long-term commitments. Japan's behavior in the past half century reflects the abrupt change in its international standing suffered because of its defeat in war. In the previous half century, after victory over China in 1894–95, Japan pressed for preeminence in Asia, if not beyond. Does Japan once again aspire to a larger role internationally? Its concerted regional activity, its seeking and gaining prominence in such bodies as the IMF and the World Bank, and its obvious pride in economic and technological achievements indicate that it does. The behavior of states responds more to external conditions than to internal habit if external change is profound.

When external conditions press firmly enough, they shape the behavior of states. Increasingly, Japan is being pressed to enlarge its conventional forces and to add nuclear ones to protect its interests. India, Pakistan, China, and perhaps North Korea have nuclear weapons capable of deterring others from threatening their vital interests. How long can Japan live alongside other nuclear states while denying itself similar capabilities? Conflicts and crises are certain to make Japan aware of the disadvantages of being without the military instruments that other powers command. Japanese nuclear inhibitions arising from World War II will not last indefinitely; one may expect them to expire as generational memories fade.

Japanese officials have indicated that when the protection of America's extended deterrent is no longer thought to be sufficiently reliable, Japan will equip itself with a nuclear force, whether or not openly. Japan has put itself politically and technologically in a position to do so. Consistently since the mid-1950s, the government has defined all of its Self-Defense Forces as conforming to constitutional requirements. Nuclear weapons purely for defense would be deemed constitutional should Japan decide to build some.[77] As a secret report of the Ministry of Foreign Affairs put it in 1969: "For the time being, we will maintain the policy of not possessing nuclear weapons. However, regardless of joining the NPT [Non-Proliferation Treaty] or not, we will keep the economic and technical potential for the production of nuclear weapons, while seeing to it that Japan will not be interfered with in this regard."[78] In March of 1988, Prime Minister Noboru Takeshita called for a defensive capability matching Japan's economic power.[79] Only a balanced conventional-nuclear military capability would meet this requirement. In June of 1994, Prime Minister Tsutumu Hata mentioned in parliament that Japan had the ability to make nuclear weapons.[80]

Where some see Japan as a "global civilian power" and believe it likely to remain one, others see a country that has skillfully used the protection the United States has afforded and adroitly adopted the means of maintaining its security to its regional environment.[81] Prime Minister Shigeru Yoshida in the early 1950s suggested that Japan should rely on American protection until it had rebuilt its economy as it gradually prepared to stand on its own feet.[82] Japan has laid a firm foundation for doing so by developing much of its own weaponry instead of relying on cheaper imports. Remaining months or moments away from having a nuclear military capability is well designed to protect the country's security without unduly alarming its neighbors.

The hostility of China, of both Koreas, and of Russia combines with inevitable doubts about the extent to which Japan can rely on the United States to protect its security.[83] In the opinion of Masanori Nishi, a defense official, the main cause of Japan's greater "interest in enhanced defense capabilities" is its belief that America's interest in "maintaining regional stability is shaky."[84] Whether reluctantly or not, Japan and China will follow each other on the route to becoming great powers. China has the greater long-term potential. Japan, with the world's second or third largest defense budget and the ability to produce the most technologically advanced weaponry, is closer to great power status at the moment.

When Americans speak of preserving the balance of power in East Asia through their military presence,[85] the Chinese understandably take this to mean that they intend to maintain the strategic hegemony they now enjoy in the *absence* of such a balance. When China makes steady but modest efforts to improve the quality of its inferior forces, Americans see a future threat to their and others' interests. Whatever worries the United States has and whatever threats it feels, Japan has them earlier and feels them more intensely. Japan has gradually reacted to them. China then worries as Japan improves its airlift and sealift capabilities and as the United States raises its support level for forces in South Korea.[86] The actions and reactions of China, Japan, and South Korea, with or without American participation, are creating a new balance of power in East Asia, which is becoming part of the new balance of power in the world.

Historically, encounters of East and West have often ended in tragedy. Yet, as we know from happy experience, nuclear weapons moderate the behavior of their possessors and render them cautious whenever crises threaten to spin out of control. Fortunately, the changing relations of East to West, and the changing relations of countries within the East and the West, are taking place in a nuclear context. The tensions and conflicts that intensify when profound changes in world politics take place will continue to mar the relations of nations, while nuclear weapons keep the peace among those who enjoy their protection.

America's policy of containing China by keeping 100,000 troops in East Asia and by providing security guarantees to Japan and South Korea is intended to keep a new balance of power from forming in Asia. By continuing to keep 100,000 troops in Western Europe, where no military threat is in sight, and by extending NATO eastward, the United States pursues the same goal in Europe. The American aspiration to freeze historical development by working to keep the world unipolar is doomed. In the not very long run, the task will exceed America's economic, military, demographic, and political resources; and the very effort to maintain a hegemonic position is the surest way to undermine it. The effort to maintain dominance stimulates some countries to work to overcome it. As theory shows and history confirms, that is how balances of power are made. Multipolarity is developing before our eyes. Moreover, it is emerging in accordance with the balancing imperative.

American leaders seem to believe that America's preeminent position will last indefinitely. The United States would then remain the dominant power without rivals rising to challenge it—a position without precedent in modern history. Balancing, of course, is not universal and omnipresent. A dominant power may suppress balancing as the United States has done in Europe. Whether or not balancing takes place also depends on the decisions of governments. Stephanie Neuman's book, *International Relations Theory and the Third World*, abounds in examples of states that failed to mind their own security interests through internal efforts or external arrangements, and as one would expect, suffered invasion, loss of autonomy, and dismemberment.[87] States are free to disregard the imperatives of power, but they must expect to pay a price for doing so. Moreover, relatively weak and divided states may find it impossible to concert their efforts to counter a hegemonic state despite ample provocation. This has long been the condition of the Western Hemisphere.

In the Cold War, the United States won a telling victory. Victory in war, however, often brings lasting enmities. Magnanimity in victory is rare. Winners of wars, facing few impediments to the exercise of their wills, often act in ways that create future enemies. Thus Germany, by taking Alsace and most of Lorraine from France in 1871, earned its lasting enmity; and the Allies' harsh treatment of Germany after World War I produced a similar effect. In contrast, Bismarck persuaded the kaiser not to march his armies along the road to Vienna after the great victory at Königgrätz in 1866. In the Treaty of Prague, Prussia took no Austrian territory. Thus Austria, having become Austria-Hungary, was available as an alliance partner for Germany in 1879. Rather than learning from history, the United States is repeating past errors by extending its influence over what used to be the province of the vanquished.[88] This alienates Russia and nudges it toward China instead of drawing it toward Europe and the United States. Despite much talk about the "globalization" of international politics, American political leaders to a dismaying extent think of East *or* West rather than of their interaction. With a history of conflict along a 2,600 mile border, with ethnic minorities sprawling across it, with a mineral-rich and sparsely populated Siberia facing China's teeming millions, Russia and China will find it difficult to cooperate effectively, but the United States is doing its best to help them do so. Indeed, the United States has provided the key to Russian–Chinese relations over the past half century. Feeling American antagonism and fearing American power, China drew close to Russia after World War II and remained so until the United States seemed less, and the Soviet Union more, of a threat to China. The relatively harmonious relations the United States and China enjoyed during the 1970s began to sour in the late 1980s when Russian power visibly declined and American hegemony became imminent. To alienate Russia by expanding NATO, and to alienate China by lecturing its leaders on how to rule their country, are policies that only an overwhelmingly powerful country could afford, and only a foolish one be tempted, to follow. The United States cannot prevent a new balance of power from forming. It can hasten its coming as it has been earnestly doing.

In this section, the discussion of balancing has been more empirical and speculative than theoretical. I therefore end with some reflections on balancing theory. Structural theory, and the theory of balance of power that follows from it, do not lead one to expect that states will always or even usually engage in balancing behavior. Balancing is a strategy for survival, a way of attempting to maintain a state's autonomous way of life. To argue that bandwagoning represents a behavior more common to states than balancing has become a bit of a fad. Whether states bandwagon more often than they balance is an interesting question. To believe that an affirmative answer would refute balance-of-power theory is, however, to misinterpret the theory and to commit what one might call "the numerical fallacy"—to draw a qualitative conclusion from a quantitative result. States try various strategies for survival. Balancing is one of them; bandwagoning is another. The latter may sometimes seem a less demanding and a more rewarding strategy than balancing, requiring less effort and extracting lower costs while promising concrete rewards. Amid the uncertainties of international politics and the shifting pressures of domestic politics, states have to make perilous choices. They may hope to avoid war by appeasing adversaries, a weak form of bandwagoning, rather than by rearming and realigning to thwart them. Moreover, many states have insufficient resources for balancing and little room for maneuver. They have to jump on the wagon only later to wish they could fall off.

Balancing theory does not predict uniformity of behavior but rather the strong tendency of major states in the system, or in regional subsystems, to resort to balancing when they have to. That states try different strategies of survival is hardly surprising. The recurrent emergence of balancing behavior, and the appearance of the patterns the behavior produces, should all the more be seen as impressive evidence supporting the theory.

Conclusion

Every time peace breaks out, people pop up to proclaim that realism is dead. That is another way of saying that international politics has been transformed. The world, however, has not been transformed; the structure of international politics has simply been remade by the disappearance of the Soviet Union, and for a time we will live with unipolarity. Moreover, international politics was not remade by the forces and factors that some believe are creating a new world order. Those who set the Soviet Union on the path of reform were old Soviet apparatchiks trying to right the Soviet economy in order to preserve its position in the world. The revolution in Soviet affairs and the end of the Cold War were not brought by democracy, interdependence, or international institutions. Instead the Cold War ended exactly as structural realism led one to expect. As I wrote some years ago, the Cold War "is firmly rooted in the structure of postwar international politics and will last as long as that structure endures."[89] So it did, and the Cold War ended only when the bipolar structure of the world disappeared.

Structural change affects the behavior of states and the outcomes their interactions produce. It does not break the essential continuity of international politics. The transformation of international politics alone could do that. Transformation, however, awaits the day when the international system is no longer populated by states that have to help themselves. If the day were here, one would be able to say who could be relied on to help the disadvantaged or endangered. Instead, the ominous shadow of the future continues to cast its pall over interacting states. States' perennial uncertainty about their fates presses governments to prefer relative over absolute gains. Without the shadow, the leaders of states would no longer have to ask themselves how they will get along tomorrow as well as today. States could combine their efforts cheerfully and work to maximize collective gain without worrying about how each might fare in comparison to others.

Occasionally, one finds the statement that governments in their natural, anarchic condition act myopically—that is, on calculations of immediate interest—while hoping that the future will take care of itself. Realists are said to suffer from this optical defect.[90] Political leaders may be astigmatic, but responsible ones who behave realistically do not suffer from myopia. Robert Axelrod and Robert Keohane believe that World War I might have been averted if certain states had been able to see how long the future's shadow was.[91] Yet, as their own discussion shows, the future was what the major states were obsessively worried about. The war was prompted less by considerations of present security and more by worries about how the balance might change later. The problems of governments do not arise from their short time horizons. They see the long shadow of the future, but they have trouble reading its contours, perhaps because they try to look too far ahead and see imaginary dangers. In 1914, Germany feared Russia's rapid industrial and population growth. France and Britain suffered from the same fear about Germany, and in addition Britain worried about the rapid growth of Germany's navy. In an important sense, World War I was a preventive war all around. Future fears dominated hopes for short-term gains. States do not live in the happiest of conditions that Horace in one of his odes imagined for man:

Happy the man, and happy he alone, who can say,
Tomorrow do thy worst, for I have lived today.[92]

Robert Axelrod has shown that the "tit-for-tat" tactic, and no other, maximizes collective gain over time. The one condition for success is that the game be played under the shadow of the future.[93] Because states coexist in a self-help system, they may, however, have to concern themselves not with maximizing collective gain but with lessening, preserving, or widening the gap in welfare and strength between themselves and others. The contours of the future's shadow look different in hierarchic and anarchic systems. The shadow may facilitate cooperation in the former; it works against it in the latter. Worries about the future do not make cooperation and institution building among nations impossible; they do strongly condition their operation and limit their accomplishment. Liberal institutionalists were right to start their investigations with structural realism. Until and unless a transformation occurs, it remains the basic theory of international politics.

Acknowledgments

I am indebted to Karen Adams and Robert Rauchhaus for help on this article from its conception to its completion. For insightful and constructive criticisms I wish to thank Robert Art, Richard Betts, Barbara Farnham, Anne Fox, Robert Jervis, Warner Schilling, and Mark Sheetz.

Notes

1 For example, Richard Ned Lebow, "The Long Peace, the End of the Cold War, and the Failure of Realism," *International Organization*, Vol. 48, No. 2 (Spring 1994), pp. 249–277; Jeffrey W. Legro and Andrew Moravcsik, "Is Anybody Still a Realist?," *International Security*, Vol. 24, No. 2 (Fall 1999), pp. 5–55; Bruce Russett, *Grasping the Democratic Peace: Principles for a Post-Cold War Peace* (Princeton, NJ: Princeton University Press, 1993); Paul Schroeder, "Historical Reality vs. Neorealist Theory," *International Security*, Vol. 19, No. 1 (Summer 1994), pp. 108–148; and John A. Vasquez, "The Realist Paradigm and Degenerative vs. Progressive Research Programs: An Appraisal of Neotraditional Research on Waltz's Balancing Proposition," *American Political Science Review*, Vol. 91, No. 4 (December 1997), pp. 899–912.
2 Michael W. Doyle, "Kant, Liberal Legacies, and Foreign Affairs, Parts 1 and 2," *Philosophy and Public Affairs*, Vol. 12, Nos. 3 and 4 (Summer and Fall 1983); and Doyle, "Kant: Liberalism and World Politics," *American Political Science Review*, Vol. 80, No. 4 (December 1986), pp. 1151–1169.
3 Francis Fukuyama, "Liberal Democracy as a Global Phenomenon," *Political Science and Politics*, Vol. 24, No. 4 (1991), p. 662. Jack S. Levy, "Domestic Politics and War," in Robert I. Rotberg and Theodore K. Rabb, eds., *The Origin and Prevention of Major Wars* (Cambridge: Cambridge University Press, 1989), p. 88.
4 Kenneth N. Waltz, "Kant, Liberalism, and War," *American Political Science Review*, Vol. 56, No. 2 (June 1962). Subsequent Kant references are found in this work.
5 Ido Oren, "The Subjectivity of the 'Democratic' Peace: Changing U.S. Perceptions of Imperial Germany," *International Security*, Vol. 20, No. 2 (Fall 1995), pp. 157ff.; Christopher Layne, in the second half of Layne and Sean M. Lynn-Jones, *Should America Spread Democracy? A Debate* (Cambridge, MA: MIT Press, forthcoming), argues convincingly that Germany's democratic control of foreign and military policy was no weaker than France's or Britain's.

6 John M. Owen, "How Liberalism Produces Democratic Peace," *International Security*, Vol. 19, No. 2 (Fall 1994), pp. 87–125. Cf. his *Liberal Peace, Liberal War: American Politics and International Security* (Ithaca, NY: Cornell University Press, 1997).

7 Christopher Layne, "Kant or Cant: The Myth of the Democratic Peace," *International Security*, Vol. 19, No. 2 (Fall 1994), pp. 5–49.

8 Francis Fukuyama, *The End of History and the Last Man* (New York: Free Press, 1992), pp. 254–256. Russett, *Grasping the Democratic Peace*, p. 24.

9 For example, Leopold von Ranke, Gerhard Ritter, and Otto Hintze. The American William Graham Sumner and many others shared their doubts.

10 Immanuel Kant, *The Philosophy of Law*, trans. W. Hastie (Edinburgh: T. and T. Clark, 1887), p. 218.

11 John Mueller, "Is War Still Becoming Obsolete?," paper presented at the annual meeting of the American Political Science Association, Washington, DC, August–September 1991, pp. 55ff; cf. his *Quiet Cataclysm: Reflections on the Recent Transformation of World Politics* (New York: HarperCollins, 1995).

12 Edward Hallett Carr, *Twenty Years' Crisis: An Introduction to the Study of International Relations*, 2d ed. (New York: Harper and Row, 1946), pp. 129–132.

13 Quoted in Anthony Lewis, "The Kissinger Doctrine," *New York Times*, February 27, 1975, p. 35; and see Henry Kissinger, *The White House Years* (Boston: Little, Brown, 1979), chap. 17.

14 See, for example, Kenneth N. Waltz, "America as Model for the World? A Foreign Policy Perspective," *PS: Political Science and Politics*, Vol. 24, No. 4 (December 1991); and Mueller, "Is War Still Becoming Obsolete?," p. 5.

15 Quoted in Walter A. McDougall, *Promised Land, Crusader State* (Boston: Houghton Mifflin, 1997), p. 28 and n. 36.

16 Doyle, "Kant, Liberal Legacies, and Foreign Affairs, Part 2," p. 337.

17 Warren Christopher, "The U.S.–Japan Relationship: The Responsibility to Change," address to the Japan Association of Corporate Executives, Tokyo, Japan, March 11, 1994 (U.S. Department of State, Bureau of Public Affairs, Office of Public Communication), p. 3.

18 Page quoted in Waltz, *Man, the State, and War: A Theoretical Analysis* (New York: Columbia University Press, 1959), p. 121. Rusk quoted in Layne, "Kant or Cant," p. 46.

19 Quoted in Clemson G. Turregano and Ricky Lynn Waddell, "From Paradigm to Paradigm Shift: The Military and Operations Other than War," *Journal of Political Science*, Vol. 22 (1994), p. 15.

20 Peter Beinart, "The Return of the Bomb," *New Republic*, August 3, 1998, p. 27.

21 Quoted in Michael Straight, *Make This the Last War* (New York: G. P. Putnam's Sons, 1945), p. 1.

22 Hans J. Morgenthau, *Politics among Nations: The Struggle for Power and Peace*, 5th ed. (New York: Knopf, 1973), p. 248.

23 Gordon Craig and Alexander George, *Force and Statecraft: Diplomatic Problems of Our Time*, 2d ed. (New York: Oxford University Press, 1990), p. 64.

24 Strongly affirmative answers are given by John R. Oneal and Bruce Russett, "Assessing the Liberal Peace with Alternative Specifications: Trade Still Reduces Conflict," *Journal of Peace Research*, Vol. 36, No. 4 (July 1999), pp. 423–442; and Russett, Oneal, and David R. Davis, "The Third Leg of the Kantian Tripod for Peace: International Organizations and Militarized Disputes, 1950–85," *International Organization*, Vol. 52, No. 3 (Summer 1998), pp. 441–467.

25 Richard Rosecrance, *The Rise of the Trading State: Commerce and Coalitions in the Modern World* (New York: Basic Books, 1986); and at times Susan Strange,

The Retreat of the State: The Diffusion of Power in the World Economy (New York: Cambridge University Press, 1996).

26 Norman Angell, *The Great Illusion*, 4th rev. and enlarged ed. (New York: Putnam's, 1913).

27 Katherine Barbieri, "Economic Interdependence: A Path to Peace or a Source of Interstate Conflict?," *Journal of Peace Research*, Vol. 33, No. 1 (February 1996). Lawrence Keely, *War before Civilization: The Myth of the Peaceful Savage* (New York: Oxford University Press, 1996), p. 196, shows that with increases of trade and intermarriage among tribes, war became more frequent.

28 On states managing interdependence to avoid excessive dependence, see especially Robert Gilpin, *The Political Economy of International Relations* (Princeton, NJ: Princeton University Press, 1987), chap. 10; and Suzanne Berger and Ronald Dore, eds., *National Diversity and Global Capitalism* (Ithaca, NY: Cornell University Press, 1996).

29 Cf. Kenneth N. Waltz, in Steven L. Spiegel and Waltz eds., *Conflict in World Politics* (Cambridge, MA: Winthrop, 1971), chap. 13.

30 Robert O. Keohane and Joseph S. Nye, *Power and Interdependence*, 2d ed. (New York: Harper-Collins, 1989).

31 Keohane and Nye are on both sides of the issue. See, for example, ibid., p. 28. Keohane emphasized that power is not very fungible in Keohane ed., "Theory of World Politics," *Neorealism and Its Critics* (New York: Columbia University Press, 1986); and see Kenneth N. Waltz, "Reflection on Theory of International Politics: A Response to My Critics," in ibid. Robert J. Art analyzes the fungibility of power in detail. See Art, "American Foreign Policy and the Fungibility of Force," *Security Studies*, Vol. 5, No. 4 (Summer 1996).

32 Kenneth N. Waltz, "The Myth of National Interdependence," in Charles P. Kindleberger ed., *The International Corporation* (Cambridge, MA: MIT Press, 1970).

33 Strange, *Retreat of the State*, pp. 46, 189.

34 Ibid., pp. 25, 192.

35 Alexis de Tocqueville, *Democracy in America*, ed. J. P. Mayer, trans. George Lawrence (New York: Harper Perennial, 1988), p. 446, n. 1.

36 See Kenneth N. Waltz, "International Structure, National Force, and the Balance of World Power," *Journal of International Affairs*, Vol. 21, No. 2 (1967), p. 219.

37 Glenn H. Snyder, *Alliance Politics* (Ithaca, NY: Cornell University Press, 1997), p. 192.

38 Kenneth N. Waltz, "The Emerging Structure of International Politics," *International Security*, Vol. 18, No. 2 (Fall 1993), pp. 75–76.

39 John Roper, "Shaping Strategy without the Threat," Adephi Paper No. 257 (London: International Institute for Strategic Studies, Winter 1990/91), pp. 80–81.

40 Joseph A. Schumpeter, writing of armies, put it this way: "*created by wars that required it, the machine now created the wars it required.*" "The Sociology of Imperialism," in Schumpeter, *Imperialism and Social Classes* (New York: Meridian Books, 1955), p. 25 (emphasis in original).

41 Gunther Hellmann and Reinhard Wolf, "Neorealism, Neoliberal Institutionalism, and the Future of NATO," *Security Studies*, Vol. 3, No. 1 (Autumn 1993), p. 20.

42 John Kornblum, "NATO's Second Half Century—Tasks for an Alliance," *NATO on Track for the 21st Century*, Conference Report (The Hague: Netherlands Atlantic Commission, 1994), p. 14.

43 Mark S. Sheetz, "Correspondence: Debating the Unipolar Moment," *International Security*, Vol. 22, No. 3 (Winter 1997/98), p. 170; and Mike Winnerstig, "Rethinking Alliance Dynamics," paper presented at the annual meeting of the International Studies Association, Washington, DC, March 18–22, 1997, at p. 23.

44 Cf. Alan S. Milward, *The European Rescue of the Nation–State* (Berkeley: University of California Press, 1992).

45 Robert O. Keohane and Lisa L. Martin, "The Promise of Institutionalist Theory," *International Security*, Vol. 20, No. 1 (Summer 1995), p. 40.

46 James M. Goldgeier, "NATO Expansion: The Anatomy of a Decision," *Washington Quarterly*, Vol. 21, No. 1 (Winter 1998), pp. 94–95. And see his *Not Whether but When: The U.S. Decision to Enlarge NATO* (Washington, DC: Brookings, 1999).

47 William D. Hartung, "Welfare for Weapons Dealers 1998: The Hidden Costs of NATO Expansion" (New York: New School for Social Research, World Policy Institute, March 1998); and Jeff Gerth and Tim Weiner, "Arms Makers See Bonanza in Selling NATO Expansion," *New York Times*, June 29, 1997, p. I, 8.

48 See Michael E. Brown, "The Flawed Logic of Expansion," *Survival*, Vol. 37, No. 1 (Spring 1995), pp. 34–52. Michael Mandelbaum, *The Dawn of Peace in Europe* (New York: Twentieth Century Fund Press, 1996). Philip Zelikow, "The Masque of Institutions," *Survival*, Vol. 38, No. 1 (Spring 1996).

49 J. L. Black, *Russia Faces NATO Expansion: Bearing Gifts or Bearing Arms?* (Lanham, MD: Rowman and Littlefield, 2000), pp. 5–35, 175–201.

50 Ibid., p. 72.

51 Keohane and Martin, "The Promise of Institutionalist Theory," pp. 42, 46.

52 Strange, *Retreat of the State*, p. xiv; and see pp. 192–193. Cf. Carr, *The Twenty Years' Crisis*, p. 107: "international government is, in effect, government by that state which supplies the power necessary for the purpose of governing."

53 Keohane and Martin, "The Promise of Institutionalist Theory," p. 46.

54 Ibid., p. 42.

55 Mearsheimer, "A Realist Reply," p. 85.

56 Keohane and Nye, *Power and Interdependence*, p. 251; cf. Keohane, "Theory of World Politics," in Keohane, *Neorealism and Its Critics*, p. 193, where he describes his approach as a "modified structural research program."

57 Robert O. Keohane, *International Institutions and State Power: Essays in International Relations Theory* (Boulder, CO: Westview, 1989), p. 15.

58 Robert J. Art, "Why Western Europe Needs the United States and NATO," *Political Science Quarterly*, Vol. 111, No. 1 (Spring 1996).

59 Quoted in ibid., p. 36.

60 Robert O. Keohane, "The Diplomacy of Structural Change: Multilateral Institutions and State Strategies," in Helga Haftendorn and Christian Tuschhoff eds., *America and Europe in an Era of Change* (Boulder, CO: Westview, 1993), p. 53.

61 Stephen D. Krasner, "Global Communications and National Power: Life on the Pareto Frontier," *World Politics*, Vol. 43, No. 1 (April 1991), p. 234.

62 Stephen D. Krasner, *Structural Conflict: The Third World against Global Liberalism* (Berkeley: University of California, 1985), p. 263 and passim.

63 Stephen D. Krasner, "International Political Economy: Abiding Discord," *Review of International Political Economy*, Vol. 1, No. 1 (Spring 1994), p. 16.

64 Quoted in Robert Tucker, *Intervention and the Reagan Doctrine* (New York: Council on Religious and International Affairs, 1985), p. 5.

65 Robert Gilpin explains the oddity. See Gilpin, "No One Loves a Political Realist," *Security Studies*, Vol. 5, No. 3 (Spring 1996), pp. 3–28.
66 William C. Wohlforth, "The Stability of a Unipolar World," *International Security*, Vol. 24, No. 1 (Summer 1999), pp. 5–41.
67 Quoted in Ted Robert Gurr, "Persistence and Change in Political Systems, 1800–1971," *American Political Science Review*, Vol. 68, No. 4 (December 1974), p. 1504, from Robert G. Wesson, *The Imperial Order* (Berkeley: University of California Press, 1967), unpaginated preface. Cf. Paul Kennedy, *The Rise and Fall of Great Powers: Economic Change and Military Conflict from 1500 to 2000* (New York: Random House, 1987).
68 "Cover Story: Communism's Collapse Poses a Challenge to America's Military," U.S. *News and World Report*, October 14, 1991, p. 28.
69 Michael Mastanduno, "Preserving the Unipolar Moment: Realist Theories and U.S. Grand Strategy after the Cold War," *International Security*, Vol. 21, No. 4 (Spring 1997), p. 88. See Josef Joffe's interesting analysis of America's role, " 'Bismarck' or 'Britain'? Toward an American Grand Strategy after Bipolarity," *International Security*, Vol. 19, No. 4 (Spring 1995).
70 Waltz, "The Emerging Structure of International Politics," p. 79.
71 Charles W. Kegley, Jr., "The Neoidealist Moment in International Studies? Realist Myths and the New International Realities," *International Studies Quarterly*, Vol. 37, No. 2 (June 1993), p. 149.
72 Jacques Delors, "European Integration and Security," *Survival*, Vol. 33, No. 1 (March/April 1991), p. 106.
73 Craig R. Whitney, "NATO at 50: With Nations at Odds, Is It a Misalliance?." *New York Times*, February 15, 1999, p. A1.
74 The following four pages are adapted from Waltz, "The Emerging Structure of International Politics."
75 Nuclear parity is reached when countries have second-strike forces. It does not require quantitative or qualitative equality of forces. See Waltz, "Nuclear Myths and Political Realities," *American Political Science Review*, Vol. 84, No. 3 (September 1990).
76 David E. Sanger and Erik Eckholm, "Will Beijing's Nuclear Arsenal Stay Small or Will It Mushroom?," *New York Times*, March 15, 1999, p. A1.
77 Norman D. Levin, "Japan's Defense Policy: The Internal Debate," in Harry H. Kendall and Clara Joewono eds., *Japan, ASEAN, and the United States* (Berkeley: Institute of East Asian Studies, University of California, 1990).
78 "The Capability to Develop Nuclear Weapons Should Be Kept: Ministry of Foreign Affairs Secret Document in 1969," *Mainichi*, August 1, 1994, p. 41, quoted in Selig S. Harrison, "Japan and Nuclear Weapons," in Harrison ed., *Japan's Nuclear Future* (Washington, DC: Carnegie Endowment for International Peace, 1996), p. 9.
79 David Arase, "US and ASEAN Perceptions of Japan's Role in the Asian-Pacific Region," in Kendall and Joewono, *Japan, ASEAN, and the United States*, p. 276.
80 David E. Sanger, "In Face-Saving Reverse, Japan Disavows Any Nuclear-Arms Expertise," *New York Times*, June 22, 1994, p. 10.
81 Michael J. Green, "State of the Field Report: Research on Japanese Security Policy," Access *Asia Review*, Vol. 2, No. 2 (September 1998), judiciously summarized different interpretations of Japan's security policy.
82 Kenneth B. Pyle, *The Japanese Question: Power and Purpose in a New Era* (Washington, DC: AEI Press, 1992), p. 26.
83 Andrew Hanami, for example, points out that Japan wonders whether the

United States would help defend Hokkaido. Hanami, "Japan and the Military Balance of Power in Northeast Asia," *Journal of East Asian Affairs*, Vol. 7, No. 2 (Summer/Fall 1994), p. 364.

84 Stephanie Strom, "Japan Beginning to Flex Its Military Muscles," *New York Times*, April 8, 1999, p. A4.

85 Richard Bernstein and Ross H. Munro, *The Coming Conflict with China* (New York: Alfred A. Knopf, 1997); and Andrew J. Nathan and Robert S. Ross, *The Great Wall and the Empty Fortress: China's Search for Security* (New York: W. W. Norton, 1997).

86 Michael J. Green and Benjamin L. Self, "Japan's Changing China Policy: From Commercial Liberalism to Reluctant Realism," *Survival*, Vol. 38, No. 2 (Summer 1996), p. 43.

87 Stephanie Neuman ed., *International Relations Theory and the Third World* (New York: St. Martin's, 1998).

88 Tellingly, John Lewis Gaddis comments that he has never known a time when there was less support among historians for an announced policy. Gaddis, "History, Grand Strategy, and NATO Enlargement," *Survival*, Vol. 40, No. 1 (Spring 1998), p. 147.

89 Kenneth N. Waltz, "The Origins of War in Neorealist Theory," *Journal of Interdisciplinary History*, Vol. 18, No. 4 (Spring 1988), p. 628.

90 The point is made by Robert O. Keohane, *After Hegemony: Cooperation and Discord in the World Political Economy* (Princeton, NJ: Princeton University Press, 1984), pp. 99, 103, 108.

91 Robert Axelrod and Robert O. Keohane, "Achieving Cooperation under Anarchy: Strategies and Institutions," in David Baldwin ed., *Neorealism and Neoliberalism: The Contemporary Debate* (New York: Columbia University Press, 1993). For German leaders, they say, "the shadow of the future seemed so small" (p. 92). Robert Powell shows that "a longer shadow . . . leads to greater military allocations." See Powell, "Guns, Butter, and Anarchy," *American Political Science Review*, Vol. 87, No. 1 (March 1993), p. 116; see also p. 117 on the question of the compatibility of liberal institutionalism and structural realism.

92 My revision.

93 Robert Axelrod, *The Evolution of Cooperation* (New York: Basic Books, 1984).

14

GLOBALIZATION AND GOVERNANCE

In 1979 I described the interdependence of states as low but increasing. It has increased, but only to about the 1910 level if measured by trade or capital flows as a percentage of GNP; lower if measured by the mobility of labor, and lower still if measured by the mutual military dependence of states. Yet one feels that the world has become a smaller one. International travel has become faster, easier, and cheaper; music, art, cuisines, and cinema have all become cosmopolitan in the world's major centers and beyond. The *Peony Pavilion* was produced in its entirety for the first time in 400 years, and it was presented not in Shanghai or Beijing, but in New York. Communication is almost instantaneous, and more than words can be transmitted, which makes the reduced mobility of labor of less consequence. High-technology jobs can be brought to the workers instead of the workers to the jobs; foreigners can become part of American design teams without leaving their homelands. Before World War I, the close interdependence of states was thought of as heralding an era of peace among nations and democracy and prosperity within them. Associating interdependence, peace, democracy, and prosperity is nothing new. In his much translated and widely read book, *The Great Illusion* (1933), Norman Angell summed up the texts of generations of classical and neoclassical economists and drew from them the dramatic conclusion that wars would no longer be fought because they would not pay. World War I instead produced the great disillusion, which reduced political optimism to a level that remained low almost until the end of the Cold War. I say "almost" because beginning in the 1970s a new optimism, strikingly similar in content to the old, began to resurface. Interdependence was again associated with peace and peace increasingly with democracy, which began to spread wonderfully to Latin America, to Asia, and with the Soviet Union's collapse, to Eastern Europe. Francis Fukuyama (1992) foresaw a time when all states would be liberal democracies and, more recently, Michael Doyle (1997) projected the year for it to happen as lying between 2050 and 2100. John Mueller (1989), heralding the disappearance of war among the world's advanced countries, argued that Norman Angell's premises were right all along, but that he had published his book prematurely.

230

Robert Keohane and Joseph Nye in their 1977 book, *Power and Interdependence*, strengthened the notion that interdependence promotes peace and limits the use of force by arguing that simple interdependence had become complex interdependence, binding the economic and hence the political interests of states ever more tightly together. Now, we hear from many sides that interdependence has reached yet another height, transcending states and making *The Borderless World*, which is the title and theme of Kenichi Ohmae's 1990 book. People, firms, markets matter more; states matter less. Each tightening of the economic screw raises the benefits of economic exchange and makes war among the more advanced states increasingly costly. The simple and plausible propositions are that as the benefits of peace rise, so do the costs of war. When states perceive wars to be immensely costly, they will be disinclined to fight them. War becomes rare, but is not abolished because even the strongest economic forces cannot conquer fear or eliminate concern for national honor (Friedman 1999, pp. 196–197).

Economic interests become so strong that markets begin to replace politics at home and abroad. That economics depresses politics and limits its significance is taken to be a happy thought. The first section of this paper examines its application domestically; the second, internationally.

The state of the state

Globalization is the fad of the 1990s, and globalization is made in America. Thomas Friedman's *The Lexus and the Olive Tree* is a celebration of the American way, of market capitalism and liberal democracy. Free markets, transparency, and flexibility are the watchwords. The "electronic herd" moves vast amounts of capital in and out of countries according to their political and economic merits. Capital moves almost instantaneously into countries with stable governments, progressive economies, open accounting, and honest dealing, and out of countries lacking those qualities. States can defy the "herd," but they will pay a price, usually a steep one, as did Thailand, Malaysia, Indonesia, and South Korea in the 1990s. Some countries may defy the herd inadvertently (the countries just mentioned); others, out of ideological conviction (Cuba and North Korea); some, because they can afford to (oil-rich countries); others, because history has passed them by (many African countries).

Countries wishing to attract capital and to gain the benefits of today's and tomorrow's technology have to don the "golden straitjacket," a package of policies including balanced budgets, economic deregulation, openness to investment and trade, and a stable currency. The herd decides which countries to reward and which to punish, and nothing can be done about its decisions. In September 1997, at a World Bank meeting, Malaysia's prime minister, Dr. Mahathir Mohammad, complained bitterly that great powers and international speculators had forced Asian countries to open their markets and had manipulated their currencies in order to destroy them. Friedman (1999, p. 93) wonders what Robert Rubin, then-U.S. treasury secretary, might have said in response. He imagines it would have been something like this: "What planet are you living on? . . . Globalization isn't a choice, it's a reality, . . . and the only way you can grow at the speed that your people want to grow is by tapping into the global stock and bond markets, by seeking out multinationals to invest in your country, and by selling into the global trading system what your factories produce. And the most basic truth about globalization is this: *No one is in charge.*"

The herd has no telephone number. When the herd decides to withdraw capital from a country, there is no one to complain to or to petition for relief. Decisions of the herd are collective ones. They are not made; they happen, and they happen because many investors individually make decisions simultaneously and on similar grounds to invest or to withdraw their funds. Do what displeases the herd, and it will trample you into the ground. Globalization is shaped by markets, not by governments.

Globalization means homogenization. Prices, products, wages, wealth, and rates of interest and profit tend to become the same all over the world. Like any powerful movement for change, globalization encounters resistance—in America, from religious fundamentalists; abroad, from anti-Americanists; everywhere from cultural traditionalists. And the resisters become bitter because consciously or not they know they are doomed. Driven by technology, international finance sweeps all before it. Under the protection of American military power, globalization proceeds relentlessly. As Friedman proclaims: "America truly is the ultimate benign hegemony" (p. 375).

The "end of the Cold War and the collapse of communism have discredited all models other than liberal democracy." The statement is by Larry Diamond, and Friedman repeats it with approval. There is one best way, and America has found it. "It's a post-industrial world, and America today is good at everything that is post-industrial" (pp. 145, 303). The herd does not care about forms of government as such, but it values and rewards "stability, predictability, transparency, and the ability to transfer and protect its private property." Liberal democracies represent the one best way. The message to all governments is clear: Conform or suffer.

There is much in what Friedman says, and he says it very well. But how much? And, specifically, what is the effect of closer interdependence on the conduct of the internal and external affairs of nations?

First, we should ask how far globalization has proceeded? As everyone knows, much of the world has been left aside: most of Africa and Latin America, Russia, all of the Middle East except Israel, and large parts of Asia. Moreover, for many countries, the degree of participation in the global economy varies by region. Northern Italy, for example, is in; southern Italy is out. In fact, globalization is not global but is mainly limited to northern latitudes. Linda Weiss points out that, as of 1991, 81% of the world stock of foreign direct investment was in high-wage countries of the north: mainly the United States, followed by the United Kingdom, Germany, and Canada. She adds that the extent of concentration has grown by 12 points since 1967 (Weiss 1998; cf., Hirst and Thompson 1996, p.72).

Second, we should compare the interdependence of nations now with interdependence earlier. The first paragraph of this paper suggests that in most ways we have not exceeded levels reached in 1910. The rapid growth of international trade and investment from the middle 1850s into the 1910s preceded a prolonged period of war, internal revolution, and national insularity. After World War II, protectionist policies lingered as the United States opened it borders to trade while taking a relaxed attitude toward countries that protected their markets during the years of recovery from war's devastation. One might say that from 1914 into the 1960s an interdependence deficit developed, which helps to explain the steady growth of interdependence thereafter. Among the richest 24 industrial economies (the OECD countries), exports grew at about twice the rate of GDP after 1960. In 1960, exports were 9.5% of their GDPs; in 1900, 20.5% (Wade 1996, p. 62; cf., Weiss 1998, p. 171). Finding that 1999 approximately equals 1910 in extent of interdependence is hardly surprising. What is true of trade also holds for capital flows, again as a percentage of GDP (Hirst and Thompson 1996, p. 36).

Third, money markets may be the only economic sector one can say has become truly global. Finance capital moves freely across the frontiers of OECD countries and quite freely elsewhere (Weiss 1998, p. xii). Robert Wade notes that real interest rates within northern countries and between northern and southern countries vary by no more than 5%. This seems quite large until one notices variations across countries of 10 to 50 times in real wages, years of schooling, and numbers of working scientists. Still, with the movement of financial assets as with commodities, the present remains like the past. Despite today's ease of communication, financial markets at the turn of the previous century were at least as integrated as they are now (Wade 1996, pp. 73–75).

Obviously, the world is not one. Sadly, the disparities of the North and South remain wide. Perhaps surprisingly, among the countries that are thought of as being in the zone of globalization, differences are considerable and persistent. To take just one example, financial patterns differ markedly across countries. The United States depends on capital imports, Western Europe does not, and Japan is a major capital exporter. The more closely one looks, the more one finds variations. That is hardly surprising. What looks smooth, uniform, and simple from a distance, on closer inspection proves to be pockmarked, variegated, and complex. Yet here, the variations are large enough to sustain the conclusion that globalization, even within its zone, is not a statement about the present, but a prediction about the future.

Many globalizers underestimate the extent to which the new
looks like the old. In any competitive system the winners are
imitated by the losers, or they continue to lose.

Many globalizers underestimate the extent to which the new looks like the
old. In any competitive system the winners are imitated by the losers, or they
continue to lose. In political as in economic development, latecomers imitate
the practices and adopt the institution of the countries who have shown the
way. Occasionally, someone finds a way to outflank, to invent a new way, or to
ingeniously modify an old way to gain an advantage; and then the process of
imitation begins anew. That competitors begin to look like one another if the
competition is close and continuous is a familiar story. Competition among
states has always led some of them to imitate others politically, militarily, and
economically; but the apostles of globalization argue that the process has now
sped up immensely and that the straitjacket allows little room to wiggle. In the
old political era, the strong vanquished the weak; in the new economic era,
"the fast eat the slow" (Klaus Schwab quoted in Friedman 1999, p. 171).
No longer is it "Do what the strong party says or risk physical punishment";
but instead "Do what the electronic herd requires or remain impoverished."
But then, in a competitive system there are always winners and losers. A few
do exceptionally well, some get along, and many bring up the rear.

States have to conform to the ways of the more successful among them or
pay a stiff price for not doing so. We then have to ask what is the state of the
state? What becomes of politics within the coils of encompassing economic
processes? The message of globalizers is that economic and technological
forces impose near uniformity of political and economic forms and functions
on states. They do so because the herd is attracted only to countries with
reliable, stable, and open governments—that is, to liberal democratic ones.

Yet a glance at just the past 75 years reveals that a variety of political-
economic systems have produced impressive results and were admired in their
day for doing so. In the 1930s and again in the 1950s, the Soviet Union's
economic growth rates were among the world's highest, so impressive in
the '50s that America feared being overtaken and passed by. In the 1960s
President Kennedy got "the country moving again," and America's radically
different system gained world respect. In the '70s, Western European welfare
states with managed and directed economics were highly regarded. In the late
'70s and through much of the '80s, the Japanese brand of neomercantilism
was thought to be the wave of the future; and Western Europe and the United
States worried about being able to keep up. Imitate or perish was the counsel
of some; pry the Japanese economy open and make it compete on our
grounds was the message of others. America did not succeed in doing much of
either. Yet in the 1990s, its economy has flourished. Globalizers offer it as the
ultimate political-economic model—and so history again comes to an end. Yet
it is odd to conclude from a decade's experience that the one best model has at

last appeared. Globalization, if it were realized, would mean a near uniformity of conditions across countries. Even in the 1990s, one finds little evidence of globalization. The advanced countries of the world have enjoyed or suffered quite different fates. Major Western European countries were plagued by high and persistent unemployment; Northeast and Southeast Asian countries experienced economic stagnation or collapse while China continued to do quite well; and we know about the United States.

Variation in the fortunes of nations underlines the point: The country that has done best, at least lately, is the United States. Those who have fared poorly have supposedly done so because they have failed to conform to the American Way. Globalizers do not claim that globalization is complete, but only that it is in process and that the process is irreversible. Some evidence supports the conclusion; some does not. Looking at the big picture, one notices that nations whose economies have faltered or failed have been more fully controlled, directed, and supported governmentally than the American economy. Soviet-style economies failed miserably; in China, only the free-market sector flourishes; the once much-favored Swedish model has proved wanting. One can easily add more examples. From them it is tempting to leap to the conclusion that America has indeed found, or stumbled onto, the one best way.

Obviously, Thomas Friedman thinks so. Tip O'Neill, when he was a congressman from Massachusetts, declared that all politics are local. Wrong, Friedman says, all politics have become global. "The electronic herd," he writes, "turns the whole world into a parliamentary system, in which every government lives under the fear of a no-confidence vote from the herd" (1999, pp. 62, 115).

I find it hard to believe that economic processes direct or determine a nation's policies, that spontaneously arrived at decisions about where to place resources reward or punish a national economy so strongly that a government either does what pleases the "herd" or its economy fails to prosper or even risks collapse. We all recall recent cases, some of them mentioned above, that seem to support Friedman's thesis. Mentioning them both makes a point and raises doubts.

First, within advanced countries at similar levels of development that are closely interrelated, one expects uniformities of form and function to be most fully displayed. Yet Stephen Woolcock, looking at forms of corporate governance within the European community, finds a "spectrum of approaches" and expects it to persist for the foreseeable future (1996, p. 196). Since the 1950s, the economies of Germany and France have grown more closely together as each became the principal trading partner of the other. Yet a study of the two countries concludes that France has copied German policies but has been unwilling or unable to copy institutions (Boltho 1996). GDP per work hour among seven of the most prosperous countries came close together between the 1950s and the 1980s (Boyer 1996, p. 37). Countries at a high level of development do tend to converge in productivity, but that is something of a tautology.

What I found to be true in 1970 remains true today: The world is less interdependent than is usually supposed.

Second, even if all politics have become global, economies remain local perhaps to a surprising extent. Countries with large economies continue to do most of their business at home. Americans produce 88% of the goods they buy. Sectors that are scarcely involved in international trade, such as government, construction, nonprofit organizations, utilities, and wholesale and retail trade employ 82% of Americans (Lawrence 1997, p. 21). As Paul Krugman says, "The United States is still almost 90% an economy that produces goods and services for its own use" (1997, p. 166). For the world's three largest economies—the United States, Japan, and the European Union—taken as a unit, exports are 12% or less of GDP (Weiss 1998, p. 176). What I found to be true in 1970 remains true today: The world is less interdependent than is usually supposed (Waltz 1970). Moreover, developed countries, oil imports aside, do the bulk of their external business with one another, and that means that the extent of their dependence on commodities that they could not produce for themselves is further reduced.

Reinforcing the parochial pattern of productivity, the famous footloose corporations in fact turn out to be firmly anchored in their home bases. One study of the world's 100 largest corporations concludes that not one of them could be called truly "global" or "footloose." Another study found one multinational corporation that seemed to be leaving its home base: Britain's chemical company ICI (Weiss 1998, pp. 18, 22; cf., Hirst and Thompson 1996, pp. 82–93, 90, 95ff.). On all the important counts—location of most assets, site of research and development, ownership, and management—the importance of a corporation's home base is marked. And the technological prowess of corporations corresponds closely to that of the countries in which they are located.

Third, the "*transformative capacity*" of states, as Linda Weiss emphasizes, is the key to their success in the world economy (Weiss 1998, p. xii). Because technological innovation is rapid, and because economic conditions at home and abroad change often, states that adapt easily have considerable advantages. International politics remains international. As the title of a review by William H. McNeill (1997) puts it, "Territorial States Buried Too Soon." Global or world politics has not taken over from national politics. The twentieth century was the century of the nation-state. The twenty-first will be too. Trade and technology do not determine a single best way to organize a polity and its economy. National systems display a great deal of resilience. States still have a wide range of choice. Most states survive, and the units that survive in competitive systems are those with the ability to adapt. Some do it well, and

236

they grow and prosper. Others just manage to get along. That's the way it is in competitive systems. In this spirit, Ezra Taft Benson, when he was President Eisenhower's secretary of agriculture, gave this kindly advice to America's small farmers: "Get big or get out." Success in competitive systems requires the units of the system to adopt ways they would prefer to avoid.

States adapt to their environment. Some are light afoot, and others are heavy. The United States looked to be heavy afoot in the 1980s when Japan's economy was booming. Sometimes it seemed that the MITI (Ministry of International Trade and Industry) was manned by geniuses who guided Japan's economy effortlessly to its impressive accomplishments. Now it is the United States that appears light afoot, lighter than any other country. Its government is open: Accurate financial information flows freely, most economic decisions are made by private firms. These are the characteristics that make for flexibility and for quick adaptation to changing conditions.

Competitive systems select for success. Over time, the qualities that make for success vary. Students of American government point out that one of the advantages of a federal system is that the separate states can act as laboratories for social-economic experimentation. When some states succeed, others may imitate them. The same thought applies to nations. One must wonder who the next winner will be.

Because technological innovation is rapid, and because economic conditions at home and abroad change often, states that adapt easily have considerable advantages.

States adapt; they also protect themselves. Different nations, with distinct institutions and traditions, protect themselves in different ways. Japan fosters industries, defends them, and manages its trade. The United States uses its political, economic, and military leverage to protect itself and manipulate international events to promote its interests. Thus, as David E. Spiro elaborately shows, international markets and institutions did not recycle petrodollars after 1974. The United States did. Despite many statements to the contrary, the United States worked effectively through different administrations and under different cabinet secretaries to undermine markets and thwart international institutions. Its leverage enabled it to manipulate the oil crisis to serve its own interests (1999, chap. 6).

Many of the interdependers of the 1970s expected the state to wither and fade away. Charles Kindleberger wrote in 1969 that "the nation-state is just about through as an economic unit" (p. 207). Globalizers of the 1990s believe that this time it really is happening. The state has lost its "monopoly over internal sovereignty," Wolfgang H. Reinecke writes, and as "an externally sovereign actor" it "will become a thing of the past" (1997, p. 137; cf., Thurow 1999). Internally, the state's monopoly has never been complete, but it seems more nearly so now than earlier, at least in well-established states. The range of governmental functions and the extent of state control over society and economy has seldom been fuller than it is now. In many parts of the world the concern has been not with the state's diminished internal powers but with their increase. And although state control has lessened somewhat recently, does anyone believe that the United States and Britain, for example, are back to a 1930s level, let alone to a nineteenth-century level of governmental regulation?

States perform essential political social-economic functions, and no other organization appears as a possible competitor to them. They foster the institutions that make internal peace and prosperity possible. In the state of nature, as Kant put it, there is "no mine and thine." States turn possession into property and thus make saving, production, and prosperity possible. The sovereign state with fixed borders has proved to be the best organization for keeping peace and fostering the conditions for economic well-being.[1] We do not have to wonder what happens to society and economy when a state begins to fade away. We have all too many examples. A few obvious ones are China in the 1920s and '30s and again in the 1960s and '70s, post-Soviet Russia, and many African states since their independence. The less competent a state, the likelier it is to dissolve into component parts or to be unable to adapt to transnational developments. Challenges at home and abroad test the mettle of states. Some states fail, and other states pass the tests nicely. In modern times, enough states always make it to keep the international system going as a system of states. The challenges vary; states endure. They have proved to be hardy survivors.

Having asked how international conditions affect states, I now reverse the question and ask how states affect the conduct of international political affairs.

The state in international politics

Economic globalization would mean tht the world economy, or at least the globalized portion of it, would be integrated and not merely interdependent. The difference between an interdependent and an integrated world is a qualitative one and not a mere matter of proportionately more trade and a greater and more rapid flow of capital. With integration, the world would look like one big state. Economic markets and economic interests cannot perform the functions of government. Integration requires or presumes a government to protect, direct, and control. Interdependence, in contrast to integration, is "the mere mutualism" of states, as Emile Durkheim put it. It is not only less close than usually thought but also politically less consequential. Interdependence did not produce the world-shaking events of 1989–91. A political event, the failure of one of the world's two great powers, did that. Had the configuration of international politics not fundamentally changed, neither the unification of Germany nor the war against Saddam Hussein would have been possible. The most important events in international politics are explained by differences in the capabilities of states, not by economic forces operating across states or transcending them. Interdependers, and globalizers even more so, argue that the international economic interests of states work against their going to war. True, they do. Yet if one asks whether economic interests or nuclear weapons inhibit war more strongly, the answer obviously is nuclear weapons. European great powers prior to World War I were tightly tied together economically. They nevertheless fought a long and bloody war. The United States and the Soviet Union were not even loosely connected economically. They coexisted peacefully through the four-and-a-half decades of the Cold War. The most important causes of peace, as of war, are found in international-political conditions, including the weaponry available to states. Events following the Cold War dramatically demonstrate the political weakness of economic forces. The integration (not just the interdependence) of the parts of the Soviet Union and of Yugoslavia, with all of their entangling economic interests, did not prevent their disintegration. Governments and people sacrifice welfare and even security to nationalism, ethnicity, and religion.

Political explanations weigh heavily in accounting for international-political events. National *politics*, not international markets, account for many international *economic* developments. A number of students of politics and of economics believe that blocs are becoming more common internationally. Economic interests and market forces do not create blocs; governments do. Without governmental decisions, the Coal and Steel Community, the European Economic Community, and the European Union would not have emerged. The representatives of states negotiate regulations in the European Commission. The Single-Market Act of 1985 provided that some types of directives would require less than a unanimous vote in the Council of Ministers. This political act cleared the way for passage of most of the harmonization standards for Europe (Dumez and Jeunemaître 1996, p. 229). American governments forged NAFTA; Japan fashioned an East and Southeast Asian producing and trading area. The decisions and acts of a country, or a set of countries arriving at political agreements, shape international political and economic institutions. Governments now intervene much more in international economic matters than they did in the earlier era of interdependence. Before World War I, foreign-ministry officials were famed for their lack of knowledge of, or interest in, economic affairs. Because governments have become much more active in economic affairs at home and abroad, interdependence has become less of an autonomous force in international politics.

In real terms, America's 1995 military budget approximately equaled the 1980 budget, and in 1980 the Cold War reached its peak.

The many commentators who exaggerate the closeness of interdependence, and even more so those who write of globalization, think in unit rather than in systemic terms. Many small states import and export large shares of their gross domestic products. States with large GDPs do not. They are little dependent on others, while a number of other states heavily depend on them. The terms of political, economic, and military competition are set by the larger units of the international-political system. Through centuries of multipolarity, with five or so great powers of comparable size competing with one another, the international system was quite closely interdependent. Under bi-and unipolarity the degree of interdependence declined markedly.

States are differentiated from one another not by function but primarily by capability. For two reasons, inequalities across states have greater political impact than inequalities across income groups within states. First, the inequalities of states are larger and have been growing more rapidly. Rich countries have become richer while poor countries have remained poor. Second, in a system without central governance, the influence of the units of greater capability is disproportionately large because there are no effective laws and institutions to direct and constrain them. They are able to work the system to their advantage, as the petrodollar example showed. I argued in 1970 that what counts are states' capacity to adjust to external conditions and their ability to use their economic leverage for political advantage. The United States was then and is still doubly blessed. It remains highly important in the international economy, serving as a principal market for a number of countries and as a major supplier of goods and services, yet its dependence on others is quite low. Precisely because the United States is relatively little dependent on others, it has a wide range of policy choices and the ability both to bring pressure on others and to assist them. The "herd" with its capital may flee from countries when it collectively decides that they are politically and economically unworthy, but some countries abroad, like some firms at home, are so important that they cannot be allowed to fail. National governments and international agencies then come to the rescue. The United States is the country that most often has the ability and the will to step in. The agency that most often acts is the IMF, and most countries think of the IMF as the enforcement arm of the U.S. Treasury (Strange 1996, p. 192). Thomas Friedman believes that when the "herd" makes its decisions, there is no appeal; but often there is an appeal, and it is for a bailout organized by the United States.

The international economy, like national economies, operates within a set of rules and institutions. Rules and institutions have to be made and sustained. Britain, to a large extent, provided this service prior to World War I; no one did between the wars, and the United States has done so since. More than any other state, the United States makes the rules and maintains the institutions that shape the international political economy.

Economically, the United States is the world's most important country; militarily, it is not only the most important country, it is the decisive one. Thomas Friedman puts the point simply: The world is sustained by "the presence of American power and America's willingness to use that power against

240

those who would threaten the system of globalization. . . . The hidden hand of the market will never work without a hidden fist" (1999, p. 373). But the hidden fist is in full view. On its military forces, the United States outspends the next six or seven big spenders combined. When force is needed to keep or to restore the peace, either the United States leads the way or the peace is not kept. The Cold War militarized international politics. Relations between the United States and the Soviet Union, and among some other countries as well, came to be defined largely in a single dimension, the military one. As the German sociologist Erich Weede has remarked, "National security decision making in some . . . democracies (most notably in West Germany) is actually penetrated by the United States" (1989, p. 225).

Oddly, the end of the Cold War has raised the importance of the American military to new heights. The United States continues to spend at a Cold War pace. In real terms, America's 1995 military budget approximately equaled the 1980 budget, and in 1980 the Cold War reached its peak. That other countries have reduced their budgets more than the United States has heightened the military dominance of one country. To say that the world is unipolar and that the world is becoming one through globalization is all too suggestive. Some say that the world is not really unipolar because the United States often needs, or at least wants, the help of others (see, e.g., Huntington 1999; Nye 1999). The truth, however, remains: The stronger have many more ways of coping with adversities than the weak have, and the latter depend on the former much more than the other way around. The United States is the only country that can organize and lead a military coalition, as it did in Iraq and in the Balkans. Some states have little choice but to participate, partly because of the pressure the strong can bring to bear on the weak and partly because of the needs of the latter. Western European countries and Japan are more dependent on Middle Eastern oil than the United States, and Western European countries are more affected by what happens in Eastern Europe than the United States is.

As expected, the beneficiaries resent their benefactor, which leads to talk of righting the imbalance of power. Yet, when the imbalance between one and the rest is great, to catch up is difficult. French leaders, especially, bemoan the absence of multipolarity and call for greater European strength, but one cannot usefully will the end without willing the means. The uneven distribution of capabilities continues to be the key to understanding international politics.

To an increasing extent, American foreign policy relies on military means. America continues to garrison much of the world and to look for ways of keeping troops in foreign countries rather than ways to withdraw them as one might have expected at the Cold War's end.[2] The 1992 draft of the Pentagon's *Defense Planning Guidance* advocated "discouraging the advanced industrialized nations from . . . even aspiring to a larger global or regional role." The United States may at times want help from others, but not too much help lest it lose its leading position in one part of the world or another. The document, when it was leaked, provoked criticism. In response, emphasis was placed on its being only a draft, but it continues to guide and describe America's policy.

William J. Perry and Ashton B. Carter, respectively the former secretary and assistant secretary of defense, have recently offered the concept of "preventive defense" as a guide to American policy. Preventive defense is conducted by American defense officials engaging in "security and military dialogue with regional states"; it calls for "a more robust defense to defense program" (1999, pp. 9, 11; cf., Carter, Perry, and Steinbruner 1992). Bismarck tried to keep Germany's military officials away from their opposite numbers in foreign countries lest the military's military policy became the country's foreign policy. In part, World War I resulted from his successors' failure to do this. In the United States, Treasury and Defense now make as much or more foreign policy than State does.

Conclusion

In a system of balanced states, the domination of one or some of them is prevented by the reaction of others acting as counterweights. The states of Europe held each other in balance through the first 300 years of the modern state system. In the next 50 years, the United States and the Soviet Union balanced each other, each protecting its sphere and helping to manage affairs within it. Since the end of the Cold War, the United States has been alone in the world; no state or combination of states provides an effective counterweight.

What are the implications for international politics? The more interdependent the system, the more a surrogate for government is needed. Who can supply it? Some Americans believe that the United States benignly provides a necessary minimum of management of the system and that, because of its moderation, other states will continue to appreciate, or at least to accept, its services (see, e.g., Ikenberry 1998/99, pp. 77–78). Benign hegemony is, however, something of a contradiction in terms. "One reads about the world's desire for American leadership only in the United States," a British diplomat has remarked. "Everywhere else one reads about American arrogance and unilateralism" (quoted in Huntington 1999, p. 42).

McGeorge Bundy once described the United States as "the locomotive at the head of mankind, and the rest of the world the caboose" (quoted in Gardner 1995, p. 178). America's pulling power is at a peak that cannot be sustained, for two main reasons. First, America is a country of 276 million people in a world of six billion. It represents 4.6% of the world's total population. The country's physical capabilities and political will cannot sustain present world burdens indefinitely. Second, other countries may not enjoy being placed at the back of the train. Both friends and foes will react as countries always have to the threatened or real predominance of one from among them by working to right the balance (Waltz 1998). The present condition of international politics is unnatural. Both the predominance of America and, one may hope, the militarization of international affairs will diminish with time.

Many globalizers believe that the world is increasingly ruled by markets. Looking at the state among states leads to a different conclusion. The main difference between international politics now and earlier is not found in the increased interdependence of states but in their growing inequality. With the end of bipolarity, the distribution of capabilities across states has become extremely lopsided. Rather than elevating economic forces and depressing political ones, the inequalities of international politics enhance the political role of one country. Politics, as usual, prevails over economics.

Notes

1 The picture of the purpose and the performance of states is especially clear in Thomson and Krasner (1989).
2 For example, Hans Binnendijk has urged Americans to develop a case for leaving American troops in South Korea even if the north should no longer be a threat (1996, p. 2).

References

Angell, Norman. 1933. *The Great Illusion*. New York: G. P. Putnam's Sons.
Binnendijk, Hans A. 1996. *Strategic Assessment 1996: Instruments of U.S. Power*. Washington, DC: National Defense University Press.
Boltho, Andrea. 1996. "Has France Converged on Germany?" In *National Diversity and Global Capitalism*, ed. Suzanne Berger and Ronald Dore. Ithaca: Cornell University Press.
Boyer, Robert. 1996. "The Convergence Hypothesis Revisited: Globalization But Still the Century of Nations." In *National Diversity and Global Capitalism*, ed. Suzanne Berger and Ronald Dore. Ithaca: Cornell University Press.
Carter, Ashton B., and William J. Perry. 1999. *Preventive Defense: A New Security Strategy for America*. Washington, DC: The Brookings Institution.
——, and John D. Steinbruner. 1992. *A New Concept of Cooperative Security*. Washington, DC: The Brookings Institution.
Doyle, Michael W. 1997. *Ways of War and Peace: Realism, Liberalism, and Socialism*. New York: W. W. Norton.
Dumez, Hervé, and Alain Jeunemaître. 1996. "The Convergence of Competition Policies in Europe: Internal Dynamics and External Imposition." In *National Diversity and Global Capitalism*, ed. Suzanne Berger and Ronald Dore. Ithaca: Cornell University Press.
Friedman, Thomas L. 1999. *The Lexus and the Olive Tree*. New York: Farrar, Straus, Giroux.
Fukuyama, Francis. 1992. *The End of History and the Last Man*. New York: Free Press.
Gardner, Lloyd. 1995. *Pay Any Price: Lyndon Johnson and the Wars for Vietnam*. Chicago: I. R. Dee.

Hirst, Paul, and Grahame Thompson. 1996. *Globalization in Question: The International Economy and the Possibilities of Governance.* Cambridge: Polity Press.

Huntington, Samuel P. 1999. "The Lonely Superpower," *Foreign Affairs* 78 (March/April).

Ikenberry, John. 1998/99. "Institutions, Strategic Restraint, and the Persistence of American Postwar Order," *International Security* 23 (Winter): pp. 77–78.

Keohane, Robert O., and Joseph S. Nye. 1977. *Power and Interdependence: World Politics in Transition.* Boston: Little, Brown.

Kindleberger, Charles P. 1969. *American Business Abroad.* New Haven: Yale University Press.

Krugman, Paul. 1997. "Competitiveness: A Dangerous Obsession." In *The New Shape of World Politics.* New York: W. W. Norton.

Lawrence, Robert Z. 1997. "Workers and Economists II: Resist the Binge." In *The New Shape of Politics.* New York: W. W. Norton.

Mueller, John. 1989. *Retreat from Doomsday: The Obsolescence of Major War.* New York: Basic Books.

McNeill, William H. 1997. "Territorial States Buried Too Soon." *Mershon International Studies Review.*

Nye, Joseph Jr. 1999. "Redefining the National Interest." *Foreign Affairs* 78 (July/August).

Ohmae, Kenichi. 1990. *The Borderless World: Power and Strategy in the Interlinked Economy.* New York: HarperBusiness.

Reinecke, Wolfgang H. 1997. "Global Public Policy." *Foreign Affairs* (November/December).

Spiro, David E. 1999. *The Hidden Hand of American Hegemony: Petrodollar Recycling and International Markets.* Ithaca: Cornell University Press.

Strange, Susan. 1996. *The Retreat of the State: The Diffusion of Power in the World Economy.* Cambridge: Cambridge University Press.

Thomson, Janice E., and Stephen D. Krasner. 1989. "Global Transactions and the Consolidation of Sovereignty." In *Global Changes and Theoretical Challenges: Approaches to Word Politics for the 1990s,* ed. Ernst-Otto Czempiel and James N. Rosenau. Lexington, MA: Lexington Books.

Thurow, Lester C. 1999. *Building Wealth: The New Rules for Individuals, Companies, and Nations in a Knowledge-Based Economy.* New York: HarperCollins.

Wade, Robert. 1996. "Globalization and Its Limits: Reports of the Death of the National Economy Are Grossly Exaggerated." In *National Diversity and Global Capitalism,* ed. Suzanne Berger and Ronald Dore. Ithaca: Cornell University Press.

Waltz, Kenneth N. 1970. "The Myth of National Interdependence." In *The International Corporation,* ed. Charles P. Kindleberger. Cambridge, MA: MIT Press.

——. "Structural Realism after the Cold War." Presented at the Annual Meeting of the American Political Science Association, Boston.

Weede, Erich. 1989. "Collective Goods in an Interdependent World: Authority and Order as Determinants of Peace and Prosperity." In *Global Changes and Theoretical Challenges: Approaches to Word Politics for the 1990s,* ed. Ernst-Otto Czempiel and James N. Rosenau. Lexington, MA: Lexington Books.

Weiss, Linda. 1998. *The Myth of the Powerless State: Governing the Economy in a Global Era*. Cambridge: Polity Press.

Woolcock, Stephen. 1996. "Competition among Forms of Corporate Governance in the European Community: The Case of Britain." In *National Diversity and Global Capitalism*, ed. Suzanne Berger and Ronald Dore. Ithaca: Cornell University Press.

15

THE CONTINUITY OF INTERNATIONAL POLITICS

On the morning of September 11, 2001, terrorists toppled the Twin Towers of the World Trade Center, symbols of world capitalism. They then struck a section of the Pentagon, symbol of America's military might. Apparently organized by Osama bin Laden and executed by members of al-Qaeda, the terrorists' acts were roundly condemned worldwide. Yet one wonders how deep and lasting the impact on American policy and on international politics will be.

The biggest early effects were felt in the policies and politics of the United States. The new Bush administration instantly turned from strident unilateralism to urgent multilateralism. The new multilateral approach, however, was adopted only to meet immediate and pressing requirements. The United States needed the police and intelligence capabilities of other states in order to track and apprehend terrorists. However, the American military response flatly refuted the subtitle of a newly published book: *The Paradox of American Power: Why the World's Superpower Can't Go it Alone*, by Joseph S. Nye. America organized and conducted the Afghanistan campaign on its own, rudely rebuffing Prime Minister Blair's offer of British troops to share in the fighting. Other indications that the Bush administration's multilateral impulses are strictly limited abound. By proclaiming a "war against terrorism," Bush raised terrorists to the dignity of soldiers, and almost casually assigned to American forces the impossible task of militarily defeating an "ism." President Bush nevertheless claimed that prisoners held at Guantanamo were criminals, not soldiers, and thus unprotected by the Geneva Convention. America's attempt to make its own international rules (in disregard of the well-being of Americans fighting abroad who may be captured by countries that refuse to call them soldiers) is an extreme example of unilateralism. New challenges have not changed old habits. I offer just two more examples. NATO foreign ministers promised to bring Russia directly into NATO consultations. Lord Robertson, NATO's secretary-general, proposed giving Russia equal status with other members, including the right of veto, on problems of terror and regional stability.[1] But America's Afghanistan campaign went beautifully, and nothing more has been heard about NATO's becoming 19 + 1. When world leaders, dressed in their Tang dynasty jackets, were bonding at the APEC conference in Shanghai last October, President Bush gave the impression that he and President Putin would find agreement on interpretations of, and modifications to, the Anti-Ballistic Missile (ABM) Treaty. Instead Bush renounced the treaty and gave notice of America's withdrawal from it.

Early in the Bush administration consultation with other countries meant that we would tell them what we intended to do and then do it whether they liked it or not. Except on limited and specific matters, the practice has not changed. Some changes, however, are more pronounced. September 11 lifted Secretary of State Colin Powell from near invisibility to prominence, though one wonders how well diplomatic prominence will translate into influence on policy. Having campaigned against nation building, President Bush now embraces it as American policy in Afghanistan, though one wonders whether he will show the same zeal for nation building that he has shown for war fighting. The war against terrorists changed Pakistan from sanctioned pariah to favoured partner, but throughout the Cold War Pakistan has risen in, or fallen from, American favour depending on the thrust of threats from the Soviet Union. One must wonder, as Pakistanis do, whether the pattern will persist. In the name of fighting terrorists, liberties of both American citizens and resident aliens have been curtailed. This, one fears, may last.

Fighting terrorists provided a cover that has enabled the Bush administration to do what it wanted to do anyway. The administration got from Congress all of the money it sought for national missile defence. Terrorist acts torpedoed the earlier cross-party agreement on reductions. The administration abrogated the ABM Treaty without strident complaints at home or abroad. The administration obtained whopping increases in the budgets for the armed services in order to fight and defend against the weak forces the terrorists can muster. Although terrorists can be terribly bothersome, they hardly pose threats to the fabric of a society or the security of the state.

Terrorists have caused America to change its policy and behavior in the near term, but the changes run in the direction that earlier policies had set. Are changes in the structure of international politics and the behavior of nations more notable? One reads in the *New York Times* that "the world has changed, developments in technology have given small groups of people the kind of destructive power once only available to national governments".[2] Supposedly the weak have become strong—but have they? By cleverly picking their targets, terrorists have often been able to use slender resources to do disproportionate damage. The diplomatic historian John Lewis Gaddis claims that national security has now become truly "national" with the homeland at risk, and calls this "a revolution in strategic thinking."[3] Have the terrorist attacks produced a strategic revolution, or do they leave the underlying conditions of international politics largely intact? For most countries throughout history, including the United States during the war of 1812, the homeland has at times been at risk.

Since the Soviet Union's disappearance, international politics has been marked by three basic facts. The first is the gross imbalance of power in the world. Never since Rome has one country so nearly dominated its world. In 1997 America's expenditure on its armed forces exceeded that of the next five big spenders; by 2000, the next eight. The defence budgets of most countries are stable or declining, while America's rises at an accelerating pace. Economically, technologically and militarily, the United States is far and away the leading country. No other country or combination of countries can hope to challenge it within a generation. After the defeat of the Soviet Union, the United States became the vengeful victor. It maintained its grip on the foreign and military policies of Western Europe and added three countries of the old Soviet empire to NATO's roster while announcing that more would follow. Old members of NATO showed no enthusiasm for, or willingness to bear the cost of, NATO's enlargement, but nevertheless supinely acquiesced in America's aggrandizement. The war on terrorists now enables the United States to establish bases on Russia's southern border and to further its encirclement of China as well as Russia. Secretary of Defense Donald Rumsfeld has announced that, if necessary to prosecute the war against terrorists, the United States will move militarily into 15 more states. In his January 29, 2002, State of the Union Address, President Bush targeted the next three countries (Iraq, Iran and North Korea) who may feel our wrath and threatened to move into any country "timid in the face of terror." Driving the threat home, he added: "And make no mistake about it: if they do not act, America will."[4] Today Afghanistan and the Philippines; tomorrow, who knows?

Terrorism does not change the first basic fact of international politics—the gross imbalance of world power. Instead, the effect of September 11 has been to enhance American power and extend its military presence in the world.

The second basic fact of international politics is the existence of nuclear weapons, most of them in the hands of the United States, and their gradual spread to additional countries. Again, terror furthers trends already in being. Having agreed with Russia to reduce its nuclear arsenal, the United States announced in January 2002 that instead of dismantling warheads it would place them in storage. And even though September 11 showed that national missile defences are irrelevant to the most likely modes of attack, the Bush administration used terror as a cover for renouncing the ABM Treaty.

The best one can say about missile defences is that they won't work. (If they did, an offence–defence race would result, with all too familiar consequences.) Missile defences are easily thwarted. In the nuclear business, offensive weapons are much cheaper than defensive ones. Other states can multiply their warheads; they can confound defences by deploying decoys and spreading chaff; they can outflank defences by delivering warheads in any of many different ways—by plane, by ships, by cruise missiles, by missiles fired on depressed trajectories. Missile defences would be the most complicated system ever mounted, and the system would have to work with near perfection in meeting its first realistic test—the test of enemy fire. Some warheads may get through, and both the attacked and the attacker will know that. No president will rely on such a system but will instead avoid actions that might provoke an attack. With or without defences, the restraints on American policy are the same.

The worst thing about nuclear defences is that, even though they will leak like a sieve, they will have damaging effects on others and on the United States as well. American intelligence reports state that American nuclear defences may prompt China to multiply its nuclear arsenal by ten and to place multiple warheads on its missiles.[5] Where China leads, India and Pakistan will follow. The result, President Putin fears, may be "a hectic and uncontrolled arms race on the borders of our country."[6] Japan, already made uneasy by China's increasing economic and military capabilities, will become uneasier still as China acts to counter America's prospective defences. Since the new Bush administration is rending the fabric of agreements that brought nuclear weapons under a modicum of control, and since nothing has been offered to replace it, other countries try harder to take care of themselves. North Korea, Iraq, Iran and others know that the United States can be held at bay only by deterrence. Weapons of mass destruction are the only means by which they can hope to deter the United States. They cannot hope to do so by relying on conventional weapons. During the Cold War the United States used nuclear weapons to offset the Soviet Union's conventional strength. Other countries may now use nuclear weapons to offset ours. On matters of nuclear weapons, as on others, American unilateralism prevails. The Bush administration refuses to ratify treaties that the United States sponsored (the Comprehensive Test Ban Treaty) and to honor treaties that it has ratified (the ABM Treaty).

Terrorists do not change the second brute fact of international politics: Nuclear weapons govern the military relations of nations that have them. Moreover, American policies stimulate the vertical proliferation of nuclear weapons and promote their spreading from one country to another.

The third basic fact of international politics is the prevalence of crises that plague the world and in most of which the United States is directly or indirectly involved. Argentina is an economic and political mess; Chechnya is a running sore on the Russian body politic; North Korea and South Korea, both heavily armed, are as usual at daggers drawn; the Taiwan problem affects every state in the region; the disintegration of Indonesia, should it occur, threatens to destabilize Southeast Asia; the longstanding Indian–Pakistani conflict over Kashmir is exacerbated by the war against terrorists, as is the unending conflict between Palestine and Israel. If the United States decides to move into other countries militarily or to strike at them, more crises will be added to the already long list.

Terrorists do not change the third basic fact of international politics: the persistence and accumulation of crises. Indeed, by pursuing terrorists and threatening to attack states that harbor them the United States will add crises to an already long list.

Rather than interrupting the continuity of international politics, increased terrorist activity is a response to changes that have taken place in the last two decades. Before the decline and disappearance of the Soviet Union, weak states and disaffected people could hope to play off one superpower against the other. Now the weak and disaffected are on their own. Unsurprisingly, they lash out at the United States as the agent or symbol of their suffering. The terrorist acts of September 11 have prompted the United States to enlarge its already bloated military forces and to extend its influence into parts of the world that its tentacles had not already reached.

Fortunately or not, terrorists contribute to the continuity of international politics. They further trends already in motion. Why, one may wonder, does the prospect of terror not change the basic facts of international politics? All states—whether authoritarian or democratic, traditional or modern, religious or secular—fear being their targets. Governments prize stability, and most of all they prize the continuation of their regimes. Terror is a threat to the stability of states and to the peace of mind of their rulers. That is why President Bush could so easily assemble a coalition a mile wide.

Yet, because terror is a weapon wielded by the weak, terrorists do not seriously threaten the security of states. States are therefore not compelled to band together to shift the balance of world power. Terrorist attacks do not change the two main bases of international politics or alter the condition of recurring crises. That is why, although a mile wide, the antiterrorist coalition is only an inch deep.

Notes

1 Patrick E. Tyler, "Gingerly, NATO Plans Broader Role for Moscow," *New York Times*, December 7, 2001, p. All; Michael Wines, "NATO Plan Offers Russia Equal Voice on Some Policies," *New York Times*, November 23, 2001, p. A1.
2 Alexander Stille, "What is America's Place in the World Now?," *New York Times*, January 12, 2002, p. B7.
3 Ibid.
4 "President Bush's State of the Union Address to Congress and the Nation," *New York Times*, January 30, 2002, p. A22.
5 Steven Lee Myers, "Study Said to Find US Missile Defense Might Incite China," *New York Times*, August 10, 2000, p. A1.
6 Patrick E. Tyler, "Putin Says Russia Would Add Arms to Counter Shield," *New York Times*, June 19, 2001, p. A1

Part III

MILITARY AFFAIRS

16

REASON, WILL AND
WEAPONS*

If it is true, as we are often told, that no problem is more important than dis-armament, it is also true that none is more difficult. The difficulties have always been present. The sense of urgency produced by the thought that war now holds the possibility not merely of death for some but of annihilation for all has seemingly led increasing numbers to the conclusion that at least some of the weapons of war, and perhaps war itself, can be eliminated. Since the days of the First Hague Peace Conference more man-hours of diplomatic negotiation have gone into the problem of securing arms limitations than have been devoted to any other international problem. Recurringly since the Second World War we have been told that a given proposal or series of negotiations represented the last hope of mankind to escape from destruction. Repeatedly little or nothing has happened. Seldom has so much effort been so ill rewarded. Yet optimism is not dead. Two of the most doggedly optimistic, The Rt. Hon. Philip Noel-Baker and Dr. Linus Pauling, have written books that are now before us.

Philip Noel-Baker, Professor of International Relations at distinguished English and American universities, long prominent in British politics, associated with the League of Nations from its inception and in the forefront of those who sought disarmament under its aegis, lays claim to qualifications on the subject of disarmament that few others can even aspire to. The richness of background, the depth of concern, the breadth of coverage make *The Arms Race* an immensely informative book, whether or not one accept its premises, ascriptions of cause, and prescriptions for cure. This reviewer does not. It is difficult to share his optimism, for it is difficult to understand or accept the basis of it. There are two major problems. They are worth discussing, for they often appear in essays on disarmament. First, he tends to write as though the important barriers to disarmament are technical ones, which intelligence is sufficient to overcome. All that remains then is for statesmen of good will to apply what others have contrived. This is apparent in his explanations of the successful disarmaments of the past. The demilitarization of the United States–Canadian border is, for example, presented as a triumph of courage and good sense on the part of British and American statesmen, producing in G. M. Trevelyan's words a border defended since 1817 "by the sole garrison of trust and good will. . . ." Pointing out that the possibility of disarmament there rested initially on the decreasing ability of Canada to invade the United States and on the abilities of the British Navy to defend Canada by striking at our East Coast does not disparage the accomplishment. It does make the case more instructive. One way of estimating the possibilities of disarmament now is by taking note of the instances in which it has come about, but the purpose is not well served if past cases are put in such a way as to lead to the conclusion that he who will, can. Where disarmament has been achieved it has depended on highly special circumstances, and it is only by looking at them carefully that we can derive lessons of present relevance. If, however, one takes the line that the successes of the past have rested simply upon intelligence, courage, and good will, the failures can be explained in similar terms. Thus persistently one finds the author saying, or at least implying, that the world would be a radically better one had a good plan been forcefully put forth at the strategic moment or a bad plan been properly amended.

When distrust and fear are great, the competitive building of arms intensifies. As the arms race intensifies, distrust and fear grow greater. The result may be to no one's taste, but even were the distaste universal, the arms race would not be eliminated. Saying to all states that reason dictates disarmament is like saying to each person that he must guard his cash box as best he can and then urging everyone to negotiate for the outlawing of revolvers. If we could assume a universal wish to forgo the use of firearms, disarmament would appear to be possible. Seemingly one can say that he will give up his revolver if everyone else will too. But if one still must guard his cash box, competition will shift to such other means as bodily force and cunning. In the use of these, some will be relatively unskilled. Foreseeing this, they may be unwilling to agree in the first place. Or, having agreed, they may perceive their disadvantage and seek to abrogate the agreement. Or they may lose their cash boxes by having unwisely entered a system that works to their disadvantage.

The second difficulty of Mr. Noel-Baker's analysis is a more general one. He does not argue simply for stopping the testing of nuclear devices, or for bringing the hydrogen bomb under control, or for reducing the numbers of men in national military establishments. Indeed he argues that no disarmament limited to one type of weapon can be successful. This is a virtue of the book, for pellucidly the point is made that limiting any one weapon will shift emphasis to competitive building of others. The partial quality of the Washington Naval Treaty is given as the reason for its passing out of existence in 1937. This is one of many examples of his pushing political reality aside, but the essential point remains. Fewer capital ships may well mean more light cruisers. Eliminating nuclear weapons may well mean more bombers for the carrying of conventional explosives. The point is intrinsically a good one, and it has the merit of prompting the author to bring within his purview all types of weapons, including gases and biologicals. But the comprehensive quality of the disarmament that is then required compounds the difficulty of achieving it. If we have been able to agree with the Soviet Union about so little, how can we ever expect to agree about so much? It does not appear this way to the author largely because of his confidence in reason and will and the stimulus given to them by present weapons technology. But what are reason and will to contrive? The answers given are varied. For anarchy must be substituted the rule of law under the United Nations. There must be an agreement not to use, test, make, or stock nuclear weapons. There must be effective inspection, and technically there can be if inspection is part of a general disarmament. Finally, to maintain the panoply he has described in detail, there must be an international atomic military force.

There is an air of reality about this. Force has to be available to control the possession and use of the instruments of power by the separate states. War is outlawed within every state. Internationally, if the instruments of war are to be effectively limited, agencies must exist to give effect to the prohibitions and a sense of security to the states abiding by them. Like international lawyers of the present, disarmers are often led to the conclusion that the better ordering and the safety of the world require international bodies possessing more and more of the qualities of government. Thus at times the author's arguments for disarmament seem to require an argument for world government. To be effective an international police force must be strong. If strong, it must be firmly controlled. The thought could be well established by pointing to instances where there has existed a strong military establishment alongside a weak national government. So long as the United Nations remains a "service organization," as Secretary-General Hammerskjold has recently and rightly described it, the problem of who will control the controllers will remain, whether one hope for an improved international law, an international inspectorate, or an international police force. Mr. Noel-Baker, however, quite clearly thinks of these matters, not as problems that could be managed only by an international authority having the essential attributes of government, but rather as problems that can be solved by arrangements reasonably made and voluntarily kept.

It is difficult to believe that any state will perform the act that would touch off a third world war. But it is comparably difficult to believe that every state of consequence will always restrain itself so nicely and calculate so precisely as to avoid the result that presumably no state wants. War is possible. In another sense, it is impossible. The impossibility of war is a major theme of Dr. Pauling's book:

> I believe [he writes] that the development of these terrible weapons forces us to move into a new period in the history of the world, a period of peace and reason, when world problems are not solved by war or by force, but are solved by the application of man's power of reason, in a way that does justice to all nations and that benefits all people (p. 3).

The impossibility of war is put not in terms of efficient causes, the conditions that could reasonably be expected to produce a world perpetually at peace. It is put instead in terms of a final cause, perception of the intolerable horror that would result were the nuclear capabilities now extant widely employed. There is an unavoidable relation between the proclaimed end of behavior and the circumstances that condition our acts. Insisting on the importance of the end may, however, do nothing to change these conditions and may consequently leave behavior unaffected. Still final cause is not irrelevant. The spur of financial need helped to make Mark Twain a prolific writer and platform speaker— we never know how much we can do until we have to. But his determination to save the family's honor by paying off its debts could not have made him either a wit or a writer had he not been endowed with certain capabilities from the start. If his most salable asset had been skill as a plumber, he might have driven himself to despair trying, or he might have decided that family honor is not so important after all. The problem, which may be insuperable, is to make the final cause efficient. Yet continually in politics we are urged to make efforts toward some goal, and the importance of the goal, not the demonstrated possibility of achieving it, is given as the basis for hoping that it can be reached. On the question of how to reach it Dr. Pauling is of no help. He points to the discrepancy between the ethical principles applied to personal behavior and the immorality of national leaders. "A military leader who is given a choice between the principles of humanity and an effective defense of his nation always abandons the principles of humanity" (pp. 151–152). Should he instead abandon the "effective defense of his nation"? Statesmen and military leaders are responsible for the security of their states; no one at all is responsible for humanity. This may be deplorable, but so long as it is true it is difficult to see how leaders can walk away from their assigned responsibilities; difficult even to believe that they should. Dr. Pauling would not have them do so. He would have them meet their responsibilities in new ways. With war ruled out as a means of settling disputes, other means must be found. How are they to be sought? Dr. Pauling proposes a "World Peace Research Organization, within the structure of the United Nations." Its purpose would be to carry out "research on how to solve . . . problems of the kind that have in the past led to war" (p. 201). With more research it may well be that solutions to some or even, as Dr. Pauling thinks, to many international problems could be found. There would still be the difficulty of getting the solutions applied. (It is carefully specified that this is to be a search-for-the-truth organization and not a policy-making body.) Nevertheless, if it were true that wars are resorted to merely to settle immediate points at issue, one might share his optimism. Optimism vanishes when one recalls that war is often the means used by states in their attempts to determine the answer to the calamitous question: Who shall dominate whom? Research, however well financed and vigorously conducted, cannot supply a generally acceptable and widely applicable answer to this question.

Where, before the Second World War, Communists ruled about one eighth of the world's people, they now control one third. The Soviet Union, having grown immensely in capabilities, shows no convincing signs of lessening its ambitions. Under the circumstances, the very attempt to discuss disarmament seriously as a proposed policy of government must somehow seem unreal. But not all discussion is irrelevant. Much is presently written and said about the deleterious effects of continued testing. Dr. Pauling's book is replete with data on and analysis of the likely effects of continued testing. If his statements are correct, and they are highly convincing, a suspension of testing all around would promise great benefits. Suspension of tests is a result that conditions have temporarily produced. An agreement to solidify the result would be useful. This would, of course, not be disarmament. Many, however, write or speak as though it would represent the first in a series of disarmament steps. President Dwight Eisenhower, Premier Nikita Khrushchev, the Soviet delegate to the Geneva Conference on banning nuclear tests, Semyon Tsarapkin, and Professors Louis Henkin and Jay Orear, the last-named, author of one of the essays in *Inspection for Disarmament*, come immediately to mind. It is more reasonable to say that a suspension of tests is possible in great part because it is not itself disarmament and none of the parties to an agreement would need fear its leading any further.

As long as the difficulties previously mentioned remain, and they will exist so long as independent states endure, armaments will be an important part of every country's foreign policy. Statesmen work within a narrow range of choice. The Columbia Inspection Study, edited and with a summary report written by Professor Seymour Melman, helps one to see what the possibilities and attendant difficulties are. In a system of self-help, trust is no substitute for certainty, as Professor William T. R. Fox points out in his Foreword, since for its protection each state must ultimately rely on its own devices. Taken together the twenty-one papers, most of them written by scientists or engineers, convince this reader that by ingeniously combining a number of techniques, an inspection system could be devised that would reduce to a fully acceptable minimum the chances of undetected evasion of a general disarmament agreement. So great would be the chances of being found out early in the stages of a clandestine attempt to rearm that it would be irrational for one state to make the effort and at the same time safe for other states to rely on the inspection system to expose the illegal effort to public view before rearmament reached dangerous proportions. The difficulties of inspected disarmament are not so much physical as they are political. Whatever system is devised will promise to the various states differential gains and losses, a thought well put by the Spanish delegate to the 1932 Disarmament Conference at Geneva in an allegory at once charming and disconcerting. When the animals met to discuss disarmament, he related, "the lion looked the eagle in the eye and said 'we must abolish talons.' The eagle looked him full in the eye and said 'we must abolish claws.' Then the bear said 'let's abolish everything but universal embraces.' "[1] Thus the United States has sought inspection without disarmament; the Soviet Union, disarmament without inspection. The more inspection we get, the more we gain; for we now know less of the Russians than they of us. The more disarmament without inspection, the more they gain; for within a system of partial disarmament they can more easily arm clandestinely and within a system of general disarmament more readily employ nonmilitary means in nearby theaters of action.

In domestic politics there are difficulties as well. It is often said that Soviet governance precludes a far-reaching system of inspection. Professor Henkin, in his *Arms Control and Inspection in American Law*, asks if our federal, constitutional system does not also pose difficulties. Could we accept and implement the control and inspection devices we have often proposed? In answering this question, he relates international events (the experience of the United Nations Emergency Force and the European Coal and Steel Community, for example) to political practice and to judicial interpretation in international as well as in domestic law. His conclusion, carefully argued and cautiously put, is that under our constitution the likely provisions of an armaments control plan could be enforced. The relevance of the conclusion depends upon one's estimate of the probability of such an agreement being made, but even for the pessimist the study makes many useful points along the way and contains a quantity of valuable information.

The Pauling, Melman, and Henkin volumes may convince one first of the importance of ending tests and then of the practical possibilities of doing so. On the more profound problem of actually securing some disarmament, the international difficulties standing in the way appear implicitly throughout and sometimes explicitly in the Melman, Noel-Baker, and Pauling books. The domestic difficulties are delineated by Professor Henkin. The conditions that will exist in the continued absence of an agreement on arms are considered in terms of catastrophe by Noel-Baker and Pauling; in terms of expenditures and future weapons development by the National Planning Association pamphlet, *1970 Without Arms Control*, which is the first of a series on "Security Through Arms Control" and contains in brief compass a large quantity of useful information. Together the five books under review provide a representative sampling of present-day writings on disarmament and, despite the note of optimism struck by some of the authors, very little encouragement. One misses the kind of analysis that along with humanitarian reason, good will, and technical knowledge would give political meaning to the information conveyed and the conclusions reached.

Notes

* This review article is based on the following books:

The Arms Race: A Programme for World Disarmament, by Philip Noel-Baker. New York: Oceana Publications, 1958. xviii, 579 pp. $6.00.

No More War! by Linus Pauling. New York: Dodd, Mead & Company, 1958. ix, 254 pp. $3.50.

Inspection for Disarmament, edited by Seymour Melman. New York: Columbia University Press, 1958. xv, 291 pp. $6.00.

Arms Control and Inspection in American Law, by Louis Henkin. With a Foreword by Philip C. Jessup, and Preface by John M. Kernochan. New York: Columbia University Press, 1958. xii, 289 pp. $5.50.

1970 Without Arms Control: Implications of Modern Weapons Technology, by the NPA Special Project Committee on Security Through Arms Control. Washington: National Planning Association, 1958. vii, 72 pp. $1.25.

1 Quoted in Hoffman Nickerson, *Can We Limit War?* (New York, 1934), p. 163.

17

TOWARD NUCLEAR PEACE

The world has enjoyed more years of peace since 1945 than had been known in this century—if peace is defined as the absence of general war among the major states of the world. Presumably features of the postwar system that were not present earlier account for the world's recent good fortune. The biggest changes in the postwar world are the shift from multipolarity to bipolarity and the introduction of nuclear weapons. This chapter focuses on the latter.

The military logic of self-help systems

States coexist in a condition of anarchy. Self-help is the principle of action in an anarchic order, and the most important way in which states must help themselves is to provide for their own security. Therefore, in weighing the chances for peace, the first questions concern the ends for which states use force and the strategies and weapons they employ. The chances of peace rise if states can achieve their most important ends without actively using force. War also becomes less likely as the costs of war rise in relation to possible gains. Strategies bring ends and means together. The effect of nuclear weapons on the chances for peace is seen by examining the different implications of defense and deterrence, the two strategies for discouraging attack. Defense dissuades by making it difficult to launch an attack and carry it home, whereas deterrence dissuades by frightening a state out of attacking because the opponent's expected reaction will result in one's own severe punishment. Purely defensive forces provide no deterrence, and purely deterrent forces provide no defense. We should expect war to become less likely when weaponry exists to make conquest more difficult, to discourage preemptive and preventive war, and to make coercive threats less credible. Do nuclear weapons have these effects? This chapter considers how nuclear deterrence and nuclear defense improve the prospects for peace.

First, wars can be fought in the face of deterrent threats; but the higher the stakes and the closer a country moves toward winning them, the more surely that country invites retaliation and risks its own destruction. States are not likely to run major risks for minor gains. Because of fears that wars between nuclear states may escalate as the loser uses larger and larger warheads, deescalation rather than escalation becomes likely. War remains possible, but victory in war is too dangerous to fight for.

Second, states act with less care if the expected costs of war are low and with more care if they are high. It is instructive here to compare the carelessness of Britain in the Crimean War with the caution of President Kennedy in the Cuban missile crisis.

Third, the question demands a negative answer all the more insistently when the deterrent deployment of nuclear weapons contributes more to a country's security than does conquest of territory. A country with a deterrent strategy needs less territory than one that relies on a conventional defense. A deterrent strategy makes it unnecessary for a country to fight to increase its security, and thereby removes a major cause of war.[1]

Fourth, deterrence depends on both one's capabilities and one's will to use them. The will of the attacked, striving to preserve its own territory, can ordinarily be presumed stronger than the will of the attacker, striving to annex someone else's territory. Knowledge of this further inhibits the would-be attacker.

Certainty about the relative strength of adversaries also makes war less likely. Many wars might have been avoided had their outcomes been foreseen. "To be sure," Georg Simmel once said, "the most effective presupposition for preventing struggle, the exact knowledge of the comparative strength of the two parties, is very often only to be obtained by the actual fighting out of the conflict."[2] Miscalculation causes wars. One side expects victory at an affordable price, whereas the other side hopes to avoid defeat. Here the differences between conventional and nuclear weapons are fundamental. With the former, states are too often tempted to act on advantages that are wishfully discerned and narrowly calculated. In 1914 neither Germany nor France tried very hard to avoid a general war. Both hoped for victory even though they believed their forces to be quite evenly matched. In 1941 Japan, in attacking the United States, could hope for victory only if a series of events that was possible but not highly probable took place.

Uncertainty about outcomes does not work decisively against the fighting of wars with conventional weapons. Countries so armed go to war knowing that even in defeat their suffering will be limited. Calculations about nuclear war are made differently, however. A nuclear world calls for a different kind of reasoning. If countries armed with nuclear weapons go to war, they do so knowing that their suffering may be unlimited. Of course, it also may not be, but that is not the kind of uncertainty that encourages the use of force. In a conventional world, one is uncertain about winning or losing. In a nuclear world, one is uncertain about survival or annihilation. If force is used and not kept within limits, catastrophe will result. That prediction is easy to make because it does not require close estimates of opposing forces. The number of one's cities that can be severely damaged is at least equal to the number of strategic warheads an adversary can deliver. Variations of number mean little within wide ranges. The expected effect of the deterrent is clear because wide margins of error in estimates of the damage one may suffer do not matter. Do we expect to lose one city or two, two cities or ten? When these are the pertinent questions, we stop thinking about running risks and start worrying about how to avoid them. In a conventional world, deterrent threats are ineffective because the damage threatened is distant, limited, and problematic. Nuclear weapons make military miscalculation difficult and politically pertinent prediction easy.

Dissuading a would-be attacker by throwing up an impressive defense may be as effective as dissuading him through deterrence. Beginning with President Kennedy and Secretary of Defense McNamara in the early 1960s, the United States has asked how it can avoid or at least postpone using nuclear weapons, rather than how it can mount the most effective defense. NATO's attempts to keep a defensive war conventional in its initial stage may guarantee that nuclear weapons, if used, will be used in a losing cause and in ways that multiply destruction without promising victory. Early use of very small warheads may stop escalation. Defensive deployment, if it should fail to dissuade, would bring small nuclear weapons into use before the physical, political, and psychological environment had deteriorated. The chances of deescalation are high if the use of nuclear weapons is carefully planned and their use limited to the battlefield. The United States has rightly put strong emphasis on strategic deterrence, which makes large wars less likely, and wrongly slighted the question of whether or not low-yield nuclear weapons can effectively be used for defense, which would make any war at all even less likely.[3]

An unassailable defense is fully dissuasive; and dissuasion is what we want, whether by defense or by deterrence. The likelihood of war decreases as deterrent and defensive capabilities increase. Nuclear weapons and an appropriate doctrine for their use may make it possible to approach the defensive-deterrent ideal, a condition that would cause the chances of war to dwindle. Concentrating attention on the destructive power of nuclear weapons has obscured the important benefits they promise to states trying to coexist in a self-help world.

Effects of the spread of nuclear weapons

Contemplating the nuclear past gives grounds for hoping that the world will survive if further nuclear powers join today's six or seven. This tentative conclusion is called into question by the widespread belief that the infirmities of some new nuclear states and the delicacy of their nuclear forces will work against the preservation of peace and for the fighting of nuclear wars. The likelihood of avoiding destruction as more states become members of the nuclear club is often coupled with the question of which states they will be.

What are the likely differences in situation and behavior of new as compared to old nuclear powers?

Nuclear weapons and domestic stability

Because of the importance of controlling nuclear weapons—of keeping them firmly in the hands of reliable officials—rulers of nuclear states may become more authoritarian and more secretive. Moreover, some potential nuclear states are not politically strong and stable enough to ensure control of the weapons and of the decision to use them. If neighboring, hostile, unstable states are armed with nuclear weapons, each will fear attack by the other. Feelings of insecurity may lead to arms races that subordinate civil needs to military necessities. Fears are compounded by the danger of internal coups in which the control of nuclear weapons may be the main object of struggle and the key to political power. Under these fearsome circumstances, it may be impossible to maintain government authority and civil order. The legitimacy of the state and the loyalty of its citizenry may dissolve because the state is no longer considered capable of maintaining external security and internal order. In sum, the first fear is that states become tyrannical; the second, that they lose control. Both fears may be realized either in different states or in the same state at different times.[4]

Four observations are relevant here. First, possession of nuclear weapons may slow arms races down rather than speed them up, a possibility considered later. Second, building nuclear arsenals requires a long lead time for less developed countries. The more unstable a government, the shorter the attention span of its leaders becomes. They must deal with today's problems and hope for the best tomorrow.

Third, although highly unstable states are unlikely to initiate nuclear projects, such projects may begin in stable times but continue through periods of political turmoil and succeed in producing nuclear weapons. True, a nuclear state may be unstable or may become so. Why, however, in an internal struggle for power, should the contenders start using nuclear weapons? At whom would they aim? How would they use these weapons to maintain or gain control? There is little more reason to fear that one faction or another in some less developed country will fire atomic weapons in a struggle for political power than that they will be used in a crisis of succession in the USSR or China.

Fourth, the possibility remains of one side in a civil war firing a nuclear warhead at its opponent's stronghold. Such an act would produce a national tragedy, not an international one. The question then arises: Once the weapon is fired, what happens next? The domestic use of nuclear weapons is, of all the uses imaginable, least likely to lead to escalation and to threaten the stability of the central balance.

Nuclear weapons and regional stability

If nuclear weapons are not likely to be used at home, are they likely to be used abroad? As nuclear weapons spread, what new causes may bring effects different from and worse than those known earlier in the nuclear age?[5]

First, new nuclear states may come in hostile pairs and share a common border. Where states are bitter enemies, one may fear that they will be unable to resist using their nuclear weapons against each other. This is a concern for the future which finds no precedent in the past. The USSR and the United States, and the USSR and China, are hostile enough; the latter pair share a long border. Nuclear weapons have caused China and the USSR to deal cautiously with each other. It is alleged that bitterness among some potential nuclear states exceeds that experienced by the old ones. Playing down the bitterness sometimes felt by the United States, the USSR, and China, however, requires a creative reading of history. Moreover, those who believe that bitterness causes wars assume a close association that is seldom found between bitterness among nations and their willingness to run high risks.

Second, some new nuclear states may have governments and societies that are not well rooted. If a country is a loose collection of hostile tribes, if its leaders form a thin veneer atop a people partly nomadic and with an authoritarian history, then its rulers may be freer of constraints than, and have different values from, those who rule older and more fully developed polities. Idi Amin and Muammar el-Khaddafy fit these categories, and they are favorite examples of the kinds of rulers who supposedly cannot be trusted to manage nuclear weapons responsibly. Despite wild rhetoric aimed at foreigners, however, both these "irrational" rulers became cautious and modest when punitive actions against them might have threatened their ability to rule. Arabs, for example, did not marshall their resources and make an all-out effort to destroy Israel in the years before Israel could strike back with nuclear warheads. We cannot expect countries to risk more in the presence of nuclear weapons than they have in their absence.

Third, many fear that states that are radical at home will use their nuclear weapons recklessly in pursuit of revolutionary ends abroad. States that are radical at home, however, may not be radical abroad. States coexist in a competitive arena, and the pressures of competition cause them to behave in ways that make the threats they face manageable and enable them to get along. States can remain radical in foreign policy only if they are overwhelmingly strong—as none of the new nuclear states will be—or if their radical acts fall short of damaging vital interests of nuclear powers. States that acquire nuclear weapons will not be regarded with indifference. States that want to be freewheelers have to stay out of the nuclear business. A nuclear Libya, for example, would have to show caution, even in rhetoric, lest it suffer retaliation in response to someone else's anonymous attack on a third state. That state, ignorant of who attacked, might claim that its intelligence agents had identified

Libya as the culprit and take the opportunity to silence it by striking a conventional blow. Nuclear weapons induce caution, especially in weak states.

Fourth, although some worry about nuclear states coming in hostile pairs, others worry that the bipolar pattern will not be reproduced regionally in a world populated by larger numbers of nuclear states. The simplicity of relations that obtains when one party has to concentrate its worry on only one other, and the ease of calculating forces and estimating the dangers they pose, may be lost. The structure of international politics, however, will remain bipolar as long as no third state is able to compete militarily with the great powers. Moreover, the USSR now has to worry lest a move made in Europe cause France and Britain to retaliate, thus possibly setting off U.S. forces. Such worries at once complicate calculations and strengthen deterrence.

Fifth, in some of the new nuclear states civil control of the military may be shaky. Nuclear wapons may fall into the hands of military officers more inclined than civilians to put them to offensive use. This again is an old worry. I see no reason to think that civil control of the military is secure in the USSR, given the occasional presence of serving officers in the Politburo and some known and some surmised instances of military intervention in civil affairs at crucial times. In the People's Republic of China military and civil branches of government are not separate but fused. Although one may prefer civil control, preventing a highly destructive war does not require it. What is required is that decisions be made that keep destruction within bounds, whether these decisions are made by civilians or soldiers. Soldiers may indeed be more cautious than civilians. *Uncertainty* about the course a nuclear war might follow, along with the *certainty* that destruction can be immense, strongly inhibits the first use of nuclear weapons.

Examining the supposedly unfortunate characteristics of new nuclear states removes some of one's worries. Still, the feeling that something terrible will emerge as new nuclear powers are added to the present group is not easily quieted. Nuclear weapons may be set off anonymously, or back a policy of blackmail, or be used in a combined conventional–nuclear attack.

Some have feared that a radical Arab state might fire a nuclear warhead anonymously at an Israeli city in order to block a peace settlement.[6] The state exploding the warhead, however, could not be certain of remaining unidentified. Even if a country's leaders persuade themselves that chances of retaliation are low, who would run the risk? Nor would blackmail be easy to accomplish, because the blackmailer's threat is not a cheap way of working one's will. The threat is simply incredible unless a considerable investment has already been made.

Although nuclear weapons are poor instruments for blackmail, would they not provide a cheap and decisive offensive force when used against a conventionally armed enemy? A country that takes the nuclear offensive, however, has to fear a punishing blow from someone. Far from lowering the expected cost of aggression, a nuclear offense even against a nonnuclear state raises the possible costs of aggression to incalculable heights because the aggressor cannot be sure of the reaction of other nuclear powers.

Deterrence with small nuclear forces

A number of problems are thought to attend the efforts of minor powers to use weapons for deterrence. This section considers how hard these problems are for new nuclear states to solve.

The forces required for deterrence

In considering the physical requirements of deterrent forces, we should distinguish between *prevention* and *preemption*. A preventive war is launched by a stronger state against a weaker one that is thought to be gaining strength. Aside from the balance of forces, a preemptive strike is launched by one state when another state's offensive forces are seen to be vulnerable.

The first danger posed by the spread of nuclear weapons would seem to be that each new nuclear state may tempt an old one to strike preventively in order to destroy an embryonic nuclear capability before it can become militarily effective. Two stages of a country's nuclear development should be distinguished: an early stage in which it is obviously unable to make nuclear weapons, and an advanced stage in which it may or may not have some nuclear weapons.

A preventive strike would seem to be most promising during the first stage of nuclear development. A state could strike without fearing that the country it attacked would return a nuclear blow. Would one strike so hard, however, as to destroy the very potential for future nuclear development? If not, the country struck could simply resume its nuclear career, and one must be prepared either to repeat the attack or to occupy and control the country. Either response would be difficult and costly.

In striking Iraq, Israel showed that a preventive strike can be made. Israel's act and its consequences, however, also demonstrate that the likelihood of useful accomplishment is low. Israel's strike increased Arab determination to produce nuclear weapons. Far from foreclosing Iraq's nuclear future, it gained Iraq the support of some other Arab states in pursuing it. Despite Prime Minister Begin's vow to strike as often as needed, the risks in doing so would rise with each occasion.

A preventive strike during the second stage is even less promising. As more countries acquire nuclear weapons and gain nuclear competence through power projects, the difficulties and dangers of preventive strikes increase. To be certain that the country attacked has not already produced or otherwise acquired some deliverable warheads becomes increasingly difficult. If the country attacked has even a rudimentary nuclear capability, one's own severe punishment becomes possible.

266

Preventive strikes against states that have, or may have, nuclear weapons are hard to imagine, but what about preemptive ones? Will states of limited and roughly similar capabilities use nuclear weapons against one another? They do not want to risk nuclear devastation any more than the United States does. Preemptive strikes nevertheless seem likely because of the assumption that their forces will be delicate. With delicate forces, states are tempted to launch disarming strikes before their own forces can be struck and destroyed. One is thus led back to the subject of deterrence.

To be effective, a deterrent force must meet three requirements. First, part of the force must appear to be able to survive an attack and launch one of its own. Second, survival of the force must not require early firing in response to what may be false alarms. Third, weapons must not be susceptible to accidental and unauthorized use. No one wants vulnerable, hair-trigger, accident-prone forces. Deterrent forces are seldom delicate because no state wants delicate forces, and nuclear forces can easily be made sturdy. Nuclear weapons are fairly small and light. They are easy to hide and to move.

It is sometimes claimed that the few bombs of a new nuclear state create a greater danger of nuclear war than additional thousands for the United States and the USSR. Such statements assume that preemption of a small force is easy. This is so only if the would-be attacker knows that the intended victim's warheads are few in number, knows their exact number and locations, and knows that they will not be moved or fired before they are struck. It is exceedingly difficult to know all these things, and to be assured of this knowledge. How can military advisers promise the full success of a disarming first strike when the penalty for slight error may be so heavy?

If the survival of nuclear weapons requires their dispersal and concealment, do not problems of command and control become harder to solve? U.S. citizens think so because they think in terms of large nuclear arsenals. Small nuclear powers will neither have nor need them. Lesser nuclear states might deploy, say, ten real weapons and ten dummies, while permitting other countries to infer that the numbers are larger. The adversary need only believe that some warheads may survive an attack and be used to retaliate. That belief should not be hard to create without making command and control unreliable. All nuclear countries must live through a time when their forces are crudely designed, but so far all have been able to control them. Relations between the United States and the USSR, and later among the United States, the USSR, and China, were at their bitterest just when their nuclear forces, in early stages of development, were unbalanced, crude, and presumably hard to control. Why should we expect new nuclear states to experience greater difficulties than those the old ones were able to cope with? Moreover, although some of the new nuclear states may be economically and technically backward, either they will have an expert and highly trained group of scientists and engineers, or they will not produce nuclear weapons. Even if they buy the weapons, they will have to hire technicians to maintain and control them. We do not have to wonder whether or not they will take good care of their weapons. They have every incentive to do so. They will not want to risk retaliation because one or more of their warheads accidentally strikes another country.

Hiding nuclear weapons and keeping them under control are tasks for which the ingenuity of numerous states is adequate. Means of delivery are not difficult to devise or procure. Bombs can be driven in by trucks from neighboring countries. Ports can be torpedoed by small boats lying offshore. Moreover, a thriving arms trade in ever more sophisticated military equipment provides ready access to what may be wanted, including planes and missiles suited to nuclear-warhead delivery.

Lesser nuclear states can pursue deterrent strategies effectively. Deterrence requires the ability to inflict unacceptable damage on another country. *Unacceptable damage* to the USSR was variously defined by Robert McNamara as requiring the ability to destroy one-fifth to one-quarter of the Soviet population and one-half to two-thirds of its industrial capacity. U.S. estimates of what is required for deterrence have been absurdly high. To deter, a country need not appear to be able to destroy one-quarter or one-half of another country, although in some cases that might be easily done.

In sum, the weak can deter one another. But can the weak deter the strong? The question of China's ability to deter the USSR highlights this issue. A major attack on the top ten cities of the USSR would destroy 25 percent of its industrial capacity and 25 percent of its urban population. Geoffrey Kemp concluded in 1974 that China would probably be able to strike on that scale.[7] And, I emphasize again: China need only *appear* to be able to do so. Not much is required to deter. What political-military objective is worth risking Vladivostok, Novosibirsk, and Tomsk, with no way to be sure that Moscow will not succumb as well?

The credibility of small deterrent forces

The credibility of weaker countries' deterrent threats has two faces. The first is physical: Will such countries be able to construct and protect a deliverable force? We have found that they can readily do so. The second is psychological: Will deterrent threats that are physically feasible be psychologically plausible? Will an adversary believe that the threatened retaliation will be carried out?

Deterrent threats backed by second-strike nuclear forces raise the expected costs of war to such heights that war becomes unlikely. Deterrent threats may not be credible, however. In a world in which two or more countries can make them, the prospect of *mutual* devastation makes it difficult or irrational to execute threats should the occasion for doing so arise. Why retaliate once a threat to do so has failed? To carry out the threat that was "rationally" made may be "irrational." The course of wisdom may be to pose a new question: What is the best policy now that deterrence has failed? One gains nothing but revenge by destroying an enemy's cities. Instead, in retaliating, one may prompt the enemy to unleash more warheads. A ruthless aggressor may strike believing that the leaders of the attacked country are capable of following such a "rational" line of thought. This old worry achieved new prominence as the strategic capabilities of the USSR approached those of the United States in the mid-1970s. The USSR, some feared, might believe that the United States would be self-deterred.

Much of the literature on deterrence emphasizes the problem of achieving the credibility on which deterrence depends and the danger of relying on a deterrent of uncertain credibility. One earlier solution of the problem was found in Thomas Schelling's notion of "the threat that leaves something to chance."[8] No state can know for sure that another state will refrain from retaliating even when retaliation would be irrational. No state can bet heavily on another state's rationality. Bernard Brodie put the thought more directly, while avoiding the slippery notion of rationality: How do governments behave in the presence of awesome dangers? His answer was "very carefully."

To ask why a country should carry out its deterrent threat once deterrence has failed is to ask the wrong question. Suggesting that an aggressor may attack believing that the attacked country may not retaliate invokes the conventional logic that analysts find so hard to forsake. In a conventional world, a country can sensibly attack if it believes that success is probable. In a nuclear world, a country cannot sensibly attack unless it believes that success is assured. An attacker is deterred even if he believes only that the attacked *may* retaliate. Uncertainty of response, not certainty, is required for deterrence because if retaliation occurs, one risks losing all. In a nuclear world, we should look less at the retaliator's conceivable inhibitions and more at the challenger's obvious risks.

One may nevertheless wonder, as people in the United States recently have, whether or not retaliatory threats remain credible if the strategic forces of the attacker are superior to those of the attacked. Will an unsuccessful defender in a conventional war have the courage to unleash its deterrent force, using nuclear weapons first against a country having superior strategic forces? Once more the question is the wrong one. It is important to shift attention not only from the defender's possible inhibitions to the aggressor's unwillingness to run extreme risks, as earlier, but also from the defender's courage to the different valuations that defenders and attackers place on the stakes. An attacked country will ordinarily value keeping its own territory more highly than an attacker will value gaining some portion of it. Given second-strike capabilities, it is not the balance of forces but the courage to use them that counts. The balance or imbalance of strategic forces affects neither the calculation of danger nor the question of whose will is stronger. Second-strike forces must be seen in absolute terms.

Emphasizing the importance of the "balance of resolve," to use Glenn Snyder's apt phrase, raises questions about exactly what a deterrent force covers.[9] Interpreting cautious U.S. and Soviet postwar behavior in terms of nuclear logic suggests that deterrence extends to vital interests beyond the homeland more easily than many have thought. The United States cares more about Western Europe than the USSR does. The USSR cares more about Eastern Europe than the United States does. Communicating the weight of one side's concern as compared with the other side's has been easy when the matters at hand affect the United States and the USSR directly. For this reason, Western European anxiety about the coverage it gets from our strategic forces, though understandable, is exaggerated. The United States might well retaliate should the USSR make a major military move against a NATO country, and that possibility is enough to deter.

The problem of extended deterrence

How far from the homeland does deterrence extend? One answers that question by defining the conditions that must obtain if deterrent threats are to be credited. The credibility of a deterrent force requires both that interests be seen to be vital and that it is the attack from outside that threatens them. Although countries may not instantly agree on the question of whose interests are vital, nuclear weapons strongly incline them to grope for de facto agreement rather than risk war. If the threat to a regime is in good part from internal factions, then an outside power may risk supporting one of them even in the face of deterrent threats.

The difficult problem for the Western alliance of stretching a deterrent does not exist for lesser nuclear states. Their problem is to protect not others but themselves. Many have feared that lesser nuclear states would be the first ones to break the nuclear taboo and that they would use their weapons irresponsibly. I expect just the opposite. Weak states find it easier than strong ones to establish their credibility. Not only are they not trying to stretch their deterrent forces to cover others, but also their vulnerability to conventional attack lends credence to their nuclear threats. Because in a conventional war they can lose so much so fast, it is easy to believe that they will unleash a deterrent force even at the risk of receiving a nuclear blow in return. With deterrent forces, the party that is absolutely threatened prevails.[10] Use of nuclear weapons by lesser states will come only if survival is at stake. This should be called not irresponsible but responsible use. Moreover, establishing the credibility of a deterrent force requires moderation of territorial claims on the part of the would-be deterrer. For modest states, weapons whose very existence works strongly against their use are just what is wanted.

In a nuclear world, conservative would-be attackers will be prudent, but will would-be attackers be conservative? A new Hitler is not unimaginable. Would the presence of nuclear weapons have moderated Hitler's behavior? Hitler did not start World War II in order to destroy the Third Reich. From the occupation of the Rhineland in 1936 to the invasion of Poland in 1939, his calculations were realistically made. In those years Hitler would probably have been deterred from acting in ways that immediately threatened massive death and widespread destruction in Germany. If Hitler had not been deterred, moreover, would his generals have obeyed his commands? In a nuclear world, to act in blatantly offensive ways is madness. Under the circumstances, how many generals would obey the commands of a madman? One man alone does not make war.

To believe that nuclear deterrence would have worked against Germany in 1939 is easy. It is also easy to believe that in 1945, given the ability to do so, Hitler and some few around him would have fired nuclear warheads at the United States, Great Britain, and the USSR as their armies advanced, whatever the consequences for Germany. When defeat appears inevitable, however, a ruler's authority may vanish. Early in 1945 Hitler apparently ordered the initiation of gas warfare, but no one responded.[11] In a nuclear world, no country will press another to the point of decisive defeat. All the parties involved are constrained to be moderate because the immoderate behavior of one makes the nuclear threats of others credible.

Arms races among new nuclear states

One may easily believe that U.S. and Soviet military doctrines set the pattern that new nuclear states will follow and that they will compete in building larger and larger nuclear arsenals while continuing to accumulate conventional weapons. For three main reasons, however, new nuclear states are likely to decrease rather than to increase their military spending.

First, nuclear weapons alter the dynamics of arms races. In a competition between two or more parties, it may be hard to say who is pushing and who is being pushed, who is leading and who is following. If one party seeks to increase its capabilities, it may seem that the other(s) must too. The dynamic may be built into the competition and may unfold despite a mutual wish to resist it. This need not be the case in a strategic competition between nuclear countries, however, if the conditions of competition make deterrent logic dominant, as it will be if the conditions of competition make it nearly impossible for any of the competing parties to achieve a first-strike capability.

Those who foresee nuclear arms racing among new nuclear states fail to make the distinction between war-fighting and war-deterring capabilities. War-fighting forces, because they threaten the forces of others, must be compared. Superior forces may bring victory to one country; inferior forces may bring defeat to another. With war-fighting strategies, arms races become difficult, if not impossible, to avoid. Forces designed for deterring war need not be compared, however, and with deterrent strategies, arms races make sense only if a first-strike capability is within reach. Because thwarting a first strike is easy, deterrent forces are quite cheap to build and maintain. With deterrent forces, the question is not whether one country has more than another but rather whether it has the capability of inflicting unacceptable damage on another, with unacceptable damage sensibly defined. Once that capability is assured, additional strategic weapons are useless. More is not better if less is enough. Deterrent balances are inherently stable. If one can say how much is enough, then within wide limits one state can be insensitive to changes in its adversaries' forces. The logic of deterrence eliminates incentives for strategic arms racing.

Allowing for their particular circumstances, lesser nuclear states confirm these statements in their policies. The British and French strategic forces are modest enough when one considers that their purpose is to deter the USSR rather than states with capabilities comparable to their own. China, of course, faces the same task. These three countries show no inclination to engage in nuclear arms races with anyone. India appears content to have a nuclear military capability that may or may not have produced deliverable warheads, and Israel maintains its ambiguous status. New nuclear states are likely to conform to these patterns and aim for a modest sufficiency rather than to vie with one another for a meaningless superiority.

Second, because strategic nuclear arms races among lesser powers are unlikely, the interesting question is whether or not countries having strategic nuclear weapons can avoid running conventional races. No more than the United States or the USSR will new nuclear states want to rely on executing the deterrent threat that risks all. Moreover, will not their vulnerability to conventional attack induce them to continue their conventional efforts?

U.S. policy since the early 1960s again teaches lessons that mislead. For two decades we have emphasized the importance of having a continuum of forces that would enable the United States and its allies to fight at any level from irregular to strategic nuclear warfare. The policy of flexible response lessened reliance on strategic deterrence and therefore increased the chances of fighting a war. New nuclear states are not likely to experience this problem. The expense of mounting conventional defenses, and the difficulties and dangers of fighting conventional wars, will keep most nuclear states from trying to combine large war-fighting forces with deterrent forces. Disjunction within their forces will increase the value of deterrence.

Israeli policy seems to contradict these propositions. From 1971 through 1978, both Israel and Egypt spent from 20 to 40 percent of their GNPs on arms. Israel's spending on conventional arms remains high, although it has decreased since 1978. The decrease followed from the making of peace with Egypt and not from increased reliance on nuclear weapons. The seeming contradiction in fact bears out deterrent logic. As long as Israel holds the West Bank and the Gaza Strip, it must be prepared to fight for them, Since they are by no means unambiguously Israel's, deterrent threats, whether implicit or explicit, will not cover them. Moreover, while large U.S. subsidies continue, economic constraints will not drive Israel to the territorial settlement that would shrink its borders sufficiently to make a deterrent policy credible.

Finally, arms races in their ultimate form—the fighting of offensive wars designed to increase national security—also become pointless. The success of a deterrent strategy does not depend on the extent of territory a state holds, a point made earlier. It merits repeating because of its unusual importance for states whose geographic limits lead them to obsessive concern for their security in a world of ever more destructive conventional weapons.

The frequency and intensity of war

The presence of nuclear weapons makes war less likely. One may nevertheless oppose the spread of nuclear weapons because they would make war, however unlikely, unbearably intense. We may be grateful for decades of nuclear peace and for the discouragement of conventional war among those who have nuclear weapons. Yet the fear is naturally widespread that if they ever go off, we may all be dead. People as varied as the scholar Richard Smoke, the arms controller Paul Warnke, and former Defense Secretary Harold Brown all believe that if any nuclear weapons go off, many will. Although this seems the least likely of all the unlikely possibilities, unfortunately it is not impossible. This scenario is quite unlikely, however, because even if deterrence should fail, the prospects for rapid deescalation are good.

Deterrence rests on what countries *can* do to each other with strategic nuclear weapons. From this statement one easily leaps to the wrong conclusion: That deterrent strategies, if they have to be carried through, will produce a catastrophe. That countries are able to annihilate each other means neither that deterrence depends on their threatening to do so nor that they will do so if deterrence fails. Because countries heavily armed with strategic nuclear weapons can carry war to its ultimate intensity, the control of force, in wartime as in peacetime, becomes the primary objective. Since the great powers are unlikely to be drawn into the nuclear wars of others, the added global dangers posed by the spread of nuclear weapons are small.

The spread of nuclear weapons threatens to make wars more intense at the local and not at the global level, where wars of the highest intensity have been possible for a number of years. If their national existence should be threatened, weaker countries, unable to defend themselves at lesser levels of violence, may destroy themselves through resorting to nuclear weapons. Lesser nuclear states will live in fear of this possibility. This, however, is no different from the fear under which the United States and the USSR have lived for years. Small nuclear states may experience a keener sense of desperation because of extreme vulnerability to conventional as well as to nuclear attack; but, again, in desperate situations what all parties become most desperate to avoid is the use of strategic nuclear weapons. Still, however improbable the event, lesser states may one day fire some of their weapons. Are minor nuclear states more or less likely to do so than major ones? The answer to this question is vitally important because the existence of some states would be at stake even if the damage done were regionally confined.

For a number of reasons, then, deterrent strategies promise less damage than war-fighting strategies. First, deterrent strategies induce caution all around and thus reduce the incidence of war. Second, wars fought in the face of strategic nuclear weapons must be carefully limited because a country having them may retaliate if its vital interests are threatened. Third, prospective punishment need only be proportionate to an adversary's expected gains in war after those gains are discounted for the many uncertainties of war. Fourth, should deterrence fail, a few judiciously delivered warheads are likely to produce sobriety in the leaders of all of the countries involved and thus bring rapid deescalation. Finally, war-fighting strategies offer no clear place to stop short of victory for some and defeat for others. Deterrent strategies do, and that place is where one country threatens another's vital interests. In sum, deterrent strategies lower the probability that wars will begin. If wars start nevertheless, deterrent strategies lower the probability that they will be carried very far.

Nuclear weapons may lessen the intensity as well as the frequency of wars among their possessors. For fear of escalation, nuclear states do not want to fight long or hard over important interests—indeed, they do not want to fight at all. Minor nuclear states have even better reasons than major ones to accommodate one another peacefully and to avoid any fighting. Worries about the intensity of war among nuclear states have to be viewed in this context and against a world in which conventional weapons become ever costlier and more destructive.

Acknowledgment

This essay is a shortened and revised version of Kenneth N. Waltz, *The Spread of Nuclear Weapons: More May Be Better*, Adelphi Papers, no. 171 (London: International Institute for Strategic Studies, 1981). Reprinted with permission.

Notes

1   Glenn H. Snyder, *Deterrence and Defense* (Princeton, NJ: Princeton University Press, 1961), p. 44; Stephen Van Evera, "Nuclear Weapons, Nuclear Proliferation, and the Causes of War," Unpublished paper, 1976.
2   Georg Simmel, "The Sociology of Conflict, I," *American Journal of Sociology* 9 (January 1904): p. 501.
3   I shall concentrate on nuclear deterrence and slight nuclear defense. A defensive nuclear doctrine, although it has not been welcomed in U.S. or NATO military circles, was at times supported by Bernard Brodie and has been persuasively expounded by Sandoval, Shreffler, and a few others. See, for example, R. R. Sandoval, "Consider the Porcupine: Another View of Nuclear Proliferation," *Bulletin of the Atomic Scientists* 32 (May 1976); R. Shreffler and R. R. Sandoval, *Nuclear Weapons, Their Role in U.S. Political and Military Posture, and an Example* (Los Alamos Scientific Laboratory, September 1975); and R. Shreffler, "The New Nuclear Force," in *Tactical Nuclear Weapons: European*

Perspectives, Stockholm International Peace Research Institute Yearbook (London: Taylor and Francis, 1978).

4 Cf. Lewis A. Dunn, "Nuclear Proliferation and World Politics," in Joseph I. Coffey ed., *Nuclear Proliferation: Prospects, Problems, and Proposals* (Philadelphia: *Annals of the American Academy of Political Science*, March 1977), pp. 102–107.

5 I use *spread*, not *proliferate*, because so far the only proliferation has been vertical; horizontal acquisition has been slow.

6 Cf. Dunn, "Nuclear Proliferation," p. 101.

7 Geoffrey Kemp, *Nuclear Forces for Medium Powers*, part I: *Targets and Weapons*, Adelphi Papers, no. 106 (London: International Institute for Strategic Studies, 1974).

8 Thomas Schelling, *Arms and Influence* (New Haven: Yale University Press, 1966).

9 Glenn H. Snyder, "Crisis Bargaining," in C. F. Hermann, ed., *International Crises: Insights from Behavioral Research* (New York: Free Press 1972), p. 232.

10 Shai Feldman, "Israeli Nuclear Deterrence: A Strategy for the 1980s?," Ph.D. diss. University of California (Berkeley), 1980, chap. 1.

11 Frederic J. Brown, in "Chemical Warfare: A Study in Restraints," In *The Use of Force*, ed. by Robert J. Art and Kenneth Waltz (Boston: Little, Brown, 1971). p. 183.

18

NUCLEAR MYTHS AND
POLITICAL REALITIES

Two pervasive beliefs have given nuclear weapons a bad name:
that nuclear deterrence is highly problematic, and that a break-
down in deterrence would mean Armageddon. Both beliefs
are misguided and suggest that nearly half a century after
Hiroshima, scholars and policy makers have yet to grasp the
full strategic implications of nuclear weaponry. I contrast the
logic of conventional and nuclear weaponry to show how
nuclear weapons are in fact a tremendous force for peace and
afford nations that possess them the possibility of security at
reasonable cost.

Nuclear weapons have been given a bad name not just by the Left, as one
might have expected, but by the Center and Right as well. Throughout the
long life of NATO, calls for strengthening conventional forces have been
recurrently heard, reflecting and furthering debate about the wisdom of relying
on nuclear deterrence. Doubts were spread more widely when McGeorge
Bundy, George Kennan, Robert McNamara, and Gerald Smith published
their argument for adopting a NATO policy of "no first use" (Bundy et al.
1982). From the Right came glib talk about the need to be prepared to fight a
protracted nuclear war in order to "deter" the Soviet Union and proclaiming
the possibility of doing so. Brigadier General Louis Guiffridda, when he was
director of the Federal Emergency Management Agency, well described the
Reagan administration's intended nuclear stance: "The administration," he
said, "categorically rejected the short war. We're trying to inject a long-war
mentality" (Dowd 1984). Such statements, which scared people at home and
abroad out of their wits, quickly disappeared from public discourse. Nevertheless, preparation to carry the policy through proceeded apace. In 1982 Secretary
of Defense Caspar Weinberger signed the five-year Defense Guidance Plan,
which was to provide the means of sustaining a nuclear war; and in March of
that year an elaborate war game dubbed Ivy League "showed" that it could be
done (Pringle and Arkin 1983, pp. 22–40). Finally, in March of 1983 President

Reagan offered his vision of a world in which defensive systems would render nuclear weapons obsolete.

With their immense destructive power, nuclear weapons are bound to make people uneasy. Decades of fuzzy thinking in high places about what deterrence is, how it works, and what it can and cannot do have deepened the nuclear malaise. Forty-some years after the first atomic bombs fell on Japan, we have yet to come to grips with the strategic implications of nuclear weapons. I apply nuclear reasoning to military policy and in doing so contrast the logic of conventional and nuclear weapons.

Uneasiness over nuclear weapons and the search for alternative means of security stem in large measure from widespread failure to understand the nature and requirements of deterrence. Not unexpectedly, the language of strategic discourse has deteriorated over the decades. This happens whenever discussion enters the political arena, where words take on meanings and colorations reflecting the preferences of their users. Early in the nuclear era *deterrence* carried its dictionary definition, dissuading someone from an action by frightening that person with the consequences of the action. To deter an adversary from attacking one need have only a force that can survive a first strike and strike back hard enough to outweigh any gain the aggressor had hoped to realize. Deterrence in its pure form entails no ability to defend; a deterrent strategy promises not to fend off an aggressor but to damage or destroy things the aggressor holds dear. Both defense and deterrence are strategies that a status quo country may follow, hoping to dissuade a state from attacking. They are different strategies designed to accomplish a common end in different ways, using different weapons differently deployed. Wars can be prevented, as they can be caused, in various ways.

Deterrence antedates nuclear weapons, but in a conventional world deterrent threats are problematic. Stanley Baldwin warned in the middle 1930s when he was prime minister of England that the bomber would always get through, a thought that helped to demoralize England. It proved seriously misleading in the war that soon followed. Bombers have to make their way past fighter planes and through ground fire before finding their targets and hitting them quite squarely. Nuclear weapons purify deterrent strategies by removing elements of defense and war-fighting. Nuclear warheads eliminate the necessity of fighting and remove the possibility of defending, because only a small number of warheads need to reach their targets.

Ironically, as multiplication of missiles increased the ease with which destructive blows can be delivered, the distinction between deterrence and defense began to blur. Early in President Kennedy's administration, Secretary McNamara began to promote a strategy of Flexible Response, which was halfheartedly adopted by NATO in 1967. Flexible Response calls for the ability to meet threats at all levels from irregular warfare to conventional warfare to nuclear warfare. In the 1970s and 1980s more and more emphasis was placed on the need to fight and defend at all levels in order to "deter." The melding of defense, war-fighting, and deterrence overlooks a simple truth about nuclear weapons proclaimed in the book title *The Absolute Weapon* (Brodie 1946). Nuclear weapons can carry out their deterrent task no matter what other countries do. If one nuclear power were able to destroy almost all of another's strategic warheads with practical certainty or defend against all but a few strategic warheads coming in, nuclear weapons would not be absolute. But because so much explosive power comes in such small packages, the invulnerability of a sufficient number of warheads is easy to achieve and the delivery of fairly large numbers of warheads impossible to thwart, both now and as far into the future as anyone can see. The absolute quality of nuclear weapons sharply sets a nuclear world off from a conventional one.

What deters?

Most discussions of deterrence are based on the belief that deterrence is difficult to achieve. In the Eisenhower years "massive retaliation" was the phrase popularly used to describe the response we would supposedly make to a Soviet Union attack. Deterrence must be difficult if the threat of massive retaliation is required to achieve it. As the Soviet Union's arsenal grew, MAD (mutual assured destruction) became the acronym of choice, thus preserving the notion that deterrence depends on being willing and able to destroy much, if not most, of a country.

That one must be able to destroy a country in order to deter it is an odd notion, though of distinguished lineage. During the 1950s emphasis was put on the *massive* in *massive retaliation*. Beginning in the 1960s the emphasis was put on the *assured destruction* in the doctrine of MAD. Thus viewed, deterrence becomes a monstrous policy, as innumerable critics have charged. One quotation can stand for many others. In a warning to NATO defense ministers that became famous, Henry Kissinger counseled the European allies not to keep "asking us to multiply strategic assurances that we cannot possibly mean or if we do mean, we should not want to execute because if we execute, we risk the destruction of civilization" (1981, p. 240). The notion that the failure of deterrence would lead to national suicide or to mutual annihilation betrays a misunderstanding of both political behavior and nuclear realities.

Introducing the Eisenhower administration's New Look policy in January of 1954, John Foster Dulles gave the impression that aggression anywhere would elicit heavy nuclear retaliation. Just three months later, he sensibly amended the policy. Nuclear deterrence, Dulles and many others quickly came to realize, works not against minor aggression at the periphery, but only against major aggression at the center, of international politics. Moreover, to deter major aggression, Dulles now said, "the probable hurt" need only "outbalance the probable gain" (1954, p. 359). Like Brodie before him, Dulles based deterrence on the principle of proportionality: "Let the punishment fit the crime."

What would we expect the United States to do if the Soviet Union launched a major conventional attack against vital U.S. interests—say, in Western Europe? Military actions have to be related to an objective. Because of the awesome power of nuclear weapons, the pressure to use them in ways that achieve the objective at hand while doing and suffering a minimum of destruction would be immense. It is preposterous to think that if a Soviet attack broke through NATO's defenses, the United States would strike thousands of Soviet military targets or hundreds of Soviet cities. Doing so would serve no purpose. Who would want to make a bad situation worse by launching wantonly destructive attacks on a country that can strike back with comparable force, or, for that matter, on a country that could not do so? In the event, we might strike a target or two—military or industrial—chosen to keep casualties low. If the Soviet Union had run the preposterous risk of attacking the center of Europe believing it could escape retaliation, we would thus show them that they were wrong while conveying the idea that more would follow if they persisted. Among countries with abundant nuclear weapons, none can gain an advantage by striking first. The purpose of demonstration shots is simply to remind everyone—should anyone forget—that catastrophe threatens. Some people purport to believe that if a few warheads go off, many will follow. This would seem to be the least likely of all the unlikely possibilities. That no country gains by destroying another's cities and then seeing a comparable number of its own destroyed in return is obvious to everyone.

Despite widespread beliefs to the contrary, deterrence does not depend on destroying cities. Deterrence depends on what one *can* do, not on what one *will* do. What deters is the fact that we can do as much damage to them as we choose, and they to us. The country suffering the retaliatory attack cannot limit the damage done to it; only the retaliator can do that.

With nuclear weapons, countries need threaten to use only a small amount of force. This is so because once the willingness to use a little force is shown, the adversary knows how easily more can be added. This is not true with conventional weapons. Therefore, it is often useful for a country to threaten to use great force if conflict should lead to war. The stance may be intended as a deterrent one, but the ability to carry the threat through is problematic. With conventional weapons, countries tend to emphasize the first phase of war. Striking hard to achieve a quick victory may decrease the cost of war. With nuclear weapons, political leaders worry not about what may happen in the first phase of fighting but about what may happen in the end. As Clausewitz wrote, if war should ever approach the absolute, it would become "imperative . . . not to take the first step without considering what may be the last" (1976, p. 584).

Since war now approaches the absolute, it is hardly surprising that President Kennedy echoed Clausewitz's words during the Cuban Missile Crisis of 1962. "It isn't the first step that concerns me," he said, "but both sides escalating to the fourth and fifth step—and we don't go to the sixth because there is no one around to do so" (R. Kennedy 1969, p. 98). In conventional crises, leaders may sensibly seek one advantage or another. They may bluff by threatening escalatory steps they are in fact unwilling to take. They may try one stratagem or another and run considerable risks. Since none of the parties to the struggle can predict what the outcome will be, they may have good reason to prolong crises, even crises entailing the risk of war. A conventional country enjoying military superiority is tempted to use it before other countries right the military balance, A nuclear country enjoying superiority is reluctant to use it because no one can promise the full success of a disarming first strike. As Henry Kissinger retrospectively said of the Cuban Missile Crisis, the Soviet Union had only "60–70 truly strategic weapons while we had something like 2,000 in missiles and bombs." But, he added, "with some proportion of Soviet delivery vehicles surviving, the Soviet Union could do horrendous damage to the United States" (Kissinger 1979, p. 18). In other words, we could not be sure that our two thousand weapons would destroy almost all of their sixty or seventy. Even with numbers immensely disproportionate, a small force strongly inhibits the use of a large one.

The catastrophe promised by nuclear war contrasts sharply with the extreme difficulty of predicting outcomes among conventional competitors. This makes one wonder about the claimed dependence of deterrence on perceptions and the alleged problem of credibility. In conventional competitions, the comparative qualities of troops, weaponry, strategies, and leaders are difficult to gauge. So complex is the fighting of wars with conventional weapons that their outcomes have been extremely difficult to predict. Wars start more easily because the uncertainties of their outcomes make it easier for the leaders of states to entertain illusions of victory at supportable cost. In contrast, contemplating war when the use of nuclear weapons is possible focuses one's attention not on the probability of victory but on the possibility of annihilation. Because catastrophic outcomes of nuclear exchanges are easy to imagine, leaders of states will shrink in horror from initiating them. With nuclear weapons, stability and peace rest on easy calculations of what one country can do to another. Anyone—political leader or man in the street—can see that catastrophe lurks if events spiral out of control and nuclear warheads begin to fly. The problem of the credibility of deterrence, a big worry in a conventional world, disappears in a nuclear one.

Yet the credibility of deterrence has been a constant U.S. worry. The worry is a hangover from the 1930s. Concern over credibility, and the related efforts to show resolve in crises or wars where only peripheral interests are at stake were reinforced because the formative experiences of most of the policy makers of the 1950s and 1960s took place in the 1930s. In rearming Germany, in reoccupying the Rhineland, in annexing Austria, and in dismantling Czechoslovakia, Hitler went to the brink and won. "We must not let that happen again" was the lesson learned, but in a nuclear world the lesson no longer applies. Despite rhetoric to the contrary, practice accords with nuclear logic because its persuasive force is so strong, and the possible consequences of ignoring it so grave. Thus, John Foster Dulles, who proclaimed that maintaining peace requires the courage to go the brink of war, shrank from the precipice during the Hungarian uprising of 1956. And so it has been every time that events even remotely threatened to get out of hand at the center of international politics.

Still, strategists' and commentators' minds prove to be impressively fertile. The imagined difficulties of deterrence multiply apace. One example will do: Paul Nitze argued in the late 1970s that, given a certain balance of strategic forces, the Soviet Union's supposed goal of world domination, and its presumed willingness to run great risks, the Soviet Union might launch a first strike against our land-based missiles, our bombers on the ground, and our strategic submarines in port. The Soviet Union's strike would tilt the balance of strategic forces sharply against us. Rather than retaliate, our president might decide to acquiesce; that is, we might be self-deterred (1988, pp. 357–360). Nitze's scenario is based on faulty assumptions, unfounded distinctions, and preposterous notions about how governments behave. Soviet leaders, according to him, may have concluded from the trend in the balance of nuclear forces in the middle 1970s that our relatively small warheads and their civil defense would enable the Soviet Union to limit the casualties resulting from our retaliation to 3% or 4% of their population. Their hope for such a "happy" outcome would presumably rest on the confidence that their first strike would be well timed and accurate and that their intelligence agencies would have revealed the exact location of almost all of their intended targets. In short, their leaders would have to believe that all would go well in a huge, unrehearsed missile barrage, that the United States would fail to launch on warning, and that if by chance they had failed to "deter our deterrent," they would still be able to limit casualties to only ten million people or so.[1] But how could they entertain such a hope when by Nitze's own estimate their first strike would have left us with two thousand warheads in our submarine force in addition to warheads carried by surviving bombers?

Nitze's fear rested on the distinction between counterforce strikes and countervalue strikes—strikes aimed at weapons and strikes aimed at cities. Because the Soviet Union's first strike would be counterforce, any U.S. president would seemingly have good reason to refrain from retaliation, thus avoiding the loss of cities still held hostage by the Soviet Union's remaining strategic forces. But this thought overlooks the fact that once strategic missiles numbered in the low hundreds are fired, the counterforce–countervalue distinction blurs. One would no longer know what the attacker's intended targets might be. The Soviet Union's counterforce strike would require that thousands, not hundreds, of warheads be fired. Moreover, the extent of their casualties, should we decide to retaliate, would depend on how many of our warheads we chose to fire, what targets we aimed at, and whether we used ground bursts to increase fallout. Several hundred warheads could destroy either the United States or the Soviet Union as ongoing societies. The assumptions made in the effort to make a Soviet first strike appear possible are ridiculous. How could the Soviet Union—or any country, for that matter— somehow bring itself to run stupendous risks in the presence of nuclear weapons? What objectives might its leaders seek that could justify the risks entailed? Answering these questions sensibly leads one to conclude that deterrence is deeply stable. Those who favor increasing the strength of our strategic forces, however, shift to a different question. "The crucial question," according to Nitze, "is whether a future U.S. president should be left with only the option of deciding within minutes, or at most within two or three hours, to retaliate after a counterforce attack in a manner certain to result not only in military defeat for the United States but in wholly disproportionate and truly irremediable destruction to the American people" (1988, p. 357). One of the marvels of the nuclear age is how easily those who write about the unreliability of deterrence focus on the possible retaliatory inhibitions and play down the attacker's obvious risks. Doing so makes deterrence seem hard and leads to arguments for increasing our military spending in order "to deny the Soviet Union the possibility of a successful war-fighting capability" (1988, p. 360), a strategic capability that the Soviet Union has never remotely approached.

We do not need ever-larger forces to deter. Smaller forces, so long as they are invulnerable, would be quite sufficient. Yet the vulnerability of fixed, land-based missiles has proved worrisome. Those who do the worrying dwell on the vulnerability of one class of weapon. The militarily important question, however, is not about the vulnerability of one class of weapon but about the vulnerability of a whole strategic-weapons system. Submarine-launched missiles make land-based missiles invulnerable since destroying only the latter would leave thousands of strategic warheads intact. To overlook this again reflects conventional thinking. In the absence of a dominant weapon, the vulnerability of one weapon or another may be a big problem. If the means of protecting sea-lanes of communications were destroyed, for example, we would be unable to deploy and support troops abroad. The problem disappears in a nuclear world. Destroying a portion of one's strategic force means little if sufficient weapons for deterrence survive.

Thinking about deterrence is often faulted for being abstract and deductive, for not being grounded in experience. The criticism is an odd one, since all statements about the military implications of nuclear weapons are inferred from their characteristics. Deterrers from Brodie onward have drawn conclusions from the all-but-unimaginable increase in easily delivered firepower that nuclear warheads embody. Those who in the nuclear era apply lessons learned in conventional warfare make the more problematic claim, that despite profound changes in military technology, the classic principles of warfare endure (Rose 1980, pp. 102–106). We all, happily, lack the benefit of experience. Moreover, just as deterrent logic is abstract and deductive, so too are the weaknesses attributed to it. Scenarios showing how deterrence might fail are not only abstract but also far-fetched. Deterrence rests on simple propositions and relies on forces obviously sufficient for their purpose.

Deterring the Soviet Union

Underlying much of the concern about the reliability of nuclear deterrence is the conviction that the Soviet Union is especially hard to deter. Three main reasons are given for believing this. First, the Soviet Union's ambitions are said to be unlimited. In 1984 Secretary of Defense Caspar Weinberger, when asked why the Soviet Union armed itself so heavily, answered the question bluntly, "World domination, it's that simple" (Rosenthal 1989). Second, her military doctrine seemed to contemplate the possibility of fighting and winning combined conventional and nuclear war, while rejecting the doctrine of deterrence. Third, the Soviet Union has appeared to many people in the West to be striving for military superiority.

These three points make a surprisingly weak case, even though it has been widely accepted. Ambitions aside, looking at the Soviet Union's behavior one is impressed with its caution when acting where conflict might lead to the use of major force. Leaders of the Soviet Union may hope that they can one day turn the world to communism. Although the Soviet Union's intentions may be extraordinary, her behavior has not been. Everyone agrees that except in the military sector, the Soviet Union is the lagging competitor in a two-party race. The Soviet Union has been opportunistic and disruptive, but one expects the lagging party to score a point or two whenever it can. The Soviet Union has not scored many. Her limited international successes should not obscure the fact that what the Soviet Union has done mostly since 1948 is lose.

The second point rests on basic misunderstandings about deterrence. It has often been argued that we could not rely on deterrence when the Soviet Union was rejecting the doctrine. One of the drawbacks of the "theory" of assured destruction, according to Henry Kissinger, was that "the Soviets did not believe it" (1981, p. 238). The efficacy of nuclear deterrence, however, does not depend on anyone's accepting it. Secretaries of defense nevertheless continue to worry that Soviet values, perceptions, and calculations may be different from ours. Thus, Secretary of Defense Harold Brown, worried by the Soviets' emphasis "on the acquisition of war-winning capabilities," concluded that we must "continue to adapt and update our countervailing capabilities so that the Soviets will clearly understand that we will never allow them to use their nuclear forces to achieve any aggressive aim at an acceptable cost" (1980, p. 83).

The belief that the Soviet Union's having an aggressive military doctrine makes her especially hard to deter is another hangover from conventional days. Germany and Japan in the 1930s were hard to deter, but then the instruments for deterrence were not available. We can fairly say that their leaders were less averse to running risks than most political leaders are. But that is no warrant for believing that had they been confronted with second-strike nuclear forces, they would have been so foolhardy as to risk the sudden destruction of their countries. The decision to challenge the vital interests of a nuclear state, whether by major conventional assault or by nuclear first strike, would be a collective decision involving a number of political and military leaders. One would have to believe that a whole set of leaders might suddenly go mad. Rulers like to continue to rule. Except in the relatively few countries of settled democratic institutions, one is struck by how tenaciously rulers cling to power. We have no reason to expect Russian leaders to be any different. The notion that Russian leaders might risk losing even a small number of cities by questing militarily for uncertain gains is fanciful. Malenkov and Khrushchev lost their positions for lesser failures.

With conventional weapons a status quo country must ask itself how much power it must harness to its policy in order to dissuade an especially aggressive state from striking. Countries willing to run high risks are hard to dissuade. The varied qualities of governments and the temperaments of leaders have to be carefully weighed. In a nuclear world any state will be deterred by another state's second-strike forces. One need not become preoccupied with the characteristics of the state that is to be deterred or scrutinize its leaders.

The third worry remains: the Soviet Union's seeming aspiration for military superiority. One might think that the worry should have run the other way through most of the years of the Cold War. In the nuclear business the United States moved from monopoly to superiority. In the late fifties Khrushchev deeply cut conventional arms, and the Soviet Union failed to produce strategic warheads and missiles as rapidly as we had expected. Nevertheless, the Kennedy administration undertook the largest peacetime military buildup the world had yet seen in both nuclear and conventional weaponry. We forged ahead so far strategically that Robert McNamara thought the Soviet Union would not even try to catch up. "There is," he said, "no indication that the Soviets are seeking to develop a strategic nuclear force as large as ours" (Interview, *U.S. News and World Report*, 12 April 1976, p. 52). The Soviet Union's giving up would have been historically unprecedented. Instead, the Soviet Union did try to compete, but to catch up with the United States was difficult. In the 1970s, the decade in which we are told the Soviet Union moved toward superiority (or, according to President Reagan, achieved it), the United States in fact added more nuclear warheads to its arsenal than the Soviet Union did.

We have exaggerated the strength of the Soviet Union; and they, no doubt, have exaggerated ours. One may wonder whether the Soviet Union ever thought itself superior or believed it could become so. Americans easily forget that the Soviet Union has the strategic weapons of the United States, Britain, France, and China pointed at it and sees itself threatened from the East as well as the West. More fundamentally, continued preoccupation with denying "superiority" to the Soviet Union, if not seeking it ourselves, suggests that a basic strategic implication of nuclear weapons is yet to be appreciated. So long as two or more countries have second-strike forces, to compare them is pointless. If no state can launch a disarming attack with high confidence, force comparisons become irrelevant. For deterrence one asks how much is enough, and enough is defined as "having a second-strike capability." This does not imply that a deterrent force deters everything, but rather that beyond a certain level of capability, additional forces provide no additional coverage for one party and pose no additional threat to others. The United States and the Soviet Union have long had second-strike forces, with neither able to launch a disarming first strike against the other. Two countries with second-strike forces have the same amount of strategic power—since, short of attaining a first-strike capability, adding more weapons does not change the effective military balance.

Why nuclear weapons dominate strategy

Deterrence is easier to contrive than most strategists have believed. With conventional weapons, a number of strategies are available, strategies combining and deploying forces in different ways. Strategies may do more than weapons to determine the outcomes of wars. Nuclear weapons are different; they dominate strategies. As Brodie clearly saw, the effects of nuclear weapons derive not from any particular design for their employment in war but simply from their presence (1973, p. 412). Indeed, in an important sense, nuclear weapons eliminate strategy. If one thinks of strategies as being designed for defending national objectives or for gaining them by military force and as implying a choice about how major wars will be fought, nuclear weapons make strategy obsolete. Nevertheless, the conviction that the only reliable deterrent force is one able to win a war or at least end up in a better position than the Soviet Union is widespread. Linton F. Brooks, while a captain in the U.S. Navy, wrote that "war is the ultimate test of any strategy; a strategy useless in war cannot deter" (1988, p. 580; see also Howard 1981, p. 15).

NATO policy well illustrates the futility of trying to transcend deterrence by fashioning war-fighting strategies. The supposed difficulties of extending deterrence to cover major allies has led some to argue that we require nuclear superiority, that we need nuclear war-fighting capabilities, and that we must build up our conventional forces. Once the Soviet Union achieved nuclear parity, confidence in our extended deterrent declined in the West. One wonders whether it did in the East. Denis Healey once said that one chance in a hundred that a country will retaliate is enough to deter an adversary, although not enough to reassure an ally. Many have repeated his statement; but none, I believe, has added that reassuring allies is unnecessary militarily and unwise politically. Politically, allies who are unsure of one another's support have reason to work harder for the sake of their own security. Militarily, deterrence requires only that conventional forces be able to defend long enough to determine that an attack is a major one and not merely a foray. For this, a trip-wire force as envisioned in the 1950s, with perhaps fifty thousand U.S. troops in Europe, would be sufficient. Beyond that, deterrence requires only that forces be invulnerable and that the area protected be of manifestly vital interest. West European countries can be counted on to maintain forces of trip-wire capability.

Nuclear weapons strip conventional forces of most of their functions. Bernard Brodie pointed out that in "a total war" the army "might have no function at all" (1957, p. 115). Herman Kahn cited "the claim that in a thermonuclear war it is important to keep the sea lanes open" as an example of the "quaint ideas" still held by the military (1960, p. 38). Conventional forces have only a narrow role in any confrontation between nuclear states over vital interests, since fighting beyond the trip-wire level serves no useful purpose. Enlarging conventional capabilities does nothing to strengthen deterrence. Strategic stalemate does shift military competition to the tactical level. But one must add what is usually omitted: Nuclear stalemate limits the use of conventional forces and reduces the extent of the gains one can seek without risking devastation. For decades U.S. policy has nevertheless aimed at raising the nuclear threshold in Europe. Stronger conventional forces would presumably enable NATO to sustain a longer war in Europe at higher levels of violence. At some moment in a major war, however, one side or the other—or perhaps both—would believe itself to be losing. The temptation to introduce nuclear weapons might then prove irresistible, and they would be fired in the chaos of defeat with little chance of limited and discriminant use. Early use would promise surer control and closer limitation of damage. In a nuclear world a conventional war-fighting strategy would appear to be the worst possible one, more dangerous than a strategy of relying on deterrence.

Attempts to gain escalation dominance, like efforts to raise the nuclear threshold, betray a failure to appreciate the strategic implications of nuclear weapons. Escalation dominance, so it is said, requires a "seamless web of capabilities" up and down "the escalation ladder." Earlier, it had been thought that the credibility of deterrence would be greater if some rungs of the escalation ladder were missing. The inability to fight at some levels would make the threat to use higher levels of force easy to credit. But again, since credibility is not a problem, this scarcely matters militarily. Filling in the missing rungs neither helps nor hurts. Escalation dominance is useful for countries contending with conventional weapons only. Dominance, however, is difficult to achieve in the absence of a decisive weapon. Among nuclear adversaries the question of dominance is pointless because one second-strike force cannot dominate another. Since strategic nuclear weapons will always prevail, the game of escalation dominance cannot be played. Everyone knows that anyone can quickly move to the top rung of the ladder. Because anyone can do so, all of the parties in a serious crisis have an overriding incentive to ask themselves one question: How can we get out of this mess without nuclear warheads exploding? The presence of nuclear weapons forces them to figure out how to deescalate, not how to escalate.

To gain escalation dominance, if that were imaginable, would require the ability to fight nuclear wars. War-fighting strategies imply that nuclear weapons are not absolute but relative, so that the country with more and better nuclear weapons could in some unspecified way prevail. No one, however, has shown how such a war could be fought. Indeed, Desmond Ball has argued that a nuclear war could not be sustained beyond the exchange of strategic warheads numbered not in the hundreds but in the tens (1981, p. 9). After a small number of exchanges no one would know what was going on or be able to maintain control. Yet nuclear weapons save us from our folly: Fanciful strategies are irrelevant because no one will run the appalling risk of testing them.

Deterrence has been faulted for its lack of credibility, its dependence on perceptions, its destructive implications, and its inability to cover interests abroad. The trouble with deterrence, however, lies elsewhere: The trouble with deterrence is that it can be implemented cheaply. The claim that we need a seamless web of capabilities in order to deter does serve one purpose: It keeps military budgets wondrously high. Efforts to fashion a defensive and war-fighting strategy for NATO are pointless because deterrence prevails and futile because strategy cannot transcend the military conditions that nuclear weapons create.

Nuclear arms and disarmament

The probability of major war among states having nuclear weapons approaches zero. But the "real war" may, as William James claimed, lie in the preparation for waging it. The logic of deterrence, if followed, circumscribes the causes of "real wars" (1968, p. 23). Nuclear weapons make it possible for a state to limit the size of its strategic forces as long as other states are unable to achieve disarming first-strike capabilities by improving their forces.

Within very wide ranges, a nuclear balance is insensitive to variation in numbers and size of warheads. This has occasionally been seen by responsible officials. Harold Brown, when he was secretary of defense, said that purely deterrent forces "can be relatively modest, and their size can perhaps be made substantially, though not completely, insensitive to changes in the posture of an opponent." Somehow, he nevertheless managed to argue that we need "to design our forces on the basis of essential equivalents" (1979, pp. 75–76). Typically, over the past three decades secretaries of defense have sought, albeit vainly, the superiority that would supposedly give us a war-fighting capability. But they have failed to explain what we can do with twelve thousand strategic nuclear warheads that we could not do with two thousand or an even smaller number. What difference does it make if we have two thousand strategic weapons and the Soviet Union has four thousand? We thought our deterrent did not deter very much and did not work with sufficient reliability just as we were reaching a peak of numerical superiority in the mid-1960s. Flexible response, with emphasis on conventional arms, was a policy produced in our era of nuclear plenty. "Superiority" and "parity" have had the same effect on our policy.

Many who urge us to build ever more strategic weapons in effect admit the military irrelevance of additional forces when, as so often, they give political rather than military reasons for doing so: Spending less, it is said, would signal weakness of will. Yet militarily, only one perception counts, namely, the perception that a country has second-strike forces. Nuclear weapons make it possible for states to escape the dynamics of arms racing; yet the United States and the Soviet Union have multiplied their weaponry far beyond the requirements of deterrence. Each has obsessively measured its strategic forces against the other's. The arms competition between them has arisen from failure to appreciate the implications of nuclear weapons for military strategy and, no doubt, from internal military and political pressures in both countries.

Many of the obstacles to arms reduction among conventional powers disappear or dwindle among nuclear nations. For the former, the careful comparison of the quantities and qualities of forces is important. Because this is not so with nuclear weapons, the problem of verifying agreements largely disappears. Provisions for verification may be necessary in order to persuade the Senate to ratify an agreement, but the possibility of noncompliance is not very worrisome. Agreements that reduce one category of conventional weapons may shift competition to other types of weapons and lead to increases in their numbers and capabilities. Because with nuclear weapons sufficiency is easily defined, there is no military reason for reductions in some weapons to result in increases in others. Conventionally, multiparty agreements are hard to arrive at because each party has to consider how shifting alignments may alter the balance of forces if agreements are reached to reduce them. In a world of second-strike nuclear forces, alliances have little effect on the strategic balance. The Soviet Union's failure to insist that British, French, and Chinese forces be counted in strategic arms negotiations may reflect its appreciation of this point. Finally, conventional powers have to compare weapons of uncertain effectiveness. Arms agreements are difficult to reach because their provisions may bear directly on the prospects for victory or defeat. Because in a nuclear world peace is maintained by the presence of deterrent forces, strategic arms agreements do not have military but economic and political, significance. They can benefit countries economically and help to improve their relations.

A minority of U.S. military analysts have understood the folly of maintaining more nuclear weapons than deterrence requires. In the Soviet Union, Mikhail Gorbachev and some others have put forth the notion of "reasonable sufficiency," defined as having a strategic force roughly equal to ours and able to inflict unacceptable damage in retaliation. Edward Warner points out that some civilian analysts have gone further, "suggesting that as long as the USSR had a secure second-strike capability that could inflict unacceptable damage, it would not have to be concerned about maintaining approximate numerical parity with U.S. strategic nuclear forces" (1989, p. 21). If leaders in both countries come to accept the minority view—and also realize that a deterrent force greatly reduces conventional requirements on central fronts—both countries can enjoy security at much lower cost.

Strategic defense

Strategic defenses would radically change the propositions advanced here. The Strategic Defense Initiative, in Reagan's vision, was to provide an area defense that would protect the entire population of the United States. Strategic defenses were to pose an absolute defense against what have been absolute weapons, thus rendering them obsolete. The consequences that would follow from mounting such a defense boggle the mind. That a perfect defense against nuclear weapons could be deployed and sustained is inconceivable. This is so for two reasons: (1) it is impossible, and (2) if it were possible, it wouldn't last.

Nuclear weapons are small and light; they are easy to move, easy to hide, and easy to deliver in a variety of ways. Even an unimaginably perfect defense against ballistic missiles would fail to negate nuclear weapons. Such a defense would instead put a premium on the other side's ability to deliver nuclear weapons in different ways: firing missiles on depressed trajectories, carrying bombs in suitcases, placing nuclear warheads on freighters to be anchored in American harbors. Indeed, someone has suggested that the Soviet Union can always hide warheads in bales of marijuana, knowing we cannot keep them from crossing our borders. To have even modestly effective defenses we would, among other things, have to become a police state. We would have to go to extraordinary lengths to police our borders and exercise control within them. Presumably, the Soviet Union does these things better than we do. It is impossible to imagine that an area defense can be a success because there are so many ways to thwart it. In no way can we prevent the Soviet Union from exploding nuclear warheads on or in the United States if it is determined to do so.

Second, let us imagine for a moment that an airtight defense, however defined, is about to be deployed by one country or the other. The closer one country came to deploying such a defense, the harder the other would work to overcome it. When he was secretary of defense, Robert McNamara argued that the appropriate response to a Soviet defensive deployment would be to expand our deterrent force. More recently, Caspar Weinberger and Mikhail Gorbachev have made similar statements. Any country deploying a defense effective for a moment cannot expect it to remain so. The ease of delivering nuclear warheads and the destructiveness of small numbers of them make the durability of defenses highly suspect.

289

The logic of strategic defense is the logic of conventional weaponry. Conventional strategies pit weapons against weapons. That is exactly what a strategic defense would do, thereby recreating the temptations and instabilities that have plagued countries armed only with conventional weapons. If the United States and the Soviet Union deploy defensive systems, each will worry—no doubt excessively—about the balance of offensive and defensive capabilities. Each will fear that the other may score an offensive or defensive breakthrough. If one side should do so, it might be tempted to strike in order to exploit its temporary advantage. The dreaded specter of the hair trigger would reappear. Under such circumstances a defensive system would serve as the shield that makes the sword useful. An offensive–defensive race would introduce many uncertainties. A country enjoying a momentary defensive advantage would be tempted to strike in the forlorn hope that its defenses would be able to handle a ragged and reduced response to its first strike. Both countries would prepare to launch on warning while obsessively weighing the balance between offensive and defensive forces.

Finally, let us imagine what is most unimaginable of all—that both sides deploy defenses that are impregnable and durable. Such defenses would make the world safe for World War III—fought presumably in the manner of World War II but with conventional weapons of much greater destructive power.

Still, some have argued that even if some American cities remain vulnerable, defenses are very good for the cities they do cover. The claim is spurious. In response to the Soviet Union's deploying antiballistic missiles to protect Moscow, we multiplied the number of missiles aimed at that city. We expect to overcome their defenses and still deliver the "required" number of warheads. The result of defending cities may be that more warheads strike them. This is especially so because both they and we, working on worst-case assumptions, are likely to overestimate the number of missiles that the other country's system will be able to shoot down. Strategic defenses are likely to increase the damage done.

Most knowledgeable people believe that an almost leak-proof defense cannot be built. Many, however, believe that if improved hard-point defenses result from the SDI program, they will have justified its price. Defense of missiles and of command, control, and communications installations will strengthen deterrence, so the argument goes. That would be a solution, all right; but we lack a problem to go with it: deterrence is vibrantly healthy. If the Soviet Union believes that even one Trident submarine would survive its first strike, it will be deterred.[3] Since we do not need hard-point defenses, we should not buy them. The deployment of such defenses by one side would be seen by the other as the first step in deploying an area defense. Strategic considerations should dominate technical ones. In a nuclear world defensive systems are predictably destabilizing. It would be folly to move from a condition of stable deterrence to one of unstable defense.

Conclusion

Nuclear weapons dissuade states from going to war more surely than conventional weapons do. In a conventional world, states going to war can at once believe that they may win and that, should they lose, the price of defeat will be bearable. World Wars I and II called the latter belief into question before atomic bombs were ever dropped. If the United States and the Soviet Union were now armed only with conventional weapons, the lesson of those wars would be strongly remembered—especially by Russia, since she has suffered more in war than we have. If the atom had never been split, the United States and the Soviet Union would still have much to fear from each other. The stark opposition of countries of continental size armed with ever-more-destructive conventional weapons would strongly constrain them. Yet in a conventional world even forceful and tragic lessons have proved to be exceedingly difficult for states to learn. Recurrently in modern history one great power or another has looked as though it might become dangerously strong (Louis XIV's and Napolean's France, Wilhelm II's and Hitler's Germany). Each time, an opposing coalition formed, if belatedly, and turned the expansive state back. The lesson would seem to be clear: In international politics, success leads to failure. The excessive accumulation of power by one state or coalition of states elicits the opposition of others. The leaders of expansionist states have nevertheless been able to persuade themselves that skillful diplomacy and clever strategy might enable them to transcend the normal processes of balance-of-power politics. The Schlieffen Plan, for example, seemed to offer a strategy that would enable Germany to engage enemies on two fronts, serially: Germany would defeat France before Russia could mobilize fully and move westward in force. Later, Hitler, while denouncing the "boobs" of Wilhelmine Germany for getting themselves into a war on two fronts, reenacted their errors.

How can we perpetuate peace without solving the problem of war? This is the question that states with nuclear weapons must constantly answer. Nuclear states continue to compete militarily. With each state tending to its security interests as best it can, war is constantly possible. Although the possibility of war remains, nuclear weapons have drastically reduced the probability of its being fought by the states that have them. Wars that might bring nuclear weapons into play have become extraordinarily hard to start. Over the centuries great powers have fought more wars, and lesser states have fought fewer: The frequency of war has correlated less closely with the attributes of states than with their international standing. Yet because of a profound change in military technology, waging war has more and more become the privilege of poor and weak states. Nuclear weapons have reversed the fates of strong and weak states. Never since the Treaty of Westphalia in 1648, which conventionally marks the beginning of modern history, have great powers enjoyed a longer period of peace than we have known since the Second World War. One can scarcely believe that the presence of nuclear weapons does not greatly help to explain this happy condition.

Notes

This essay was presented as the presidential address at the annual meeting of the American Political Science Association in Washington, 1988. David Schleicher's penetrating criticisms and constructive suggestions helped me greatly in writing it.

1 Nitze blandly adds that if we do launch on warning, "the estimates in the Soviet civil defense manuals are overoptimistic from the Soviet viewpoint" (1988, p. 357).
2 Quaint ideas die hard. In the fall of 1989 NATO resisted discussing naval disarmament with the Soviet Union because of the need for forces to guard the sea-lanes to Europe (Lewis 1988).
3 An Ohio-class Trident submarine carries twenty-four missiles, each with eight warheads.

References

Ball, Desmond. 1981. "Counterforce Targeting: How New? How Viable?," *Arms Control Today* 11: pp. 1–9.
Brodie, Bernard ed. 1946. *The Absolute Weapon*. New York: Harcourt, Brace.
Brodie, Bernard. 1957. "More about Limited War." *World Politics* 10:112–22.
Brodie, Bernard. 1973. *War and Politics*. New York: Macmillan.
Brooks, Linton F. 1988. "Naval Power and National Security." In *The Use of Force*, 3d ed., ed. Robert J. Art and Kenneth N. Waltz. Lanham, MD: University Press of America.
Brown, Harold. 1979. *Annual Report, Fiscal Year 1980*. Washington: U.S. Department of Defense.
Brown, Harold. 1980. *Annual Report, Fiscal Year 1981*. Washington: U.S. Department of Defense.
Bundy, McGeorge, George F. Kennan, Robert S. McNamara, and Gerard Smith. 1982. "Nuclear Weapons and the Atlantic Alliance," *Foreign Affairs* 60: pp. 753–768.
Clausewitz, Carl von. 1976. *On War*. Trans. Michael Howard and Peter Paret. Princeton: Princeton University Press.
Dowd, Maureen. 1984. "Ferraro Suggests Reagan Go Home," *New York Times* 22 September.
Dulles, John Foster. 1954. "Policy for Security and Peace," *Foreign Affairs* 32: pp. 353–364.
Howard, Michael. 1981. "On Fighting a Nuclear War," *International Security* 5: pp. 3–17.
James, William. 1968. "The Moral Equivalent of War," In *War: Studies from Psychology, Sociology, Anthropology*, 2d ed., ed. Leon Bramson and George W. Goethals. New York: Basic Books.
Kahn, Herman. 1960. *On Thermonuclear War*. Princeton: Princeton University Press.

Kennedy, Robert F. 1969. *Thirteen Days.* New York: Norton.

Kissinger, Henry. 1979. "Kissinger's Critique," *Economist,* 3 February.

Kissinger, Henry. 1981. *For the Record: Selected Statements, 1977–1980.* Boston: Little, Brown.

Lewis, Paul. 1938. "Soviet Official Says Talks on Arms Should Emphasize Cuts in Navies," *New York Times,* 19 October.

Nitze, Paul H. 1988. "Deterring Our Deterrent," In *The Use of Force,* 3d ed., ed. Robert J. Art and Kenneth N. Waltz. Lanham, MD: University Press of America.

Pringle, Peter, and William Arkin. 1983. *S.I.O.P.: The Secret of U.S. Plan for Nuclear War.* New York: Norton.

Rose, John P. 1980. *The Evolution of U.S. Army Nuclear Doctrine, 1945–1980.* Boulder: Westview.

Rosenthal, Andrew. 1989. "Pentagon Report Softens Soviet Menace," *New York Times,* 28 September.

Warner, Edward L. III. 1989. "New Thinking and Old Realities in Soviet Defense Policy," *Survival* 31: pp. 13–33.

19

A REPLY (TO CRITICS OF SAGAN AND WALTZ)

Authors can always find something to carp about in evaluations made of their work. I shall forego the pleasure of doing so and take notice only of the basic misapprehensions that mar the comments of Steven R. David and especially of Peter D. Feaver.[1]

In seven pages, Feaver offers a critique of my chapters in *The Spread of Nuclear Weapons: A Debate*[2] and of neorealist theory as well. Given the scope of the critical task, its faulty execution is hardly surprising, but the distance by which Feaver's salvoes miss their mark is. He identifies three flaws in my recent and earlier writings on the spread of nuclear weapons. First, my "nuclear optimism theory," he says, explains "the absence of nuclear war" and nothing else ("Optimists, Pessimists," pp. 754–755). In a way, this is fair enough. I set out to explain why nuclear weapons work strongly to keep peace among those who have them and why they may be expected to continue to do so as nuclear weapons slowly spread from country to country. I can hardly quarrel with someone who says I succeeded. I do want to point out, however, that I have not developed a theory about nuclear weapons. Theories explain, but not every explanation is a theory. I do believe that in the past fifty years the United States has grossly overspent on nuclear weapons, but I do not see why my failure to account for this when writing about the spread of nuclear weapons exposes either a weakness in an unidentified theory, or an omission in an argument about a quite different question.

Second, Feaver claims that I unduly depreciate problems of command and control and of civil-military relations ("Optimists, Pessimists," p. 757). He fails, however, to consider my main point: Namely, that although large and complex nuclear arsenals are hard to control, the relatively small and simple forces of new nuclear states are not. That proposition is indeed hard to disagree with.

Third, Feaver, wandering into the realm of structural theory, censures me for believing at once that the spread of nuclear weapons promotes peace and that multipolarity is unstable. Believing that "the spread of nuclear weapons fosters multipolarity," he sees a contradiction ("Optimists, Pessimists," p. 760). Yet few can believe that weak states become great powers merely by getting nuclear weapons. Weak states armed with nuclear weapons can, however, deter strong states having much larger forces. Feaver apparently doubts this; I long ago ceased doing so and have abundantly explained why.

These three criticisms, according to Feaver, generate a fourth one, which exposes a "damning" inconsistency ("Optimists, Pessimists," p. 760). His reasoning is this: If, as I say, nuclear weapons restore the clarity and simplicity of a bipolar world, then polarity, along with structural realism, is "largely irrelevant in a multipolar world." This, he believes, is the logical conclusion of nuclear optimism ("Optimists, Pessimists," p. 761). It is so, however, only if security defined in purely military terms is the only problem states confront and if nuclear weaponry is a complete solution to that problem. Structural realism depicts international politics as a realm of self-help. The instruments available to states for helping themselves make their lives more or less precarious. Nuclear weapons are a big help to states that have to maintain their own security. Nuclear weapons clarify security relations among nations that have them, and clarity is all the more helpful as the waning of bipolarity increases the complication of international life. States continue to compete for wealth and security even while nuclear weapons alter some of the terms of the competition. Where is the inconsistency?

Steven R. David makes two major criticisms, one about terrorists, the other about weak states. According to him, I believe that "all terrorists will fit" my "rational model" ("Risky Business," p. 775). I have, however, offered no model, rational or other. Instead, I ask why terrorists behave the way they do, and especially why they have limited the damage they have chosen to do. I answer those questions by looking at their presumed aims and their actual situations, rather than by drawing conclusions from an assumed rationality. Asserting that terrorists will destroy all they can, David dwells on the well-known destructive power of nuclear weapons, while avoiding the pertinent question—why have terrorists not used easily available means to increase the damage they have done? Since they have not, one wonders why they would want to take the fateful step into the world of nuclear weapons. So far, at least, ends not means have placed limits on their acts. Anyway, fear of nuclear terrorism has little to do with the spread of nuclear weapons. Since the disintegration of the Soviet Union, nuclear materials have apparently not been hard to come by.

David believes, as I suppose most citizens of strong states do, that weak states pose the greatest threat to world peace. He points out, as I do, that during the past fifty years weak states have done most of the fighting, adding that more people have been killed in internal than in external wars ("Risky Business," p. 775). Since many weak states experience internal conflict, he reasons, we should be all the more fearful of their getting nuclear weapons. Moreover, the Saddam Husseins of this world would "face few inhibitions" in using nuclear weapons where "a domestic threat . . . could be defeated" by them ("Risky Business," p. 778). In saying this, David ignores the inhibitions inherent in the very possession of nuclear weapons. For the cruelest of leaders, inhibitions will not be moral, but no leader of any state can bet that the use of nuclear weapons whether at home or abroad will not bring punishing attack from other states. Even the most troublesome and cruel leaders have shown themselves susceptible to deterrence *(Spread,* pp. 12–13). Contrary to David, it is not obvious that "[c]ountries beset by conflict are obviously more likely to use their weapons . . . than countries at peace" ("Risky Business," p. 777). Many countries at peace are beset by conflict, nuclear states among them. Since 1945, none of the latter has tried to use nuclear weapons to solve their internal or external problems, however pressing they have been.

Both David and Feaver believe that the policy relevance of "nuclear optimists" approaches zero. They further believe that the nuclear arming of countries against which the United States may want to bring pressure runs counter to our interests. Both beliefs are problematic. Clearly they are so when viewed historically. The United States has treated different potential and actual nuclear states differently. We act on the belief that the spread of nuclear weapons is not always to be opposed, at least not very strongly. The belief that another country or two going nuclear is not always so bad already informs our policy.

The argument that we must not let such countries as Libya, Iraq, and North Korea have nuclear weapons does, however, appear to be unassailable. Yet I wonder. Is the world worse off, and indeed is the United States worse off, because the Soviet Union and China became nuclear powers? In these archetypical cases, the peace-producing effects of nuclear weapons have been beneficial to all of us. Benefits have not come without costs, but the costs have been incalculably lower than the cost of fighting major wars. Limitations of America's policy choices has been one of the costs, but David and Feaver forget that limitations apply to those who would use their weapons for aggression as well as to those who would oppose them.

From fifty years of experience, one may conclude that nuclear weapons effectively preserve a country's vital interests, but are of little use in extending one country's control over others. David and Feaver nevertheless fear that a nuclear Iraq would be able to dominate its oil-rich region. They repeat a common error of believing that weak nuclear states will be able to do with their weapons what strong states have not been able to.

The notion that weak states want nuclear weapons to use for aggression has taken hold of the imagination of policymakers. To disabuse them of odd notions is hardly an idle task.

Notes

1 Peter D. Feaver, "Optimists, Pessimists, and Theories of Nuclear Proliferation Management," *Security Studies* 4, no. 4 (summer 1995): pp. 754–772; Steven R. David, "Risky Business: Let Us Not Take a Chance on Proliferation," *Security Studies* 4, no. 4 (summer 1995): pp. 773–778.
2 Scott D. Sagan and Kenneth N. Waltz *The Spread of Nuclear Weapons: A Debate* (New York: Norton, 1995).

Part IV

POLICY

20

THE POLITICS OF PEACE*

The striking characteristics of world politics since the war have been these: peace among the powerful; their occasional use of force against others; war at times within and among the weak; the failure of such force as has been used to lead to wider wars at higher levels of violence. If one measures time from the termination of wars, 1967 stands to 1945 as 1940 does to 1918. Never in this century have so many years gone by without the great powers fighting a general war. Small wars have been numerous, but somehow violence has been controlled and limited. Despite dreadful dangers, a relative peace has prevailed. How has peace been prolonged and what are the prospects of extending our blessings?

I

"The end of the Cold War" is an emergent theme of political studies, and those who proclaim its demise usually do so with a sigh of relief. I am tempted to predict, perversely, that in the coming years students of politics will look back on the era of the Cold War, if indeed it has ended, with the nostalgia that diplomatic historians have long felt for nineteenth-century Europe.

Only four years ago it was written that "The West, instead of dealing with Russia in terms of a world policy, persists in the attempt to deal with the world in terms of a Russian policy, this being in essence the policy of containing Russia all over the world. The underlying orientation is faulty."[1] This is a fair description and a false judgment. The United States did fashion and follow a "Russian" foreign policy. We have been willing to act or to support the action of others in order to counter the outward thrust of the Soviet Union and associated states: for example, in Greece, Berlin, Korea, and Cuba. We were not willing to support the Dutch in Indonesia in 1946 and 1962, the British and French in Suez in 1956, or the French in Indochina in the spring of 1954. The American pursuit of a "Russian" foreign policy was not an error; it was instead the reversal of old and erroneous American habits. America's mistake prior to two world wars lay not in her failure to pay attention to little states but in her disregard of the course of great-power relations. Interests have to

299

be guarded where they exist in greatest magnitude, as in Western Europe; threats have to be met when they emanate from a state whose strength may endanger one's own security. By her military and other capabilities, the Soviet Union—and only the Soviet Union—has constituted such a threat. In sensible response, America pursued a "Russian" foreign policy; and the reverse can be said of the Soviet Union.

The term "bloc" at times misled us, both because we exaggerated the likely coherence of the two blocs and because we misunderstood their meaning. Associated states added little if anything to the strength of the respective bloc leaders; each bloc was an extension of the leader's power. Antagonism between the United States and the Soviet Union shaped the politics of peace in the period that began with the conclusion of the Second World War. The stark dangers of a nuclear world and the simplicity of relations between two powerful adversaries produced clarity in the definition of their national interests. Each can lose heavily only in war with the other; in power and in wealth, both can gain more by the peaceful development of internal resources than by wooing and winning—or by fighting and subduing—other states in the world. A five percent growth rate sustained for three years adds to the American gross national product an amount greater than the entire gross national product of Britain or France or West Germany or Japan. Whether measured in economic or in military terms, the distance in power between the superpowers and any other state has enabled the United States and the Soviet Union to pursue their own interests without adjusting their strategies to the fears and wishes of associated states.

The United States and the Soviet Union influence each other more than any of the states living in their penumbra can possibly hope to do. In the last analysis, what the United States had to do in the world was determined not by calculation of how to gain new allies or please old ones, but by gauging the power and disposition of the Soviet Union. In a hot war or a cold war—as in any close competition—the external situation dominates. In the middle 1950s, John Foster Dulles inveighed against the immoral neutralists. Russian and Chinese leaders, at the same time and in similar spirit, described neutralists as either fools themselves or dupes of capitalist countries. But ideology did not long prevail over interest. Both Russia and America quickly came to accept neutralist states and even to lend them encouragement. The Soviet Union aided Egypt and Iraq, countries that kept their communists in jail. From 1957 onward, the United States, which had already given much assistance to Communist Yugoslavia, made neutralist India the most favored of aid recipients.

According to the rhetoric of the Cold War, the root cleavage in the world was between capitalist democracy and godless communism. But by the size of the stakes and the force of the struggle, ideology was subordinated to interest in the policies of America and Russia, who behaved more like traditional great powers than like leaders of messianic movements. In a world in which two

300

states united in their mutual antagonism far overshadow any other, the incentives to a calculated response stand out most clearly, and the sanctions against irresponsible behavior achieve their greatest force. Thus two states, isolationist by tradition, untutored in the ways of international relations, and famed for impulsive behavior, soon showed themselves—not always and everywhere, but always in crucial cases—to be wary, alert, cautious, flexible, and forbearing.

Some have believed that a new world began with the explosion of an atomic bomb over Hiroshima. In shaping the behavior of nations, the perennial forces of politics are as important as the new military technology. States remain the primary vehicles of ideology. The internationalist brotherhood of autocrats after 1815, the cosmopolitan liberalism of the middle nineteenth century, international socialism before World War I, international communism in the decades following the Bolshevik revolution—in all of these cases international movements were captured by individual nations, adherents of the creed were harnessed to the nation's interest, international programs were manipulated by national governments, and ideology became a prop to national policy. So the Soviet Union in crisis became Russian, and American policy, liberal rhetoric aside, came to be realistically and cautiously constructed. By the force of events, they and we were constrained to behave in ways belied both by their words and ours.

Such were the healthful effects of the Cold War, defined as the approximate balance of the two most powerful states, whose interactions formed the politics of peace.** If, however, the world balance has now tilted in America's favor, then domestic aspects of foreign policy become more important in the study of the politics of peace.

II

Partly for reasons of policy and partly because changes in military technology have lately been less rapid and far-reaching, the United States in the past half-dozen years has converted superior economic resources into military capability at a pace that the Soviet Union apparently has not matched. Close competition subordinates ideology to interest; states that enjoy a margin of power over their closest competitors can more readily pursue their fancies abroad and indulge aspirations that reach beyond the fulfillment of interests narrowly defined in terms of security. Deterrence that rests on second-strike forces makes small wars safe by diminishing the chances of uncontrolled escalation. The possibilities of action, by military and other means, are thus made large for any state that disposes of a surplus of power. Under such circumstances, national impulses shape foreign policy with lesser constraint than prevails when power is more evenly balanced.

Habits shaped by international conditions may continue to inform a nation's policy even when conditions have changed. The United States, once reflexively isolationist, has become almost reflexively internationalist. Where we once

301

assumed that changes in the configuration of world power were of no interest to us, we now behave as though any of many events in the world must elicit our vigorous response. Moreover, with American foreign policy less closely guided by the Russian danger, impulses frozen by the Cold War may thaw out in today's warmer climate and lead to unfortunate actions. When foreign dangers are less pressing, more attention must be paid to national inclinations.

Herbert Hoover and Woodrow Wilson, whose preferences in foreign policy moved in opposite directions, nevertheless illustrate a basic quality of American thinking. The one found evil rife in the world and would have had us insulate ourselves from it; the other agreed about the unsatisfactory condition of the world and would have had us act to change it. In the foreign policy of the country since the Second World War, the latter tendency has not been absent.

An imbalance of international forces may give one state the opportunity to dominate, singly or in combination with others—that is, to use its own power to control the use of power by other states. At times this has been the half-articulated dream of American policy. One critic has discerned it in the threat of massive retaliation, the message conveyed being: Cross the line we have drawn—or, in more general terms, violate the rules we have laid down—and you will be erased.[2] Not so long ago, Senator J. William Fulbright, along with other artificers of an Atlantic imperium, aspired to a condition of world hegemony that would provide the material basis for managing the world. "If the West goes on to realize its fullest possible strength in an Atlantic partnership, it can," the Senator wrote, "bring about a decisive shift in the world balance of power and permanently foreclose the possibility of significant Communist expansion."[3] President Kennedy, speaking on the Fourth of July, 1962, remarked that: "Acting on our own by ourselves, we cannot establish justice throughout the world. We cannot insure its domestic tranquility, or provide for its common defense, or promote its general welfare, or secure the blessings of liberty to ourselves and our posterity. But joined with other free nations, we can do all this and more. . . . We can mount a deterrent powerful enough to deter any aggression, and ultimately we can help achieve a world of law and free choice, banishing the world of war and coercion."[4] Such would be the benefits of an American–European union. Put more simply in the down-to-earth prose of President Johnson: The purpose of American military strength is "to put an end to conflict."[5] A continuous strand in American thinking runs from Presidents Wilson and Hoover to President Johnson— if we cannot insulate ourselves from the world, then we should seek to control it.[†]

The humane rhetoric and obvious good intention of the above statements disguise what should worry us greatly. One cannot assume that the leaders of a nation superior in power will always define policies with wisdom, devise tactics with fine calculation, and apply force with forbearance. The possession of great power has often tempted nations to the unnecessary and foolish employment of force. For one state or combination of states to foreclose others' use of force in a world in which grievances and disputes abound, to end conflict in a contentious world, would require as much wisdom as power. Since justice cannot be objectively defined, the temptation of the powerful nation is to claim that the solution it seeks to impose is a just one.

Illustrations are dismayingly abundant. For example, in Senator Edward W. Brooke's maiden speech to the Senate, he first defined the question of justifying our presence in Vietnam as academic and then went on to resolve that issue. The development of his logic well illustrates what scares me. This is what he said: "Once we . . . begin to rationalize the struggle in Vietnam as a necessary sacrifice to the global balance of power, I believe that we cross the line between a just and an unjust war. While we may recognize the wider implications of the war, we can never justify the conflict on those grounds. In my judgment it would be plainly immoral to expect the South Vietnamese to suffer today's violence in order to ward off tomorrow's war somewhere else."[6]

We fight not to ward off a bigger war but, again in the words of Senator Brooke, to secure what is "best for South Vietnam, and most honorable and decent for ourselves." This is apparently true; we surely do not fight out of necessity. Spokesmen for the Administration have asserted the vital importance of showing that insurgencies are costly, damaging, and doomed to defeat; they have argued that one setback may lead to another; they have averred that China must be contained for a time as the Soviet Union was earlier. A strong case, however, cannot result from adding up weak reasons. The revolutionary guerrilla wins civil wars, not international ones, and no civil war can change the balance of world power unless it takes place in America or Russia. In any event, the potency of irregular warfare and the ability of communists to bore from within have been grossly exaggerated—as the record of events in Greece, Malaya, the Philippines, Laos, and Indonesia makes clear. Nor does one setback necessarily lead to another. We are misled by the vision of dominoes. States in the area of the fighting lack the solidity, shape, and cohesion that the image suggests. Externally illdefined, internally fragile and chaotic, they more appropriately call to mind sponges; and sponges, whatever their other characteristics, do not from the transmission of impulses neatly fall down in a row. As for China, mesmerized by the magic of mere numbers, we have led ourselves to believe that 800 million people must be able to do something highly damaging to somebody. They have in fact hardly been able to do anything at all; and any increase in Chinese strength would anyway be first and foremost a worry for the Soviet Union, not for the United States.

The term "bloc" has fallen into desuetude; instead it is the term "polycentrism" that now misleads us. Though the communist movement is no longer effectively directed by the Soviet Union, we still think in terms of an international conspiracy and talk as though interest and duty require us to counter its machinations. It can, however, no longer be said that a communist government newly come to power in some minor state will enhance Russia's strength or somehow add to the power of a now mythical world communist movement. Nor can we believe, if we look at Eastern Europe, that the triumph of communism permanently enslaves a people. Let us be blunt. Who will say for sure that Ho Chi Minh and his associates are the worst of the possible future rulers of Vietnam? And when I say "for sure," I mean with enough assurance to merit the killing of some hundreds of thousands of people over the issue.

The United States has been able to commit nearly 500,000 men to war in Vietnam with no increase in the percentage of gross national product that goes into defense and no weakening of our strategic position vis-à-vis the Soviet Union. With such vast capability, the United States can act, not against the Soviet Union, but aside from the threat that her power entails. Senator Brooke is indeed right. We do not fight for our interest; not enough is at stake to bring important American interests into question. We must then be fighting for such abstractions as honor and decency and on behalf of somebody else's welfare as we see it.

A state that enjoys a margin of power in its favor is able to make choices. It can seek to bring orderly government to those unable to govern themselves, to give freedom to people whose unhappy history and present condition make them unable to use it; it can kill people in the name of their liberty and seek to build a polity and shape a society by the use of B-52s.

But which is the better basis of policy—to kill people in order to free them, or to undertake war only out of apprehension for one's own security? The first amounts to deducing necessity from a liberal principle[7] and wrapping the mantle of justice around a national cause in order to legitimate the bloodshed. The second amounts to doing what necessity dictates and eschewing force except where vital interest dictates its use. If developments in Vietnam might indeed tilt the world balance in America's disfavor, then we ought to be fighting. But by Senator Brooke's logic such fighting would be immoral. If the dominant balance of power in the world is not in question, then we need not fight. But, according to Senator Brooke, only under such a circumstance, where the nation fighting abroad has risen above its interest, can wars be considered just. War undertaken on calculations of what the security of the country requires is said to be crass and narrowly selfish. "War is either a crusade or a crime" is a slogan that idealists find attractive. But the crusader, who acts on his definition of another's interest, may then commit crimes in the name of humanity. Statesmen of the nineteenth century, it has been said, "fought 'necessary' wars and killed thousands; the idealists of the twentieth century fight 'just' wars and kill millions."[8]

The perils of weakness are matched by the temptations of power. Good intentions, backed by great power, have often led to persecution, unnecessary violence, and widespread destruction. The pattern is uncomfortably common, whether in the relation of believers to infidels, of one race to another, or of nation to nation.

War is a blunt instrument. Once begun, it is hard to control. As more blood is spilled, more resounding reasons must be given for the carnage until finally unimportant wars fought for doubtful causes are justified in the name of high principle. The escalation of justifications in the war in Vietnam is as impressive as the escalation of force—and may be ultimately as dangerous. The loftier the principles invoked, the more difficult it becomes to stop the war and disentangle the nation. Given the luxury of choice that vast power provides, the question of the criteria of commitment, far from being academic, becomes vital. And if the restraints of international politics press less closely, the question of internal restraint looms ever larger. To study the politics of peace, then, requires examination of domestic politics, especially the politics of the world's most powerful nation.

III

Democracies, and especially the American democracy, have often been thought defective in the making and conduct of foreign policy. To maintain large foreign-aid programs, to sustain heavy defense spending in years of peace, to garrison odd corners of the world, to fight on occasion in distant lands without prospect of tangible gains—these tasks were thought to exceed the political capacity of the nation. They have all been steadily accomplished.

Weaknesses were thought to inhere in the structure of American politics; strengths were much underestimated. In the American system of government, political struggles for office and arguments over policy take place among individuals and groups who openly clash and compete. Competition among interests and the clash of perspectives heightens issues and strengthens the institutions that express them. The Congressman, who is a political generalist, becomes an expert in one realm of policy or another in order to advance his career and forward his policy preferences. The executive official, who may be an expert in policy, schools himself in the political arts in order to protect his department and advance its programs. The American system is one of contention among strong institutions whose cutting edges have been honed in recurrent conflict. Should one say then that the President is weak because Congress is strong, or should one say that the American government is powerful because its component parts are strongly constituted and active? Those who define power according to differences in the amount of force wielded by each of two entities—who think of power as a residue of strength—will surely reply in the negative. It is, however, more useful to think of the power of a government in terms of its effectiveness. May it not be that the government gains power from the strength of each of its component institutions?

The strength of the Presidency facilitated the remarkably rapid and felicitous adjustment of the nation to its postwar role in the world. But there is no end to one's worries. In the 1950s we wondered whether the nation would support the waging of limited wars. We may now fear that the government is unable to admit its errors and bring wars to an end when force has outrun its objectives. No governmental system, however well constructed, can guarantee a satisfactory policy product. More than other systems, the American government provides opportunity for leadership combined with encouragement to critics who oppose the nation's policy. Many Congressmen, powerful in their constituencies, are not easily amenable to the executive's wishes. Because opposition to the President's policy cannot bring the government down, members of both parties are free to criticize loudly. The presence of inquisitive Congressmen gives dissident executive officials a chance to express their misgivings. The investigations of congressional committees provide private citizens with a public platform.

President Johnson has shown an unusual ability to keep issues closed, to prevent arguments from occurring in publicly conspicuous places. The susceptibility of the President to criticism is nevertheless indicated by his efforts to win over some critics and to blanket the voices of others through skillful timing of his own newsworthy activities.

Though one would not expect Presidents to admit it—or even to believe it—opposition to foreign policy may not only be permissible; it may even be a patriotic duty. Opposition in some ways makes the President's life harder; in other ways, it improves his position. If one state is hard pressed by others, the wide and willing support of its people is needed. Though widespread support of leaders and their policies enhances the strength of a state, it also decreases the government's opportunity for maneuver. Dissent from policy and opposition to the actions of the government provide a chance for the President to choose among different policies. Should we bomb more in Vietnam, try harder to withdraw, or carry on as at present? If each option enjoys a fair amount of support, the President can more easily choose among them. By raising their voices, the critics have helped to "maintain the options"; they have not persuaded the President to make a more precise adjustment of power to political purpose, nor are they likely to do so.

A government's policy and its public standing are closely identified, perhaps more so in democracies than in other political systems. At this point, the relation of a government to its policy must be considered with care. Two cases are especially instructive: first, the Korean War and the American election of 1952. The Democratic Administration, having begun the Korean War, was unable to end it either by military victory or diplomatic settlement. A President steadily losing public support may find himself boxed in, as to a considerable extent President Truman did. After months of inconclusive and costly fighting, withdrawal would have been humiliating, and to threaten the use of unlimited means in order to achieve a limited end, as Eisenhower and Dulles did later, would have failed of acceptance at home and lacked credibility abroad. The Korean case is one in which the President and his closest advisers had failed to sustain the nation's confidence in their integrity and competence. Under such circumstances, if a change of persons and parties can be easily and gracefully made, policies that remain necessary though they have become unpopular can more easily be continued. The election of 1952, by bringing a change in government, promoted the continuity and success of a policy. This is hardly what is wanted by the critics of America's policy in Vietnam.

If one looks further and makes a second comparison, another possibility emerges. France pursued a costly course, and one that could never return a profit, for sixteen years in Indochina and Algeria. During the Fourth Republic, policy remained constant so long as governments were formed by the shuffling of party leaders and groups, all of whom were deeply implicated in old policies. It took exceptional political events, the emergence of Mendès-France and then of de Gaulle, to make the redirection of policy possible. In the United States elections provide a routine way of changing leaders, parties, the cabinet, and many public officials. Would-be governors customarily argue that they can do what present governors cannot, whether this be to carry old programs to a successful conclusion or to contrive new and better policies. Any government that commits itself to a policy whose costs come to exceed possible benefits will have trouble admitting its error. A government cannot reassess national interests if its costly policies have been based on dramatic statements of their importance. At the same time, a government in such a position appears to the adversary as an unattractive negotiating partner precisely because its large investment in war makes its acquiescence in a moderate settlement unlikely. Both for internal and external reasons, a change of government facilitates the contrivance and application of new policies.

In the years of the Korean War, it appeared that Russia and China united were bent upon extending their sway. America resisted for the sake of her future security. Now, with communist nations in disarray, America's war in Southeast Asia threatens to heal communist rifts, to call forth Russian or Chinese military intervention, and to destroy North Vietnam's ability to resist Chinese control. Continued fighting works against American interests and seems to have only the purpose of determining who shall misrule Vietnam next. To settle on almost any terms available is the course that wisdom would dictate. In American domestic politics, a new government would have more to gain by concluding a peace than by waging General William C. Westmoreland's "war of attrition" with all of its costs and attendant risks.[9] One cannot predict that a new President would seek to disentangle the nation more earnestly than President Johnson has done; one can only say that a new President would be freer to do so. The critics of American policy in Vietnam help to make a policy of disentanglement possible. They widen the range of choices, especially for the next government which they may help to bring into power.

IV

If the United States is militarily so powerful that we need not at the moment follow a "Russian" foreign policy but instead are free to pursue peripheral objectives in Asia, then, by the same logic, the opposition is free to oppose that policy without earning the charge of seriously weakening the nation. Strong nations have often abused their power to the detriment of themselves and of others. A nation as powerful as America may become impatient with the defensive pose it has struck and long maintained. Senator Fulbright, frightened by the temptations posed by the plenitude of power that he once hoped we would generate, has warned us against "that fatal presumption, that overextension of power and mission, which brought ruin to ancient Athens, to Napoleonic France and to Nazi Germany." He has cautioned his country not to become "what it is not now and never has been, a seeker after unlimited power and empire."[10]

Two dangers now threaten especially. With multiplication of the arenas of major contention, it will become more difficult to remember that American security interests require military engagements only where the adversary is of such strength that he is or may become a threat to the nation. Beyond that, though the margin of power that America enjoys over any other contender may be a source of comfort to her citizens, it may also worry the observer. The temptations of power arise from its surplus, and that same surplus of power makes dissent at once acceptable and politically useful. To a considerable extent, the restraint of the nation must now be self-imposed.

The politics of peace is primarily the internal and external politics of the powerful. We should not hastily assume that the Cold War has ended; the relation of underlying antagonism between America and Russia will remain. This must be so since each is and will long continue to be the only state that can grievously damage the other. Substantial imbalance between the United States and the Soviet Union is not likely to endure, for especially in a two-party competition the laggard is stimulated to increase its efforts. All the more so, then, we should pay attention first and most to the Soviet Union and not gear our actions to wayward political movements in states of minor consequence.

Notes

* This is a revised version of a paper delivered at a conference on "The Requirements of Peace" at the University of New Hampshire, March 31–April 1, 1967.
** This is not the usual definition of "Cold War"; it is the most useful one both for understanding past events and for gauging future possibilities.
† I do not contend that this is uniquely an American way of thinking. One might draw comparisons with Russia and with many other nations.
1 Robert C. Tucker, *The Soviet Political Mind: Studies in Stalinism and Post-Stalin Change* (New York: Praeger, 1963), p. 183.
2 Robert W. Tucker, *The Just War: A Study in Contemporary American Doctrine* (Baltimore: Johns Hopkins Press, 1960), pp. 190–193.
3 J. William Fulbright, *Prospects for the West* (Cambridge: Harvard University Press, 1963), p. 27.
4 "The Goal of an Atlantic Partnership: Address by President Kennedy," *The Department of State Bulletin*, Vol. XLVII, No. 1204 (July 23, 1962), p. 133.

5 "Excerpts From Speech to Coast Guard," *New York Times*, June 4, 1964.
6 "Report on Vietnam and East Asia." Reprinted from the *Congressional Record* (March 23, 1967), p. 8.
7 Cf. Tucker, *The Just War*, pp. 20–21.
8 A. J. P. Taylor, *Rumours of War* (London: Hamish Hamilton, 1952), p. 44. Taylor refers specifically to Bismarck.
9 See "Text of Westmoreland's Address at A. P. Meeting and of His Replies to Questions," *New York Times*, April 25, 1967.
10 "Excerpts From Fulbright's Speech on Vietnam War," *New York Times*, April 29, 1966.

21

AMERICA'S EUROPEAN POLICY VIEWED IN GLOBAL PERSPECTIVE*

In this essay, I look at American foreign policy in broad perspective. I do so partly because other essays in this volume will treat immediate American and European problems and policies and will do so in considerable detail. That, I admit, is more an excuse than a reason, for it seems to me that only by going back to questions about American assumptions and world realities can one understand the past and likely future evolution of our policy. Answers to the questions I raise apply, then, to American policy globally. That is necessarily the case when one's concern is with the bases of all policies rather than with the fashioning of particular ones. I have, however, indicated how my examination of America's world situation applies to European needs and desires.

The questions I raise and try to answer in the five sections of this essay are these: What is America's view of the world? What is the world really like? What do other countries want from us? How can we know what to do? What are we to conclude?

What is America's view of the world?

A country's perceptions of international politics are not determined entirely by what the world is like. Its perceptions are also affected by the circumstances of its birth and development, by its experiences at home and abroad, by its public philosophy and national ideology. We have to understand how America sees the world in order to understand how it has acted, and is likely to act, in it.

In some respects, how American assumptions about foreign policy and aspirations for the world have been shaped by its experience is well known. The impulse to isolation, a normal one for any state, was strengthened by early unhappy experience. In the colonial period, every time European countries went to war, Americans were drawn into an imperial war in the new world, usually with little profit to themselves. Early American statesmen—most notably Alexander Hamilton and John Jay—keenly appreciated the advantages of isolation and the possibility of realizing those advantages.[1] If America became united while Europe remained divided, the United States would be able to

310

insulate itself from European quarrels. Because European states would have to continue to watch each other warily, none would be able to turn westward and direct all of its military force against the United States. Under those circumstances, the United States was able to follow a quite consistent policy of isolation for more than a hundred years, from the early nineteenth century onward.

In its origin, isolationist policy had been situationally based and situationally explained. A century's happy experience turned an appreciation of one's good fortune into a feeling of moral superiority. In coming to believe that we remained aloof from the power-political games of the Old World because we were enlightened and uplifted, we turned the policy of isolation into an ideology.

The principal elements of the ideology, and the ways in which it was formed during a century of isolation, can be stated in summary form. Though all men are born equal, some men are rich and others are poor. This apparent contradiction is eliminated by defining equality, as liberals of the eighteenth and nineteenth centuries did, in purely legal terms. Americans generally accepted the definition. Those unequal in material goods or in capabilities remain intrinsically equal. Absence of established rank in a land of golden opportunity gave meaning to the definition domestically. It was applied internationally as well. Because America's foreign-policy experiences were largely with dependent states, an egalitarian international ideology easily developed. When small and weak states deal with large and strong ones, the former are conscious of the power in the relation and the latter often are not. With power left out of the equation, national and international experiences combined to establish the American conviction that foreign policy is an extension of, and that international relations are dependent upon, what states are like internally. All causes are seen as clustering at the level of the state, and the international political system becomes a dependent variable. Only through this view could national self-determination be seen as a fundamental principle of foreign policy and as the necessary basis of a proper world order.

So deeply rooted is the American ideology that it informs policies that at the surface are sharply opposed. Beneath the contrary foreign policies of Woodrow Wilson and Herbert Hoover, to take the most striking examples, lay a common conviction. Both Wilson and Hoover looked at the world and saw evil rife in it. Hoover concluded that we must isolate ourselves in order to develop the unique virtues of the new world free of contamination from the old one. Wilson concluded that we must act to change the world. As he put it:

No injustice furnishes a basis for permanent peace. If you leave a rankling sense of injustice anywhere, it will not only produce a running sore presently which will result in trouble and probably war, but it ought to produce war somewhere.[2]

Through their contrary policies, both Wilson and Hoover renounced old-fashioned, European-style diplomacy and power politics. They agreed that the United States could not live in the world as it was.

Neither the First nor the Second World War did much to change our basic view of the world. In both of those wars, our enemies could be personified in the characters of their rulers: of the Kaiser, Hitler, Mussolini, and Tojo. To our good fortune, moreover, the Czar abdicated in March of 1917 just in time to permit us to declare war in April of that year without thereby joining a coalition having Czarist Russia as one of its principal members. In World War II, we tried to turn Stalin into "Uncle Joe," an aspiring democrat whose application of the admirable provisions of the constitution adopted in 1936 was delayed by difficult conditions at home and abroad. In both wars, we could think of ourselves as fighting authoritarian or totalitarian states in the name of justice and democracy. Whether or not we were also fighting for reasons of security, whether or not there was an element of power politics in our policy, was a question that the lineup of forces permitted us to avoid.

How are the habits and assumptions of American foreign policy, formed in prolonged isolation, reflected in the interventionist policies followed from 1945 onward? Most commentators, whether they praise or condemn American postwar policy, explain our quick move from isolationist habits to sustained international action by pointing to our concern, or obsession, with Communism. We did indeed substitute a simple cry against Communism for more difficult and more useful thought about foreign-policy problems. We do, however, misinterpret postwar policy by forgetting that more than anti-Communism went into it. If we say that at the height of the Cold War our policy was to oppose all Communist states, we have to add quickly—unless the state was named "Yugoslavia." In a decade and a half beginning in 1949, we gave Yugoslavia more than $2,700 million in economic and military aid. Much of our policy toward the third world is, moreover, ill-explained by recalling the crude political rhetoric of that day. John Foster Dulles remains famous for condemning godless Communism and those immoral neutralist states who refused to stand up and be counted as favoring the free world. And yet in 1956, with Dulles still Secretary of State, we began a major program of assistance to India, and the foremost neutral state soon became the most favored recipient of American aid. Anti-Communism was the trigger of action, which, once pulled, released older and deeper impulses. They were compounded of exaggerated security worries, natural to a country that had never before been seriously threatened, and of ideological preferences, especially devotion to the right of national self-determination. These more enduring impulses of our policy are obscured by facile explanations of American motivation as merely obsessive opposition to Communism.

Another old American habit, that of attributing good or bad international outcomes to the merits or defects of somebody's internal politics, is widely reflected in political commentaries from various quarters. The most severe and

extended criticisms of American policy have been written by revisionist historians and by those who have labelled American policy "imperialist" and offered
economic explanations of it. They look back and find Truman and Acheson
hardliners and leaders of a hardline pack. They accuse them of having created
a cold war. They forget that Truman and Acheson were to the left, or soft side,
of much domestic opinion, especially on the question of China. They forget
that the strong and innovative policies of the United States were in accord
with, and indeed were often in response to, the demands of European and
other states. But most important for the present theme, these critics reveal
themselves as dreadfully American. They imply that some American error, or
sinister interest, or faulty assumption about Russian aims is what created a
cold war. They appear as the mirror image of many earlier American writers
who had thought of the Soviet Union as being the country that created
the Cold War by the actions that followed necessarily from the nature of its
society and government. Both critics and defenders imply a claim to American
uniqueness. They deny the continuity of international politics and that America
is part of that continuity. Instead they say, in effect, that the United States and
the Soviet Union could have escaped from the tensions and the competition in
power that have marred the relations of all other great powers in world history
if only we or they had not done certain wrong things.

Any country is likely to develop ideological predilections that shape its view
of the world. Since intellectuals, like political leaders, are influenced by the
unspoken assumptions that lie behind policies; piercing the ideological veil
becomes difficult. Having dwelt on important notions about policy that are
peculiarly American may help us to answer the next question.

What is the world really like?

C. L. Sulzberger announced in November of 1972 that "the U.S. finds itself
no longer the global giant of twenty years ago." Our share of global production, he claimed, "has slipped from 50 to 30 percent."[3] Such a misuse of
numbers would be startling had we not become accustomed to hearing about
America's steady decline. In the summer of 1971, President Nixon had
remarked that twenty-five years ago "we were number one in the world militarily" and "number one economically" as well. The United States, he added,
"was producing more than 50 percent of all the world's goods." But no
longer. By 1971, "instead of just America being number one in the world
from an economic standpoint, the preeminent world power, and instead of
there being just two superpowers, when we think in economic terms and
economic potentialities, there are five great power centers in the world
today."[4]

The trick that Sulzberger and Nixon have played on us, and no doubt on
themselves, should be easily apparent. In 1946, Nixon's year of comparison,
most of the industrial world except for the United States lay in ruins. By 1952,

Sulzberger's year of comparison, Britain, France, and Russia had regained their prewar levels of production, but the German and Japanese economic miracles had not yet been performed. In the years just after the war, the United States naturally produced an unusually large percentage of the world's goods. Now again, as before the war, we produce more than a quarter of the world's goods. And that somehow means that rather than being number one, we have become merely one of five. The United States produced about 30 percent of the world's goods in 1971, the Soviet Union about 15 percent, and Japan about 7 percent, they being the three largest producers. If we are no longer number one, who is?[5]

Why has it been so difficult for us to assess the distribution of world power sensibly? One reason is that we have been misled by the customary American pragmatically-formed and technologically-influenced definition of power—a definition that equates power with control. A person's power is then measured by his ability to get people to do what he wants them to do when otherwise they would not do it.[6] That definition may serve for some purposes, but it ill fits the requirements of political analysis. According to the definition, a failure to get one's way is proof of weakness. In politics, powerful agents often fail to work their wills upon others. Politics is preeminently the realm of unintended and unexpected consequences. The intention of the act and its result will seldom be identical because the result will be affected by the person or object acted upon and conditioned by the environment within which it occurs.

What, then, can be substituted for the practically and logically untenable definition? I offer the old and simple notion that one is powerful to the extent that he affects others more than they affect him.[7] The weak understand this; the strong may not. Prime Minister Trudeau once said that, for Canada, being America's neighbor "is in some ways like sleeping with an elephant. No matter how friendly or even-tempered is the beast . . . one is affected by every twitch and grunt."[8] As the leader of a weak state, Trudeau understands the meaning of our power in a way that we easily overlook. Because of the weight of our capabilities, American actions have a tremendous impact whether or not we fashion effective policies and put power behind them in order to achieve certain ends.

To identify power with control is to assert that only power is needed in order to get one's way. That is obviously false, but thinking that way leads one to see weakness whenever one's will is thwarted. How is power distributed? What are the effects of a given distribution of power? These two questions are distinct, and the answers to each of them are extremely important politically. In the notion of power just rejected, the two questions merge and become hopelessly confused. If power and the effects of power are equated, then those who find themselves frustrated can be said to be weak. The paradox that some have found in the so-called impotence of American power disappears if power is given a politically sensible definition. Thus only in a parochial, indeed a cruelly egocentric, American view can it be said, as sometimes it is, that America demonstrated its weakness in Vietnam. True, we did not show any impressive ability to get our way. We did affect Vietnam more than the Vietnamese affected us. One can get around that only by equating political disruptions in the one country with hundreds of thousands of deaths in the other.

Students of international politics tend to think that wars in the past brought territorial and economic gains to the victors and that in contrast the United States now cannot use its vast military might for positive accomplishment.[9] Such views rest on the incidental error of overestimating the profits of imperialist and military ventures in the past. They rest also on a more important error: exaggeration of the importance that external gains could have for the United States. This exaggeration in turn arises from misunderstanding America's position in the world, a misunderstanding that derives directly from the confusions examined above. America's 1971 GNP was about one trillion dollars. An economic growth rate of 5 percent adds $50 billion yearly to the GNP, which is about 20 percent of Japan's entire GNP, 40 percent of Britain's, and at least that much of China's.[10] These comparisons suggest that America's internal efforts add much more to her wealth than could any imaginable gains scored abroad. Why, then, should we think of using force for positive international accomplishment? We seem to be in the happy position of needing to worry only about the negative, or defensive, use of force.

With increased frequency, one hears that the bipolar world has become a world in which five great powers contend. To get that result requires some odd counting. The inclination to count in funny ways is rooted in the desire to arrive at a particular answer. Scholars feel a strong affection for the balance-of-power worlds of Metternich and Bismarck, on which many of their theories are grounded. That was a world in which five or so great states manipulated their neighbors and maneuvered for advantage. Confusing the distribution of power with its effects has made it easy to overlook the peculiarity of the ways in which the counting is now often done. Great powers used to be defined according to their physical capabilities. Students of international politics now seem to look at other conditions. The ability or inability of states to solve problems is said to raise or lower their rankings. The relations of states may be examined instead of their capabilities, and since the latter are always multilateral, the world is said to be multipolar. Thus the dissolution of blocs was said to signal the end of bipolarity even though to infer bipolarity from the existence of blocs in itself confuses the relations of states with their capabilities. The world was never bipolar because two blocs opposed each other, but because of the preeminence of bloc leaders.

In addition to confusion about what to count, one often finds that the measurement is strange even when the effort is correctly made to identify great powers by gauging their capabilities. Three variations are common. A country's most prominent assets may be singled out and weaknesses simply ignored. A country is then said to be a superpower even though it has only some of the necessary characteristics. China has 800 million people; Japan has

315

a magnificent economic growth rate; Western Europe has everything that is needed demographically and economically and lacks only political existence. As commonly, the desired number of great states is reached by projecting the future into the present. When Europe unites . . .; if Japan's economy continues to grow . . .; once China's industrious people have developed their resources. . . . And then, although the imagined future lies some decades ahead, we hear that the world is no longer bipolar. A further variant is to infer another country's status from our policy toward it. Thus one scholar worries that if we do not adopt proper policies the five-power world won't emerge, but instead "we might, at best [i.e., worst?], have a tripolar world."[11] In the same vein, President Nixon slips easily from talking of China's becoming a superpower to conferring superpower status upon her. In one of the statements that smoothed the route to Peking, he accomplished this in two paragraphs.[12] And the headlines of various news stories before, during, and after the visit confirmed China's new rank. This is the greatest act of creation since Adam and Eve, and a true illustration of the superpower status of the United States. A country becomes a superpower if we treat it like one. We are able to create other states in our image.

We seem to believe our own rhetoric. In January of 1973, Richard Helms, then director of the CIA, said that China's progress in nuclear weaponry would soon make her a superpower. Earlier, Secretary of Defense, Melvin Laird, had been saying that if there were no SALT Agreements, and if the United States did not build more ABMs, and if the Soviet Union continued to deploy SS-9 missiles, then the United States would be a second-rate power. Notice the fantasy. The People's Republic of China was about to become a superpower with an expected ten to thirty intercontinental ballistic missiles by 1976, while at the same time the United States was ceasing to be one because of the Soviet Union's SS-9s.

For years Walter Lippmann wrote of the bipolar world as being perpetually in the process of rapidly passing away.[13] Many others now carry on in the tradition he so firmly established. Since any simple and direct statement that a third, fourth, or fifth superpower has joined the big two is palpable nonsense, complicated language is used. In terms of nuclear weapons the world is bipolar, one often hears, but not so in terms of conventional military capabilities. Another common formulation is this: Militarily the world is bipolar, but economically it is not so. The United States and the Soviet Union dispose of more powerful and more varied nuclear arsenals, and also of more powerful and more varied conventional military instruments, than do any other states. They are able to do so because their economic capabilities far exceed those of other states. Economic capacity, though it does not automatically transform itself into military might, is an essential condition for it. It is misleading to say that the United States and the Soviet Union are strong because they have built immense and varied arsenals without adding that they would not have been able to surpass others in military strength had their economic capabilities not been proportionately large. Any look at pertinent economic and military data can lead only to one conclusion: Whether by military or by economic measurement, the world since the war has been, and remains, bipolar.

In economic matters, as in military ones, the tendency to merge and confuse capabilities with effects has made America's position in the world harder to understand. The recent vogue of "transnationalism," the word favored by political scientists, and of "interdependence," the word favored by economists, contributes to the confusion. I take "interdependence" as describing a situation in which two or more parties depend about equally on each other for important goods and services. A relation of interdependence then rests on an underlying condition of approximate equality. If the underlying condition is not one of approximate equality, then the relation is not one of interdependence but is some compound of relatively high dependence for one or some of the parties and of relatively high independence for others. In recent American discourse, however, the word "interdependence" has been used to obscure inequalities of national capability, to point pleasingly to a reciprocal dependence, and to suggest strongly that all states are playing the same game. This usage, as might be expected, corresponds to the levelling ideology that America lives by. In its light, we appear to be plagued by the same difficulties that beset other states. From our much greater capabilities we do not gain the clout that would help us get our way, nor do the extent and variety of our resources help to insulate us from the effects of others' policies, or so we are told. Monetary problems and energy shortages may seem to bear this out. Instead, looked at more closely, they indicate that our common view of our collective plight is badly distorted.

Twice in a period of fourteen months, beginning in December of 1971, the dollar was devalued, by 10 percent each time. For a country that imports goods amounting to 15 or 20 percent of its GNP, as many states do, devaluations are serious, even traumatic affairs. In the United States, one might have expected that political waves would be set in motion that would engulf the government in crisis, the more so since four decades had passed since America had devalued its currency. Why instead was the reaction quite mild? Simply because it is hard to get excited about changes in the value of one's currency when the country's imports yearly amount only to 4 percent of GNP. Devaluation raises the price of those imported goods. It does cost something. The dependence of the country on others does not reduce to zero. But that dependence is heavier proportionately for states that do a good part of their business abroad. The United States is in a doubly fortunate position. First, it does only a small percentage of its business abroad and thus is more insulated than most states from adverse economic movements internationally. Second, because of the size of its economy, that business looms large in the world's economy and thus gains us some leverage.[14]

We are nevertheless warned of the dangers entailed by our dependence on others as markets for our goods and as suppliers of materials for our industries.

Here is one example: "The dependence of Europe and Japan, and soon the United States, on Middle Eastern oil is becoming the overpowering strategic fact of this decade, comparable to the threat of Soviet expansionism in the first years after World War II."[15] So writes a member of the editorial board of *The New York Times*. The United States has been so well set up in the world for so long that the threat of a little adversity brings panic, at least in the press. Japan now imports slightly more oil than we do and her imports will increase much faster than ours will. Western Europe already imports much more oil than we do and her imports continue to increase. We, moreover, are much better able to develop alternate sources of supply and to turn to other fuels.[16] We, like others, will face increased energy costs, but we can bear those costs more easily than others simply because we are richer.

Just as we depreciate our power, so we easily persuade ourselves of our dependence. Actually the terms of trade have moved in our favor for decades and against the primary producers. Rather than seeing America's excessive dependence, one can more objectively say that the United States does not consume enough raw materials to provide primary producers with an adequate market for their products.

Though still preeminent, we have had to adjust to a situation in which the gap between us and the other major industrial states of the world has narrowed somewhat from its extraordinary postwar width. Sensitivity about losing some ground has led us to exaggerate the strength of other states. The interest of the stronger may lie in depreciating its power in the eyes of others while continuing to benefit from it. This habit becomes a dangerous one if the policymakers' and the critics' view of the world also becomes distorted.

Given the decentralized character of international politics, the distortions introduced through the American perspective are especially serious. By definition, a decentralized system lacks specified relations of super- and subordination among its constituent units; units are differentiated primarily according to their greater or lesser capabilities for performing similar tasks. International politics is such a realm. Inequalities across states are, moreover, much greater than inequalities within them. Under these circumstances, the unequal capabilities of states are of principal importance for understanding the operation of the system and the fate of its units. The intricacies of diplomacy are often compared to those of chess. The game cannot be successfully played unless the chessboard can be accurately described. Odd notions about the distribution of world power have had debilitating effects upon policy.

What do other countries want from us?

At times it may have been thought that the answer to the above question was suggested by the slogan chalked on walls in many foreign cities: "Americans go home." Instead we find that we are asked as often to come as to go, as often to intervene as to stay out, as often to supply capital as to stop imperialist activity, as often to fight as to refrain from using force. Obvious examples abound. Arabs want us to bring pressure on Israelis. Israelis want us to supply and support them. South Koreans want us to keep two divisions in their country. The reader can easily extend the list; I shall mention only a few revealing examples from Asia for the sake of placing a more extended examination of West European needs and desires in perspective.

During the American war in Indochina, the stern moral rhetoric of India concealed the belief of many leading figures that her security depended on our fighting. C. Rajagopalachari, independence leader and Governor-General from 1948 to 1950, expressed Indian fears in this way: "There is not the slightest doubt that if America withdraws and leaves Southeast Asia to itself, Communist China will advance and seize the continent. All the people of Asia will soon be intimidated to pay homage to the Communist parties in each of the regions in Asia and the empire of China under Mao and his successors will be firmly established."[17] Prince Sihanouk of Cambodia, though not conspicuously friendly toward us, nevertheless believed that American withdrawal from Vietnam would turn neighboring countries, including his own, into Chinese satellites, "Czechoslovakias of Asia." All Asia, he added, "remains persuaded of the domino theory."[18] And now Chinese officials suggest that America should not remove its military forces from Asia too far and too fast.[19] An American military presence helps to balance off Russia.

This is an age-old pattern. The weak, when threatened, seek aid and protection from the strong, even though the weak may suffer as well as benefit from the aid, and chafe under as well as enjoy the protection. America as the world's premier power, and the only state that has been able to operate on a global scale throughout the postwar period, is turned to most often.

Western Europe provides the most protracted case of a region relying on America for major contributions to its well-being and security. In addition to loans and grants for relief and rehabilitation following the war, the United States supplied some $12 billion from 1948 to 1952 under the European Recovery Program. The economic recovery of Western Europe increased its security worries. Would not the Soviet Union's presumed hope of taking over European countries from within wither as they began to prosper? Might not the Soviet Union then resort to direct military pressure? The Atlantic Defense Treaty of 1949 was a response to such worries. The war in Korea, which soon followed, was taken as further evidence of aggressive Communist intentions that would soon be directed against the main target, Europe. The worries of West European states, insistently added to our own, led us in 1951 to dispatch two national guard divisions to join the four divisions we already had in Europe. Ever since, a large number of American troops, backed by air and sea power and soon armed with tactical nuclear weapons, have been stationed in Europe. Peak strength of more than 400,000 men was reached in the 1960s, and later run down to its present level of about 300,000.

The worries of West European states have varied across countries and over time. Through all the variations, one theme has persisted: concern for insuring the reliability of American commitments. This concern has done more to shape the size and nature of Western Europe's own military forces than have thoughts about participating in a military division of labor in ways that would contribute best to a united defense. As Hugh Gaitskell said when he was leader of the British Labour Party: "I do not believe that when we speak of our having to have nuclear weapons of our own it is because we must make a contribution to the deterrent of the West." As he indicated, no contribution of consequence was made. Instead, he remarked, the desire for a nuclear force derives in large part "from doubts about the readiness of the United States Government and the American citizens to risk the destruction of their cities on behalf of Europe."[20] The thought was echoed widely in England during the later 1950s and repeated in France in the 1960s. André Beaufre, retired general and director of the French Institute of Strategic Studies, justified nuclear diffusion in part with the argument that the uncertainty produced by a third power's nuclear force "considerably augments the opponent's belief in the possibility of a *first* strike" (italics added).[21] The rationale for small nuclear forces reflects doubt that America's deterrent threat will always reliably cover European interests. And yet, as President de Gaulle himself once said, uncertainty about their use "does not in the least prevent the American nuclear weapons, which are the most powerful of all, from remaining the essential guarantee of world peace."[22] Given a sense of uncertainty combined with dependence, Europeans understandably strive to fashion their forces so as to insure our commitment.

They also wish to determine the form the commitment takes and the manner of its likely execution. The wish is evident in the response of Pierre Gallois, a retired officer of the French Air Force and its most eloquent spokesman, to a remark by President Kennedy. In a speech in July of 1961 on the Berlin crisis, Kennedy had said: "We intend to have a wider choice than humiliation or all-out nuclear action." What could be wrong, one may wonder, with wanting choices between those two ugly extremes? Gallois nevertheless focused on "choice" as the word that scares Europeans. If America herself were threatened, he reasoned, the government "would not 'choose'; it would strike, and with all its might."[23] An American choice about how to respond to threats in Europe is a choice that affects the lives, and may bring the death, of Europeans. At the least, Europeans want to have a large voice in American policies that may determine their destiny.

West Germany's concerns are similar, though being militarily on the front line of Western Europe she is more inclined to express them in the form of demands for the maintenance of America's troop strength in Europe. Georg Leber, the German Defense Minister, has warned us that for our military commitment to Europe "there is neither a political nor a military nor a psychological substitute—not one provided by a single European state nor by various European states together."[24] Leber is saying quite simply that if the

United States does not continue to maintain its troops in Europe nothing can be put in their place. Helmut Schmidt, the previous defense minister, was even said to believe that the effect of further unilateral American troop withdrawals would be compounded by a reduction of defense spending in Bonn. Publicly he ruled out a greater German effort because "lack of money, manpower and popular support would preclude such a solution—quite apart from the grave political effects it would have in the East as well as in the West."[25]

One more piece needs to be fitted into the European policy puzzle before we reflect on its pattern. That piece will fall into place once we answer these questions: How do approaching negotiations over Mutual and Balanced Force Reductions (MBFR), and how do the Soviet Union's interests and attitudes, bear upon European policy?

We know, of course, that the prospect of disarmament talks signals the need to increase, or at least to maintain, military strength. One cannot bargain without chips, and the chips are military troops and equipment. President Nixon and Secretary Laird earnestly taught us that lesson in preparing the country for Strategic Arms Limitation Talks with Russia. It applies as well to the question of MBFR. Indeed, one may surmise that one of the principal reasons for advancing that notion was to head off or to moderate further unilateral reduction of American forces in Europe.

Not only West Europeans, and not only Nixon and Laird, but also Leonid I. Brezhnev, General Secretary of the Soviet Communist Party, seem to uphold the military status quo in Europe. Could Brezhnev have failed to realize that his offer of troop talks in May of 1972 would decrease support for unilateral American reduction? Senator Gaylord Nelson's reaction was typical: "If Mr. Brezhnev had not spoken on the subject, I would have been prepared to vote . . . to cut our forces in half in accordance with the Mansfield amendment." Moscow appears to agree with West Germany's leaders that continued détente depends on America's troop strength in Europe being kept in its present proportion to Russia's. How can one explain this unexpected conclusion? Russia may very well fear that less American strength in Europe would provoke further West German armament and stimulate her desire to control nuclear weapons. Russia may also fear that a decrease in America's commitment would stimulate further moves toward the political union of Western Europe.[26] Whether or not Russia's fears are matched by Europe's hopes, it nevertheless seems that Brezhnev sees America's military policy in Europe as serving Russia's interests.

Our European policy serves West European purposes and even some Russian ones. How does it serve our own? The status quo in Europe has come to be associated with stability, a much wanted condition in a world where destructive power is unlimited. All of the interested parties may fear the possibly disruptive effects of any but measured and marginal changes in military arrangements. Beyond that we are often reminded of two dangers. The one is an old fear, dating from Czarist times, of Russian mass combining with

German technological and organizational skills. This is apparently the spectre that is limned when German leaders warn that unilateral American withdrawal of troops will tilt the balance of power in Russia's favor. More recently, another fear has appeared; this one known as "Finlandization." If West European states do more of their business with Russia, they will supposedly become more and more susceptible to her will.

One wonders how either of these dangers might come into being. Fears that Western Europe may one day find itself politically beholden to the Soviet Union because of economic dependence upon her are nightmares dreamt by people who fail to look at the data. France, West Germany, and England send less than 2 percent of their total exports to the Soviet Union. Countries have done vastly more business with each other than the states of Western Europe and the Soviet Union are ever likely to do without some of them slipping into excessive dependence.

The danger of military imbalance, though easier to understand, is usually much exaggerated. American military assistance to Europe resumed after World War II when European countries were economically unable to mount a large military effort with the requisite speed. It continues even though they are now easily able to do more for themselves. In 1970, only England of all the West European states spent more than 4 percent of its GNP on defense. Schmidt, in arguing that politically and economically West Germany could not increase its efforts, might have added that the defense cost she was struggling to bear amounted to 3.3 percent of GNP. At the same time, we were spending almost 8 percent of GNP on defense with about 2 percent of GNP going for military personnel and equipment that we keep either in or for Europe. Yet supposedly a unilateral further rundown of America's European force would be disastrously destabilizing because it could not be made up for by the efforts of European states. The wonder is not that they make the arguments but that we believe them.[27]

We are often told that we gain security through our European expenditures. No doubt, but not as much as Europeans do. If it is true that in the absence of our contribution Europe would be out of balance with the Soviet Union, then it is true only because of a lack of effort, not of ability, on the part of Europeans. In 1971, the nine states of Western Europe had a population of more than 250 million, and the sum of their GNPs amounted to $705 billion. Historically, Western Europe has always been able to stand up to Russia. Indeed, the difficulty was always the other way around. The extent of Russian inferiority to Western Europe has lessened over the decades. Nevertheless, her population now is slightly smaller than that of the nine states of the EEC and her GNP is barely more than three-fourths of theirs. Nor is the military situation inherently unfavorable. Because of a presumed danger from China, the Soviet Union has about a third of her troops in the Sino-Soviet border area. Our strategic nuclear forces, moreover, provide considerable deterrence against Russian military action in Western Europe. No matter what our policies and our commitments may say, Russians will believe that there is some noticeable chance of our swift and strong response to any major threat from the Soviet Union in a theater so important.

As the expert authors of a study of American–European military arrangements have noticed, "neither time nor circumstance has altered the bipolar character of the European security system."[28] 'West Europeans continue to see their security as involving a possible threat from the East and a necessary military guarantee from the West, that is, from us. A decrease of military support for Europe would apparently leave European states feeling less secure. In Europe we are now as ever in the postwar world asked to act not for our own sake but for someone else's. If we did less, we should ask, might Europeans not do more despite what their leaders have said? And if they did not, should we be concerned or should they? These questions entail profound problems about the criteria we should apply to our policies, problems to which I now turn.

How can we know what to do?

The immensity of American power, along with the perennial difficulty of controlling great power and insuring its benign use, makes it imperative to examine the principles of foreign policy that we might adopt or have in fact acted upon. The foreign policies of states may be guided by notions of national interest, by a preference for remaining uninvolved in others' affairs, or by aspirations to make the world over in some important respect. The policies of great powers have most often been grounded on the first and third of these principles.

Hans Morgenthau, more than any other scholar, has insisted that interest must be the touchstone of policy if it is to be realistically made and conducted. Numerous critics have found his formulations too general to be of much use. I am not one of those critics. When a country is said to act according to its national interest, all that is meant is that, having examined its security requirements, it tries to meet them. That is simple; it is also important. Entailed in the concept of national interest is the notion that diplomatic and military moves must be carefully calculated lest the very survival of the state be put in jeopardy. The necessary state action is deduced from the situation in which the state finds itself. That, of course, is not to say that statesmen's perceptions will be correct or that deductions will be properly made. No standard can eliminate error from human action, and yet some standards of action are useful.

The second principle of policy—noninvolvement—requires little comment, especially since it can be assimilated to the notion of national interest. If interest is defined in terms of security and if one's security can be assured without acting internationally, then the prudent policy is a quiescent one.

Since the war, the first two principles have been limited in their application to American foreign policy. The notion of interest does serve well as the rationale for America's major postwar policies—that is, for those policies designed to guard against the threat implicit in the Soviet Union's possession of great power. The landmarks of American policy—the Truman Doctrine, the Marshall Plan, NATO, the Korean war—were responses that can fairly be said to be in accordance with traditional notions of national interest, although of course without claiming that we always got everything right. No state other than the Soviet Union has been close to having a military capability that threatens us. In military terms, the question then has to be: Why should we ever act other than in response to the threat of a gain by the Soviet Union that would tilt the world balance? One might think, moreover, that the gain for the Soviet Union would have to be such that, added to her own resources, it would enable her to generate a first-strike capability. Where and how could she score such a gain? Put differently, with a GNP twice Russia's and with a triad of second-strike forces, we are hardly in the position of having to worry much about military security.

But, someone will hasten to say, if Russia, or anyone, should be able to foreclose American trade and investment in successively more parts of the world, we could be quietly strangled to death. To believe that, one has to think not in terms of politics but in terms of the apocalypse. If some countries want to deal with us less, others for related reasons are likely to move economically closer to us. It has ever been thus, and why it has been is so easy to see that I shall say nothing further. One can, moreover, transcend estimates about reliable access to supplies since economically the United States can get along without the rest of the world better than most of its parts can get along without us. Robert W. Tucker is the person best-known for making the argument that nothing that goes wrong in the rest of the world can affect American security very much—not even the loss of Japan or Western Europe. More recently, Herman Kahn and William H. Overholt have concluded that if the United States were completely isolated from the rest of the world, if there were no economic exchange of any kind between us and others, we would suffer initial pains of adjustment, but in the long run only a slowing down of our growth rate. Tucker drives logically ahead to the conclusion that isolation is the proper American policy. Kahn and Overholt shy away from accepting the logic by arguing that for psychological and political reasons—a sense of identification with Europe, for example, and our commitments to her—an isolationist policy cannot be sustained.[29]

If we want to act where we need not, then some principle other than interest or isolation will naturally come into play. Like some other great powers before us, we have found that principle by identifying the presumed duty of the rich and the powerful to help others with our own beliefs about what a better world would look like. England claimed to bear the white man's burden; France spoke of her *mission civilisatrice*. In like spirit, we say that we act to make and maintain world order.

The United States could justify acting abroad, aside from the Russian danger, in either of two ways. First, we could exaggerate our security worries and overreact to slight dangers. The domino theory was a necessary one if a traditional rationale for state action in terms of security was to be offered for peripheral military actions. Second, we could act for the presumed good of others. The conviction that we must be concerned with every remote danger is analytically distinguishable from the world order theme that developed out of old American ideas about national self-determination. In practice, however, they have been closely connected. The interest of the country in security came to be identified with the maintenance of a certain order.

A few examples, grouped to bring out different aspects of the world-order theme, will make its importance clear. Early postwar expressions of the theme, and some even today, incorporate the anti-Communist concern in quite simple ways. As early as September of 1946, Clark Clifford, in a memorandum written for President Truman, argued that "our best chances of influencing Soviet leaders consist in making it unmistakably clear that action contrary to our conception of a decent world order will redound to the disadvantage of the Soviet regime whereas friendly and cooperative action will pay dividends. If this position can be maintained firmly enough and long enough the logic of it must permeate eventually into the Soviet system."[30] Anti-Communism is not merely an end in itself; it is also a means of making a decent world. More recently, Adam Ulam has remarked that postwar history can suggest "which changes in Russian behavior favor a rapprochement with the United States, which developments in America threaten her influence in the world and hence the future of democratic institutions."[31] Both Clifford and Ulam link opposition to the Soviet Union and the maintenance and development of a proper world order. Both of them, moreover, accept the proposition that the dangers of war and the prospects for peace depend mainly on what the Soviet Union becomes like in its internal governance.

A second set of examples transcends the anti-Communist theme, without eliminating it, by concentrating directly on the importance of building a world order. Our responsibility for reordering the world became America's theme song during the presidencies of Kennedy and Johnson. President Kennedy himself, speaking on the Fourth of July, 1962, remarked that: "Acting on our own by ourselves, we cannot establish justice throughout the world. We cannot insure its domestic tranquility, or provide for its common defense, or promote its general welfare, or secure the blessings of liberty to ourselves and our posterity. But joined with other free nations, we can do all this and more. . . . We can mount a deterrent powerful enough to deter any aggression, and ultimately we can help achieve a world of law and free choice, banishing the world of war and coercion."[32] Such would be the benefits of an American–European union. A few years later, Senator J. William Fulbright, ever an effective spokesman for the developing trends of the day, conveyed a full sense of our world aspirations. In *The Arrogance of Power*, an aptly titled book, he urged that because the world is able to destroy itself, it is "essential that the competitive instinct of nations be brought under control." And he added that America, "as the most powerful nation in the world, is the only nation equipped to lead the world in an effort to change the nature of its politics."[33] Never have the leaders of a nation expressed more overweening ambitions.

Whether because of a change in national mood or because of a caution born of conservatism, Republicans in power have expressed national aspirations more modestly. Still, there is aspiration enough. In the spring of 1973, President Nixon continued to describe the war in Vietnam as a war fought on behalf of "the right" of South Vietnamese people "to choose their own government."[34] The right in question is one that they could not enjoy unless we fought for it. Why, one wonders, should we see ourselves as the guarantors of the rights of others, unless we also see ourselves as the upholders of a world order in which the rights of all people are secured? The Nixon doctrine does not change that goal though it may limit the means that we supply for achieving it.

A final example shows how the grandiose version of the domino theory fits into the larger world order theme. That fit is nowhere more evident than in statements made by Dean Rusk when he was Secretary of State. On one occasion he remarked that we are criticized "for endeavoring to impose the international interest upon other nations." This criticism, he proudly added, is a sign "of our strength and of the strength of international law." On another occasion he remarked that we are secure only when "the total environment is safe."[35] One might think that the environment will never be safe if the world's most powerful nation takes that attitude and insists upon imposing its notion of the international interest on others. In the statements of Dean Rusk, the world order and the domino themes unite and find their ultimate expression.

The urge to act for the good of other people as we define it became especially dangerous in the early 1960s when we converted superior economic resources into military capability at a pace that the Soviet Union did not match. Close competition subordinates ideology to interest; states that enjoy a margin of power over their closest competitors are naturally led to pay undue attention to minor dangers and to pursue fancies abroad that reach beyond the fulfillment of interests narrowly defined in terms of security. Worrying about remote dangers, we prepared to act on short notice in response to them. We maintained a large number of options. If the means of acting on many options are at hand, strong inclinations to use those means will develop. Capabilities seek missions; the capability of doing something leads easily to its being done.

Our policies toward Indochina bear out these thoughts. In the spring of 1954, when it appeared that Russia and China were able to act in concert, it was at least vaguely plausible to argue for military intervention in Indochina to save the French. We stayed out. In 1965, when old-style security arguments could not conceivably apply, we went in. Why? In the earlier case, military action was inhibited by the fact that we did not have the needed instruments in being; a politically unpleasant measure of military mobilization would have been required. In the later instance, our military intervention was facilitated by the fact that conventional troops and lift capabilities were more readily available.

Just as capabilities develop their missions, so the ability to strike swiftly leads easily to instant response. Thus our Dominican expedition in April of 1965 put 23,000 troops—a force larger than the Dominican army—onto the island within one week in response to events of ambiguous political meaning. We have been able to act militarily faster than we are able to think politically.[36]

The perils of weakness are matched by the temptations of power. Examination of the rationales of state action may, by exposing pretension and folly, induce a greater caution. Still, we might wish to develop a more secure ground for policy. I offer, therefore, something safer than a revised rationale. I offer a recipe, which in a first and simple statement can be put this way: If power is dangerous to its possessor as well as to others, then it would be well to be weaker.

It is too much to say that some military moves are made simply because they are possible. A negative version of the proposition is more tenable: Namely, if you cannot, you will not. The notion is widespread that, when a military approach to a crisis is imaginable, military leaders will be inclined to say: "Yes, commit troops." That is a false generalization, as can easily be shown. In the Moroccan crises of 1905 and 1911, for example, military ministers and military officers in France and Russia strongly advised that war be avoided. American military leaders prior to World War II urged softer diplomacy and less economic pressure precisely because they feared that a stronger policy would goad Japan into a war that they did not want at that time. Generals Marshall and Bradley opposed General MacArthur's policy of carrying the Korean war across the Yalu and into Manchuria. The Pentagon in 1958 opposed sending the marines to Lebanon, a policy that the State Department favored.

There is nothing odd about these examples. In each case, the military felt that the means at its disposal were insufficient to the task at hand or that proposed moves entailed risks that the present military strength of the nation could not safely bear. The common quality of military advice is conservatism. Strength may lead military leaders to counsel preventive war while the moment of superiority lasts. Weakness generates the advice: be cautious; don't plunge into war; wait to see how the situation develops.

I can now more fully spell out the recipe that American policy should follow. It goes this way: If you can, you very well may; if you cannot, you will not; we should not be able to because we need not. And we need not according to the definition of being powerful that I gave earlier. Because we affect other states more than they affect us, we need not be prepared for instant action in most parts of the world. By our vast economic and military capabilities, we are quite well insulated from the wayward events of the world. We have at once a high capability of acting and little need to do so. With many choices and little need for action, wisdom dictates long deliberation before deciding to use military force.

We have recently worried too much about too many problems. In doing so we have first exaggerated their importance and then fashioned elaborate means of solving them. Worrying about problems may promote their solution. Some of the biggest problems for the United States, however, have arisen from our overreactions. I have, therefore, written my recipe for American policy as a prescription to do less, a prescription more likely to be filled if military forces are appropriately designed.

What are we to conclude?

The tasks that remain in this essay are to apply the recipe just suggested to our European policies and in doing so to show how economic, military, and political considerations come into play.

Our yen for the military ability to do all manner of things instantly finds its diplomatic counterpart in the presumed requirements of our foreign policy. The imagined emergence of a world of five centers is said to require a subtlety of calculation and a flexibility of policy that our governmental system supposedly finds difficult to achieve. These requirements are said to arise as much from economic problems as from military dangers.

Stepping back in order to gain a clearer perspective enables one to see that here, as in military matters, we exaggerate problems, some of which we have ourselves created. For years we have spent more on imports and on governmental and private operations abroad than our exports have earned. We were able to do so because foreigners were willing to accept the dollars we printed. American economic investments abroad were acquired partly in this way. President de Gaulle used to emphasize that foreigners in financing our deficit helped build up our holdings abroad. His resentment was understandable. Foreign assets were also acquired through local borrowing and the reinvestment of earnings. Little export of American capital was required. What flowed outward most importantly was technological and managerial know-how.

Foreign investments bring in more yearly than additional acquisitions cost us. We have not been willing, however, to run a trade deficit and balance accounts through an inflow of profits as a creditor nation might be expected to do. We have been unwilling to do that because of our desire to continue costly political-military operations abroad and our wish to maintain and increase foreign holdings. We have been able to do all that, which is impressive; we are beginning to feel the pressure of costs, which is hardly surprising.

Our economic difficulties derive from our chosen roles rather than from the emergence of additional superpowers. The point must be emphasized, since it is usually misunderstood. The major powers of the world, with their health restored, do vie economically with the United States as they could not two decades ago. Noting that our dependence on them has increased, we overlook the fact that their dependence on others and on us is much greater. Because we fail to think of the comparative plights of nations, we tend to talk as though our problems are unique. The habit in itself reflects our preeminent international position and the fact that our vast holdings abroad loom small in relation to our internal economy. Our position in the world provides relatively wide margins for dealing with economic problems. One can immediately get a sense of this simply by comparing our past policies with the restrictive economic measures England has so frequently taken because of balance-of-payments problems. With two exceptions, 1957 and 1968, the United States has run a balance-of-payments deficit yearly since 1950. What country other than the United States would be able to do this over a period of two decades before devaluing its currency? Much more than most countries, we have been able to unload the costs of economic adjustment on others.

Countries that are economically interdependent will want some control over each other. The United States, since it is largely independent economically, should refrain from seeking control where it is not needed. We will, one must add, become somewhat more dependent on others as time goes by. Income from foreign investment has gradually increased and now amounts to a little more than one percent of GNP. Imports have also edged upward. In 1935, they amounted to 2.8 percent of our GNP, a figure that stood at 3.1 percent in 1950, and increased to 4.3 percent in 1971. We can expect further increases, but we should not fail to notice that compared to the world's middle-rank states, China excepted, we will continue to be a small trader if external is measured against internal business. We will remain relatively little dependent on the rest of the world. Moreover, we can take steps, and might wish to, in order to keep our dependence on certain primary products from growing too rapidly.

Europe has been, and will continue to be, an area of major economic importance for us. Beginning in 1961, our exports to and imports from Western Europe, measured as a percentage of our world totals, have varied narrowly around the 30 percent mark. That statement holds also for our direct investments there from 1966 onward.[37] In 1969, Western Europe replaced Canada as the principal location of our direct investments. On economic grounds, as on others, Western Europe will continue to rank second only to the Soviet Union in the hierarchy of American concerns.

In saying "Western Europe," we must be careful not to slip into thinking of it as a political unit. Because many do so, it has become all the easier to mistake the maturation of bipolarity for its passing. "Maturation" is meant here in two senses. First, the earlier, extraordinary position of American dominance in a world heavily damaged by war has diminished through a less drastically skewed distribution of national capabilities. Second, the United States and the Soviet Union have more and more often shown that they have learned to behave as sensible duopolists should—moderating the intensity of their competition and cooperating at times to mutual advantage while maintaining deterrent capabilities against each other. This condition, if properly seen and exploited, permits some reversal of America's global expansion, an expansion undertaken ironically in the name of opposing Communism. The United States and the Soviet Union, as the only two truly global powers, have a responsibility for world stability commensurate with their interest in it. Each must, therefore, be concerned to maintain a rough balance of forces between them. They can be relied upon to take that duty seriously. To maintain a global balance does not necessarily require either of them to keep large forces abroad. Surely we will make further withdrawals of troops. In doing so we will be accused of acting irresponsibly and of retreating into isolationism. That should neither surprise us nor bother us very much.

In the old days, our commitment to isolationism was condemned because we were unwilling to act even in the face of threats that could plausibly be thought of as being dangerous to us. Where we once were reflexively isolationist, we have now become reflexively internationalist. Neither isolationism nor internationalism is good in itself. The United States with its far-flung economic and other interests is hardly in danger of retreating too far. That statement is reinforced by two considerations. First, other countries will continue to ask for our help. South Korea, with a strong economy and more than twice the population of the North, will continue to insist that two American divisions are a necessary guarantee of her security. West Europeans, despite an imbalance of economic assets favoring them rather than Russia, will continue to make similar, though larger, claims. Second, we have become accustomed to acting on behalf of others and to believing that the external, and even the internal, affairs of other states will be improperly attended to unless we lend a hand. Too often we have gauged our actions by our presumed capability for doing good rather than by our interest. Minding much of the world's business for a quarter of a century has made it easy for us to believe that the world will be worse off if we quit showing such solicitude for it. Too much American involvement continues to be more likely than too little of it.

I have argued that the United States need worry little about wayward movements and unwanted events in weak states. We do have to be concerned, however, with the implications of great power wherever it may exist. The principal pains of a great power, if they are not self-inflicted, arise from the effects of the policies pursued by other great powers, whether or not the effects are intended. That thought suggests that European unity, should it ever come, would be troublesome. Henry Kissinger has noticed this. Ambivalence runs through his *Troubled Partnership*, a book about NATO. United, Europe would be a bastion against the Soviet Union. But a Europe of separate states is easier for an alliance leader to deal with. That ambivalence may explain why in calling for a new "Charter" for Europe, he did not himself chart anything. He did, however, make this remark: "We knew that a united Europe would be a more independent partner. But we assumed, perhaps too uncritically, that our common interests would be assured by our long history of cooperation."[38] He might have added, as few do when discussing the prospects of European unity, that students of international politics, who do not agree on much else, have always expected that a world of three great powers would be the most unstable of all. These fears should make us worry about the effects of withdrawing American support from Europe. Brezhnev's apparent belief that America's absence from Europe would promote its unity may be well founded.

NATO has always been an arrangement by which the United States guarantees European security, rather than an old-style alliance in which the partners contribute comparably to each other's protection. The imbalance of capabilities among the parties has made equality of contribution impossible. Withdrawal of the guarantee would seem to be inadvisable, not only because withdrawal might stimulate Europeans to find the strength for their own defense through political unity, but also because they might instead move in the opposite direction, toward what George Kennan once described as the inclination to commit suicide for fear of death. America's ties to Europe are her oldest and most important by any criteria. Even if Robert W. Tucker is right in saying that the "loss" of Europe could be sustained by us economically and militarily, still psychology remains important politically. If we were to witness the crumbling of political will in a succession of West European states, might we not be provoked to sudden action that would pose unpredictable and grave danger?

We should continue to guarantee Western Europe's security, not only through the deterrent forces that we maintain for our own sake, but also through the earnest of our interest in Europe provided by the presence of our troops. And yet the logic of forbearance, a logic supported by the analysis of this essay, should be applied in Europe as elsewhere. In applying it, we should question, not the necessity of a continued American guarantee for Europe, but the wisdom of keeping such large American forces there. Why should we have more than a thin trip-wire force in Europe? If more is needed militarily, Europeans can well provide it. What would be wrong with expecting the nine nations of Western Europe to bear the major burden of their own defense? If more than a token ground force as a symbol of a deterrent strategy is needed and if Europeans choose not to provide it, that is their concern, not ours.

West Europeans could be expected to act more effectively in their own interest if we defined our interests more accurately and acted accordingly. A measure of American withdrawal will leave various parts of the world with more to do in order to take care of themselves. It will leave us with fewer self-assumed duties and unnecessarily-run risks.

Notes

* For criticisms, suggestions, and help in research I am grateful to Harry Kreisler; for research support, to the Institute of International Studies, University of California, Berkeley.

1 The desire for an effective unity in the face of foreign dangers was a principal reason for replacing the Articles of Confederation with the Constitution. About a quarter of the Federalist Papers are concerned with foreign affairs in some important way.

2 Reprinted in Joseph Tumulty, *Woodrow Wilson as I Knew Him* (printed for the *Literary Digest*, 1921), p. 274.

3 C. L. Sulzberger, "New Balance of Peace," *The New York Times* (November 15, 1972), p. 47. Cf. James Reston, "Tanaka, Nixon and Haldeman," *The New York Times* (August 1, 1973), p. 39.

4 "President's Remarks to News Media Executives," Kansas City, Missouri, July 6, 1971, in *Weekly Compilation of Presidential Documents* (July 12, 1971), p. 1035.

5 In addition to choosing odd base lines for comparison, Nixon and Sulzberger overestimate American postwar economic dominance. W. S. and E. S. Woytinsky credit the United States with 40.7 percent of world income in 1948, compared to 26 percent in 1938. Theirs seems to be a better estimate. See *World Population and Production* (New York: Twentieth Century Fund, 1953), pp. 389, 393–395.

6 Cf. Robert A. Dahl, "The Concept of Power," *Behavioral Science*, II (July 1957), pp. 201–215. Dahl's definition is not without ambiguity.

7 Obviously this notion does not constitute a formal and complete definition of power. I mean merely to emphasize an aspect of power that is at once widely ignored and essential to understanding international politics.

8 Quoted in Louis Turner, *Invisible Empires* (New York: Harcourt Brace Jovanovich, 1971), p. 166.

9 See, for example, Hans J. Morgenthau, "The Impotence of American Power," *Truth and Power* (New York: Praeger, 1970), p. 325; and A. F. K. Organski, *World Politics*, 2nd ed. (New York: Alfred A. Knopf, 1968), pp. 328–329.

10 Unless otherwise indicated, economic and military data are from *The Military Balance*, a yearly publication of The International Institute for Strategic Studies, London, or from various editions of the following publications issued by the US Government Printing Office, Washington, DC: *Statistical Abstract of the United States, Survey of Current Business, Historical Statistics of the United States, Colonial Times to 1957.*

11 Stanley Hoffmann, "Statecraft Demands Imagination," *The New York Times* (March 7, 1952), p. 37.

12 "Transcript of the President's News Conference on Foreign and Domestic Matters," *The New York Times* (August 5, 1971), p. 16.

13 See, e.g., Walter Lippmann, "Breakup of the Two-Power World," *Atlantic Monthly*, CLXXXV (April 1950), p. 30; "NATO Crisis—and Solution: Don't Blame de Gaulle," *Boston Globe* (December 5, 1963), p. 26.

14 For a demonstration of the low dependence of the United States in matters of trade and investment, see Kenneth N. Waltz, "The Myth of National Interdependence," in Charles P. Kindleberger ed., *The International Corporation* (Cambridge, MA: MIT Press, 1970), pp. 205–223.

15 Peter Grose, "Oil: Delay and Disunity," *The New York Times* (May 15, 1973), p. 37.

16 For a useful survey, see "Enough Energy—If Resources Are Allocated Right," *Business Week* (April 21, 1973), pp. 50–60. Discussions of our problems often fail to mention that our foreign petroleum investments have been unusually profitable and that the increase of petroleum prices has been below average. The Consumer Price Index for all items moved from 72.1 in 1948 to 121.3 in 1971, while gasoline moved from 70.4 to 106.3. *Handbook of Labor Statistics, 1972* (Washington, DC: GPO, 1972), pp. 277 and 291.

17 C. Rajagopalachari, letter to the *The New York Times* (June 6, 1965), p. E-11.

18 "Sihanouk's Warning on Vietnam Pullout," *San Francisco Chronicle* (February 28, 1970) (Times-Post Service).

19 T. C. Rhee, "Implications of the Sino-American Détente," *Orbis*, XVI (Summer 1972), pp. 504–505. William Beecher, "Chou is Said to Have Given Japan Military Assurances," *The New York Times* (December 14, 1972), p. 14.

20 *House of Commons Debates*, Vol. 618 (March 1, 1960), cols. 1136–1138.

21 André Beaufre, "Nuclear Deterrence and World Strategy," in Karl H. Cerny and Henry W. Briefs eds., *NATO in Quest of Cohesion* (New York: Praeger, 1965), p. 221.

22 Ambassade de France, *Speeches and Press Conferences*, No. 185 (January 14, 1963), p. 9.

23 Pierre M. Gallois, "U.S. Strategy and the Defense of Europe," *Orbis*, VII (Summer 1963), p. 231. The latest evolution of French policy, reflecting the above concerns but in a somewhat changed form, is well expressed in Colonel Lucien Poirier, "Dissuasion et Puissance Moyenne," *Revue de Défense Nationale* (March 1972), pp. 356–381.

24 *The Bulletin*, XXI (February 27, 1973), 50. Published in Bonn by the Press and Information Office of the Government of the Federal Republic of Germany.

25 Quoted in John Newhouse, et al., U.S. Troops in Europe: Issues and Choices (Washington: The Brookings Institution, 1971), p. 83.

26 Senator Nelson's statement and the above analysis are from Congressman Benjamin Rosenthal, "America's Move," *Foreign Affairs*, LI (January 1973), p. 384.

27 Cf. Newhouse, et al., U.S. Troops in Europe: Issues and Choices, p. 71. They accept the argument and conclude that more than a further 5 to 10 percent cut in America's European effort would be unsupportable.

28 Ibid., p. 79.

29 Robert W. Tucker, *A New Isolationism: Threat or Promise?* (New York: Universe Books, 1972). Herman Kahn and William H. Overholt, *The Future of the Nixon Doctrine in Pacific Asia* (Croton-on-Hudson: Hudson Institute, 1972), unpublished manuscript, pp. 25–27 and 49–50.

30 Arthur Krock, *Memoirs* (New York: Funk and Wagnalls, 1968), Appendix A, p. 480.

31 Adam Ulam, *The Rivals* (New York: Viking, 1971), p. vi.

32 "The Goal of an Atlantic Partnership: Address by President Kennedy," *The Department of State Bulletin*, XLVII (July 23, 1962), p. 133.

33 J. William Fulbright, *The Arrogance of Power* (New York: Random House, 1966), p. 256.

34 "Text of Nixon's speech on Indochina and Economy," *The New York Times* (March 31, 1973), p. 18.

35 "The Control of Force in International Relations," Address by Secretary Rusk before the American Society of International Law, *The Department of State Bulletin*, LII (May 10, 1965), p. 695. The final phrase is quoted from Robert W. Tucker, *Nation or Empire* (Baltimore: Johns Hopkins Press, 1968), p. 47.

36 Cf. Colonel James A. Donovan, who also develops and illustrates the proposition that capabilities seek missions. See his *Militarism USA* (New York: Charles Scribner's Sons, 1970), esp. pp. 88–100.
37 With slight trends downward for imports and upward for investment from 1969 through 1971, the last year for which data are available.
38 "Text of Kissinger's Talk at A.P. Meeting Here on U.S. Relations with Europe," *The New York Times* (April 24, 1973), p. 14.

22

ANOTHER GAP?[1]

Robert Osgood divides analyses of the Soviet Union's behavior into two parts. Anyone who is on neither Team A nor Team B is, he says, too far left or right to merit attention. He defines the two positions in terms of the Soviet Union's intentions. This is common practice. Yet surely William Graham Sumner was right in saying that our intentions seldom have much to do with the results that our behaviors produce.[2] This is because behaviors and outcomes are affected by our situations and because the forces set loose by our acts often escape our control. We should pay considerable attention to situations because they alter outcomes whether or not motives and strategies change.

For a decade and a half the Soviet Union has steadily improved its conventional and strategic forces. To explain this Osgood looks to "the inner dynamics and motives of the Soviet system." In doing so, he pays little attention to how the Soviet Union is placed in the world. By shifting our focus, we can transcend the given categories without being either a left-wing innocent or a right-wing ideologue. If we contemplate the situation of the Soviet Union, her military buildup appears less ominous than Osgood believes it to be, and categories A and B cease to represent the range of legitimate evaluations of the Soviet Union's behavior.

In the 1970s, the United States added more warheads to its strategic arsenal than did the Soviet Union. In 1980, the United States had about 9,200 strategic warheads and the Soviet Union had about 6,000. The Soviet Union has an advantage in the weight its missiles can lift; we, in their accuracy and reliability. By the K index, a measure of lethality, the United States probably remains in a superior position. The strategic question, however, is not who leads by any of these measures. The question instead is whether either side can develop the ability to destroy all but a few of the other side's warheads with practical certainty. To do so is beyond the capability of either state. For the foreseeable future the balance of strategic power between the United States and the Soviet Union is indestructible.

At this point many will say that strategic stalemate shifts the competition to lower military levels, where the Soviet Union has an advantage. Thus Fred Charles Iklé, now Undersecretary of Defense, believes that if in some future conflict the expected horrors of nuclear war should make political leaders unwilling to cross the nuclear threshold, "then conventional arms would presumably carry the day, and we would presumably lose."[3] Such conclusions rest on mistaken notions about deterrence and on a distorted view of the overall balance between the Soviet Union and the rest of the world.

We thought our deterrent did not deter very much and did not work with sufficient reliability just as we were reaching a peak of numerical superiority in the mid-1960s. Flexible response, with emphasis on conventional arms, was a policy produced in our era of nuclear plenty. "Superiority" and "parity" have had the same effect on American policy. Something has gone wrong with our reasoning. We invented the logic of deterrence, and now we fail to live by it.

Two worries plague us. We worry that neglect of our strategic forces is opening a window of vulnerability that the Soviet Union can climb through and from which it can gain military and political advantage. Many have been concerned about the vulnerability of our strategic system because its land-based component can be struck and perhaps largely destroyed by the Soviet Union in the mid-1980s. If the Soviet Union launched a strike that utterly destroyed our ICBMs, we would still have thousands of warheads at sea and thousands of bombs in the air. The number of cities that can be severely damaged if not destroyed is at least equal to the number of strategic warheads an adversary can deliver. The Soviet Union, if it contemplated making a strike, could not be sure that we would fail to launch on warning or fail to strike back after having been struck. A would-be attacker is deterred if it believes only that the attacked *may* retaliate. What de Gaulle said in 1963 remains true today. Uncertainty about the use of the American deterrent force, he remarked, "does not in the least prevent the American nuclear weapons, which are the most powerful of all, from remaining the essential guarantee of world peace."[4] Uncertainty of response, not certainty, is enough to deter because if retaliation takes place one risks losing all. In a nuclear world, we should look less at the retaliator's conceivable inhibitions and more at the challenger's obvious risks. War has to find a political objective that appears commensurate with its cost. What political objective is worth the risk of losing one, two, or ten cities, let alone hundreds?

If no state can launch a disarming attack with high confidence, force comparisons are irrelevant. That we have 9,000 warheads to the Soviet Union's 6,000 makes us no worse and no better off than we were when the ratio was even more favorable. That the throw-weight of the Soviet Union's missiles exceeds ours by several times makes the Soviet Union no better and no worse off than it would be were the ratio reversed. For deterrence, one asks how much is enough, and enough is defined as having a second-strike capability. This statement does not imply that a deterrent force deters everything, but rather that beyond a certain level of capability additional forces provide no additional coverage for one party and pose no additional threat to other parties. Both the United States and the Soviet Union have long had second-strike forces, with neither able to launch a disarming strike against the other. More-over, given second-strike capabilities, it is not the balance of forces but the courage to use them that counts. The balance or imbalance of strategic forces affects neither the calculation of danger nor the question of whose will is the stronger. Second-strike forces have to be viewed in absolute terms. In the case of a conflict, the question of whose interests are paramount determines whose will is perceived as being the stronger. Nuclear deterrence depends on the "balance of resolve," and not on the balance of forces, once countries have second-strike forces.[5]

Emphasizing the importance of the "balance of resolve" raises questions about what a deterrent force covers and what it does not. In answering these questions, we can learn something from the experience of the last three dec-ades. The United States and the Soviet Union have limited and modulated their provocative acts, the more carefully so when major values for one side or the other were at issue. This can be seen both in what they have done and in what they have not done. Whatever support the Soviet Union gave to North Korea's initial attack on South Korea was given after Secretary of State Acheson, the Joint Chiefs of Staff, General MacArthur, and the Chairman of the Senate Foreign Relations Committee all explicitly excluded both South Korea and Taiwan from America's defense perimeter. To give another example, the United States could fight for years on a large scale in Southeast Asia because neither success nor failure mattered much internationally. Victory would not have made the world one of American hegemony. Defeat would not have made the world one of Russian hegemony. No vital interest of either great power was at stake, as both Kissinger and Brezhnev made clear at the time.[6] One can fight without fearing escalation only where little is at stake. And that is where the deterrent does not deter.

Actions at the periphery can safely be bolder than actions at the center. In contrast, where much is at stake for one side, the other side moves with care. Trying to win where winning would bring the central balance into question threatens escalation and becomes too risky to contemplate. By political and military logic, we can understand why nuclear weapons induce great caution, and we can confirm that they do by observing the differences of behavior between great powers in nuclear and great powers in conventional worlds. Contemplating American and Russian postwar behavior, and interpreting it in terms of nuclear logic, suggests that deterrence extends to vital interests beyond the homeland more easily than many have thought. The United States cares more about Western Europe than the Soviet Union does. The Soviet Union cares more about Eastern Europe than the United States does. Com-municating the weight of one side's concern as compared to the other side's has been easily enough done where the matters at hand affect the United States and the Soviet Union directly.

Strategic stalemate shifts military competition to the tactical level. Iklé is right about that. But he fails to add that nuclear stalemate limits the use even of conventional force and reduces the extent of the gains one can seek without risking devastation. Amassing military force is what the Soviet Union is best at. And military force now finds its greatest use and highest benefit in deterring. This condition works for a status quo power and against an expansive one.

We underestimate the benefits of deterrence. We also exaggerate the extent of the conventional imbalance.[7] The countries of NATO have 50 percent more people than the countries of the Warsaw Treaty Organization (WTO) have. Year after year NATO countries have spent more on defense than the WTO countries have. The troops of NATO and of WTO are roughly equal in numbers. Although in my view NATO's strategy and force deployment are woefully defective, one nevertheless wonders how any leader of the Soviet Union could order an attack knowing that NATO forces dispose of 7,000 tactical nuclear weapons, many of them larger than Hiroshima size. Much has recently been made of the growth of the Soviet Union's navy, but it is seldom mentioned that, except for attack submarines, this is the growth of a navy that not many years ago had little more than a coast guard capability. In tonnage the Soviet Union's navy is about half the size of ours, and NATO has a third more major surface ships than does the WTO.[8] The United States has thirteen large aircraft carriers. The Soviet Union has five small ones. As the Pentagon's Director of Net Assessment has said, the Soviet Union has only "embryonic military power projection capabilities."[9]

Even some who agree broadly with my appraisal of the world military balance nevertheless resist the conclusion that we are in, and will remain in, a superior position. They resist the conclusion because of certain advantages enjoyed by the Soviet Union and because of certain vulnerabilities suffered by the United States and associated countries. The patterns that are important in weighing the strengths and weaknesses of states, however, are ones in which advantages and disadvantages balance each other to some extent but ordinarily favor the stronger party. The Soviet Union's defense spending, for example, is said to be larger than it looks because the Soviet Union relies on cheap conscripted manpower and therefore has more money left over for other things. True, but then the Soviet Union has had more difficulty producing technologically sophisticated items of military equipment than we have and devotes proportionately higher percentages of scarce scientific and techno-logical resources to them. Some of our military materiel, the CIA estimates, would be of infinite cost to the Soviet Union. In other words, she lacks the ability to produce some of the items in our military inventory. To cite another example, the vulnerability of oil flowing from OPEC to the industrial dem-ocracies is sometimes thought of as making the "free world" a hostage to the Soviet Union with her plentiful attack submarines. Technically this is true, but politically it is hardly relevant. The story of relations between great powers is written in terms of mutual vulnerabilities. The Office of Technology Assess-ment, for example, estimates that an attack on Russian refineries using seven

Poseidon and three Minuteman III missiles would destroy 73 percent of her refining capability.[10]

The Soviet Union, though not without strengths, is in the weaker position overall. Her ideology has lost its appeal. Her demographic situation is difficult. The non-Russian proportion of the population, now just under half, rises relentlessly. This must concern the leaders of a country whose elite is overwhelmingly Russian. Her political system makes it hard to break old patterns and to adopt new policies. Her economy has slowed down. Her technology lags. Her exports and imports display the pattern of a less developed country, exporting raw materials, including fuel, along with simple manufactured goods in exchange for high technology items and occasionally for large quantities of food. To have to compete economically and militarily with America and with much of the rest of the world while producing only a half of the American GNP, and less than a fifth of the American, West European, and Japanese GNPs combined, is an unenviable task. The Soviet Union is surrounded by hostile countries in a friendless world. If her plight were ours, one may wonder whether we would arm less heavily and behave more moderately than she does.

The Soviet Union behaves much as any great power in her unfortunate position would be expected to do. Still, I agree with Osgood and others: We cannot assume that the Soviet Union is an ordinary power. The leaders of the Soviet Union may hope that they can one day turn the world to communism. Although the Soviet Union's intentions may be extraordinary, her behavior has not been. The Soviet Union has been opportunistic and disruptive, but one expects the lagging party in a two-party competition to score a point or two whenever it can. The Soviet Union has not scored many. Her sporadic successes should not obscure the fact that what the Soviet Union has done mostly since 1948 is lose. Most of her successes have been sporadic, of little value if not of high cost, and evanescent. Contrary to Osgood's claim, the recent projection of "Soviet arms and forces into the Third World" has not been very impressive, and her recent slight successes bear no more promise of longevity than earlier ones did. The Soviet Union has not penetrated the Third World nearly so widely and deeply as have non-Communist industrial countries—especially the United States.

No doubt the Soviet Union has moderated her behavior largely because we and others have acted to contain her. We should continue to do so, but modestly, as in the Carter years, rather than obsessively, as we now seem inclined to do. That is, we should act where our vital interests are threatened and not react to every wayward movement in peripheral parts of the world merely because the Soviet Union is in some way involved in them.

For two main reasons we should be slow to use force to counter the Soviet Union in peripheral areas. First, since World War II, no state other than the Soviet Union has been close to having a military capability that threatens us. We should therefore react to the Soviet Union's action abroad only if it might tilt the world balance. Big gains could be made by the Soviet Union in Western Europe, in Northeast Asia, and in the Persian Gulf area. Yet we have reacted in other places even when the Soviet Union's involvement was problematic. When in such cases we have wanted to use security interests to justify action, we have invoked the "domino theory." A single loss does not matter, so the reasoning goes, but a string of losses would; and if one thing leads to another, a string of losses may be suffered. In international politics, however, the "domino theory" does not hold. In international politics, winning leads to losing. No country wants to be dependent on another. If a country becomes dependent because of weakness, its neighbors will resist suffering a similar fate. We have been misled by the vision of falling dominoes. The so-called domino theory rests on a profound misunderstanding of international politics. States try to balance each other off; they do not climb on the bandwagon of a winner. Contrary to the theory's counsel, we need not react to prospective victories for the Soviet Union unless they threaten vital interests.

Second, whether as a new vision or merely a new version of the domino theory, Americans now worry that the Soviet Union may pose a double or triple threat to American interests by making military moves or feints against Western Europe, the Persian Gulf area, and Northeast Asia at the same time. The worry may come from holding our own policy up to the mirror. In response to an attack by the Soviet Union in the Middle East, the Republican platform of 1980 calls for our taking "military action elsewhere at points of Soviet vulnerability—an expression of the classic doctrine of global maneuver."[11] Accordingly, Secretary of Defense Caspar Weinberger, in explaining his first budget, said this: "We must not pursue a defense strategy that anticipates a point-to-point response to [the Soviet Union's] actions, but rather one that permits us to take full advantage of Soviet vulnerabilities."[12] A state that is relatively weak and surrounded suffers many vulnerabilities. In a world without nuclear weapons, Weinberger's thinking would make sense for us, but not for the Russians. They would not want their actions to prompt us to strike at their multiple weak points. In a world with nuclear weapons, Weinberger's thinking makes no sense for either country.

As I have noted, nuclear weapons provide the strongest incentive to tread gently when vital interests are at issue. Thomas J. Watkins, our recent Ambassador to the Soviet Union, understood this. "My own feeling," he said, "is that the Russians are very realistic about the Persian Gulf and that we don't need to make any noise or lay down any ultimatums at all. They understand that that is a national and vital interest of the United States of America and I believe they will be very cautious there."[13] Because of her weakness, and even more so because the world is a nuclear and not a conventional one, the Soviet Union is in no position to exploit the military strength she so expensively maintains. Russian leaders have to worry about political uprisings and unrest in Afghanistan and Eastern Europe; they have to worry about four separate strategic nuclear forces pointed at them; they have to worry generally about the strength amassed against them. I see no reason to believe that they would be inclined to challenge American vital interests in the Persian Gulf or elsewhere, much less be tempted to begin a multifront war.

Ever since Peter the Great, Russians have been trying to catch up with somebody. They are still trying. The mystery then is why so many people, especially so many Americans, exaggerate the strength of the Soviet Union's position. Four reasons combined offer a sufficient explanation.

First, theories about organizations explain why the United States and the Soviet Union overspend on defense. Strong organizations get relatively larger slices of the budgetary pie than weak ones do, and American and Russian military organizations are very strong. Moreover, obviously in the United States and presumably in the Soviet Union, interservice rivalry accentuates the effect. Each of the American services exaggerates the Soviet Union's capability in attempting to increase its own. Budgetary claims were made with ever greater effect when President Carter began to lose control of military policy. Hard-line critics took the initiative from a wobbly president and a weakly led Pentagon. With remarkable skill, the critics convinced the majority of Americans that our government was permitting the Soviet Union to gain a military edge. Attributing unwanted events abroad to military weakness reinforced the point, even though greater military strength would not have prevented or reversed them.

Second, by the logic of deterrence, variations in numbers of deliverable warheads do not matter, short of one side's achieving a first-strike capability. Overwhelming numerical superiority, when we had it, did not overwhelm anyone, as is shown by the history of the postwar world. Nevertheless, we slip into playing irrelevant numbers games based on myths created about the past. A myth still popular is that strategic superiority, as W. Scott Thompson put it, "enabled President Kennedy to compel the Soviets to remove the missiles" they had planted in Cuba.[14] At the time, most everyone thought that a strategic standoff obtained, despite the Soviet Union's gross inferiority in numbers of warheads, while overwhelming naval superiority in local waters enabled the United States to prevail. The better explanation, I believe, is that the United States and the Soviet Union shared a mortal fear of the destruction nuclear weapons can wreak.

Third, those who proclaim the Soviet Union's military superiority usually talk as though the United States and the Soviet Union exist in isolation, that direct comparisons of the two tell us all we need to know. Although I firmly believe that political and military realism requires that the world be seen as bipolar, this does not imply that other states have no importance. They are important, and some of them greatly worry the Soviet Union. While he was Ambassador to Moscow, Malcolm Toon referred to the Russians' "panic fear" of China. The Russians also exaggerate the German danger and the threat posed by NATO in general. They work on worst-case assumptions, as we do, and they are influenced by centuries of experience with invasions from east and west. Their apprehensions, although excessive, should be easily understood.

Fourth, the Soviet Union has narrowed the margin of strategic "superiority" that we have enjoyed. When the Russians narrow a gap, we are inclined to say that they are creating one. We create gaps in their favor, gaps which later prove to be illusory. This was the case with the bomber gap of the mid 1950s, with the missile gap of the late 1950s, with the ABM gap of the late 1960s, and with the biggest gap of all—the general strategic and tactical gap that is now said to confront us. Persistence in creating gaps appears odd only until one realizes that gaps are created to be filled in a way that preserves American "superiority." Military establishments—theirs and ours alike—are uncomfortable with deterrence. One heard in the 1960s that the United States must "reconstitute its usable war-fighting capability." While a member of the House of Representatives, Melvin Laird wrote that American "strategy must aim at fighting, winning, and recovering," a strategy that, as he said, requires the ability to wage nuclear war and the willingness to strike first. The Republican platform pledged that a Republican administration would reestablish American strategic "superiority." Reagan softened the aspiration without eliminating it by making it his goal to establish a "margin of safety" for us militarily.[15] Expression of such aspirations is commonplace. If we follow the route they mark out, instead of worrying about having enough to deter the Soviet Union, we shall strive, albeit hopelessly, for enough to prevail. Those who trumpet our inferiority seem in fact to be seeking a lost and largely mythical superiority.

That the Soviet Union is internally weak is widely accepted. I have concentrated on the Soviet Union's external position, where her weakness is often mistaken for strength.

Concentrating on the Soviet Union's situation rather than on her motives, and concentrating on the outcomes of her actions rather than on her often disturbing behavior, leads to four conclusions pertinent to Osgood's paper.

First, I differ with Osgood's argument that the military balance needs redressing. A-B thinking tends to support that argument and to support the Reagan administration's policy of spending more on defense without rethinking the strategy that should guide us. Osgood does emphasize the need for strategic reassessment. I strongly concur. Yet only by seeing the two great powers in global perspective can we identify the dangers we face and find better ways of meeting them.

Second, by exaggerating American weakness and Russian strength, we have persuaded ourselves to run faster, while our allies continue to stroll. West Germany would have had to spend 50 percent more just to bring her defense budget proportionally up to the level of ours in the last Carter year, and Japan would have had to spend more than five times as much. Some countries should spend more on defense, but ours is not one of them. Viewing the world in A-B terms, however, we frighten ourselves into bearing such heavy defense burdens that we remove the incentive for allies to do more. We should have learned by now that exhortation will not persuade them to bear proportionate burdens. Only by doing less in Europe and in the Pacific will we get others to do very much more. We can follow such a policy only if we first realize that we can safely do so.

Third, given the awesome array of countries and resources the Soviet Union faces, we can believe that we suffer an interest-power gap only if we grossly inflate our interests. Our vital interests are to achieve an effective but modestly defined containment of the Soviet Union and to maintain access to critical raw materials. The only raw material that poses much of a problem is oil. Oil aside, the industrial democracies produce about 45 percent of the world's raw materials; the less developed countries and the Communist countries about equally account for the rest. In 1977, for example, two-thirds of our imports of twenty-five critical materials came from Canada, Australia, South Africa, and other more developed countries—over half from Canada alone.[16] If we define our vital interests sensibly, we shall have not a paucity but a plenitude of power to serve them. Inflating our interests will produce an endless arms race and will lead us to adopt a war-fighting doctrine even though a defensive-deterrent doctrine would better serve us. With a defensive-deterrent doctrine, we can say roughly how much is enough and place a ceiling on arms. With a war-fighting doctrine, we shall need ever more and more.

Fourth, the belief that we suffer an interest-power gap distorts the world and ill serves our interest. Overspending on defense weakens our economy. The economic game is our best one. The military game is the Soviet Union's best one. We should play our best game and use our economic capabilities to moderate Soviet behavior. We should act in ways that increase the Soviet Union's stake in a stable international political system, while tending militarily to our vital interests sensibly defined.

Notes

1 This essay uses some material from a paper I wrote for the Leonard Davis Institute of the Hebrew University.
2 William Graham Sumner, "War," in *War and Other Essays* (New Haven: Yale University Press, 1911).
3 Fred Charles Iklé, "What It Means to be Number Two," *Fortune*, November 20, 1978.
4 Charles de Gaulle, *Speeches and Press Conferences*, no. 185 (January 14, 1963), p. 9.
5 Glenn H. Snyder, "Crisis Bargaining," in *International Crises: Insights from Behavioral Research*, ed. C. F. Hermann (New York: Free Press, 1972).
6 John G. Stoessinger, *Henry Kissinger: The Anguish of Power* (New York: W. W. Norton, 1976), ch. 8.
7 See William Kaufman, "Defense Policy," in *Setting National Priorities: Agenda for the 1980s*, ed. Joseph A. Pechman (Washington, DC: Brookings Institution, 1980), pp. 283–316.

8 Department of Defense, *Annual Report*, Fiscal Year 1981 (Washington, DC, 1981); John E. Moore ed., *Jane's Fighting Ships, 1979–1980* (London: Jones Yearbooks, 1980), pp. 784–815; International Institute for Strategic Studies, *The Military Balance, 1980–1981* (London: IISS, 1980), pp. 7–9.

9 Andrew Marshall, "Sources of Soviet Power: The Military Potential in the 1980s," in *Prospects of Soviet Power in the 1980s*, ed. Christoph Bertram (London: Archon Books, 1980), p. 68.

10 Office of Technology Assessment, *The Effects of Nuclear War* (Washington, DC: GPO, May 1976).

11 "Excerpts from Platform to be Submitted to Republican Delegates," *New York Times*, July 13, 1980.

12 Quoted in Flora Lewis, "Military Horse or Cart," *New York Times*, March 16, 1981.

13 Thomas J. Watson, Interview on "Issues and Answers," ABC News, February 4, 1981.

14 W. Scott Thompson, "Letter to the Editor," *New York Times*, June 5, 1979.

15 Melvin R. Laird, *A House Divided: America's Strategy Gap* (Chicago: Henry Regnery, 1962), pp. 53, 78–79; Reagan quoted in Murrey Marder, "The Superpowers—III," *Washington Post*, January 3, 1981.

16 Council on International Economic Policy, *International Economic Report of the President* (Washington, DC: GPO, 1977), p. 137; *Twenty-Third Annual Report of the President of the United States on the Trade Agreement Program—1978* (Washington, DC: GPO, 1978), pp. 140–141.

23

AMERICA AS A MODEL FOR THE WORLD?
A Foreign Policy Perspective

If the United States, or if any country, could serve as a model for the world, we would have to believe that most of the impetus behind foreign policies is internally generated. But if the foreign policies of nations are affected in important ways by the placement of countries in the international-political system, or more simply by their relative power, then no country can adequately serve as a model for others.

I How the placement of states affects their policies

Because throughout most of the years since the second World War the United States and the Soviet Union were similarly placed by their power, their external behaviors should have shown striking similarities. Did they? Yes, more than has usually been realized. The behavior of states can be compared on many counts. Their armament policies and their interventions abroad are two of the most revealing. On the former count, the United States in the early 1960s undertook the largest strategic and conventional peacetime military buildup the world has yet seen. We did so even as Khrushchev was trying at once to carry through a major reduction in the conventional forces and to follow a strategy of minimum deterrence, and we did so even though the balance of strategic weapons greatly favored the United States. As one should have expected, the Soviet Union soon followed in America's footsteps, thus restoring the symmetry of great-power behavior. And so it was through most of the years of the Cold War. Advances made by one were quickly followed by the other, with the United States almost always leading the way. Allowing for geographic differences, the overall similarity of their forces was apparent. The ground forces of the Soviet Union were stronger than those of the United States, but in naval forces the balance of advantage was reversed. The Soviet Union's largely coastal navy gradually became more of a blue-water fleet, but one of limited reach. Its navy never had more than half the tonnage of ours. Year after year, NATO countries spent more on defense than the Warsaw Treaty Organization countries did, but their troops remained roughly equal in numbers.

The military forces of the United States and the Soviet Union remained in rough balance, and, as we should have expected, their military doctrines converged. We accused them of favoring war-fighting over deterrent doctrines, while we developed a war-fighting doctrine in the name of deterrence. From the 1960s onward, critics of our military policy urged the United States to "reconstitute its usable war-fighting capability." Before he became Secretary of Defense, Melvin R. Laird wrote that "American strategy must aim at fighting, winning, and recovering," a strategy that requires the ability to wage nuclear war and the willingness to strike first. One can multiply military and civilian statements to similar effect over the decades. Especially in the 1970s and 1980s, we accused the Soviet Union of striving for military superiority. In turn, the Republican platform of 1980 pledged that a Republican administration would reestablish American strategic "superiority."[1] Ronald Reagan as president softened the aspiration without eliminating it by making it his goal to establish a "margin of safety" for the United States militarily. Military competition between the two countries produced its expected result: the similarity of forces and doctrines.

Comparison on the second count, interventionist behavior, requires some discussion because our conviction that the United States has been the status quo, and the Soviet Union the interventionist, country distorts our view of reality. The United States, like the Soviet Union, has often intervened in others' affairs and has spent a fair amount of time fighting peripheral wars. Most Americans saw little need to explain our actions, assumed to have been in the pursuit of legitimate national interests and of international justice, and little difficulty in explaining the Soviet Union's, assumed to have been aimed at spreading communism across the globe by any means available. Americans usually interpreted the Soviet Union's behavior in terms of its presumed intentions. Intentions aside, our and their actions have been similar. The United States, for example, intervened militarily to defend client states and supported their ambitions to expand in China, Korea, and Vietnam. The Soviet Union, for example, acted in Afghanistan as we did in Vietnam and intervened directly or indirectly in Angola, Mozambique, and Ethiopia.

Before World War II, both the United States and the Soviet Union had developed ideologies that could easily propel them to unilateral action in the name of international duty: interventionist liberalism in the one country, international communism in the other. Neither, however, widely exported its ideology earlier. The postwar foreign policies of neither country can be understood aside from the changed structure of international politics, exercising its pressures and providing its opportunities. More so than the Soviet Union, the United States has acted all over the globe in the name of its own security and the world's well-being. Thus, Blechman and Kaplan found that in roughly 30 years following 1946 the government of the United States used military means in one way or another to intervene in the affairs of other countries about twice as often as did the Soviet Union.[2]

II The implications of unbalanced power

François Fénelon, who lived from 1651 to 1715, was a French theologian and political adviser and one of the first to understand balance of power as a general phenomenon rather than as merely a particular condition. He argued that a country disposing of greater power than others do cannot long be expected to behave with decency and moderation.[3] His theorem has been well illustrated by such powerful rulers as Charles V, Louis XIV, Napoleon, and Kaiser Wilhelm II. There was not necessarily something wrong with the character of those rulers or of their countries. At a minimum, it was a surplus of power that tempted them to arbitrary and arrogant behavior.

So long as the world was bipolar, the United States and the Soviet Union held each other in check. With the crumbling of the Soviet Union, no country or set of countries can presently restore a balance. One expects two results to follow. Despite abundant good intentions, the United States will often act in accordance with Fénelon's theorem. Balance of power theory leads one to predict that other states, if they have a choice, will flock to the weaker side, for it is the stronger side that threatens them.

In recent years have we seen what theory leads us to expect? A few examples will help to answer the question. President Reagan, when asked at a press conference how long we would continue to support the Contra's effort to overthrow the Nicaraguan government, began to give a fumbling answer. Then, impatient with himself, he said: Oh well, until they say "uncle." Vice President Bush in February of 1985 explained the meaning of "uncle." He laid seven stipulations upon the Nicaraguan government, which in sum amounted to saying that until Nicaragua developed a government and society much like ours, we would continue to support the opposition.[4]

Senior officials in the Reagan administration elevated the right to intervene to the level of general principle. As one of them said, we "debated whether we had the right to dictate the form of another country's government. The bottom line was yes, that some rights are more fundamental than the right of nations to nonintervention, like the rights of individual people. . . . [W]e don't have the right to subvert a democratic government but we do have the right against an undemocratic one."[5] In managing so much of the world's business for so long, the United States developed a rage to rule, which our position in the world now enables us to indulge. Thus, Charles Krauthammer looks forward to an overwhelmingly powerful America "unashamedly laying down the rules of world order and being prepared to enforce them."[6] Seeming to reflect the same spirit, President Bush, in a speech of August 2, 1990, a speech lost in the excitement of Iraq's invasion of Kuwait, announced that we would prepare for regional threats "in whatever corner of the globe they may occur." But how do threats arising in odd corners of the globe constitute dangers for us, and how many threats of what sort would we need to prepare to meet if our concern were to protect only our vital interests?

With benign intent, the United States has behaved, and until its power is brought into a semblance of balance, will continue to behave in ways that annoy and frighten others.

The powerful state may, and the United States does, think of itself as acting for the sake of peace, justice, and well-being in the world. But these terms will be defined to the liking of the powerful, which may conflict with the preferences and the interests of others. In international politics, overwhelming power repels and leads others to try to balance against it. With benign intent, the United States has behaved, and until its power is brought into a semblance of balance, will continue to behave in ways that annoy and frighten others.

America's management of the war against Iraq, and the subsequent reaction of others, provide telling examples. The United States skillfully forged a wide coalition of states in opposition to Iraq's invasion of Kuwait, but the United States opposed the efforts of France and others to find a peaceful settlement along the way. The United States pressed other states to agree that the embargo would expire on January 15, unless Iraq complied with the United Nations' resolutions, when many other states preferred to give the embargo more time to work. The United States chose the day when the war should begin and determined how it should be fought, raining well more destruction from the air than immediate military objectives required.

Many states reacted as one would expect to America's making the decisions. I give only a few examples. Philippine foreign minister Raul Manglapus called the United States "constable of the world" and wondered whether "it was necessary or even if it is just" for America to impose a new world order. Professor Sakuji Yoshimura of Waseda University expressed his distress this way: "America is a mighty country—and a frightening one . . . for better or worse the Gulf war built a new world order with America at the head . . . this will be fine as long as the rest of the world accepts its role as America's underlings." An opposition member of the Diet, Masao Kunihiro, observed that the "feeling that America is a fiercesome country is growing in Japan."[7] In France, fears of American imperialism were widely expressed and debated. In early September of 1991 foreign minister Roland Dumas remarked that "American might reigns without balancing weight," and Jacques Delors, president of the European Community Commission, cautioned that the United States must not take charge of the world. Both of them called on the United Nations and the European Community to counterbalance American influence.[8]

Professor Michael Doyle has shown that rarely do democracies fight democracies, but adds rightly that they fight plenty of wars against undemocratic states. The first generalization is not as strong as many have thought it to be. Not only was Germany a democracy in 1914 but also its being a democracy helped to explain the outbreak of war. As Chancellor Bethmann Hollweg lamented before the event, interests supporting the ruling majority pushed for policies sure to accumulate enemies for Germany. Junkers in the east demanded a tariff against Russian grain. Industrial interests in the northwest supported the Berlin to Baghdad railroad and the building of a battlefleet that could challenge the British navy. Russia and Britain were annoyed and frightened by German policies that helped to forge and strengthen the Triple Entente, which in turn made German political and military leaders entertain thoughts of fighting a preventive war before the enemies of Germany would become still stronger. One might add that in 1812 the United States chose to fight a war against the only other country that could then be called democratic, and that later in the century the northern American democracy fought the southern one.

Still, peace has prevailed much more reliably among democratic countries than elsewhere. On external as well as on internal grounds, I hope that more countries will become democratic.

III Conclusion

Yet for all of the reasons given above, we cannot take America or any other country as a model for the world. We might remind ourselves that in the past decade alone we have initiated three wars beginning with the one against Grenada and ending with the one against Iraq. In the intervening war against Panama, we not only violated international law but we violated laws that we had largely written: namely, the charter of the Organization of American States. I believe that America is better than most nations, I fear that it is not as much better as many Americans believe. In international politics, unbalanced power constitutes a danger even when it is American power that is out of balance.

Notes

1 Melvin R. Laird, *A House Divided: America's Strategy Gap* (Chicago: Henery Regney, 1962), pp. 53, 78–79.
2 Barry Blechman and Stephen S. Kaplan, *Force without War: U.S. Armed Forces as a Political Instrument* (Washington: Brookings Institution, 1978).
3 Herbert Butterfield, "The Balance of Power," in Butterfield and Martin Wight eds., *Diplomatic Investigations* (London: George Allen & Unwin, 1966), p. 140.
4 "Excerpts from Remarks by Vice President George Bush," Press Release, Austin, Texas, February 18, 1985.
5 Quoted in Robert W. Tucker, *Intervention and the Reagan Doctrine*, (New York: Council on Religion and International Affairs, 1985), p. 5.
6 In Christopher Layne, "The Unipolar Illusion: American Foreign Policy in the Post Cold War World." Presented to the Washington Strategy Seminar, April 25, 1991, p. 21.
7 Quotations are from ibid., pp. 21–22.
8 *New York Times*, "France to U.S.: Don't Rule," September 3, 1991, p. A8 (no byline).

PERMISSIONS AND ACKNOWLEDGEMENTS

"America as a Model for the World? A Foreign Policy Perspective," *PS: Political Science and Politics*, Vol. 24, No. 4 (Dec, 1991), pp. 667–670. Copyright Cambridge University Press. Reprinted with permission.

"America's European Policy in Global Perspective," *The United States and Western Europe: Political, Economic and Strategic Perspectives*, Wolfram F. Hanrieder ed., Winthrop Publishers, Inc. Cambridge, MA, 1974. Reprinted with permission of author.

"Another Gap?," *Containment, Soviet Behavior, and Grand Strategy*. Robert E. Osgood, Berkeley: Institute of International Studies, University of California, 1981. Copyright Regents of the University of California. Reprinted with permission.

"Assaying Theories, Reflections on Imre Lakatos." In Colin and Miriam Elman eds., *Progress in International Relations Theory: Appraising the Field*, pp.vii–xi. © 2002 by The Massachusetts Institute of Technology. Reprinted with permission of The MIT Press.

"Conflict in World Politics," in Steven Spiegel and Kenneth Watlz eds., *Conflict in World Politics*, Winthrop: 1971. Reprinted with permission of author.

"The Continuity of International Politics," Ken Booth and Tim Dunne eds., *Worlds in Collision: Terror and the Future of Global Order*, Palgrave Macmillan, 2002, Chapter 31, pp. 348–354. Reprinted with permission of Palgrave Macmillan.

"Contention and Management in International Relations," *World Politics*, 17:4 (1965), pp. 720–727, 729, 731. © The Johns Hopkins University Press. Reprinted with permission of The Johns Hopkins University Press.

"The Emerging Structure of International Politics," *International Security*, Vol. 18, No. 2 (Autumn, 1993), pp. 44–79. © 1993 by the President and Fellows of Harvard College and the Massachusetts Institute of Technology. Reprinted with permission of MIT Press Journals.

"Evaluating Theories," *The American Political Science Review*, Vol. 91, No. 4 (Dec., 1997), pp. 913–917. Copyright Cambridge University Press. Reprinted with permission.

"Globalization and Governance," *PS: Political Science and Politics*, Vol. 32, No. 4 (Dec., 1999), pp. 693–700. Copyright Cambridge University Press. Reprinted with permission.

"International Structure, National Force, and the Balance of World Power," *Journal of International Affairs* 21: pp. 215–231, 1967. © 1967 Cambridge University Press. Reprinted with permission.

"Kant, Liberalism, and War," *The American Political Science Review*, Vol. 56, No. 2 (Jun., 1962), pp. 331–340. Reprinted with permission.

"The Myth of National Interdependence," In Charles P. Kindleberger ed., *The International Corporation: A Symposium*, pp. 205–223, © 1970 by The Massachusetts Institute of Technology. Reprinted with permission of The MIT Press.

"Nuclear Myths and Political Realities," *The American Political Science Review*, Vol. 84, No. 3 (Sep., 1990), pp. 731–745. © 1990 Cambridge University Press. Reprinted with permission.

"The Origins of War in Neorealist Theory," *Journal of Interdisciplinary History*, XVIII (1988), pp. 615–628. Reprinted with the permission of the editors of The Journal of Interdisciplinary History and The MIT Press, Cambridge, Massachusetts. © 1996 by The Massachusetts Institute of Technology and The Journal of Interdisciplinary History, Inc.

"The Politics of Peace," *International Studies Quarterly*, Vol. 11, No. 3 (Sep., 1967), pp. 199–211. © 1967 Blackwell Publishing. Reprinted with permission.

"Realist Thought and Neorealist Theory," *Journal of International Affairs*, 44:1 (1990: Spring). Copyright © Columbia University. Reprinted with permission.

"Reason, Will and Weapons," *Political Science Quarterly*, Vol. 74, No. 3 (Sep., 1959), pp. 412–419.

"The Spread of Nuclear Weapons: Good or Bad? A Reply," SECURITY STUDIES Volume 4 Number 4 Summer 1995. Reprinted with permission.

"The Stability of a Bipolar World," DÆDALUS *Journal of the American Academy of Arts and Sciences*, Summer 1964, issued as Vol. 93, No. 3. © 1964 by the President and Fellows of Harvard College and the Massachusetts Institute of Technology. Reprinted with permission of MIT Press Journals.

"Structural Realism after the Cold War," *International Security*, Vol. 25, No. 1 (Summer 2000), pp. 5–41. © 2000 by the President and Fellows of Harvard College and the Massachusetts Institute of Technology. Reprinted with permission of MIT Press Journals.

"Toward Nuclear Peace," D. Brito and M. Intrilligator eds., In *Strategies for Managing Nuclear Proliferation: Economic and Political Issues*. Lexington, MA: Lexington Books, 1983. Copyright 1983 by Lexington Books. Reproduced with permission of Lexington Books in the format Textbook via Copyright Clearance Center.

INDEX

Gallois, Pierre 320
Geneva Disarmament Conference
(1932) 257
Genoa Conference (1922) 34
Germany: alliances 60, 107, 127; Berlin
blockade (1948–49) 62, 100, 101,
150; Berlin crisis (1961) 25, 143,
320; economic growth 108, 115,
178–80; nineteenth century
unification 54, 109; reunification 27,
184; self-defence 182; situations/
strategies 32; Third Reich xiii, 87,
112, 118, 124, 270–1, 280; Weimar
Republic 198; World War I 60,
109–10
Gilpin, Robert 48, 49, 52, 160, 189
globalization: competition 178;
governance 230–45; investment
232–3; money markets 233; new
looks like old 233–6
Goethe, Johann Wolfgang von 4, 84,
93
Gooch, G.P. 4
Gorbachev, Mikhail Sergeyevich 170,
176, 178, 288, 289
great-power politics: Japan 174;
multipolarity 61; rise and fall of great
powers 170–8; war 64; zero-sum
game 28–9
Greece: Truman Doctrine (1947) 62,
100
Guifridda, Louis 276
Gurr, Ted Robert 214

Hamilton, Alexander 201, 310
Hammarskjöld, Dag 255
Hanami, Andrew 181
Hanrieder, Wolfram xi
Hardinge, Henry (Lord) 7
Harris, Errol 47, 90, 92
Hata, Tsutumu 219
Havel, Vaclav 209
Hegel, Georg Wilhelm Friedrich 7
Hellmann, Gunther 208
Helms, Richard 316
Henkin, Louis 257, 258
Herz, John 49, 140–1
Hinsley, F.H. ix, 123–8, 131, 135
Hitler, Adolf xiii, 61, 63, 87, 88, 101,
117, 124, 214, 270–1, 280, 291
Hobbes, Thomas 78–9, 130–1,
147

Hobson, John 76, 94
Hoffmann, Stanley 108
Hollings, Ernest F. 181
Holloway, David 168
Home of the Hirshel (Sir Alec
Douglas-Home) 105
Hoover, Herbert Clark (31st
President) 302, 311–12
Hotelling, Harold 86
Hötzendorf, Conrad von 144
Hume, David 8, 92, 146, 200

Iklé, Fred Charles 335, 337
impressment 5
independence: alliances 60
India: relations with China 319;
relations with Pakistan 25–6
industrial espionage 177
integration: close association of states
28–31; mutual involvement 33
interdependence: alliances 60; close
interdependence 204; historic
comparison 233; investment
157–61; less than supposed 236;
meaning 152–3, 317; myth of
national interdependence 152–65;
rhetoric and reality 161–3; trade
153–7; weak effects 203–6
interest rates 67–8, 233
international institutions: explanation
207–12; limited role 206–13;
national aims 212–13; NATO see
North Atlantic Treaty Organization;
perpetuation 208
International Monetary Fund (IMF)
206, 216, 240
international politics: Athens xii; blocs
113, 178, 207, 300, 303, 315;
conflict 19–36; continuity 246–50;
economic growth 108, 115, 300;
emerging structure 166–96; essays
viii–x, 99–250; interest power gap
335–44; international pressures
178–85; national preferences
178–85; placement of statements
345–6; reflections on theory 37–55;
states 238–42; structural realism
57–8; structures and units 37–43;
systems theory 58–9; terrorism
246–50; theoretical pale 70–3
international relations: contention and
management 123–36

Mearsheimer, John 166, 189–90, 209, 211
Mechanical societies 38–9
Melman, Seymour 257, 258
Mercantilism 174, 175
military affairs: essays x–xi, 253–96; reason/will/weapons 253–9
military expenditure: Israel 272; NATO 167, 338; pointless expenditure 173; United States xiii, 108, 239–42
military power: France 106–7; *ultima ratio* 138; United Kingdom 106
military technology: nuclear *see* nuclear weapons; unit level change 41
Mill, John Stuart 203
Miyazawa, Kiichi 181
Mohammad, Mahathir 231
Moltke, Helmuth Karl Bernard von (Reichsgraf) 109
Monroe, James (5th President) 201
Montesquieu 3
Morgenthau, Hans J. 49, 56–7, 67, 70–1, 76–9, 83, 86–7, 112, 202
Mosaddeq, Mohammed 104
Mueller, John 189, 200, 230
multinational corporations 236
multipolarity: great-power politics 61; miscalculation/overreaction 62
Murray, James xi
Mussolini, Benito (il Duce) 87

Nagel, Ernst 85
naïve falsification 46
Napoleon Bonaparte 63, 88, 188, 214, 215
national behavior: international structure 21–3
Nelson, Gaylord 321
neorealism: anarchy 59; bandwagoning 87; critique 49; historicism 51; origins of war 56–66; security 59; theory and realist thought 67–82
Neuman, Stephanie 221
Newtonian science 9, 86, 94
Nicaragua: relations with United States 169, 347
Nicholas II (Tsar of Russia) 312
Niebuhr, Reinhold 52
Nigeria: Biafra conflict (1967–79) 27
Nitze, Paul 67, 281, 282

Nixon, Richard Milhous (37th president) 100, 213, 313–14, 316, 321, 326
Noel-Baker, Philip 253, 254, 255, 258
North American Free Trade Agreement (NAFTA) 178
North Atlantic Treaty Organization (NATO): balance of power 188–9; conventional war 262; expansion 209–10, 246, 248; flexible response 277; military expenditure 167, 338; no first use policy 276; partnerships 139; realism 206–13; Russian Federation 246; US guarantees 140
nuclear weapons: absolute weapons 65; alliances undermined xiii; arms races 271–3; balance of power 187; better weapons 264; China 217; conventional weapons compared 63–5, 187–8, 286; deterrence 63–4, 110, 116, 127, 143, 171, 266–74, 277–89; domestic stability 263; effect of spread 262–6; equalizers 108, 110; escalation 141, 286–7; first strike capability 171, 285, 320; France 106–7, 108, 116; inhibitions 182, 295–6; Iraq 182; Japan 181–3, 219; massive retaliation 142–3; modern states 124–6; mutual assured destruction (MAD) 278; myths 276–93; new nuclear states 271–3; no first use 276; nonproliferation treaty (NPT) 30–1, 219; nuclear peace 260–75; pointless expenditure 173; political realities 276–93; preemptive strikes 267; preventive strike 266; regional stability 264–6; second strike capacity 148, 171, 184, 187, 268, 269, 285, 337; small forces 266–74; state competition 41; stalemate 105; strategic defense 289–90; strategic nuclear weapons 143; strategy domination 285–7; test ban treaty (1963) 25; testing 257; unacceptable damage 268, 272
Nye, Joseph S. ix, 84, 205, 211, 231, 246

Official Development Assistance (ODA) 176
Ohmae, Kenichi 231
oil crisis (1973): petrodollars 237